Certification Study Companion Series

The Apress Certification Study Companion Series offers guidance and hands-on practice to support technical and business professionals who are studying for an exam in the pursuit of an industry certification. Professionals worldwide seek to achieve certifications in order to advance in a career role, reinforce knowledge in a specific discipline, or to apply for or change jobs. This series focuses on the most widely taken certification exams in a given field. It is designed to be user friendly, tracking to topics as they appear in a given exam and work alongside other certification material as professionals prepare for their exam.

More information about this series at https://link.springer.com/bookseries/17100.

Administering Microsoft Azure SQL Solutions

Hands-on Preparation and Practice for Exam DP-300

Geoff Hiten

Apress®

Administering Microsoft Azure SQL Solutions: Hands-on Preparation and Practice for Exam DP-300

Geoff Hiten
Johns Creek, GA, USA

ISBN-13 (pbk): 979-8-8688-1584-3   ISBN-13 (electronic): 979-8-8688-1585-0
https://doi.org/10.1007/979-8-8688-1585-0

Managing Director, Apress Media LLC: Welmoed Spahr
Acquisitions Editor: Shaul Elson
Development Editor: Laura Berendson
Coordinating Editor: Gryffin Winkler

Cover image designed by eStudioCalamar

Distributed to the book trade worldwide by Springer Science+Business Media New York, 1 New York Plaza, Suite 4600, New York, NY 10004-1562, USA. Phone 1-800-SPRINGER, fax (201) 348-4505, e-mail orders-ny@springer-sbm.com, or visit www.springeronline.com. Apress Media, LLC is a California LLC and the sole member (owner) is Springer Science + Business Media Finance Inc (SSBM Finance Inc). SSBM Finance Inc is a **Delaware** corporation.

For information on translations, please e-mail booktranslations@springernature.com; for reprint, paperback, or audio rights, please e-mail bookpermissions@springernature.com.

Apress titles may be purchased in bulk for academic, corporate, or promotional use. eBook versions and licenses are also available for most titles. For more information, reference our Print and eBook Bulk Sales web page at http://www.apress.com/bulk-sales.

Any source code or other supplementary material referenced by the author in this book is available to readers on GitHub. For more detailed information, please visit https://www.apress.com/gp/services/source-code.

If disposing of this product, please recycle the paper

Table of Contents

About the Author

Geoff Hiten began his SQL journey with Microsoft SQL Server version 4.2 for Windows NT in 1993 and hasn't had the good sense to find an easier way to earn a living. Prior to that, he worked on dBase and other ISAM data systems. Geoff is a graduate of the University of Alabama (also in 1993). He has worked for many different organizations, managing their SQL Infrastructure. He built his first production SQL Cluster in 2002 using Microsoft SQL Server 2000. In 2005, in recognition of his SQL community leadership and involvement, Geoff was invited to become a Microsoft SQL (later Data Platform) MVP. That recognition lasted until 2018 when he joined Microsoft. In 2007, Geoff got tired of filling out new W-4 forms when finding new SQL problems and started working as a consultant. He now advises Microsoft customers on how to understand and adopt Azure SQL technologies as a Senior Data Solution Engineer.

About the Technical Reviewer

Rick Heiges has been focused on IT and especially data for 35+ years. His past titles include Developer, Analyst, DBA, Faculty Member, Consultant, and Architect, and he is now a Cloud Solution Architect with Microsoft. While career accomplishments are terrific, he is most fond of his time with leading on the Board of Directors for the Professional Association for SQL Server. During his stint on the board, the conference grew 3× plus, and he spearheaded the "24 Hours of PASS" events to reach more people and fuel growth. Today, he is helping customers migrate their data to Azure and leverage it for business process evolution.

CHAPTER 1

About the DP-300 Exam, This Book, and Azure

The DP-300 exam is one of the current-generation role-based certification exams from Microsoft. If you have taken prior certification exams from Microsoft, they were likely specific to a version of a product. New exams were tied to new product releases and often focused on specific features that were new to that version. The DP-300 exam and its peers are different. This exam seeks to test your knowledge regarding the ability to perform a specific role, not how well you have memorized marketing slides on new product features.

The original DP-300 exam and related course materials were assembled from existing tests and courses when the exam was first created. Technical certification exams take a lot of time and effort to create. There are many rules regarding question format and structure to eliminate bias and ensure accuracy, fairness, and accessibility. Reusing already valid test materials to form the foundation of a new series of tests allowed Microsoft to rapidly change its entire approach to certification in just a few months.

This rapid change left us with tests and course materials that no longer were strictly aligned to each other. The biggest shortcoming in the exam and the existing support materials is a lack of a single, coherent theme that explains how all the parts fit together into the role of Cloud Database Administrator (DBA). My intent is for this book to complement the existing material available from Microsoft Learning by teaching context, depth, and perspective about Azure SQL Database (DB) Services. Microsoft Learning Paths do a good job of conveying facts regarding specific technologies, but do not assemble those facts into a single coherent story. Even though Microsoft has updated both the test and the Learning Path modules since inception, they still do not tell the story of what it means to be a cloud database administrator. People learn and remember best when knowledge has context. Very few people are good at memorizing random facts.

© Geoff Hiten 2025
G. Hiten, *Administering Microsoft Azure SQL Solutions*, Certification Study Companion Series,
https://doi.org/10.1007/979-8-8688-1585-0_1

I fully intend for you to use the free online material to do much of the technical learning. This book is a supplement, not a substitute. As such, I will often refer to Microsoft documentation or training materials. You should use this book and the free online study materials together. Here are the first two links to Microsoft Learning resources that you should open now:

- *Microsoft Certification Landing Page for the DP-300 Exam* – `https:// learn.microsoft.com/en-us/certifications/exams/dp-300`

- *Microsoft Study Guide for the DP-300 Exam* – `https://query.prod. cms.rt.microsoft.com/cms/api/am/binary/RE4q3yZ`

This book is not a beginner's guide to Azure nor to Microsoft SQL Server. Readers, especially those planning to take the DP-300 exam, are expected to have fundamental on-premises DBA skills and have a basic understanding of Azure. You should be able to navigate around the Azure portal, find and deploy services, understand the basics of Azure networking, and generally be able to use Azure resources. SQL operational skills equivalent to a junior DBA will be sufficient to understand and learn from this book. You will need to understand and operate both SQL Server Management Studio (**SSMS**) and Azure Data Studio (deprecated).

When Microsoft assembled the study guide material from multiple existing training materials, it inevitably created some topic duplication and overlap. Several topics are covered in multiple sections since the underlying repurposed study guides mentioned those topics. I have elected to pull topics together into the most relevant chapter or part of the book rather than try and split topics up or cover them twice from slightly different perspectives. The below list shows where topics have been consolidated into a single chapter or part:

- *Deploy Hybrid Solutions* – Chapter 4

- *Patching and Updates* – Chapter 14

- *Evaluate Security Aspects* – Part 2 (Chapters 5–7)

- *Database Partitioning* – Chapter 3

- *Database Sharding* – Chapter 3

Any discussion regarding Azure must consider costs. For the purposes of this book, all costs are in US Dollars (USD) for resources deployed in a US-based region. You can check for current costs in any region and local currency using the Azure Pricing Calculator: `https://azure.microsoft.com/en-us/pricing/calculator/`.

You will need an Azure subscription to complete the Learning Path and effectively use this book. If you have access to an MSDN-based subscription or a dev/test subscription from your company, that will be sufficient. Worst case, in most of the world, you can open an Azure account using a personal credit card. As long as you follow the advice you were hopefully taught as a child and turn the lights out when you leave the room, you should be fine. I used a personal account to create the examples and screenshots for this book and averaged spending less than $10/month.

Taking the Test

Some parts of the test-taking experience haven't changed since Microsoft first started offering certification exams. You still make an appointment to go to a testing center, take the test on a kiosk-mode PC, and get your results right away. Passing on the DP300 exam is 750 out of 1,000 possible points. The standard advice – get a good night's sleep, be comfortable, arrive early to sign in – still applies.

One of the largest consumers of the Microsoft certification exams is Microsoft itself. Many roles at Microsoft, including mine, require employees to obtain and maintain a wide array of certifications as well as take a great deal of internal-only technical and non-technical training. We can learn a lot about how to take certification exams from the Microsoft technical test-taking community.

Much of the test-taking at Microsoft happens at large gatherings such as their Ignite conference. Microsoft sponsors pop-up testing facilities where attendees can go take required exams. This is where Microsoft often debuts new exams in their Beta format. Beta testing a test is a thing. Beta testing exams is slightly different in that you don't find out your results until the Beta period is over, often weeks or months after you take the test. The official reason is so Microsoft can eliminate problematic questions and re-balance results before releasing the test to the public. Questions that deviate from the standard results profile are deleted or revamped before final release.

Many Microsoft employees take the Beta exams as a learning opportunity, not caring whether they pass or fail. At Microsoft, there is no penalty for failing a test, unless you fail repeatedly *and* it is a core role requirement. Many folks start studying by taking a test with no intention of passing it, treating it as an assessment to help plan their study regime.

Another oddity of Microsoft test-taking culture is what I call "The Price Is Right" philosophy. *The Price Is Right* is a TV game show where contestants "bid" on a prize. The winner is the closest to the actual retail price without going over. At Microsoft, people try and get barely over the passing score for a particular exam. Recall that passing for the DP-300 exam is 750 out of 1,000. The only time very high scores are considered a "win" is if it is in your core technology area and you didn't study for the exam. Scores above 850 where you took time to study mean that you wasted study time where you could have been learning something else.

While these Microsoft test-taking cultural oddities are interesting, we need to ask how these practices can help inform your test-taking. The biggest takeaway is don't sweat the test. Plan to fail successfully. Do a reasonable amount of preparation so you feel comfortable, but don't cram like this is finals week at school. Set up your training and testing schedule so you have an opportunity for a retake before any key deadlines. If you do not pass the first time, create a new training plan based on the results and try again. If you pass, congratulations. Time to start learning for the next one.

The second takeaway is once you pass *you are done*. Scores of 751 and 999 are the same as far as Microsoft is concerned. You passed. There is no stack-ranking or extra achievements for high scores. This is not a competition. If your organization ranks people according to certification exam scores, they are abusing the certification process. A passing score indicates Microsoft believes you have the essential knowledge and skills to perform the role of cloud database administrator. That is the sole determination that the test measures. It does not measure relative ability or skills, nor is it intended to.

Time Management

For a long time, the advice on taking certification exams was to quickly answer what you could and then go back to work on questions that take more time. This was when tests allowed people to skip around or go back to previous questions. Most people would read a question once or twice, and if the right answer didn't "appear," they would mark down the question number and come back after answering all the questions they could quickly answer. One unfortunate side effect of the amalgamation of multiple exams into the DP-300 exam is that questions are often set as no-return. Once you leave, your answers are locked, and you cannot go back. I believe this is because the setup of some questions provides guidance to other questions, but I have not been able to confirm this suspicion. "No-Return" questions change the entire dynamic of test time management.

First, be on the lookout for this type of question. Always read through everything twice, slowly, especially the instructions for each question or section. Know the type and structure of the questions and whether you can return. Obviously, if you can return to a question, go back and review your answers if you have time. Only change an answer if you are sure you are wrong. Treat the question you are returning to like an instant replay review of a sporting event – there must be incontrovertible evidence to overturn the ruling on the field. This is because as long as you fully read the question and considered the possible answers, your first instincts are most often correct. Just because you are uncertain about the answer you chose doesn't mean another answer is right.

Regardless of whether you can return, don't get bogged down on a single question. Use the techniques described below to analyze the structure of the question and get as close to the right answer as possible. Some questions will take longer than others to work out, and that's fine. Be aware of your time and when you started. You won't be able to take your watch or phone into the testing room, but the testing facility is required to put a clock in the room visible from all seats, and the test shows the time remaining on-screen. If you have trouble managing time on practice exams, start noting the time on the scratch paper provided as you start each question and check your watch or a clock frequently.

The Questions

Questions on certification exams must adhere to a rigid structure. We can give ourselves a better opportunity to succeed by understanding those rules. Let's start with the standard multiple-choice question – the bread and butter of the test. Each multiple-choice question must have one and only one answer. All the other answers, called *Distractors* in the testing world, must have at least one element that renders them incorrect. Start by eliminating Distractors rather than looking for the "right" answer. Often this works completely and eliminates all wrong answers quickly. Mark your answer and move on. If you can get it down to two or three candidate answers, break down the remaining candidate answers into specific elements and match them up to the question or scenario. If the instructions say "choose the best option," order the answers by whatever criteria (cost, speed, etc.) is in the question. Treat the question like the query in Example 1-1.

Example 1-1. SQL Query Characterization for Choosing Test Answers

```
SELECT TOP 1 * from ANSWERS
ORDER BY (importance described in question)
```

There are always one or more elements in each candidate answer that make it less than the "best" answer. It is important to remember that this is based on best generic practice and your experience may be different. Don't get caught up in trying to think about the questions in context of the databases you take care of daily.

One format of exam questions is to put items into a specific order. This is to see how well you recall a particular process. This is usually easy if you have done the task before. I emphasize the importance of working through the Learning Path examples found in the study guide link at the beginning of this chapter to gain this experience. One variation of this question format is to add extraneous items in the candidate list. The question should be clear as to whether you need to include all the items (sort the list) or just the correct items (select and sort).

Do not be surprised if Microsoft adds new types of questions, including sandbox problems where you click and type your way to a solution. Those are rare due to the high cost to develop that type of question, but they are not unheard of.

During the editing process for this book, I allowed my certification to lapse. I had to schedule and retake the exam. I wish I could say it was intentional, but it was an honest mistake. I did see many questions updated to current technology, so Microsoft is definitely maintaining and updating this exam. It was a positive experience for me in helping finalize content for this book and a reminder to track renewals more closely. And, yes, I passed the exam.

Limits, Boundaries, and Constraints

One of the easiest ways to guarantee a book about Cloud Computing becomes obsolete almost before it is finished is to quote some limit, boundary, or constraint about a specific Azure service. At one time, the limits on Azure SQL Database were a kind of "Gotcha" trivia on product-specific certification exams. Rote memorization of these constraints was a fundamental requirement to pass many early tests. Fortunately for us, the tests have evolved past that and are much more functional and practical. Having said that, we still need to know the limits of what the various technologies can do.

Instead of quoting current constraints, I am providing links to public Azure documentation that describes these limits. These links are updated as Azure technology gets updated. Some service limits are dependent on other configuration selections. Storage maximums often are limited by Virtual Machine (VM) Stock Keeping Unit (SKU) selection or compute size selection for Platform as a Service (PaaS) services. Certain features are only enabled on certain services or service tiers. We will first see some examples of this in Chapter 3. These links are being provided here without context so you can find them easily. As you read the book and study the other material, you will discover which links you need to explore further to answer specific questions about a problem or scenario.

Do not try and memorize all the material in the links. First, it is a waste of your time since the tests do not cover every limit and constraint. Second, by the time you complete memorizing the contents, they will have changed. Azure in general and Azure SQL specifically are constantly evolving and changing. Microsoft is constantly updating Azure SQL functionality, including adjusting existing limits. Knowing where they are and some general information about limits, boundaries, and constraints will serve you well for taking the DP-300 exam and as a practical Azure SQL DBA.

- *Azure SQL Database vCore-Based Limits* – `https://learn.microsoft.com/en-us/azure/azure-sql/database/resource-limits-vcore-single-databases`

- *Azure SQL Database DTU (Database Transaction Unit) - Based Limits* – `https://learn.microsoft.com/en-us/azure/azure-sql/database/resource-limits-dtu-single-databases`

- *Azure SQL Database Manage Instance Limits* – `https://learn.microsoft.com/en-us/azure/azure-sql/managed-instance/resource-limits`

Cloud Computing Fundamentals

If you tickle your favorite search engine with the phrase "Cloud Computing Characteristics," you will get pages and pages of lists. Each list is marginally different in content and length, but if you browse enough of them, you notice some common elements. Here is my list of five cloud computing characteristics that conveniently maps to what you need to know about Azure for the DP-300 exam. None of this is going to be on the test, but it is key foundational information for building your mental model of how Azure and Azure SQL services work.

1. On-Demand Self-Service

2. Resource Abstraction

3. Usage-Based Pricing

4. Elasticity and Scalability

5. Broad Network Accessibility

Let's briefly examine each characteristic and expand our understanding beyond just the titles.

On-Demand Self-Service

On-Demand Self-Service is the first item on almost every cloud computing characteristics list. It is first because it is the biggest change from how computing resources have been provisioned in the past. The default is that any end user can create any service at any scale by accessing an easy-to-use web portal or writing code against an open, documented API. Every cloud service provider including Microsoft Azure has this capability. Enterprise customers can restrict certain services and control access via Enterprise Identity management.

Resource Abstraction

Cloud computing resources are not visibly mapped to underlying physical machinery. Every resource is abstracted and virtualized. Many of these abstractions look like familiar computing resources, but they are not necessarily mapped to specific underlying hardware. We will discuss specific technology virtualization and abstraction in later chapters as it becomes relevant.

Usage-Based Pricing

Everything in Azure has a meter. Some of those meters have price tags. Each service has a measurable cost, either in a service-specific metric such as Lookups for DNS or as a combination of Compute, Storage, and Licensing. There are two common ways to measure usage-based pricing. The first is to simply bill for however much usage is consumed. The early days of web hosting were like this. Hosting providers didn't always put limits in place. Small, hobby websites that suddenly got "Internet Famous" found themselves getting billed thousands of dollars for unexpected traffic. This led to the creation of provisioned capacity–based pricing. You choose the maximum capacity for your service when you provision it, much like sizing a physical server or VM, setting both a minimum and a maximum bill rate for that service. Almost every service in Azure is based on Provisioned Capacity, but some services offer consumption-based billing. All the Azure SQL Services are provisioned capacity based or at least have provisioned limits for on-demand usage.

Elasticity and Scalability

Cloud services are elastic. They can rapidly adjust to workload changes with minimal or no downtime. You no longer must plan and purchase systems for your busiest day in the next three to five years. The cloud provider has reserve capacity that you can provision at will. This can mean more web servers in a farm (horizontal elasticity) or larger database servers/services (vertical scalability). Elasticity changes the way we think about our systems. We used to get nervous when CPU capacity edged up over about 70%. We worried about peak loads and whether our systems could cope. If you told your management chain you needed a larger server tomorrow, that would have been a failure on your part not to plan adequately. Telling management you need a new server next fiscal year means you are a genius. Cloud Elasticity means you get to accelerate the cycle for when you need to adjust to increasing or decreasing workloads. As long as you adjust your capacity ahead of time, you can scale up or down as your workload changes. This is especially beneficial for organizations that operate seasonal workloads.

Broad Network Accessibility

Cloud services are available through well-known Internet protocols. Web services are available via port 80 (HTTP) or 443 (HTTPS). Azure SQL platform services are available via port 1433 – the well-known Microsoft SQL service port. The actual network connection between the user and the service can use either a public or private network model. Neither model is better or worse; they are simply different options for different use cases. They are both simple abstractions on top of the same software-defined networking that is fundamental to Azure. Azure networking is not covered in the DP-300 exam except for firewall rules on Azure SQL Platform services, which we will cover in Chapter 6, but you do need to know a bit about the two network models. We will discuss that a little later in this chapter.

Cloud vs. On-Premises

"Cloud Breaks IT" is probably the most fundamental axiom of cloud computing. Early cloud services were adopted by either small businesses that had no IT shop, called "Born in the Cloud" businesses, or by teams within larger enterprises that were not able to obtain the services they needed via their in-house IT shops, called "Shadow IT." When modern cloud computing first got its start shortly after the start of the twenty-first century, many large companies had outsourced IT, sometimes to an overseas provider, as a cost-saving measure. This often led to lower explicit costs, but the rigid constraints of service contracts often made innovation a challenge. Projects had to span multiple budget cycles and could not adapt to rapidly changing conditions. If IT did not estimate your particular need and budget well in advance, you simply had to do without.

Cloud changed this completely. Anyone with a credit card could procure specific IT services. If Marketing needed infrastructure to analyze data and create a campaign in response to unexpected events, they could rent and provision cloud services to do this, as long as someone with budget authority made sure the bill got paid. This led to many organizations having Shadow IT alongside their regular IT. This in turn led to its own series of problems as very few of the shadow services were properly configured for Security, Privacy, Scalability, or Recoverability – all of which are core principles of Enterprise IT operations.

Cloud computing taught end users that provisioning virtualized resources takes minutes or hours, not weeks. All the rest of the time was consumed by each team executing their architecture, build, and deploy processes largely independently of each other. Certainly, each team in traditional IT executed projects on their own priorities. If you needed storage for a new database server and the Storage team was in the middle of a SAN refresh, then you just waited. End users didn't know any different and senior management was okay with this arrangement, so that is just how things worked – until end users had other options.

Enterprises have responded to this challenge in many ways. Some have sought to forbid Cloud and Shadow IT with varying degrees of success. Some have sought to impose standards on Shadow IT or lock it out of core IT systems, leading to a wider gulf between IT and Shadow IT. The strongest organizations have learned from Shadow IT and adopted the best parts of cloud computing while keeping core IT principles. Doing so has often required a complete re-engineering of IT. IT is no longer a collection of technology silos that carefully craft individual systems for end users. Gone are the days of the Storage Team, the Virtualization Team, the Windows/Linux Operating System (OS) Teams, the Security Team, and, yes, the Database Team having strict boundaries on what they do and what they are responsible for.

Modern IT shops that are "cloud-enabled" tend to create frameworks, policies, and blueprints for end users. End users can select from task-specific toolkits that are ready to be deployed and resized for specific workloads. Deployment is largely still self-serve, but with all the proper IT guardrails in place for allowed services. Some shops have taken this to an extreme, requiring all cloud "deployments" to be through validated and approved DevOps teams and processes. This includes minor operational changes such as adjusting storage allocations or backup retentions. Teams have jokingly referred to this as "Click-Ops" since the DevOps team simply updates their designs but often implements the changes directly on the normal self-serve portal since these are one-off items that do not automate well. While the boundary between Infrastructure and Operations can be an endless source of debate and sometimes friction, we should focus on working together to provide a stable and secure data platform for our organizations.

Azure Fundamentals

The DP-300 exam prep materials assume a certain basic knowledge of Azure. At Microsoft, taking and passing the DP-300 exam and other Azure role tests will exempt you from taking the AZ-900 exam on Azure fundamentals. The implicit knowledge check of Azure fundamentals is good enough to show you have that basic understanding.

This section strives to give a solid overview of two key Azure topics: Storage and Networking. Both Storage and Networking are essential underpinnings of Azure SQL, and you need to understand enough of both topics to make sense of some of the options and choices you have when deploying Azure SQL Services. The goal here is to give you a solid foundation on how Azure services work, specifically in how they interact or affect Azure SQL Data Services. Just like having good operational knowledge of how SAN storage works or how networking can impact your systems, this knowledge can only help your understanding of Azure SQL Data Services.

Azure Storage Basics

Before we dive into specific services or features, we need to have a broad understanding of one of the core resources consumed by Azure SQL in all its forms, Storage. Storage is where our data persists outside of compute and memory, regardless of the form or method. Almost all services in Azure require some type of Storage Account to persist data. In the case of Azure SQL DB, Azure SQL Managed Instance (MI), and other higher-level PaaS services, the storage is provisioned automatically via the service resource provider and consumed by the service. Billing is rolled up into the top-level service, sometimes as a line item if storage size becomes a variable billing item. For our exploration, let's start with general Azure Storage and drill into how storage is used by Azure SQL.

The first type of Storage many of us use in Azure for SQL Server is backup storage. Azure offers a convenient, native backup solution for SQL Server that works directly from on-premises SQL Servers and Azure Virtual Machines. Azure Blob Storage is where you can back up your existing on-premises database and where Azure SQL Services (DB, VM, and MI) store backups as well. Binary Large Object (*Blob*) Storage is a cloud-native type of storage. It is directly accessible from any computer via a URL endpoint, although Microsoft offers optional private networking endpoints for Storage Containers as well as Public endpoint URLs.

Microsoft Azure Storage Containers are the layer between the Storage Account and the actual blob. URLs are in the format shown in Example 1-2.

Example 1-2. Storage Blob URL Format

```
https://storageaccountname.blob.core.windows.net/containername/blobname
```

StorageAccountName in this example must be globally unique across all of Azure. The "blob.core.windows.net" namespace is a *public* namespace that can be resolved via DNS and is accessible to any Internet-connected device. While that sounds scary, the service firewall blocks all connections by default. You can enable specific IP addresses or ranges to control who can connect to the public endpoint or use private endpoints and normal network protections. We will go deeper into Storage Security in Chapter 6, but for now just accept that there are multiple layers and types of security features that protect data even with known public endpoints. While there are other types of cloud-native storage such as table, file, queue, and others – to create them just replace the "blob.core" with "table.core," "file.core," or "queue.core" in the above URL – we won't be discussing them here in detail as they are not used for any SQL services nor will they be on the exam.

One of the more important considerations for configuring Azure Blob Storage for SQL backups is provisioning the Storage Account. The Storage account determines the Redundancy of all the storage containers inside the account. Much like we have RAID (Redundant Array of Independent Disks) storage for locally attached and SAN-attached disks on-premises, we have various degrees of redundancy for Azure Storage. The minimum Azure Storage Redundancy available is Locally Redundant Storage (LRS). LRS is triple redundant, meaning it takes a minimum of two unrecovered failures to lose any data. While Azure does not explicitly use RAID technology, there is redundancy encoded in the data using technology similar to that used for streaming media. This is mathematically equivalent to three independent copies of the data – no, I am not going to do the math here. Azure Storage is also self-healing. If Azure detects any failures in the underlying hardware, it automatically copies data from the undamaged systems to re-establish full redundancy.

The next tier of Storage Redundancy is Zone-Redundant Storage (ZRS). Like LRS it is triple redundant, but the data is spread across multiple Zones within a single Azure Region. Recall that a Region is a collection of physical data centers that act and appear as a single pool of raw resources that can be deployed and configured for your use. Zones are internal divisions of the region with independent power, cooling, and, most importantly, maintenance schedules. Only one Zone in a region ever gets maintenance at a time, guaranteeing that resources which are Zone Redundant are not affected by maintenance outages, except for a few seconds of resource failover.

The next tier is Geographically Redundant Storage (GRS). Microsoft operates multiple Regions around the world. These regions are configured in pairs with extra data connectivity between designated pairs. Region pairs are always in the same Sovereignty Zone (Sovereignty Zone is a fancy way of saying a single legal environment like a country) but at least 300 miles apart. GRS is automatically replicated from the primary region to the peer or secondary region. While Microsoft does not offer a Service-Level Agreement (SLA) on how fast data is replicated from region to region, it is typically well under an hour. Simply selecting a configuration option when you deploy a Storage Account for backups is the easiest way I have seen to automatically have off-site backups. No extra maintenance, no changing tapes, and no getting an emergency retrieval at holiday rates are needed. You can use LRS or ZRS for backups, but you should have a use case that supports that level of redundancy.

There is a variant on GRS called RA-GRS where you have read-only access to the data in the peer region at all times. GRS data is only made available if Microsoft deems the primary to be unavailable. Recall that the endpoint URLs are globally accessible, so the purpose of Read Access on another region would be for data that is going to be heavily read since the Data Egress Charge – the charge for data leaving a region – has already been paid. If you only use an occasional blob, then accessing it directly from the primary region is cheaper than replicating everything all the time.

Warning   Do not use GRS or RA-GRS for web logs, performance logs, or other dynamically updated data. These may use Queue or Table containers depending on the source. GRS is very cost-intensive for these types of frequently updated containers.

GRS is the default Storage for most all SQL Service backups. SQL 2016 and later all use the same method for saving credentials and writing backups to blob storage. SQL 2014 and earlier have a different mechanism since they cannot use a URL as a target for a native SQL backup. Chapter 15 discusses the mechanics of backing up SQL Services in Azure, including Azure SQL Virtual Machines. SQL Server is agnostic to the Storage Redundancy configured in the underlying Storage Account. All levels work exactly the same as far as SQL can tell. Understanding the various levels of Storage redundancy is foundational to understanding how Azure SQL stores its data files.

Azure Networking Fundamentals

Azure networking, like all cloud networking, is Software-Defined Networking. Since all resources are abstracted and virtualized, the physical network connections inside Azure are completely invisible to Azure users. Users are presented instead with a choice of networking models. These models aren't exclusive and can both be used for many services. These models are constantly evolving with new features and capabilities like everything else in Azure. We will dig a little deeper into a few specific areas of networking in Chapter 6. For now, let's look at the two networking models and see how each has certain advantages and disadvantages.

Public Networking

At first glance the idea of Public networking for anything involving data is quite frightening. There is a world of difference between creating a Public Endpoint for a service and exposing that service to the entire world. Earlier in this chapter we talked about Storage and described how the Public endpoints (URLs) allowed universal access to Storage resources. This is because the *Namespace* is publicly listed but the networking layer defaults to no access allowed. All Public endpoints in Azure begin with no allowed access. Access is controlled by a simple IP address firewall that only allows specific source IP addresses or ranges to establish connections. If you have ever tried to connect to an Azure SQL Database Service in Azure but got the error shown in Figure 1-1, you have run into this particular security protection.

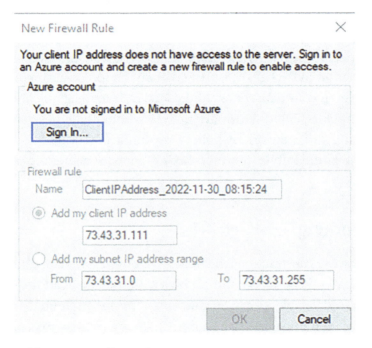

Figure 1-1. *IP Address Not Allowed*

While Azure refers to the "firewall," it is technically just a configuration option for software-defined networking. "Opening a firewall port" is just configuring Azure virtual networking to establish a connection path.

SQL Server Management Studio 18 and later helpfully allow you to provide credentials to log in to Azure and open the firewall for either your specific IP address or for a whole range of IP addresses. If you already have the Azure SQL Database Server Networking blade open, you can also add your IP address or range directly from there. Source IP protection is just the first layer of defense on a Public Endpoint, but it is an important one.

Lest you think that Public Networking is still unsafe and you would never use it, let me point out a few relevant facts. Our entire Public Key encryption infrastructure rests on Public Endpoints as do Linux updates. Systems must be able to universally and securely access peer and higher endpoints to establish and validate certificates or to download updates and patches. Modern microservices apps utilize well known endpoints to connect their various components. We need abstracted endpoints to implement cloud-native services.

Another key point to remember is that endpoints are typically hosted on Gateway servers that are specifically hardened for intrusion detection and Denial of Service (DoS) attacks. It's a lot harder to DoS all of Azure SQL than it is for just a single virtual machine running SQL Server in your data center. Microsoft tends to react quickly and decisively when it sees an attack. Finally, it is important to remember that these endpoints follow the "Azure stays in Azure" networking policy. Any traffic that originates and terminates in Azure never traverses the Public Internet, making "man in the middle" attacks virtually impossible.

Private Networking

Private networking uses abstractions that resemble physical networking used in on-premises systems. Virtual networks and subnets with specific IP address ranges can be defined and deployed. Networks can be connected (*Peered* in cloud terminology) across or within regions with traffic filters, very similar to how a router works on-premises. Platform Services can create private endpoints on specific subnets for other services to connect. Traffic is routed through and between subnets using predictable rules. Firewalls, load balancers, and custom routing tables round out the network toolkit.

Since Private networking is simply defining the abstractions for connectivity, most of the basic artifacts like networks, subnets, firewalls, and load balancers do not have a defined cost. The cost for network traffic is included with whatever service connects and moves data. There are exceptions. One popular networking model used on-premises has extended itself to the cloud. Companies will put a security appliance that does stateful packet inspection at the core of their network. Azure offers a wide array of virtual appliances from most any provider so customers can simply treat Azure networking as if it is just another part of their data center network. These virtual security appliances are not free. A desire for a network topology is the primary driver for many companies to require Private networking.

Data leaving a region is subject to an *Egress Charge*. Many customers hear about network Egress Charges and are immediately worried about unexpected costs since those charges are not something they have ever explicitly paid for before. Plus, Egress charges use the "on-demand" billing model that charges you what you consume without any predefined limits, which can scare some customers. Egress Charges are Microsoft's way of offsetting top-level Internet Peering Charges. The top-level Internet providers, including Microsoft, manage costs by paying each other to accept traffic. There is no charge for receiving data. This is one of many reasons Microsoft does not charge to bring data into Azure.

While this seems backward to our normal understanding based on residential Internet access, it works for top-level providers. The key is the only actual charge is for the net difference in traffic. If two providers each send out 10 PB of data to each other, the charges zero out. In essence each has paid half the cost of the shared connection. Top-level connections are often long-distance fiber-optic links that have a heavy initial cost to build out. Egress Charges exist to cover these costs when the data egress amounts are significant enough to warrant them. Pricing varies considerably based on the originating Region, but it is typically pennies per GB. You will only see significant billing costs if you are moving TB or more of data between regions or out of Azure entirely on a daily basis.

How About Both

As noted earlier on, the two networking models aren't mutually exclusive. Most Azure services support both public and private endpoints. Azure SQL Database and Azure SQL Managed Instance both have public and private networking capability. You can grant a Public IP address to a specific SQL Virtual Machine and expose that to the Internet, but that is strongly discouraged. Microsoft offers other, more secure ways to connect to a virtual machine from outside the private network. Azure services often can only access the Public endpoints for other Azure services, leading to Public endpoints that are enabled but only allow other Azure services to connect. These endpoints have no IP addresses or ranges allowed, only other Azure connections.

Chapter Summary

You now have a good idea of how this book will approach teaching you about Azure SQL and preparing you for the DP-300 exam. Hopefully, the insights on the new test structure and how to view taking the exam will be helpful. You should be able to identify where your company is along the "Cloud Journey" from the discussion on how cloud has impacted traditional IT organizations. Finally, you have a basic foundation on Azure Storage and Networking that should be sufficient to continue extending your SQL skills into Azure. Let's continue.

PART I

Plan and Implement Azure SQL Data Platform Resources

CHAPTER 2

Plan and Implement Azure SQL Database Solutions

The first step in becoming an Azure Cloud Database Administrator is to plan how to deploy your databases into Azure. Planning database deployments has always been a highly complex undertaking. Our SQL data systems are almost always at the core of our company's business operations. We are often tasked with achieving challenging levels of performance, scalability, and availability, all within limited budgets. Most of us have habits and practices for designing new platforms that we have developed over our careers. Several of these practices start well before the first bit of gear gets racked and stacked. We have these practices because many of the characteristics of our platforms become almost immutable once they have been deployed, or at least very expensive to change. We must get certain things right the first time in the on-premises world.

Cloud database operations, whether in Infrastructure as a Service (*IaaS*) or Platform as a Service (*PaaS*) environments, require us to have a different list of important questions and answers we need before we start deploying services. The basic concept is the same; certain things must be determined up front before taking any deployment actions. It is the actual list of decisions we make that changes for Azure SQL services.

Tip Until your cloud solution is live with a workload supporting business users, you can always delete everything and start over. Unlike on-premises solutions, you are not stuck with your platform decisions until the hardware cycle is at end of life.

In the cloud, it is important to understand the fundamental differences between various service offerings to select the best platform for your workload. It is easy to adjust different elements of a service without disrupting that service to meet workload or business requirement changes, but changing the actual service type may require creating

21

© Geoff Hiten 2025
G. Hiten, *Administering Microsoft Azure SQL Solutions*, Certification Study Companion Series,
https://doi.org/10.1007/979-8-8688-1585-0_2

new resources and migrating data, resulting in service interruptions to your users. This is not to say we need to go all in on the traditional Waterfall design pattern. Cloud is Agile by nature, and our planning needs to reflect that.

Introduction to Azure Database Administration

Let's begin our journey in Azure Database Administration by examining how Microsoft views the roles and responsibilities of Azure data professionals, followed by a deep dive into the various Azure SQL Service offerings.

Azure Database Roles

Many SQL data professionals self-identify under the catch-all label of "Database Administrators" – DBAs for short. Those of us in smaller organizations handled many of the roles and responsibilities within this title, while those at larger companies had more narrowly defined duties and tasks. Microsoft has defined specific roles within the traditional Data Professional field as it relates to Azure. These roles are

- Azure Data Engineer

- Azure Data Analyst

- Azure Data Scientist

- Azure Artificial Intelligence (AI) Engineer

- Azure Database Administrator

While this book and corresponding DP-300 exam focus on the Azure Database Administrator role, it is important to be aware of the other roles and how they also provide data services to business users. These roles are critical for *RBAC* – Role-Based Access Control – an important security methodology in Azure. Security is discussed in more detail in Part 2, Chapters 5–7, of this book.

Azure Database SQL Offerings

The first decision in using SQL in Azure is to decide which service to use. To understand the various service offerings and how they fit into the SQL Server family, we need to look at the history, origin, and evolution of Azure SQL Services. This section serves as introduction and overview of the various services. We will dive into specific functional areas of each service in later chapters as those features become relevant to the chapter topics. It is critical to understand the features and functionality of each service so we may recommend the best technical solution for new and existing workloads on Azure SQL Services. This is a pinnacle skill that must be mastered to successfully pass the DP-300 exam as well as function as an Azure Cloud SQL Database Architect.

Note   We will not be discussing Azure Synapse in this book even though it has a SQL engine at its core. Synapse skills are considered Data Analyst or Data Engineer role centric and are out of scope for the DP-300 exam.

Azure SQL Database

When Azure first went live in October 2008, Microsoft believed it was essential to offer some form of its flagship database product, Microsoft SQL Server, as a service. This was the beginning of what is currently the Azure SQL Database service, commonly referred to as **Azure SQL DB**. Since this service has existed for the longest time, it is the most mature of the services, and most new functionality surfaces here first. Azure SQL DB is a PaaS offering; the service offered is a SQL database.

The initial target customer for Azure SQL DB was not the traditional DBA nor any of the database roles listed earlier. The ideal target customer was a developer, either citizen or professional, who wanted *database as a service* for their application. This meant there would be no DBA and no hardware or platform provisioning, simply a service endpoint to connect to and interact with. Billing was on a single scale. If you needed more storage, you had to buy more compute and memory at the same time. Simple was the overriding design criteria. This has evolved to more complex billing models as Microsoft's customer needs grew and changed.

Azure SQL Database was not intended to be a migration target for fully mature on-premises SQL Servers. Some folks at Microsoft hoped it would be, but there are too many fundamental differences in the *surface areas* – the parts of the applications you interact with – for that to happen in all but a very few cases.

One of the largest differences between Azure SQL DB and an on-premises or Azure VM is the function and role of the *Server*. Different SQL services use the same word to mean very different things in Azure. Canonically, the *Server* is the first element in a four-part name for a SQL object:

`Server.Database.Schema.Object`

The Server name may be a short name or a fully qualified domain name (FQDN) for on-premises or Azure SQL VMs. "MySQLServer01" is a perfectly valid SQL Server name for an on-premises SQL Server. An Azure SQL Database Server name is **always** a fully qualified domain name (**FQDN**). `mydemodbserver.database.windows.net` is a valid FQDN for an Azure SQL DB Server. All Azure SQL Database service FQDNs end with ".database.windows.net."

Caution   Do not conflate the four-part name of a SQL Database Object with the FQDN of the Server. While they both use the "." character as delimiters, the FQDN is the first part of the four-part name. Combining the above examples gives us

`[mydemodbserver.database.windows.net].Database.Schema.Object`

FQDNs are case-insensitive like URLs, while the SQL elements of Database, Schema, and Object depend on the case sensitivity settings of the target Server and Database.

The second difference is that the Server is not actually the Server. This sounds confusing and is a major break from the mental model most of us have for SQL Server. The Server name in Azure SQL Database is an Endpoint, not the actual server. Connections are redirected within Azure to the actual host system for the target database. Azure acknowledges this by labeling the resource a *Logical Server* (Figure 2-1) in the Azure Marketplace.

Figure 2-1. *Azure Logical SQL Server*

Our existing understanding of an on-premises SQL Server is that it is the physical system the databases are hosted on. We connect to a server and can access any database – with appropriate permissions – hosted on that server. If we have sysadmin role rights to the server, we can access any data on that server. Databases can easily refer to objects in other databases on the same server in a single query with a simple three-part name `Database.Schema.Object`. The current Server is assumed. Since the Azure SQL Server is now a logical server, not a physical server, cross-database queries are now cross-server queries. We don't know what host a different database on the same logical server is actually hosted on. Microsoft SQL Server has never done well at cross-server queries, and Azure SQL DB is no exception. In fact, a multi-part name reference is disallowed and will generate an error in a query (Figure 2-2).

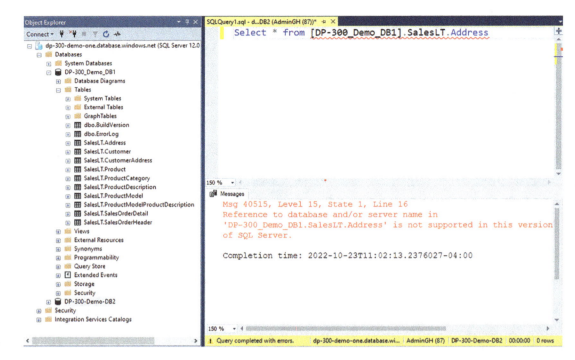

Figure 2-2. *Error Message*

Tip   Cross-database queries are one of the most frequent blockers for workloads migrating from on-premises SQL Server to Azure SQL DB.

There are many more implications of the physical/logical server disconnect, which we will explore later in this book. The basic concept of the Server as a connection endpoint manger and not a physical host is foundational to understanding Azure SQL Database.

Virtual Machines in Azure

The next SQL offering in Azure is "retail" SQL Server running in an Azure VM (Virtual Machine). This is the exact same version of SQL Server licensed and sold for on-premises operation. Microsoft provides extra services to improve the provisioning and operations experience vs. running SQL on VMs anywhere else. Additionally, Microsoft packages images of SQL Server that can be provisioned directly from the Azure

Marketplace, eliminating the need for installing SQL manually after deploying a VM. It's all one process with a helper service shouldering the configuration duties of the SQL Installer. If you need to run an older, unsupported version of SQL Server, you still must install it manually, and the helper service will have very limited functionality.

Tip   The DP-300 exam focuses on aspects of SQL Server on Azure Virtual Machines that are unique to Azure, specifically provisioning, backup, storage, and high availability (HA). These aspects will be covered in the relevant sections of this book. Deploying a VM in Azure for general purposes is not covered in this exam, nor in this book, but is an assumed base Azure skill.

Azure SQL IaaS Extension

The unique experience of SQL Server on Azure Virtual Machines is enabled by a resource provider, the Azure SQL Virtual Machine Resource. A resource provider is the software in Azure than enables a specific service, much like a DLL in Windows. There are hundreds of such resource providers with more continuously created and enhanced. The Azure Resource Manager (**ARM**) handles deploying resources according to the corresponding resource provider.

The Azure SQL Virtual Machine Resource Provider is more often referred to by its common name, the **IaaS extension**. The IaaS extension handles the following ten tasks to improve the Azure SQL Virtual Machine operations and deployment experience:

- *License Model Selection (LW)* – Select or change to pay-as-you-go, Hybrid Benefit, or HA/DR (high availability/disaster resilience) (LW).

- *Version/Edition Licensing (LW)* – Correctly recognize the version/ edition of SQL Server for supported versions/editions.

- *Automated Patching for SQL* – Define a maintenance window for automated SQL Server patching.

- *SQL Server Backup* – Schedule and execute SQL Server backups to a selected Azure storage location using a default or custom schedule.

- *Azure Key Vault Integration* – Store encryption keys in a virtualized Hardware Security Module (HSM).

- *Portal Management* – Enable feature configuration for SQL Server directly from the Azure portal.

- *tempdb Configuration* – Configure tempdb file size, count, and placement from the Azure portal.

- *Azure Defender Cloud Portal Integration (LW)* – View Azure Defender for SQL (if enabled) recommendations directly from the SQL Virtual Machine resource page.

- *SQL Best Practices Assessment* – Azure policy-based assessment for SQL Server configuration and operation.

- *Disk Utilization* – Capture and view disk utilization per data file in the Azure portal.

The Azure IaaS extension relies on least privileges to limit potential attack surface area and vulnerability. The Agent does not require a reboot or restart of the SQL Server under any circumstances: install, update, or uninstall. Least Privileges mean that only core functionality is configured and authorized by default. As you enable specific functionality, the underlying capabilities are installed and permissions granted.

Azure can be configured to scan and automatically deploy IaaS extensions if it detects SQL Server is running on a Virtual Machine. This can be enabled on selected subscriptions or for the entire Azure tenant but require customer authorization. Automatic deployment will select the license mode "Hybrid Benefit" by default to avoid changing the cost of the running VM. We will explore Azure SQL licensing models after the section "Azure SQL Managed Instance."

The Azure SQL IaaS extension exists to provide a PaaS-like experience for IaaS SQL deployments in Azure. Microsoft is continually adding to the feature set for the IaaS extension to bring IaaS and PaaS offerings closer together in functionality.

Azure SQL Managed Instance

Azure SQL Managed Instance – usually shortened to **Azure SQL MI** – became generally available on October 1, 2018. Microsoft developed Azure SQL MI specifically to give DBAs a PaaS service that is highly compatible with a typical on-premises SQL Server. SQL Server 2008/2008R2 was reaching end of extended support in just over eight months, and customers were asking for options other than climbing the upgrade treadmill again. Customers wanted an "evergreen" version of SQL that automates all the infrastructure tasks like Azure SQL DB but allows cross-database functionality, has a traditional SQL Agent, and supports as much of the surface area of on-premises or virtualized SQL Server as possible. From the beginning, Azure SQL MI was intended to be a PaaS service that could support a migration of most existing on-premises SQL Servers with little or no remediation needed. It has held to that promise remarkably well.

Recall our earlier discussion about Azure SQL Database and the Server object. Unlike Azure SQL DB, in Azure SQL MI the *Server* actually **is** the physical server the databases are connected to. You can use Server DMVs to look inside the system similar to on-premises SQL Server. Cross-database queries work as expected without any code changes. Three-part names are fully supported.

Most of the differences between SQL VM and Azure SQL MI are the result of isolating the operating platform from the database service. You can't use xp_cmdshell to call external applications because that might break the underlying cloud OS. Likewise, the SQL Agent Service does not have the Command Shell job step type.

The following example illustrates how Azure SQL MI maintains maximum compatibility while still protecting the PaaS service internals. RESTORE DATABASE is one of the most commonly used commands in Transact-SQL (T-SQL). We do a deep dive on that functionality in Chapter 15. DBAs use it to manually create copies or to migrate databases, both common management tasks. One of the clauses in the command is the WITH MOVE clause, which tells the system where to place the individual files when restoring a SQL Server backup. WITH MOVE is not an allowed clause in Azure SQL MI. SQL Data File Storage is managed as part of the service. The exact placement of data and log files is handled internally and is not something the DBA can override. Trying to use a WITH MOVE clause will generate an error. Simply eliminating the WITH MOVE clause will allow the RESTORE DATABASE command to complete normally.

Note   You can add additional SQL data files to a database on Azure SQL Managed Instance. You cannot determine where the files are placed. The Azure SQL Resource Provider determines where the data files are placed.

Azure SQL MI has one particular limitation that many organizations regularly stumble over. Azure SQL MI only supports 100 databases per instance. This limitation is due to the use of Always-On Availability Groups (**AOAGs**) behind the scenes. On-premises and Azure SQL VMs also have a recommended limit of 100 databases per instance if you are using AOAGs. Microsoft has taken its own recommendation and implemented it as a hard limit to provide guaranteed Service-Level Agreements (**SLAs**). This limit is an important consideration when choosing Azure SQL MI as a candidate for a workload.

Azure PaaS SQL Services

Azure SQL DB has grown a lot over the intervening years since its initial release. Storage is now calculated independently from compute for billing purposes, making workloads where storage and compute are not proportional more cost-efficient. Multiple tiers of the service are available to reflect desired service levels. System capabilities like High Availability, In-Memory OLTP, or Storage Performance are no longer infrastructure components; they are merely features provided at certain Service Tiers. We will map the connection between tiers and features as we explore specific features later in this chapter and throughout the remainder of this book.

Billing Models

When you provision an Azure SQL Database, you select from a range of options that impact your billing. The good news is if you get this wrong, you can change it later. You just pay the bill for what you initially provisioned until you change or delete the service. In fact, the ability to change service tiers is a key element that distinguishes cloud operations from on-premises operations: We discussed **elasticity** in Chapter 1. Elasticity is the ability to adjust the amount of processing power and its corresponding cost in response to or anticipation of workload changes.

Azure SQL DB was originally billed in units called Database Transaction Units (**DTUs**). DTUs are abstract units of database processing power and represent a specific quantity of compute and memory. One important characteristic is that DTUs are approximately linear; 200 DTUs has twice the processing power of 100 DTUs and costs twice as much. You can change the DTUs "on the fly," but there will be a brief service disruption as the system adjusts. Without going into the exact mechanics here, it is equivalent to an Availability Group failover for on-premises SQL Server.

Note   When we use the term "Compute" in Azure, we include memory and other supporting resources. Billable resource consumption in Azure is expressed in some combination of Compute, Storage, Licensing, and possibly a service-specific metric, for example, number of lookups for a directory service. Not all services have all metrics. Open source software does not have a licensing cost, neither does SQL Server Developer Edition.

When Azure SQL Managed Instance was introduced, Microsoft also introduced a new billing unit called a *Virtual Core* (**vCore**). vCores are cloud virtualized cores that map 1:1 back to physical cores on a processor. Each vCore carries a corresponding amount of memory that varies with specific hardware choices – another set of options you select at deployment and can adjust later. Like DTUs, vCores are billed by the hour.

The choice of billing model has no effect on any other functionality of Azure SQL DB. It is simply a representation of how you want to measure compute and memory consumption. Regardless of your billing model, all Azure SQL Database tiers (with one exception we will talk about later when we discuss cost optimization) are billed by the hour. For each hour the service runs, you pay for the top provisioned level for that entire hour. Azure SQL DB can use either the DTU or the vCore model and can migrate between the two as desired.

Tip   Azure Cloud resources are typically billed by the hour, but prices are quoted on a monthly basis. Microsoft as well as the other cloud providers use a standard 730-hour month for estimating costs. Be aware that exact cost per month will vary.

Azure SQL Managed Instance **only** uses the vCore (virtual Core) model for billing. Recall our original premise that Azure SQL DB is intended for developer-centric projects, while Azure SQL MI is intended as a migration target for on-premises SQL Servers. The target user for Azure SQL MI is going to be a traditional on-premises DBA, not a Developer. It was important for Microsoft to provide a billing metric that is close to how on-premises SQL Servers are sized and licensed. This also allows Microsoft to offer Azure SQL Hybrid Benefit, enabling the application of existing or newly purchased SQL licenses to offset the license portion of the Azure SQL Service bill. Using Hybrid Benefit does not change any service feature, only the per-hour bill rate.

At one time, Microsoft published a guide stating approximately how many DTUs were equivalent to a vCore. This number was different on each service tier and rapidly proved unworkable. SQL System overhead was counted differently, so the two metrics didn't exactly scale together well. Eventually the documentation article was deleted, and no equivalence is currently stated or supported. One advantage the DTU model has over the vCore model is that vCores are not available as fractions. The smallest increment is a single core. DTUs are available in values that are much smaller than any vCore equivalence, providing savings for very small workloads and development systems.

Service Tiers

Azure SQL Database and Azure SQL Managed Instance share nomenclature and underlying features for service tiers using the vCore billing model. Azure SQL DB has a different set of names for DTU-based billing, but the features correspond to the vCore named tiers. For clarity, the vCore billing model names will be used going forward.

General Purpose/Business Critical

The General Purpose service tier of Azure SQL DB and Azure SQL MI is intended for most "typical" uses. Business Critical (BC) is intended for databases requiring higher performance or availability requirements. While they are not the same as the on-premises Standard and Enterprise Editions, there are some rough correlations. The two big differentiators between General Purpose and Business Critical tiers are Storage and Availability. General Purpose uses Azure Premium Storage, which is based on Solid-State Drives – SSDs. This gives adequate IO and throughput performance for many SQL Server implementations. Azure Premium Storage is triply locally redundant storage. It takes three unrelated failures to break the underlying storage. Any storage element failure is immediately detected and a replacement copy started by the Azure Storage Infrastructure.

The Business Critical service tier uses local SSDs on the Compute host hardware to provide exceptional storage performance. This storage performance is a foundational requirement for In-Memory OLTP due to the intense read workload required at startup. An entire In-Memory OLTP table must be loaded into memory before it can be used in any type of query, thus delaying database startup until the table has been read completely. The storage performance limitations of Azure Premium Storage are such that database recovery becomes unworkably long. Therefore, the use of In-Memory OLTP tables is disallowed in the General Purpose tier.

Since local host storage has statistically low availability, Azure SQL DB and Azure SQL MI Business Critical tier uses multiple replicas to provide database redundancy. Each database for Azure SQL DB has a local availability replica running in synchronous mode available for failover. This replica is available for read-only workloads using the same `ApplicationIntent=ReadOnly` connection string parameter as with on-premises availability groups. All activity for the replica such as initialization, synchronization, connectivity, etc. is managed by the service and is largely invisible to the user. Failovers are automatic as is replica replacement after failover. A more detailed discussion of Azure SQL High-Availability solutions will be provided in Chapter 14.

Caution   Synchronous replication refers to data protection, not data availability. Data is considered protected when it is written to the log on the replica. Data availability requires completion of any transactions *and* recovery of the transactions via the REDO thread(s). The typical minimum lag for data availability on well-performing systems is three to five seconds after transaction completion. Some systems perform much worse. Your mileage *will* vary. If this lag is material to your application, test thoroughly before deploying such a solution to production.

DTU Standard/Premium

As mentioned earlier, the DTU billing model uses different names for equivalent functions. Standard is equivalent to General Purpose and Premium is equivalent to Business Critical when comparing functionality. Azure SQL DB also has a Basic tier that has severe restrictions on size and performance but is an excellent option for developing a data model or learning Azure SQL. The most attractive feature of the Basic tier is its cost, approximately 5.00 USD per month. Databases in the Basic tier can be scaled up to any other tier but cannot be scaled back down once they exit the Basic tier.

Azure SQL DB Special Cases

Azure SQL Database has three special cases, Elastic Pool, Hyperscale, and Serverless that we need to explore for a complete understanding of all the available Azure SQL Database options.

Elastic Pool

An Azure SQL Database **Elastic Pool** is a collection of Azure SQL databases that share a set of provisioned resources. An Azure SQL Database typically has a set amount of compute/memory and storage allocated. When you run out of compute or memory, queries queue up or run slower. Running out of storage prevents new data from being inserted. Managing resources on an individual database level isn't always easy or possible; we would often prefer to manage databases as a set. This is a very common scenario for organizations hosting SaaS – Software as a Service – applications. Databases that are structurally identical but may host different-sized customers then follow different activity patterns. Elastic pools give us the capability to provision resources for Azure SQL Database at scale.

Elastic pools can be altered in certain ways without incurring downtime. Databases can be added to or removed from pools fully "online." Pools can have resources added or removed without interrupting any databases in the pool.

Caution   While a specific elastic pool can only exist on a single logical SQL Server, membership in the pool and connection to the server are not equivalent. A database can join or exit the pool without impacting its database server connection.

Mixing workloads within an elastic pool has risks. High-resource-consuming databases can squeeze out low-impact databases when they hit peak activity. Azure allows you to set minimum and maximum resource allowances per database both in DTU and vCore modes. Setting these values to anything other than 0 (no limits) may impact the maximum capacities of the pool if the total of the minimum values for all pool members exceeds the maximum possible pool resource limit.

Hyperscale

Azure SQL Hyperscale is a highly specialized variant of Azure SQL Database. The internals are worthy of a book just in themselves, but our analysis will focus on the differences in functionality between Hyperscale and the other tiers of Azure SQL DB regarding operations and service selection.

Azure SQL DB Hyperscale is an attempt to provide a suitable SQL platform for VLDB – Very Large Database – deployments. Due to the internals, the fundamental system can be slower for smaller workloads but gain in efficiencies as the size increases. The improvements begin to surface as databases cross the 1 TB size threshold and continue as the database grows to the current 128 TB limit.

One challenge that Hyperscale attempts to mitigate is certain actions such as backup and restore have been proportional to the size of the database. A 2 TB database takes twice as long to restore as a 1 TB database for any SQL Service prior to Hyperscale. By using storage snapshots and a separate log service, Azure SQL Hyperscale can restore most databases, regardless of size, in about ten minutes. As with any Azure SQL Database, backups are automatic, but retention time choices are user-configurable.

Hyperscale is the only tier that cannot migrate to any other tier directly. The only way to migrate out of Hyperscale is to migrate to General Purpose, and only then if the database has not exceeded the maximum size supported on the General Purpose tier and only in the first 45 days since the initial migration. Once on General Purpose, the database can be further migrated, again assuming it fits the size constraints, into the Business Critical tier.

Hyperscale offers Read-Replica databases at a lower cost than Business Critical/Premium databases. Hyperscale can have multiple internally managed read replicas active at one time. These are called HA Replicas since any replica can be quickly "promoted" to replace the primary replica should the primary fail. The current limit is four HA replicas. Each HA replica must be the same size as the primary replica. Hyperscale also has much higher storage input/output operations per second (**IOPS**) and throughput than other tiers, so it is highly suitable for very active SQL Server databases.

Azure SQL DB Hyperscale also offers **Named Replicas**. Named replicas appear as separate databases in Azure SQL DB. These can be attached to the same logical server as the original or any other logical server in the same geographic region. Unlike

HA replicas, users connect directly to the named database instead of setting the `ApplicationIntent=ReadOnly` connection string property. Azure SQL DB Hyperscale supports up to 30 named replicas per primary database.

Serverless

Some SQL databases have very low or zero activity for extended periods of time. Keeping them online all the time is wasteful and expensive. Elastic pools can help, but not completely mitigate the cost. Azure SQL DB Serverless allows the database to *suspend* after a set inactivity time. Suspended databases only incur storage costs but no compute costs; however, the per-second operating cost is higher than the per-hour rate for the same compute level. Serverless also allows for a range of compute that auto-scales between set minimum and maximum values when it is not suspended. Serverless only supports the vCore purchasing model.

The following Azure SQL DB functionality runs on background threads that prevent auto-pausing. Auto-scaling will still work:

- Geo-replication and auto-failover groups
- Long-term backup retention (LTR)
- Sync database (used in data sync)
- DNS alias on the logical server
- Elastic Jobs (preview)

Serverless databases still connect via a logical server, the same as with any other Azure SQL Database. When you connect to a suspended database, there is a short pause while the database is brought online. Applications must be able to tolerate this delay, or Serverless is not an option for that workload. In addition, memory is more aggressively reclaimed on Serverless databases, even when not suspended. You can move databases from Serverless to any other tier seamlessly without changing logical servers.

Deploying Azure SQL Services

Microsoft has thoughtfully provided online labs that can be deployed in any Azure subscription, Free or Paid, if you have the correct permissions. Microsoft has also created example labs for deploying Azure SQL Database and Azure SQL VM services. These can be accessed via the Learning Path link referenced in Chapter 1.

Tip   I strongly suggest executing the deployment lab steps provided for Azure SQL DB and Azure SQL VM even if you choose to do none of the other learning modules. However, you really should do all the exercises if you plan to take the exam.

Azure SQL Managed Instance

Microsoft has not included a lab for deploying Azure SQL MI in the Learning Path training modules, likely due to the cost and complexity of such a lab. Azure SQL Managed Instance has a non-trivial minimum cost. The smallest instance supported in Azure SQL MI is four vCores. Using the Azure Pricing Calculator (`https://azure.microsoft.com/en-us/pricing/calculator/`), the cost is around 1 USD/hour and, deployed in a US region, not including any discounts or Hybrid Benefit. This adds up to $730 per month, which is well above most individual training budgets.

Azure SQL MI also takes a long time to deploy for the first instance, but Microsoft has worked around that by pre-provisioning instances so you may only see it take 20 minutes or so if you choose a common configuration in a popular region. The Azure SQL MI resource provider must first create a Virtual Cluster resource. This resource typically takes around four hours to deploy. Once the Virtual Cluster and first instance are in place, it only takes a few minutes to deploy additional instances. The time and resource consumption for deploying any Azure resource is not billable. Azure does not start billing for the service until it is completely deployed and usable.

Networking

Azure SQL Managed Instance also requires some Azure Networking infrastructure configurations to be in place before beginning deployment. You must have an Azure Network Subnet that can be dedicated to Azure SQL MI. It is best if all your Azure SQL Managed Instances share the same subnet within a Subscription due to the dedicated subnet requirement and the provisioning time and complexity of the Virtual Cluster. Microsoft limits the number of subnets you can use within a subscription for Azure SQL MI to encourage this design pattern.

Caution   Azure SQL MI has specific guidance on how large a dedicated subnet must be. Creating a subnet too small will prevent scale-up or scale-down operations and may inhibit maintenance operations. Microsoft does not charge for IP addresses by the each, so there is no cost penalty for larger subnets *(https:// learn.microsoft.com/en-us/azure/azure-sql/managed-instance/ vnet-subnet-determine-size)*.

Azure SQL Edge

Azure SQL Edge allows IoT – Internet of Things – developers to use SQL Server to store data locally on small IoT devices. As IOT devices get a lot smarter and are being tasked with more complex workloads than just relaying data, the software has evolved to require modern relational database storage. Microsoft SQL Edge is how Microsoft puts SQL Server into IoT devices. SQL Edge is considered part of Azure SQL because it is managed and deployed via the Azure portal and Azure's IoT management features. SQL Edge is a barebones SQL engine deployed in containers onto IoT devices ranging from full servers to small ARM-based devices and runs on both Windows and Linux devices. Patching and servicing are done automatically as with any Azure IoT device supported via the Azure IoT Hub. Azure SQL Edge has some specific optimizations for IoT devices. These include support for connected, semi-connected, and disconnected scenarios using incremental data synchronization. Data streaming and machine learning (ML) (model execution only – you don't want to develop ML models on IoT devices) are supported as well as many security features such as encryption, classification, and access controls. Azure SQL Edge is the modern SQL platform that can and should replace SQL Express in IoT-type devices.

Preview Features

As Microsoft develops new technologies and improves Azure services, they release those services in a gradual and controlled manner. The first step in release is a Private Preview. Private previews are run directly by product teams and require individual nomination and acceptance for the feature. Organizations accepted into a Private Preview will have one or more subscriptions enabled for a specific service available in only one or two regions worldwide.

Public Previews can usually be opted in by anyone via a Portal option. Public Previews are typically where Microsoft has largely completed functional testing and is preparing to operate the service or feature at scale. Public previews often have availability or geographic restrictions.

Unless otherwise specified, Preview services do not have any Service-Level Agreements and are not recommended for production use. Preview features on existing services do not have any SLAs, but do not invalidate SLAs for existing features if such SLAs exist. Microsoft strongly discourages using Preview features for production workloads. The upside is that preview features are offered at steep discounts, so you can explore capabilities cheaply.

Elastic Jobs

Azure SQL Elastic Jobs is an attempt to bring SQL Agent–like functionality to Azure SQL Database. Elastic Jobs uses an Azure SQL Database (S1 or higher for DTU based, any vCore size) to host the functionality the MSDB database does for on-premises SQL Server. After provisioning the database, you can create Agent-like jobs with some extra cloud functionality. We will explore Elastic Jobs in detail in Chapter 13.

Elastic Jobs was introduced in June 2018 and languished in Public Preview until released for General Availability (GA) in 2024 with multiple "it's going to be GA Real Soon Now" announcements over the intervening years. Elastic Jobs is covered in the DP-300 study guide, so we will study it here in Chapter 13.

Chapter Summary

You should now be comfortable understanding the fundamentals of each of the Azure SQL Services, including service tiers, billing models including Hybrid Benefit, and the general use case for each. You have the beginning knowledge to recommend an Azure SQL Solution candidate based on some basic requirements of the existing or newly proposed workload. You can see how Azure SQL has branched into several specialized services as Microsoft has adapted the general-purpose database engine to specific cloud-enabled workloads. Furthermore, they are all members of the same family with the same SQL Server database engine at the core of each service, yet each member of the family offers unique ways to provide that engine as a service. We will build on this foundation going forward as we explore various tasks required of an Azure Cloud SQL Database Administrator. Figure 2-3 shows SSMS Object Explorer connected to the various members of the SQL Family. Each has a very different surface area.

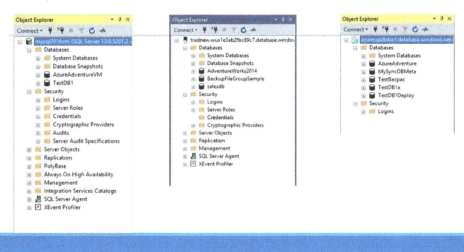

Figure 2-3. *Azure SQL Family Surface Area*

CHAPTER 3

Configure Resources for Scale and Performance

Scale and performance are two highly complex challenges facing nearly every database administrator, whether your systems are in the cloud or on-premises. People often see scalability and performance as the same problem, but they are not. Performance is the ability of the system to respond to queries within an expected time. Scalability is the ability to meet performance goals at specific workload levels and data sizes. One of the key indicators of success for scalability is if the resource consumption of the system increases at or below the rate of data and workload increase. Performance is therefore a pre-condition or element of scalability. A system that performs poorly will almost always perform even worse when faced with increasing data sizes or workloads.

A quick glance at the DP-300 study guide linked in Example 3-1 will make it abundantly clear that scalability and performance management in Azure is different from managing scalability and performance on-premises.

Example 3-1. DP-300 Study Guide Link

```
https://query.prod.cms.rt.microsoft.com/cms/api/am/binary/RE4q3yZ
```

Not only is the title "Configure Resources for Scale and Performance", every single sub-topic begins with the word "configure." In Azure, we set or change configurations to meet the demands of our workloads. Some configuration changes require more effort and potential outage times to implement. All configuration changes require an understanding of the underlying technology and, most importantly, what is the constraint on scalability or performance that is currently limiting your workload. Adding CPU and memory to a system that is constrained by Storage will not improve scalability

© Geoff Hiten 2025
G. Hiten, *Administering Microsoft Azure SQL Solutions*, Certification Study Companion Series,
https://doi.org/10.1007/979-8-8688-1585-0_3

or performance, but it will cost more money. In this chapter we will explore how to make certain adjustments to Azure services to remove or expand scalability and performance constraints and why you would make such changes.

SQL Data File Storage: Azure VMs

SQL Server has always been one of the most intensive users of Storage since the beginning days of the product. Entire companies have been created to provide products that meet the extreme Storage performance and scalability requirements of SQL Servers. While SQL Server contains a lot of lines of code for optimizing Storage input–output operations per second (IOPS) and throughput via some very smart caching algorithms as well as dedicating most of the host system memory to data cache, sometimes you still must go read a page of data off the disk to resolve a query. You must always write a log record to Storage before you can report a transaction as complete. Eventually you must write all the dirty pages out to disk to create a checkpoint for recovery purposes. These time-critical Storage input–output tasks all create a need for high-performance file storage for SQL data and log files. Fortunately, Microsoft has done a lot of the heavy lifting for us when we need to provision Azure Storage for SQL Services.

Size, IOPS, and Throughput

We need to carefully define some terms and set some expectations on how Storage is provisioned and billed in Azure before we can explore using storage and its impact on scalability and performance. In Azure, all Storage is completely abstracted. There is a near-total disconnect from the physical hardware and the Storage Abstraction Stock Keeping Units (SKUs) available to be provisioned in Azure. The one similarity that is typically exposed is the type of physical media – Hard Disk Drives (HDDs) or Solid-State Drives (SSDs) – that embodies the storage. This book and the Microsoft training materials consistently reinforce this distinction by referring to Storage and not Disks until they are abstracted to be attached to a host system. Disks are how abstracted Storage looks like to certain OSes and users, but that is simply because it is convenient to map new functionality to existing abstractions, much like how on-premises SAN storage looks like locally attached disks to a Server OS.

When we talk about on-premises Storage, whether traditional disks or abstract SAN storage, we begin by focusing on the size of the disks we need. Physical disks are shipped with labels clearly indicating the size on the case. What they do not show are how many IOPS each disk unit supports nor how much throughput each disk is capable of, even though those metrics are more critical to SQL performance and scalability than the storage capacity. In Azure, all three metrics are defined as part of the provisioned capability of each Premium Storage SKU.

Up to now, this book has referred to IOPS and throughput as singular metrics, but each counter has both Provisioned and Burst metrics as well as Burst duration metrics. For convenience, we will continue to refer to Provisioned IOPS and Throughput as just IOPS and throughput. We will refer to the same metrics the same way while discussing capacities for Premium SSD-based storage as that is what is most commonly used for Azure SQL Services when scalability or performance is a concern.

On-premises, we often test SAN storage by running common stress tests such as IOMeter or DBHammer. These use relatively small data files and expect to receive the entire IOPS or throughput performance of the entire Storage system, or at least the capacity of the underlying tray or physical aggregation of drives and caching. Storage does not work the same way in Azure. Provisioned IOPS and throughput are directly linked to the size of each Premium Storage SKU. Therefore, we refer to the size of an Azure Premium Disk by its SKU, not its size in MB/GB/TB. Azure Premium Storage sizes are denoted by a P*n* format where *n* is a number between 1 and 80. P1 disks have a 4 GB size limit and can support 125 IOPS and a throughput of 25 MB/second. These IOPS and throughput numbers sound very low compared with what we are used to from on-premises systems. That is because they *are* low. You must provision a minimum of a P30 disk to get IOPS and throughput that are sufficient for most SQL workloads. This is the Microsoft Best Practices recommendation for Azure SQL Database Storage. This is also the starting point for production-grade systems, not the perfect number for everyone. A P30 disk supports 5,000 IOPS and 200 MB/second of throughput and provides 1 TB of storage. This leads to what often appears to be overprovisioning storage for SQL, but only by legacy metrics of size alone. The combined capacities (size, IOPS, throughput) of a P30 or greater disk are what need to be compared to the workload requirements. The complete chart of P-sizes with their corresponding metrics is linked here in Example 3-2.

Example 3-2. Premium Storage Capacities

https://learn.microsoft.com/en-us/azure/virtual-machines/premium-storage-
performance#premium-storage-disk-sizes

These IOPS and throughput limits are hard limits. You get what you pay for, but
not a single bit more. One good thing is that any data remapping such that is needed
for scaling up to the next tier does not come out of your performance pool. That comes
from the internal Storage Stamp (what Microsoft calls a Physical Storage Host in
Azure). You still get the full IOPS and throughput capacity you have provisioned, even if
maintenance activities are happening "under the covers." The same rule applies if there
is an underlying hardware fault and the system self-repairs using the built-in storage
redundancy.

Microsoft recommends starting with P30 Premium Disks as the minimum size for
adequate SQL performance and expanding as necessary based on whichever metric
becomes a limiting factor. Actual storage capacity is very seldom the limiting factor.
Microsoft continues to recommend separate data and log disks. The original separation
was for recovery isolation and redundancy, but that does not apply here on fully abstract
redundant Storage. Microsoft recommends different disks for data and log so that each
disk can have an appropriate caching configuration. Unless you configure SQL to use the
local ephemeral drive D: for tempdb, a third disk is recommended for tempdb due to its
unique IO pattern.

One on-premises practice that helps maximize performance and scalability has a
detrimental effect on Azure SQL VMs. Creating multiple data disks to separate different
databases is something often done to optimize performance for on-premises systems.
Since disk performance is now inexorably tied to disk size, we are better off consolidating
data files into fewer, larger disks that have greater performance. Disks that are size
optimized will inevitably be short on performance. Such disk choices will hinder us
or lead us to have to provision far more storage than we need to get the performance
characteristics we require for each data or log file.

Another practice that has led many DBAs to conclude that Azure SQL VMs or
PaaS services simply won't hold up to their expected workloads is improperly using
benchmarking tools. While Microsoft Azure's Terms and Conditions prohibit publishing
unauthorized benchmarks, many people try it themselves for consumption within their
organizations. If you configure your benchmarks the same way you do on-premises
using IOMeter or DBHammer, these benchmarks will inevitably fail, as the Storage will

be provisioned by size rather than performance. You can achieve very good SQL storage performance in Azure, but you must understand that all Storage metrics except Latency are proportional to the allocated size of the disk.

SQL Data File Storage: Managed Instance

One of the key design principles of Azure is that when higher-level services consume foundation services like Storage or Compute, they consume the same services that are offered to any Azure customer as stand-alone services. In the case of Azure SQL Managed Instance, the service consumes Azure Premium Storage on SSD as its SQL Data and Log Store. Since these are the same Premium Disks we use on Azure SQL VM, we can use the same technique of provisioning larger disks to improve IOPS and throughput.

With Azure SQL MI, the storage is managed directly by the service. You do not have any direct control over its provisioning or management. However, we can rely on the characteristics of Azure Storage to indirectly influence some storage metrics. Since we know the size tiers of Azure Premium Storage, we can expand the allocated storage in Azure SQL MI up to the next largest tier and receive the IOPS and throughput benefits just like with Azure SQL VMs.

SQL Data File Storage: Business Critical Storage

Azure SQL DB and Azure SQL MI Business Critical (or Azure SQL DB Premium when billing via DTUs) use the same type of storage for all SQL data and log files. The Business Critical service tier uses local SSDs on the underlying physical host. Therefore, hardware generation selection affects the maximum storage capacity and overall performance. Local SSDs have higher IOPS and throughput, as well as lower latency, which are all critical for high-performance workloads. This higher performance comes with additional costs, and I don't mean just the bill.

Since local disks on a hardware host have the same recoverability as the host, that is to say very limited, we need something else to provide storage redundancy and recoverability. We will address this in greater depth in Chapter 14. Business Critical Instances and Databases have internal replicas similar to Always-On Availability Groups running traditional SQL Server on-premises or in Azure SQL VMs. Since the system always has at least two replicas running (one Primary and one Secondary), the cost is significantly higher. Also, hosts must have significant storage built in to support local

45

SQL files, costing more to build and operate. Finally, the number of cores allocated for a service (database, instance, or pool) is loosely coupled to the storage maximum size and performance. These limits exist to keep workloads roughly in balance so the host storage is not consumed before all the available cores can be provisioned.

These internal replicas all require significant management overhead. While this is handled internally, certain changes like scaling up or down require copying the data twice, one for each replica. This can significantly delay the implementation of a provisioning change, especially with larger databases.

Now that we have a solid foundation on Storage in general and SQL data file storage in particular, we can examine how to configure the various SQL Services for improved scalability and performance, including storage options.

Configure Azure SQL Database for Scale and Performance

Azure SQL Database has many different options for managing scale and performance. Most of these reside on the *Compute + Storage* blade of the Azure SQL Database portal page. The most obvious way to scale Azure SQL Database is to simply add more cores or DTUs. That has the unfortunate effect of also increasing the price. Sometimes there is no way to avoid increasing the provisioned allocation for a database. The good news is we can adjust the compute allocation "on the fly" while our database is serving workloads.

We can change the Service Tier of a database while it is running. Since changing service tiers requires creating a full copy of the database on the new service tier, this will take time, with longer times for larger databases. You can choose when to initiate any change, but the actual switchover happens automatically when the new data copy is ready. You do not get billed for the new tier until the copy is ready and the new service tier is serving connections. If the new tier is a provisioned tier, you will be billed for a minimum of one hour at the new service tier.

We can also increase the maximum allowed storage size for a database on the Compute + Storage blade. As with any storage, the larger the storage allocation, the greater the IOPS and throughput it can support. As always, there are limits on storage size based on current compute allocation that cannot be exceeded. If you manipulate the slider for Compute, you can see the slider for Storage move relative to its total capacity. These limits change over time, so refer to the "Limits, Boundaries, and Constraints" section of Chapter 1 for links to these limits.

Scaling works in two directions, up and down. We almost always think of scaling up because when we have purchased hardware and licenses for on-premises SQL Servers, we are fully invested. We have already paid for the capacity; taking it in and out of service does not save us anything. Since Compute scale is directly tied to cost in Azure, we can benefit by scaling down during off-peak times. There are many businesses that have peak and slack seasons. Some companies do nearly all of their business during a short window of a few days or weeks each year. Other businesses have cycles that match various calendar events like month-end closing for accounting firms or divisions. Any of these predictable events can be accommodated by scaling up in preparation and scaling down once the peak workload is completed. Scaling can even be automated, which we will discuss further in Chapter 12.

Compute + Storage Blade Details

Let's explore the Compute + Storage blade on the Azure portal. You can access this blade during deployment on the Basics page, the very first page displayed. Figure 3-1 shows the Basics blade, scrolled down to the options we need to consider for performance and scalability. This figure also shows the option to add the database to an elastic pool at deployment.

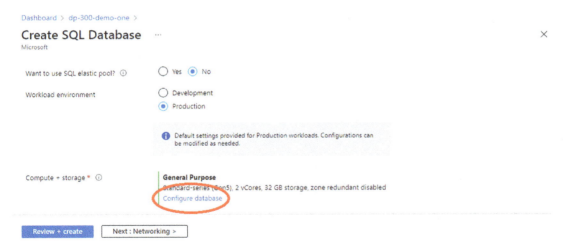

Figure 3-1. *Azure SQL DB Deployment Basics Blade (Scrolled Down)*

Clicking the Configure database link takes you to the full Compute + Storage blade as shown in Figure 3-2. This blade is *Dynamic*. Dynamic pages change layout and format top-down. As you make or change selections, the page may add, remove, or adjust options below your current selections. Figure 3-2 displays the layout based on default values for production workloads. Since we are deploying a database, Apply saves changes. If we accessed this blade for a running database, Apply would immediately begin changing to the new settings.

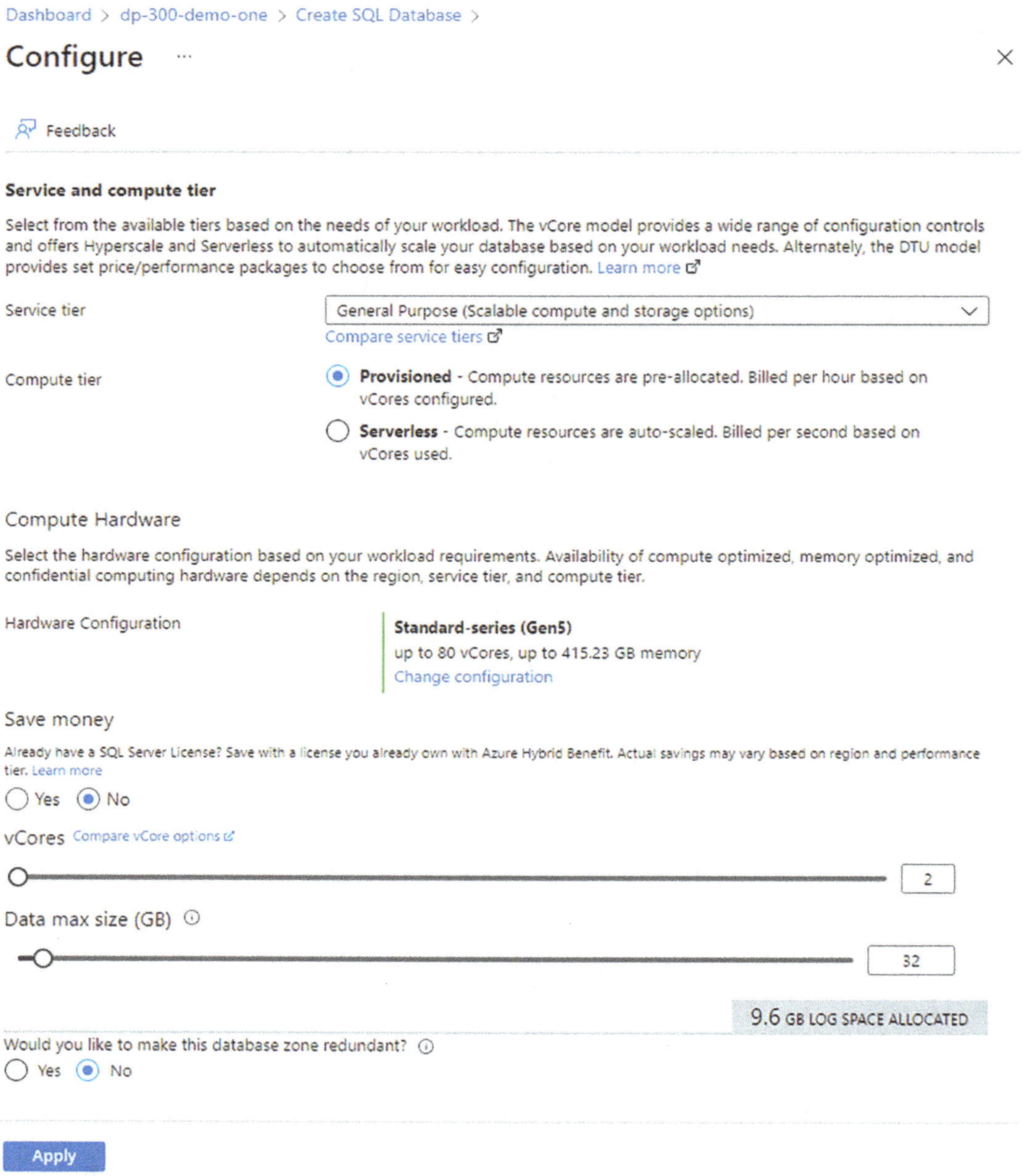

Figure 3-2. *Azure Compute + Storage Blade (Defaults)*

Since these changes have a potential cost impact, Azure shows a helpful cost estimation pane like the one shown in Figure 3-3, either to the left or the bottom of the page. Cost estimations in Azure are always based on a 730-hour month, so your actual bill will vary depending on the number of days in each calendar month. Billing is generally by the hour, but there are exceptions, notably the Serverless tier. Notice that Compute and Storage are separate sections of the estimate, letting you easily determine which resource is incurring costs. License costs (if any) are included in the Compute cost since they are directly related to Compute.

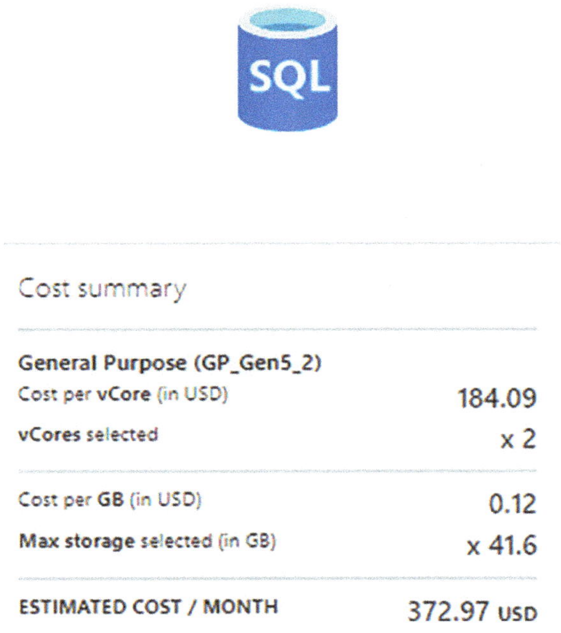

Cost summary

General Purpose (GP_Gen5_2)	
Cost per vCore (in USD)	184.09
vCores selected	x 2
Cost per GB (in USD)	0.12
Max storage selected (in GB)	x 41.6
ESTIMATED COST / MONTH	372.97 USD

Figure 3-3. *Azure SQL DB Service Cost Estimation*

Let's start by changing the Service Tier. Figure 3-4 shows the complete list of service tiers available for Azure SQL DB.

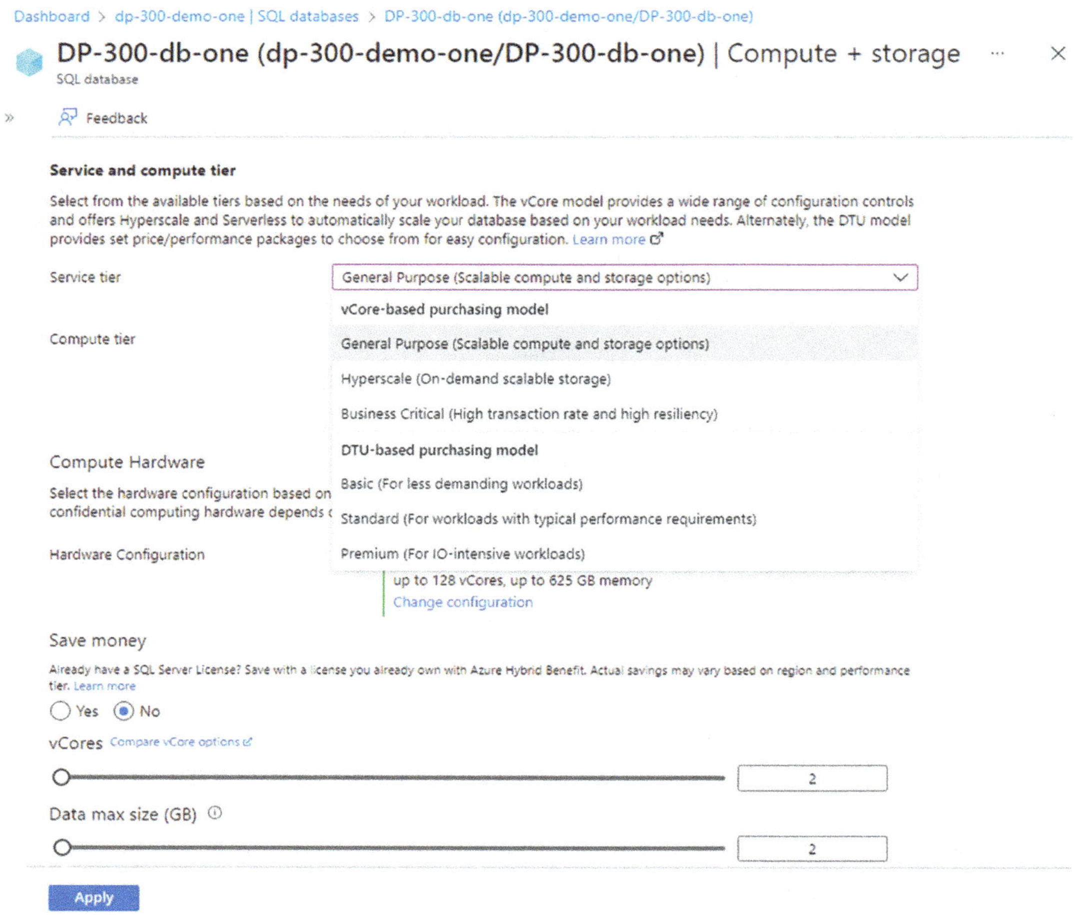

Figure 3-4. *Azure SQL DB Service Tiers*

This is where you choose the Service Tier. By choosing a Service Tier, you also choose its associated billing model. Notice if you change the tier, other options lower on the page change. If I select a DTU-based Service Tier, I can no longer choose Hyperscale or Serverless or select my Hardware Configuration. This is reflective of the fact that the DTU billing model is a legacy artifact and most new development is being done under the vCore billing model. The Basic Service tier shown in Figure 3-5 has almost no options – you get a fixed service at a very low price.

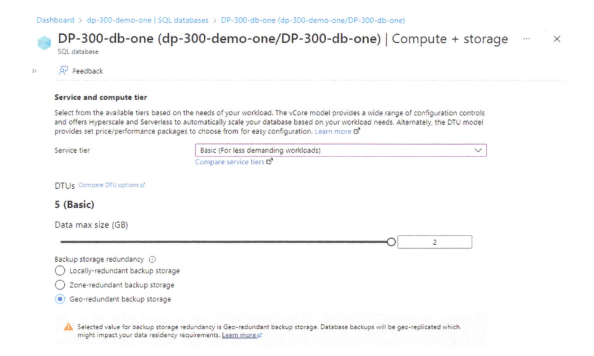

Figure 3-5. *Azure SQL DB Basic Service Tier*

Once you have selected a Service Tier, you can choose how much compute to apply. We will discuss Hardware selection in the "Azure SQL Managed Instance Scalability and Performance" section later in this chapter.

We will use the Business Critical tier in the vCore billing model for illustrative purposes. Down toward the bottom of the page are two sliders representing Compute and Storage. Recall that License cost is dependent on vCore count, so there is no need for a third slider. If you have access to the Azure portal, here is where hands-on experience is best. If not, you can look back at Figure 3-2 to see the sliders.

Simply move the sliders to the new Compute and Storage levels desired, or you can directly enter amounts in the box on the right end of the slider. Entering an invalid number will select the next lowest valid vCore count. Notice that the choice of Compute affects the maximum Storage possible. You can change multiple items at the same time such as Service Tier and vCore count.

> **Warning**   Some changes are one-way only. Exiting the Basic service tier means you cannot return. You would need to create a new database with the same content, either imported from DACPAC/BACPAC or from an Azure SQL DB backup, to return to a Basic tier database. The Hyperscale service tier can only transition to the General Purpose tier, provided the database has not exceeded the maximum capacity of that tier and is within 45 days of the migration to Hyperscale. Once in General Purpose, you can transition to either Business Critical, again assuming the database is within the BC tier constraints, or back to Hyperscale.

Once you hit "Apply," the changes begin immediately. Behind the scenes, either the existing database resource limits are adjusted or a new database is created and populated, depending on the level of change required. Once the new database (if required) is ready, the system performs an internal Availability Group–like failover, and the new database is now servicing on the workload. This marks the time when you will start getting billed for the new level. Allocating more storage to a database without changing the service tier will not cause any service interruption and takes effect immediately.

Once the system is satisfied the new database is working properly, the old one is deleted. Just like an on-premises failover, all connections are dropped, and client applications must reconnect during the internal failover. Most modern applications have connection retry logic built in, but many legacy systems do not. Any long-running queries will be dropped when their connection is killed. Plan carefully when making any compute changes as you will almost certainly get a brief service transition shortly after initiating a change. Changing Service Tiers for larger databases (1 TB and larger for this purpose) may take considerable time as the entire database must be copied to the new service tier – twice in the case of transitioning to Business Critical from another tier.

Elastic Pool

As we discussed in Chapter 2, an Azure SQL Database can be a member of an elastic pool. Entering and exiting a pool changes the resources available to the database; it does not change the logical Server or any other connection properties. An elastic pool is scaled using the same controls as an individual database, only the new resources are available to the entire pool.

Scaling an elastic pool has one major advantage over scaling individual databases. Adding or removing resources does not cause any service interruptions, provided you are not changing the service tier. Since changing the service tier involves copying all the databases, a service interruption during failover is inevitable. Elastic pools can be billed using either the DTU or the vCore model. Elastic pools are not available for Serverless Azure SQL Databases.

Hyperscale

Azure SQL Database Hyperscale is a specific service tier designed to solve VLDB (Very Large Database) challenges. As the name implies, it is a solution to many common Azure SQL Database scalability constraints. Microsoft originally only recommended Hyperscale for 1 TB and larger databases, but, due to customer experience, has removed that restriction and now supports and recommends Hyperscale for all database sizes. Hyperscale scalability applies more to storage limitations than it does to compute constraints. If your workload is CPU bound, the only solution is to either reduce the CPU demand or increase the CPU supply. If you are constrained at the storage layer, either by size, throughput, or both, then Hyperscale can help.

Hyperscale breaks the monolithic SQL Server into independent subsystems, which can be hosted in separate host environments. These are the Primary and HA replica compute nodes, the Storage layer (using Azure Premium Storage), the Log Ingestion Subsystem, and the Page Servers. Page Servers replace direct storage reads and writes from the compute nodes with large internal page buffer pools. Each page server manages a single SQL data file. Transaction Log Writes are written to the log subsystem, which aggregates the small IOPS into larger blocks for writing to persistent Storage.

RBPEX (Resilient Buffer Pool EXtensions) is the "Secret Sauce" of Azure SQL Database Hyperscale. RBPEX is very fast SSD-backed local storage that presents as RAM extensions to SQL Server memory. The underlying Buffer Pool Extension technology allowing this ultra-fast storage to be used as clean Buffer Pool pages was first introduced in SQL 2014 as a means of getting larger read caches into SQL Standard Edition without allowing for absurd memory sizes. The technology didn't receive wide adoption but did get some niche uses. Using that technology with the split-subsystem architecture of Hyperscale landed some interesting scalability improvements.

The first major difference between Hyperscale and other service tiers is the separate log subsystem. One detail we didn't examine closely during our discussion on storage was that you can generally max out either IOPS or throughput of any storage device (Azure or otherwise) but not both. You can either have a lot of small storage activities or fewer, larger ones. Azure SQL Hyperscale's log subsystem converts IOPS to throughput by accepting log writes, which are typically small in a high-IOPS environment persisting them via NVBPE and exporting them to longer-term General Purpose Premium Storage in larger batches. This allows Hyperscale to have the largest log ingestion rate of any Azure SQL DB service tier. This ingestion rate is loosely coupled to the service level (number of vCores), assuming your workload isn't CPU bound or log ingestion is throttled to ensure recoverability.

The second scalability benefit is by forcing individual file sizes to stay below 1 TB; data is forcibly sharded across multiple page servers with each page server adding to the total Storage capacity in size, IOPS, and throughput. With each page server also contributing to the RPBEX pool, the likelihood of a second-tier cache miss stays about the same as the data set size grows. The only place that compute allocation affects cache size is with the primary compute or HA replicas as RAM and cache sizes are both dependent on the number of vCores allocated. Page server size is independent of the provisioned capacity.

The final scalability enhancement in the Hyperscale tier is the ability to scale horizontally. Azure SQL Database Hyperscale can have multiple secondary replicas in addition to the primary replica. Secondary replicas are either HA (High-Availability) replicas or Named Replicas. HA replicas have the exact same size of compute node provisioned as the primary compute node and are attached to the same Page Servers. As the name implies, HA replicas act as failover partners in case the primary replica becomes unresponsive. HA replicas are accessed via the `APPLICATIONINTENT=READONLY` connection string option just like other Azure SQL Database replicas. Named Replicas are attached under different database names to a logical SQL Server, either the same as the primary or another logical SQL Server. Named Replicas can be differently sized than the original Primary replica but still use the same set of page servers. Named replicas can also have different network connectivity and security contexts than the primary as they are logically a separate database on possibly a separate server.

Azure SQL DB Hyperscale offers unique capabilities for scalability and performance for Azure SQL Databases. Hyperscale should be one of the first solutions you explore if ordinary resource increases do not resolve your scalability or performance challenge.

Serverless

When we think about scalability and performance, our first instinct is to solve for "bigger." Low-end scalability has just as many challenges as does the high end of scalability. In Azure, the challenge we face for low-end or intermittent database use is how can we economically provide sufficient service without paying for unused provisioned compute during long idle times. Azure SQL Database Serverless addresses these challenges with two differences from the Provisioned billing model. First, compute is allocated with minimum and maximum CPU allocations. Instead of hourly billing, compute use is calculated "on demand" as it is consumed, with the upper bound being an absolute limit on maximum compute capability that is billed by the second, not the hour. The rate per second is roughly twice what the equivalent provisioned rate per hour would be for the same core count, so Serverless is only useful if the average CPU use is less than half the maximum provisioned capacity.

The second difference between Azure SQL DB and Azure SQL DB Serverless is that the database can be paused if the service detects zero activity for a specified period of time. This time window is user-configurable within certain boundaries. When the database is paused, you are not billed for any compute, just for storage. When a connection arrives, the database is made active and begins processing requests. Microsoft maintains a list of activities that will prevent auto-pausing or will trigger auto-resuming. This list is part of the documentation in the link provided in Example 3-3.

Example 3-3. Serverless Documentation

```
https://learn.microsoft.com/en-us/azure/azure-sql/database/serverless-tier-
overview?view=azuresql
```

It is essential to examine any candidate databases before migrating to Serverless and to monitor Serverless databases to ensure that auto-pause and auto-resume are working as expected. Many Azure SQL Database customers wait for one or two months after initial provisioning before optimizing costs with Serverless so they can base the decision on actual usage patterns. The Azure Advisor will recommend Serverless if it detects an appropriate usage pattern for a specific Azure SQL Database.

Azure SQL Managed Instance Scalability and Performance

Scaling and performance for Azure SQL Managed Instance is largely the same as for Azure SQL Database. Storage allocation on the General Purpose tier allocates Azure Premium Storage behind the scenes. The P-disk values for size, IOPS, and throughput apply, subject to a maximum log ingestion rate for the service. The discussion on storage performance optimization for SQL VMs applies to Azure SQL Managed Instance – General Purpose tier. The Compute + Storage configuration blade shown in Figure 3-6 looks very familiar to the earlier example for Azure SQL Database if you are reading this book in order.

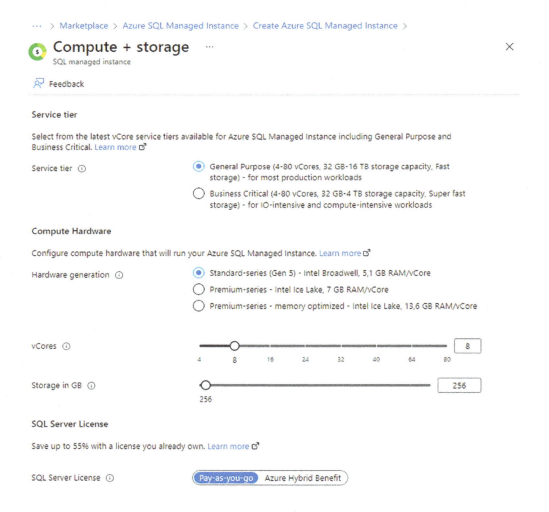

Figure 3-6. *Azure SQL Managed Instance Compute + Storage*

There are only two service tiers – General Purpose and Business Critical. In the General Purpose tier, storage and compute are only slightly interdependent. Below 16 vCores, maximum storage is limited by the number of vCores. 4 vCores maxes out at 2 TB, while 8 vCores will allow 8 TB. Only at 16 vCores and above can you access the service maximum capacity of 16 TB. As with all limits stated in print, check the current limits – they typically grow over time.

The Business Critical tier has a much stronger correlation between storage capacity and vCore allocation. 16 or fewer vCores can only allocate a maximum of 1 TB storage. 24 vCores will allow for 2 TB. 32 or larger will allow for the full 4 TB of storage using Standard-series hardware. While these values are subject to revision, it is likely that these values will not change until future-generation hardware is deployed as that has been the case so far.

Hardware selection directly impacts scalability and performance by altering the amount of RAM per vCore and by changing the maximum amount of storage available in the Business Critical tier by selecting Premium-series memory-optimized hardware. Figure 3-7 shows the maximum storage capacity is 16 TB when choosing the Business Critical Service Tier with Premium-series memory-optimized hardware.

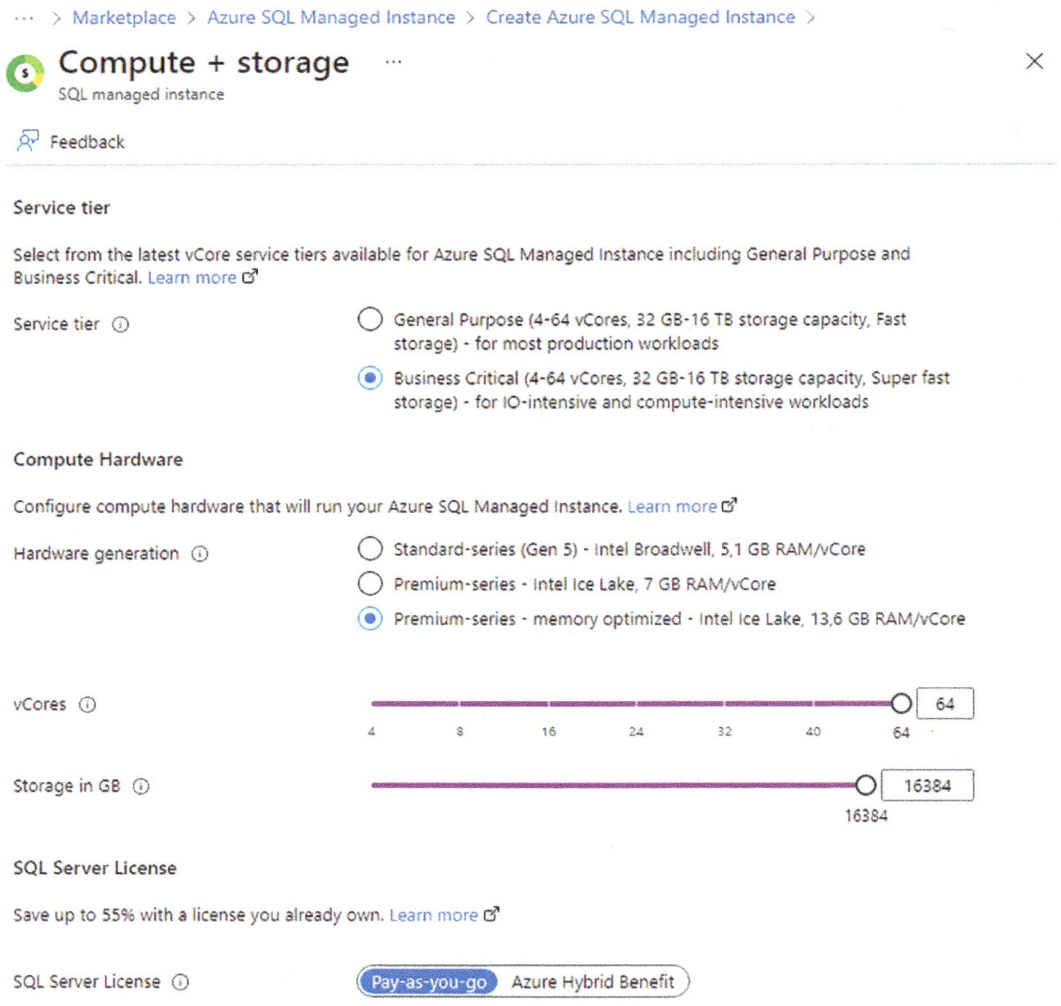

Figure 3-7. *Azure SQL Managed Instance Premium-Series Memory-Optimized Maximum Scalability and Performance Capacity*

The 16 TB capacity is only available at 64 vCores. Reducing the compute slider to 40 vCores (not shown) changes the maximum storage capacity to ~5.5 TB (5,632 GB). Any compute allocation below 40 vCores follows the same storage size restrictions as the other Azure SQL Managed Instance hardware generations.

Azure SQL VM Scalability and Performance

Azure SQL on Virtual Machines is very much like SQL Server on-premises. It uses the same retail release software and patches as you currently use outside of Azure. Microsoft makes prepared Marketplace images available for rapid deployment, but the end result is the same. In Chapter 2 we discussed the Azure SQL IaaS Extension service and how it helps run SQL better in Azure. Any examples regarding Azure SQL VMs will assume you have this service deployed and available. All Marketplace images rely on this service to configure SQL Server during deployment, removing the need to run the SQL Installation media.

Two major factors that affect the scalability of an Azure VM running SQL are the Virtual Machine size and the virtual machine series. Machines can be sized up or down within a series, sometimes with only minimal disruption. Moving machines across series takes a minimum of a full reboot and can require deprovisioning and reprovisioning the entire virtual machine. The *VM series* reflects specific hardware selections and options on the virtual host platform.

VM Series

The series of a Virtual Machine determines its built-in capabilities. The list of machine types and combinations of features would exhaust the capacity of this book several times over, so we won't be going over every possible option. It is important both for the test and as an Azure SQL Database administrator to understand a few of the most used options for SQL VMs and where to look up everything else. The Azure VM naming convention is documented in the link in Example 3-4.

Example 3-4. Azure VM Naming Conventions

```
https://learn.microsoft.com/en-us/azure/virtual-machines/vm-naming-
conventions
```

Azure began with the "A" series of VMs, a shared-resource model that did not map underlying physical compute cores to vCores and was highly vulnerable to cross-VM resource contention. "A"-series VMs have been replaced by the "B" series with similar capabilities. Many people use "B"-series VMs for SQL development. It wasn't until the

"D" (Dedicated) series of VMs was created that we could count on a specific amount of non-conflicted cores for our servers. Azure VMs were now ready for SQL Server production workloads.

Over the years, many more Virtual Machine series have been developed that also use Dedicated cores. Every series is a compromise between various features, primarily memory optimization, compute optimization, bandwidth optimization, local storage availability, and GPU or other specialized hardware availability. Some series are highly specialized, while some are more generally applicable. It is unlikely that we will need the "N" series of VMs with multiple GPUs for SQL Server VM hosting. It certainly would not be cost-effective.

Two of the more common series of VMs used for SQL besides the "D" series are the "M" series and the "E" series. The "M"-series VMs are Memory-Optimized. They have more memory than a "D"-series VM with the same core count. This is useful when you are running very large SQL VMs that may not need a lot of CPU capacity, but can benefit from high amounts of RAM for buffer cache. This also helps manage costs by biasing to lower core counts while still keeping a larger memory footprint.

The "E" series is Bandwidth-Optimized (because "B" was already taken) and is great for SQL Servers with high-IOPS or high-throughput needs. Earlier we discussed the Storage system limitations on IOPS and throughput, but there is a corresponding limit on the VM side as well. Each VM (size and series) has a specific maximum capacity for aggregate Storage IOPS and throughput. To reach desired target IOPS and throughput, both the VM and the Storage must support your desired levels. The "E" series, especially in the latest version, has higher IOPS and throughput than any other machine at the same core allocation size. This series was specifically developed for high-performance SQL Virtual Machines. Microsoft has iteratively improved the "E" series with different versions. As of publication, the current version is v5.

The other element indicating specific VM series for SQL Performance and Scalability is the lower-case letters between the core count number and the version in the VM series name. These letters indicate specific capabilities of the VM. Microsoft refers to these as "Additive Features." The three most important for our purposes are indicated by the letters "d," "s," and "b."

Additive feature "d" indicates "diskfull." Machines with a "d" attribute have a local D: drive backed by host-based SSDs. The D: drive gets reset every time the VM restarts, so do not use it for anything permanent. However, since it is local, it is not subject to the

IOPS and throughput limitations of standard storage and has the lowest latency of any Azure Storage, making it ideal for tempdb, provided the disk is large enough to meet your needs. Disk size is proportional to the provisioned core count.

Additive feature "s" indicates the machine is capable of using Azure Premium and Ultra storage. This is generally a requirement for most Azure SQL VMs, assuming you follow Microsoft Best Practices. Microsoft recommends using only "s"-capable VMs for SQL Server workloads with Premium or Ultra Storage.

Additive feature "b" is relatively new. This was added when the E-series v5 machines were created to indicate "Block Storage Performance," although it may be easier to think of this as "Bandwidth-Optimized." These machines typically have higher IOPS and throughput limits than other machines with the same core counts. This is important when your SQL Server VM needs more storage bandwidth, but you don't need or want more CPU capacity.

Data Engineering for Scale and Performance

SQL DBAs in Azure and on-premises have several tools we can use as data engineers to improve the scale and performance of SQL Server Systems without needing to change the application tier. This is critical since many times we do not have the ability to change the application. The three methods we will focus on here are Table Partitioning, Data Sharding, and Data Compression. Each method has specific use cases where the feature can benefit performance. The goal here is not to make you an expert on these features, but to improve your ability to understand how they can increase performance and scalability.

Table Partitioning

Table Partitioning is a Data Engineering Mechanism that primarily addresses scalability rather than performance. Partitioning is applied to very large tables, typically 1 TB or larger or with over 100 million rows. Below this size, the effort to manage Partitioning is usually more than the benefit Partitioning returns. SQL Table Partitioning is a Horizontal Partitioning mechanism whereby rows of data are sorted into partitions based on one column value.

Partitioning a table creates multiple internal "sub-tables" that are treated as a single logical table for Data Manipulation Language (*DML*) operations but can be addressed individually for certain Data Definition Language (*DDL*) operations. DML operations change the data of a table, while DDL operations change the definition of the table.

First, we will discuss the mechanics of partitioning. Once we are comfortable with how it works, then we can explore how partitioning helps manage scalability. The first step in partitioning is to create a Partition Function. A Partition Function defines the boundaries for the individual sub-tables. Most tables are partitioned on a Date, DateTime, or DateTime2 column, typically the date the record was created, but that is not an absolute requirement. What is essential is the partitioning key be as immutable as possible. Creating partitions based on a column that change as the row of data updates causes partition movement. This increases the work overhead of each DDL statement and works counter to our goals of increasing scalability. Created_Date is a better column choice than Last_Updated_Date as the former is generally immutable while the second is changeable and can potentially cause data movement when updated.

Partitioning begins with the CREATE PARTITION FUNCTION command. This function determines the boundaries of each partition. Partition Functions imply two outer bounds values that exist but are not included in the CREATE PARTITION FUNCTION statement. These are the upper and lower maximum values for the partition column Data Type. As a quick but useless example, consider the following PARTITION FUNCTION in Example 3-5.

Example 3-5. Partition Function Simple Example

```
CREATE PARTITION FUNCTION Useless_Partition_Function (int)
RANGE LEFT
FOR VALUES (2)
```

This CREATE PARTITION FUNCTION statement defines a partition function that divides a table into two partitions. The actual boundaries of the two partitions are (–2147483648 through 2) and (3 through 2147483647), even though we never specified the outer boundaries. Since we declared RANGE LEFT, the boundary values are included in the left partition. Values are considered ascending from left to right. If we had used RANGE RIGHT, the partitions would have been (–2147483648 through 1) and (2 through 2147483647). RANGE LEFT and RANGE RIGHT become important in date-based partitioning schemes as to which partition the boundary date falls into.

Notice what we haven't done. We have not specified any table to actually partition. We have merely defined the PARTITION FUNCTION that can be applied to any table with an integer-valued column that we desire to partition. In fact, we don't refer to the partition function directly as part of a table definition. Instead, we use an object called a Partition Scheme. The Partition Scheme maps partitions to FileGroups. Example 3-6 shows a Partition Scheme for the Useless_Partition_Function we defined in Example 3-5.

Example 3-6. Partition Scheme Simple Example

```
CREATE PARTITION SCHEME Useless_Partition_Scheme
AS PARTITION Useless_Partition_Function
TO (FileGroup1, FIleGroup1)
```

A couple of things we need to note here. We always have one more filegroup in the Partition Scheme than we have boundaries in the Partition Function since there is always one more Partition than there are enumerated boundaries. The repeated use of FilegGroup1 as the target is not a typo. You can map more than one partition to a single filegroup. Consider a very large table that is partitioned by day but stored on Monthly or Yearly filegroups. You would repeat each Monthly FileGroup name for every day of that month. There is also the issue of Azure SQL Database that does not allow multiple filegroups. Only the PRIMARY filegroup exists in Azure SQL Database. In that case you would use code like Example 3-7 and the ALL keyword. You have a Partition Scheme, but it is irrelevant for the storage layer.

Example 3-7. Partition Scheme Example with Primary FileGroup

```
CREATE PARTITION SCHEME Useless_Partition_Scheme
AS PARTITION Useless_Partition_Function
ALL TO (Primary)
```

When you CREATE a TABLE or INDEX, you reference the Partition Scheme, and the table partitions are automatically created. Creating an index that references the Partition Scheme of the underlying table is referred to as creating a Partition-Aligned Index. Partition-Aligned Indexes have attributes that help scalability and performance.

We can perform interesting tricks with partitions under certain circumstances. If we have a table and associated indexes that exactly match the characteristics of a particular partition, we can perform a SWITCH function and swap the table with the partition. One of the key elements here is that the data in the table doesn't have to match the data in the partition, only the boundary conditions of the partition and data in the table. Empty tables automatically match all boundary conditions. We can also SPLIT and MERGE partitions by executing an ALTER PARTITION FUNCTION command. While it is possible to split or merge partitions with data, it is not a recommended practice as it can take considerable time to move that data. Splitting and merging empty tables is a metadata-only exercise since there is no data to move or copy.

Now that we know how to create partitions, we need to understand how they can help improve performance and scalability. The exact answer depends on the type of data operations we intend to do with the data in our table. Most of the time, Table Partitioning data is based on a monotonically increasing time column, creating a constantly increasing record of events. Most of the time, we don't want to keep every data point forever. Summary and aggregate data is fine after a certain period, often months or years. After the data is aggregated or archived, we can delete it. This is referred to as a Sliding Window. By switching empty tables for full partitions at the beginning of the table, we can easily delete large chunks of data without blocking. We can even truncate the old partition (now a table) and use it to swap for the next partition we want to empty. We can MERGE empty partitions without any data movement as there is no data to move.

Tip   Always leave empty partitions at the beginning and end of your table so you can SPLIT and MERGE those empty partitions without data movement.

Once a partition is settled, that is, there are no changes to the rows, the filegroup it resides on can be marked as READ ONLY. This can reduce the backup and recovery duration for Very Large Databases (VLDBs). You can configure SQL to back up only the active filegroups as its regular backup operation. The READ ONLY filegroups are backed up once and the backups archived. When you restore the database, you can restore the READ ONLY backups after the live portion is restored and running. This gives a much better Recovery Time for VLDB operations. Most users won't even notice that older partitions are still restoring.

One final minor benefit of Partitioning is the Query Optimizer is aware of partitioning when the indexes are Partition Aligned. The optimizer will attempt to eliminate partitions that cannot hold candidate rows during query execution, reducing potential scan sizes. This is particularly helpful when executing aggregation queries over ranges of data that have over 20% estimated match rate. Under these conditions SQL will scan an index or table rather than do an index lookup, but with partition elimination the number of rows scanned can be drastically reduced.

Data Sharding

Data Sharding is splitting a database workload into shards or chunks so that multiple SQL engines can operate the workload. Shards typically are divided based on hash functions so that each SQL Server carries an even proportion of the entire load, but some systems use other functions to shard. Sharding is the opposite of Partitioning in that workload is spread across shards rather than concentrated into one or two active partitions.

Sharding is how Azure SQL DB Hyperscale achieves its scalability and performance metrics. The overhead of Sharding can slow the system down on smaller workloads, but eventually sharded systems are faster with large enough workloads. Azure SQL, with the noted exception of Hyperscale, does not have any native tools to shard data across multiple databases. Many people have developed tools to do this via custom code, but that tends to focus on very specific workloads.

One variation on Sharding is single tenancy, where each database has the same schema but contains different data, often split along customer lines with each customer getting their own database. This is a very common scenario for hosting companies where they may be running hundreds or thousands of copies of the same application for their customers while hosting the SQL databases on a private cloud or an Azure service. Automated deployment and management are keys to handling such large-scale SQL farms. Ultimately, this model is more scalable and manageable than the monolithic application where many customers are mixed into a single database. Some companies operate a hybrid model where some large customers have their own tenant database while very small customers share a multi-tenant database.

Sharding is also a key element of Azure Synapse scalability, but that is a topic for another book, another test, and another day.

Data Compression

At first thought, Data Compression doesn't seem to be a scalability or performance enhancement technique, but examining modern computing hardware, cloud or otherwise, tells us differently. Every facet of computing has grown by multiple orders of magnitude over the past 30–40 years except one. Compute speed, memory speed and size, and storage capacity have all grown by at least a factor of 10,000 in the past 30 years. However, storage bandwidth has only grown by a couple of orders of magnitude at best. This leaves us with a lot of computing capacity and a lot of data but with a very thin pipe connecting the two.

When discussing Scalability and Performance, Storage Compression becomes a way to maximize the capacity of that thin pipe, in essence trading CPU capacity for storage bandwidth. Of course, for this to be a successful trade that increases scalability or performance, the system must have available CPU capacity as well as be bandwidth constrained to storage. This is most common in analytics workloads where large data sets are scanned and aggregated but less common in transaction-processing scenarios where the individual transactions tend to be relatively small, involving very few rows at a time.

Azure SQL offers multiple types of compression, including some that don't seem to be compression at first glance. Row compression and Page compression are the same as their counterparts in on-premises SQL and are the first types of compression we typically think about, but most people don't put Column Store compression in the compression category. Technically it is compression in that the overall data footprint is reduced from a raw representation, but many DBAs do not think of it as a form of compression. We tend to look at it as more of a data storage transformation that works to improve Scalability and Performance for specific workloads. But it is still a form of data compression.

Chapter Summary

Azure SQL Scalability and Performance is a very broad topic, probably one of the more wide-ranging topics we will explore in our certification journey. Do not let the complexity of the topic discourage you. The primary purpose of this chapter was to give you not only facts but context to help you determine the factors that are either contributing to or limiting your Azure SQL Database scalability and performance and then adjust the correct element appropriately.

You should now feel comfortable in understanding the elements that go into Scalability and Performance in Azure for all three SQL Database services. This chapter covered "what" and "how," not "why" or "when." We will talk about how to measure and detect performance issues, other than via the volume of end user complaints, in Chapter 8. I continue to recommend completing all the exercises in the Microsoft Learning Path linked in Chapter 1. This becomes critical the deeper we get into Azure SQL.

CHAPTER 4

Plan and Implement a Migration Strategy

Now is the time for you to put your knowledge to the real test: migrating a workload to Azure. Or at least answer exam questions about migrating workloads to Azure. Migrating workloads is particularly challenging for several reasons. Your customers have come to expect a certain level of service from your database operations. You expect to be able to deliver that level of service or better. Your employment success may depend on your project success, especially if you are a consultant brought in to guide or execute a migration. Fortunately, there is a well-tested process you can learn and follow that has a solid track record of success. As we get into details of the process, specific techniques and technologies are "plugged in" at the right time to execute a particular step. The process is the same for every migration, but the exact execution may vary depending on the source systems, target systems, existing SLAs and workloads, and other variables that are outside our control. With a few exceptions, migrating to Azure is no more or less complicated than migrating all your database servers to another data center. Like any other large and complex IT task, we break it down into simpler phases and steps and execute them in order.

Cloud Adoption Framework Process

Microsoft has published and maintained a process for migrating on-premises workloads to Azure called the Cloud Adoption Framework (CAF). This CAF process includes both business and technical migration elements. The business elements focus on the economic justification for Azure adoption and are typically not part of the responsibilities of a SQL database administrator whether in Azure or on-premises. We will focus on the technical elements of migrating SQL Server workloads to Azure.

© Geoff Hiten 2025
G. Hiten, *Administering Microsoft Azure SQL Solutions*, Certification Study Companion Series,
https://doi.org/10.1007/979-8-8688-1585-0_4

The DP-300 test focuses on the SQL data tier for migration as those are the particular skills necessary for an Azure SQL database administrator, but in reality, a workload consists of web and application tiers that have to be migrated as well. Our SQL migrations are often part of a larger Azure Cloud Migration Strategy that we need to support. The CAF is structured accordingly.

Example 4-1 links to the landing page for the overall Cloud Adoption Framework.

Example 4-1. Azure Cloud Adoption Framework Landing Page

```
https://learn.microsoft.com/en-us/azure/cloud-adoption-framework/
```

Much of the CAF focuses on business goals and outcomes including the financial aspects of an Azure migration. We need to pay close attention to these factors since they generate business and technical requirements we must meet during the migration process. Common requirement types are service levels, downtime allowed for cutover, schedule, and even potential target landing architectures. Gathering and documenting these requirements is usually the difference between a successful migration and an unsuccessful one. Once we have our requirements from the business, we can begin with the technical phase of the migration.

Evaluate Requirements for the Migration

Migrations to Azure happen for a variety of reasons. Ultimately, they are all driven by business needs. Knowing and understanding what the business drivers are is essential to a successful migration. If your goal is to "just get it there," you won't know how to measure success or failure. Without predetermined goals there is so much room for interpretation that the perception of success becomes unrelated to the actual migration outcome.

The Microsoft Cloud Adoption Framework helps define a successful outcome by determining essential goals that must be met during the migration. The DP-300 exam often has questions that rely on understanding and applying business goals to technical scenarios to determine the "best" answer. Some questions may be structured to emphasize low downtime during migration, while others may have a much longer outage window to shift workloads. Understanding the right techniques and technologies to meet specific business migration goals is essential to real-world and exam-world success.

Broadly speaking, migrations fall into two buckets, lift-and-shift or migrate-and-modernize. Lift-and-shift is exactly what it sounds like. You take the existing workload and move it "as is" into Azure with as little change as possible. Often this means taking snapshots of virtual machines and provisioning them in Azure. This has the advantage of rapid execution and is typically used when there is a short business deadline such as an office or data center closing or a merger/divestiture operation that must be completed by a specific date. Lift-and-shift migrations with SQL Server almost exclusively use SQL IaaS as the target Azure SQL Service.

Migrate-and-modernize examines the workload and partially or completely replaces IaaS services with Azure-native services during the migration process. Instead of Azure IaaS SQL, you might choose Azure SQL DB or Azure SQL Managed Instance as the target SQL host technology in Azure. Similar PaaS options exist for web, application, storage, and networking tiers and are part of a complete cloud modernization. Some migrations choose to modernize only part of the application stack during migration to address specific known shortcomings with the existing architecture. The Microsoft Inventory and Assessment tools offer recommendations and support for both migration types.

Inventory and Assessment

The first technical step in a migration is to determine exactly what we are migrating. As database administrators, we should have a solid inventory of systems we are responsible for. These databases and servers may not cleanly map into workloads for migration. We often have databases sharing host servers to optimize licensing costs or simply because we had spare hardware capacity when it came time to deploy that workload onto a SQL Server host.

Your inventory (assuming you have one) is a good starting point but may not provide enough information to properly plan a migration. When you migrate IT systems to Azure, the unit of migration is the *Workload*. The definition of *workload* is deliberately vague. A good working definition is that a workload is s a single, identifiable application or set of applications that perform a defined business task. It may be as simple as a single web application with web, app, and data tiers that is largely self-contained, or it can be as complex as a suite of hundreds of apps, microservices, and databases that together run the Enterprise Resource Platform (ERP) of a large corporation. Regardless of size, the defining characteristic is that the workload is treated as a single entity for purposes of hosting and migration. Everything in the workload gets migrated and managed as a set.

One of the primary ways of identifying a workload is to look at the communication coupling rate of the various components. Data and application tiers are *tightly* coupled. They engage in frequent communication where high reliability and low latency are essential. *Loosely* coupled components connect intermittently and do not require low latency. FTP file transfers, periodic data loading to analytic systems, and export to external applications are examples of loosely coupled systems. A workload consists of a set of tightly coupled components that need to reside in a single geographic location (Azure Region) to work correctly.

Azure Migrate

The first tool in our migration toolbox is called *Azure Migrate*. Azure Migrate has multiple parts that will inventory, assess, and migrate workloads to Azure. Sounds like we can just hit a button and all our work gets done for us, right? Unfortunately, life isn't that easy. Azure Migrate is not aware of SQL as a specific server workload; it evaluates systems in terms of compute, storage, networking, and memory consumption. Azure Migrate consists of a cloud service in Azure and a *Virtual Appliance* that runs in your on-premises data center.

Everything in Azure Migrate begins with a *Project*. A project is where data is collected and shared from various inventory and assessment tools. Note that Projects are assigned to *Geographies*, not specific regions. Migrations that include Business Continuity and Disaster Recovery (BCDR) capability are multi-region, by definition, but generally keep within a same geography or sovereignty boundary. Note the Project Details Geography selection control on the Create project blade shown in Figure 4-1.

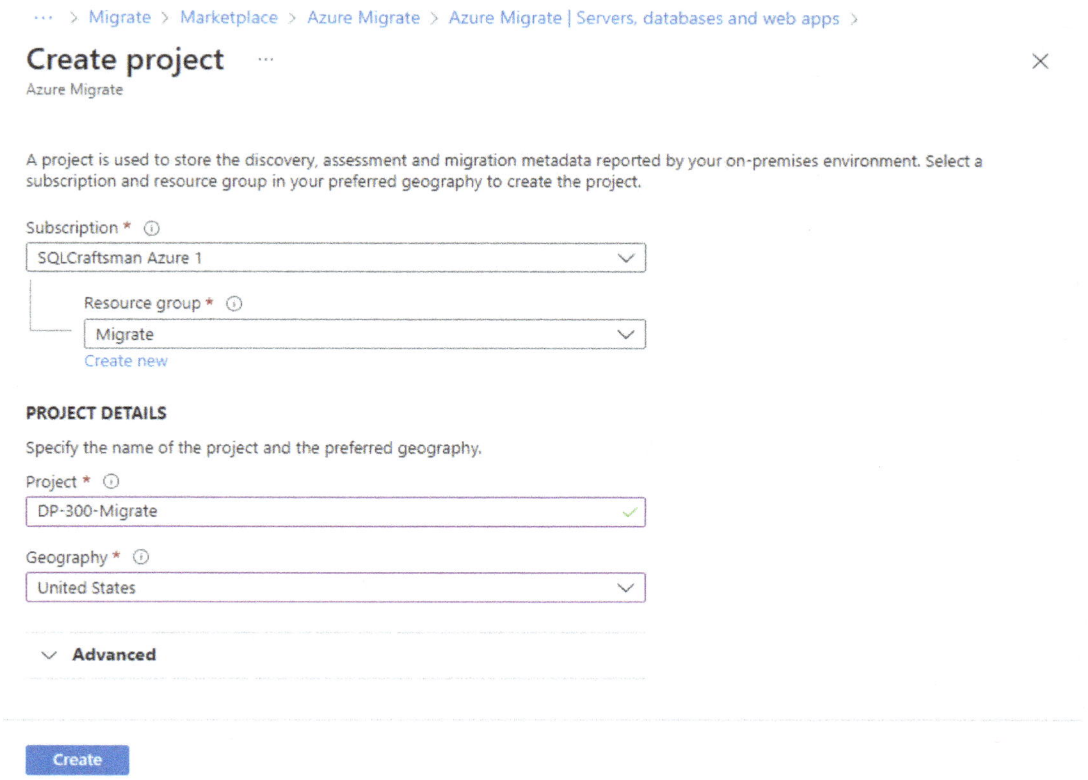

··· > Migrate > Marketplace > Azure Migrate > Azure Migrate | Servers, databases and web apps >

Create project ···

Azure Migrate

A project is used to store the discovery, assessment and migration metadata reported by your on-premises environment. Select a subscription and resource group in your preferred geography to create the project.

Subscription * ⓘ

| SQLCraftsman Azure 1 | ∨ |

Resource group * ⓘ

| Migrate | ∨ |

Create new

PROJECT DETAILS

Specify the name of the project and the preferred geography.

Project * ⓘ

| DP-300-Migrate | ✓ |

Geography * ⓘ

| United States | ∨ |

∨ **Advanced**

Create

Figure 4-1. *Create an Azure Migrate Project*

Once we have an Azure Migrate project, we can begin to use the tools to inventory and assess our workloads. You can use an existing inventory and upload a CSV file, or you can use a virtual appliance to discover the components of a workload.

Note   Our discussion on migration tooling may deviate slightly from the official curriculum, including screenshots and actual functionality. Azure migration is constantly evolving and improving, especially in the various tools available. The Learning Path modules may still show and discuss older version capabilities and limitations. This book will discuss current software version capabilities but will also note older technology where it has been known to show up on the DP-300 exam.

Azure Migrate Appliance

The component of Azure Migrate is the Azure Migrate appliance. The Azure Migrate virtual appliance is a repurposed enhancement of Microsoft's Azure Site Recovery virtual appliance since the two appliances do almost the exact same thing. Technically, an Azure migration is just a planned failover to a permanent Disaster Recovery site in Azure with no expectation of failing back. The overall event is called a *cutover* and refers to all the parts of the workload, while a *failover* is the technical process of switching data. We will explore those concepts in more detail in Chapters 14 and 15.

The Azure Migrate Virtual Appliance can be deployed to VMware, Hyper-V, or even physical infrastructure. If your SQL migration is part of a larger migration, this appliance should have already been deployed by the Infrastructure or DevOps teams. If it has not been deployed, you need to spearhead getting it deployed as soon as possible, especially if your migration is going to be a lift-and shift.

The Azure Migrate Virtual Appliance is an Agentless system that will monitor systems and networks in your infrastructure to develop your inventory (*discovery*) and your assessment. The inventory and assessment documentation support each other. The inventory becomes your "master list" for what is running in your on-premises infrastructure along with two key supplemental pieces of information, a target migration inventory and a dependency map. This inventory often highlights missing or incomplete inventory information you already may have.

The dependency map shows what systems communicate to other systems. Systems that communicate constantly (tightly coupled) are almost always part of the same workload and should be migrated together. Systems that infrequently communicate may be possible to separate into different migration waves or may be "left behind" as part of infrastructure modernization.

Azure Migrate looks at IaaS solutions when making recommendations for moving workloads. The Azure Migrate appliance checks performance metrics once every five minutes on each system it discovers. By comparing the provisioned compute capacity and the actual usage, the Azure Migrate service will recommend appropriate target compute (VM) sizes for your workloads. Metrics do include CPU, memory, and IOPS/throughput usage, so the recommendations are accurate and comprehensive. Azure Migrate has updated capabilities that enhance its ability to analyze SQL Server workloads. Azure Migrate will also often recommend M- or E-series VMs for SQL IaaS hosts due to memory and Storage IOPS/throughput requirements.

> **Caution** Azure Migrate recommendations are not cluster aware. If you are using standby nodes in a shared storage or Availability group cluster, Azure Migrate will recommend significantly less compute for these nodes. Use the sizing recommendation for the primary active node(s) to determine the correct VM size for your failover cluster nodes.

The Azure Migrate Virtual Appliance provides significant information for sizing your target systems as well as providing dependency information essential for a successful workload migration. Other tools in the Azure Migrate toolbox can help provide other, necessary information for a successful migration, particularly if you are considering migrating to one of Microsoft's PaaS SQL Services.

The Azure Migrate appliance performs migrations by copying a VM image to Azure and keeping changes at the storage layer synched via periodic snapshots. The good news is the snapshots do engage the Volume Shadow Service (VSS) and are SQL transactionally consistent. You don't have to worry about database corruption due to inconsistent snapshots. The bad news is these snapshots happen at a maximum frequency of once per 15 minutes. This means your cloud copy is up to 30 minutes behind, giving you a large Recovery Point Objective (RPO) during a cutover. You need to allow either for data loss or for time to sync the cloud copy with a quiesced on-premises source system before any cutover.

Data Migration Assistant

The Azure Data Migration Assistant (DMA) is the direct descendant of the SQL Server Upgrade Advisor tool. The tool has been significantly enhanced and updated for Azure Migration use. The tool has two primary uses: assessment and migration. Most DBAs use the assessment tool more than the migration helper. The assessment tool uses a rules engine to analyze existing servers and databases for migration compatibility. DMA is the authority on whether a deployed workload is or is not compatible with a target SQL Service. DMA will test for SQL version compatibility, if you are migrating from an older version of SQL Server to a more current one during your migration. DMA will also test for compatibility to Azure SQL Managed Instance or for compatibility to Azure SQL Database. Compatibility tests must be run separately for each targeted service since they have different surface areas and supported features.

These compatibility tests are essential to guarantee your workload is supportable by Azure SQL Managed Instance. If your workload passes compatibility tests and successfully lands on Azure SQL Managed Instance using a particular target compatibility level, Microsoft will guarantee that future changes to Azure SQL Managed Instance will still support your target compatibility level.

The migration support capability is useful for small or test migrations but suffers from some critical limitations that may limit its usefulness for enterprise migrations. First, the system running DMA must have access to both the source and target SQL platforms as well as a shared file location for the data to transit through. Second, DMA runs as a console application and must stay online and connected during the entire migration. Third, DMA can only perform an offline migration. Finally, DMA cannot migrate databases to Azure SQL Managed Instance. Its only valid targets are Azure SQL Virtual Machines or Azure SQL Database. Given these restrictions, you can see why DMA is not necessarily the best option for migrating enterprise SQL workloads to Azure.

Azure Database Migration Service

The strongest tool in the Azure Migration Toolbox for actual migration is the Azure Database Migration Service (DMS). DMS is an Azure service that addresses several of the shortcomings of the DMA tool, specifically in that it runs as an Azure service to remove the dependency on a constantly running console application. DMS can also perform online and offline migrations to any valid Azure SQL target service except for online migrations to Azure SQL Database. DMS can execute multiple migration projects simultaneously so large sets of servers can be migrated at once.

A DMS project consists of a Source Server, a Destination Server or Service, and a set of objects to be migrated. DMS uses two possible storage locations, one on-premises to land data coming out of your source system and a storage container in Azure so the Azure services can load data directly. DMS handles copying the files from on-premises to Azure Storage. DMS can also migrate SSIS packages from a source server to a target server, although best practice is to define the new server as a deployment target and redeploy the packages from source control. Many organizations do not properly source-manage their SSIS packages and thus cannot redeploy, making the migration tool necessary.

DMS once was able to do online migrations to Azure SQL DB, but due to other company acquisitions, Microsoft no longer has access to the third-party drivers that enabled online migrations and had to remove the online migration capability to Azure SQL Database from the Azure Database Migration Service.

Azure Data Studio

Many of Microsoft's customers found the array of tools for assessment and migration to be very confusing. One tool is a console app, while another is an Azure service. One gets provisioned, while another must be downloaded and installed. Microsoft is addressing this by bringing together all the tools under the Azure Data Studio (ADS) umbrella via the use of ADS extensions. ADS runs on the Visual Studio Code (VS Code) platform and is therefore natively extensible. The ADS extension for migration is sensibly named the Azure SQL Migration Extension for Azure Data Studio.

The Azure SQL Migration Extension for Azure Data Studio doesn't do much by itself. It is a wrapper or control for the DMA test suite and for the Azure Data Migration Service. It is important in that it brings assessment and migration together into one desktop tool running on a modern, extensible platform. Azure Data Studio is currently deprecated and will no longer be supported starting February 2026. The Migration Functionality appears to be transferring to Azure Arc for SQL, but Arc is beyond scope for this book.

Third-Party Tools

One glaring omission in the Microsoft Azure SQL Migration Toolkit is the inability to perform an online migration to Azure SQL Database. The Azure Database Migration Service used to have this capability by licensing Attunity drivers strictly for online SQL Migrations. This capability was withdrawn after Qlik acquired Attunity in 2019, and no comparable replacement technology has yet been included in the Azure Database Migration Service. There are several third-party incremental SQL synchronization tools in the marketplace. Some use Change Data Capture (CDC), while some read transaction logs to harvest changes. One of the more popular and successful products is from Striim and is the tool of choice for online migration to Azure SQL Database. While the DP-300 exam will not test you on knowledge of third-party tools, this is essential knowledge to perform the actual migration tasks required by a cloud database administrator role.

Evaluate Offline or Online Migration Strategies

One of the first elements you need to determine when migrating SQL Servers to Azure is answering the question "How much downtime can I take during a migration?" The answer to this question along with the size of your data set will determine which migration strategy is best for you. Small data sets may be able to simply have the entire database copied during an offline migration outage. Large databases that could take days across VPN or even ExpressRoute connections must be prepared for online migrations.

Tip   Correctly choosing online or offline migration is often the determining factor for which possible answer is "best" both on the test and in real life.

Unlike web or application host systems, SQL databases are highly stateful. The state of the database changes constantly as the system ingests and processes transactions. A copy of a web or application server from a few hours or even days ago is usually fine, requiring only a possible code deployment refresh to bring it up to current. Databases, particularly transaction-processing engines like SQL Server, cannot "roll back" to an earlier time point during a migration without incurring business consequences. Migrating SQL requires that the data be in a known good consistent state with no data loss.

Implement an Offline Migration Strategy

The detailed outline for the DP-300 Learning Path shows online migrations before offline migrations. I have elected to swap online and offline migrations in teaching order since performing an offline migration is a prerequisite to performing an online migration and should be taught first. Part of the Cloud Adoption Framework involves standing up all the elements of a production site and exercising the components. This requires an offline copy of data in your target Azure SQL Database Service. This copy will be deleted and overwritten during the final migration and cutover.

An offline migration is simply copying a database to your choice of target Azure SQL Database platform using any appropriate technology. For an enterprise migration, you need to pick a tool that can reliably repeat the process at scale such as the Database Migration Service. "One-off" or test migrations can be done manually with SQL Server Management Studio or Azure Data Studio. The key to choosing an offline strategy is that you do not care about transactions past when the database copy is made. This is appropriate for development environments or for populating candidate production environments prior to go-live for testing purposes.

The steps for an offline migration are as follows:

1. Extract a copy of the database.

2. Copy those file(s) to Azure.

3. Apply the copy to the target platform.

The exact work required for each step changes depending on the target platform. If you are targeting Azure SQL VM or Azure SQL Database, the most common method for steps 1 and 3 is using SQL-native Backup and Restore commands. If you are targeting Azure SQL Database, there is no user-accessible Backup or Restore command, so migration must be done via BACPAC or other data export/import mechanisms such as BCP. For all three targets, Azure Blob Storage is generally used for the storage necessary in step 2, but you can copy to a local file system or file share when targeting SQL VMs. Since the SQL IaaS extension uses Azure Blob Storage for Managed SQL Backups, it is best if you get familiar with backing up to and restoring from URL. The recommended solution is to always use Azure Blob Storage. We will go over that process in detail in Chapter 15.

You can use the Azure Database Migration Service to orchestrate migrating multiple SQL databases and servers simultaneously, but be aware that you may hit bandwidth limits coming out of your data center. DMS gives the benefit of being repeatable as many times as necessary for testing and data refresh prior to final cutover. Simply rerun the project, choosing to replace any existing target databases. You can also manually script the backup/copy/restore if you desire as another automation technique. Regardless of the tooling you choose, test the process repeatedly. Get familiar with how the tools work, the normal runtimes, and variances for each test iteration.

Implement an Online Migration Strategy

Online migrations to Azure are more technically complex than offline migrations to Azure. They require significant planning, preparation, and testing to succeed. Success not only depends on migrating the entire workload, including SQL components, to Azure without data loss; it typically must be done within strict and often tight time frames.

An Online Migration is one that includes an initial sync, similar to an offline migration, combined with an ongoing data refresh. For on-premises migrations, this has traditionally been done with a `RESTORE DATABASE WITH STANDBY` command followed up by a combination of Log restores and optional Differential restores. We use a similar process in migrating to Azure, but the exact mechanism for initial sync and incremental updates is different depending on the target SQL service. You cannot restore transaction logs directly to Azure SQL DB or to Azure SQL MI.

Online migrations do not imply zero downtime. They do require zero data loss and a specified, minimal downtime for the actual cutover. This downtime is often 30 minutes or less from the time the workload is stopped until it is resumed. This is rarely enough time to completely copy the database from source to target, especially with large, production databases, hence the initial sync and incremental update process. Planning an online migration requires that not only is the SQL database migrated but the rest of the workload "stack" be deployed and ready to accept traffic. Online migrations require a high degree of planning and cooperation with the entire IT organization to minimize disruptions and hit specified migration downtime windows. The choice of online vs. offline migration is determined by the amount of outage time the business allows compared to the time to copy the entire data set for a workload. If the data is much to copy during the cutover outage window, an online migration is required.

All Azure SQL Services can be subscribers for good, old-fashioned Transactional Replication. Replication can therefore be used as a data transfer and synchronization method for all target SQL services. This is a valid solution according to Microsoft and actually works for many workloads. The major drawback is that Transactional Replication does not include all schema objects, resulting in an incomplete database. Transactional Replication synchronizes *data*, not *databases*.

You will have to do some schema patches during cutover after you bring in the final data changes. Specific objects not transferred include unique constraints, views, and stored procedures. If you choose to use Transactional Replication to implement an online migration, you will need to perform a schema comparison during testing and have a schema update/repair script ready to deploy during the cutover. This applies to all Azure SQL Services as migration target services.

Online Migrate to Azure SQL VM

Migrating to an Azure SQL Virtual Machine is the closest process to an ordinary on-premises data center migration of any Azure SQL Migration targets. The only complexities beyond the usual SQL Migration Challenges involve Azure-specific conditions, typically connectivity, identity, and policy. We have previously discussed proper configuration of Azure SQL VMs, so the target server should be properly configured and healthy based on your work from earlier chapters. Any online migration will require a direct network connection between your source and target systems.

Microsoft does not have *Azure*-native tools to online migrate a SQL database from on-premises servers to Azure SQL VMs, but the native SQL Server Log Shipping capability built into SQL Server Management Studio works very well for this purpose. If the target server has a different identity framework, that is, no common domain, you may need to "roll your own" log shipping scripts or download a set from a reliable Internet source.

Online Migrate to Azure SQL Managed Instance

You cannot directly log ship to an Azure SQL Managed Instance to implement an online migration. Microsoft does provide the Azure SQL MI Log Replay Service that works like a Log Restore and uses Transaction Logs generated from your source database. You must call Azure APIs instead of executing SQL Scripts to apply the logs. Fortunately, Microsoft has wrapped all this functionality into the Azure Database Migration Service. DMS can implement both online and offline migrations. Online migrations require generating and entering an application ID/key pair for the DMS to authenticate to the target Managed Instance to call the Log Replay Service APIs. As we noted earlier, you can use the Azure Data Studio migration to Azure SQL Wizard to drive the Azure Database Migration Service. Azure Data Studio is the current preferred method.

One important point to remember is that regardless of whether you use DMS directly or through Azure Data Studio, you should not run the ongoing synchronization process for extended periods of time. Microsoft recommends 36 hours or less. The reason is the underlying Log Replay Service cannot survive an internal cluster failover within Azure SQL Managed Instance. SQL MI uses SQL Always-On Availability Group–like technology "behind the scenes" to minimize downtime during software updates. A new internal replica is created and synchronized with any updates already applied. The system then fails over to this replica. After a short time to ensure the new system is stable and working correctly, the old replica is discarded. This happens automatically inside the Managed Instance service. The process is throttled to not impact overall system stability and is completely automated. This failover process breaks the Log Replay Service and thus the ongoing synchronization. The longer the run window, the greater the risk of it breaking. I personally have seen systems running in sync for up to two weeks, but this is highly dependent on Microsoft's update cadence and release schedule, something that is not generally published for PaaS services.

Azure SQL Managed Instance Link

Microsoft released SQL Server 2022 to General Availability in November 2022. This release included a feature called "Azure SQL Managed Instance Link" usually called "SQL MI Link" for short. This feature allows a DBA to create an online copy of an on-premises database to an Azure SQL Managed Instance and keep that database in sync indefinitely using the SQL Server Distributed Availability Group (DAG) technology.

Any SQL Server 2016 or higher can be the source server. The following requirements must be met for a SQL Server to participate in Azure SQL Managed Instance Link:

- Always-On enabled

- Trace Flag T1800 (>4K storage block size correction)

- Trace Flag T-9567 (compress Always-On seeding data stream)

- TCP 5022 port open to sqlservr.exe (for default instance)

- Database master key created – master database

The instance does not have to be part of a Windows Server Failover Cluster nor even be domain-joined. Everything can be accomplished via SQL logins, provided both the SQL Server and the Managed Instance have SQL logins enabled. This is not to say the machines cannot be clustered or domain-joined; they certainly can be, but neither condition is a requirement. The target SQL Managed Instance must have the November 2022 Feature Wave enabled.

SQL Server Management Studio 19.0.0 or greater is required to run the Azure SQL Managed Link Wizard, but command scripts can be run through any supported version of SSMS or Azure Data Studio.

Configure Replication

Using SQL Server Management Studio, select a database to extend to Azure and right-click. You can select additional databases later in the wizard. The wizard has two functional branches, one for initializing the Replication and another for executing the Failover as seen in Figure 4-2.

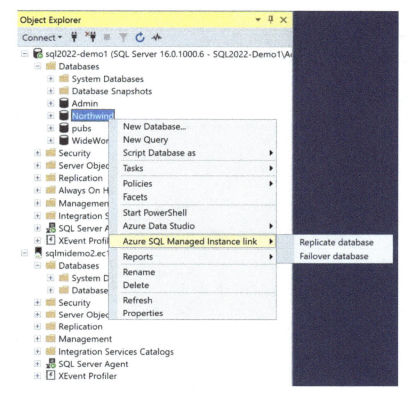

Figure 4-2. *Azure SQL Managed Instance Link SSMS Start*

We will start with the "Replicate database" wizard first. That starts with the Introduction page shown in Figure 4-3.

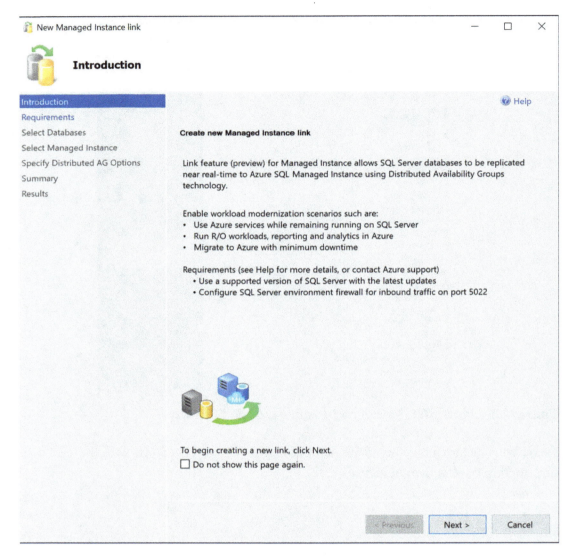

Figure 4-3. *Azure SQL Managed Instance Replication Introduction*

The next page has two panes: Server Requirements and Availability Group Requirements shown in Figures 4-4 and 4-5, respectively. These are the same requirements listed at the beginning of this walkthrough. You can often remediate any issues and retest without restarting the wizard. Some remediations (trace flags change and Availability Groups enabled) require a SQL Server Service restart.

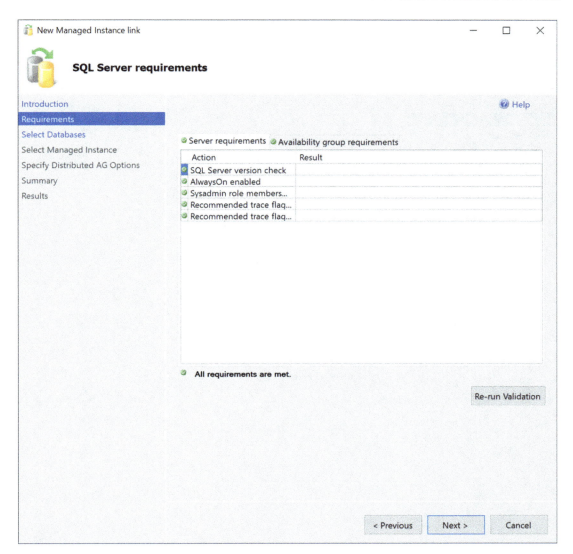

Figure 4-4. *Azure SQL Managed Instance Link Wizard Server Requirements*

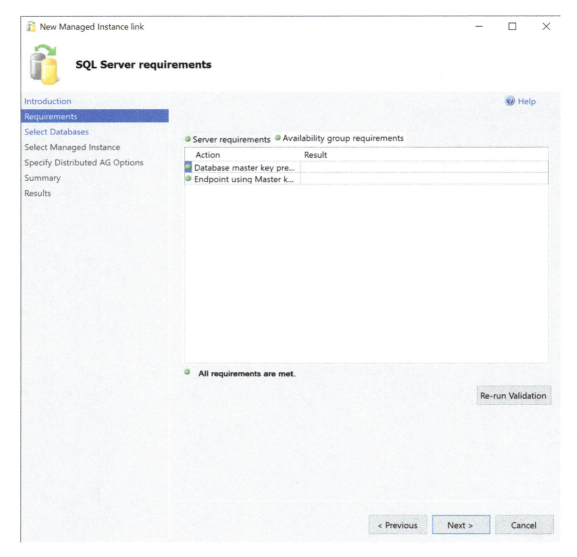

Figure 4-5. *Azure SQL Managed Instance Link Wizard AG Requirements*

Next, we select our target database(s) as shown in Figure 4-6. The database you initially chose is not automatically selected, nor are any others. Eligible databases must be in full recovery *and* have had a full backup to initialize the log sequence. In this example database "pubs" is in simple recovery and cannot be replicated. This is a fundamental requirement inherited from Always-On Availability Groups. The "All requirements are met" status tells us that the database on the SQL 2022 instance is ready to replicate.

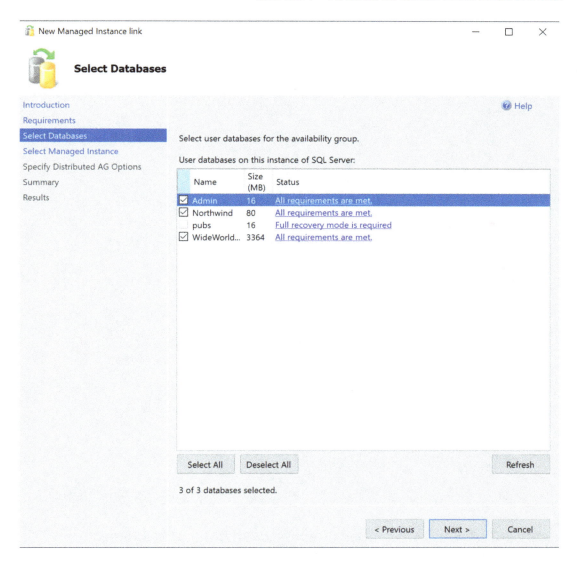

Figure 4-6. *Azure SQL Managed Instance Link Wizard Select Databases*

Now we have reached the Azure portion of the migration. You must log in to Azure and select a target instance as shown in Figure 4-7. Note the requirement for the Business Critical tier. This is because we selected the "WideWorldImporters" database on the previous page. This database has an In-Memory OLTP table, which is only supported on the *Business Critical* tier of Azure SQL Managed Instance. This resource group currently contains only *General Purpose* tier Managed Instances.

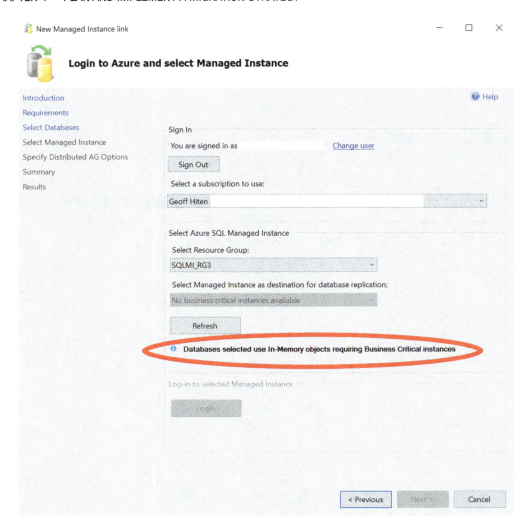

Figure 4-7. *Azure SQL Managed Instance Link Wizard Select Managed Instance –Business Critical Required*

If we remove WideWorldImporters from the database list *or* we switch to a resource group that contains a Business Critical tier Managed Instance, the result looks like Figure 4-8. The login to Managed Instance can be an Azure Active Directory identity or a SQL login, provided the Managed Instance supports that login type.

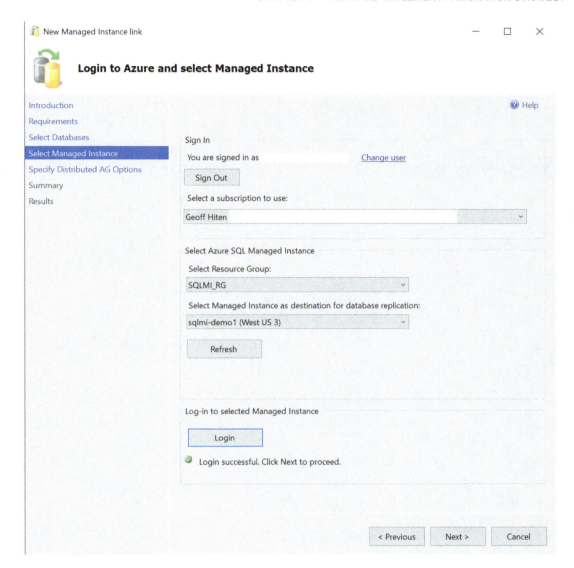

Figure 4-8. *Azure SQL Managed Instance Link Wizard Select Managed Instance*

Figure 4-9 shows the key data for the Distributed Availability Group (DAG). Since this is not the first time these two SQL services have been used for a DAG, the wizard automatically reuses the security certificate. If it was the first time, it would automatically generate a certificate. Note also that since there are no existing Availability Groups to leverage, the wizard will create groups with one AG for each database.

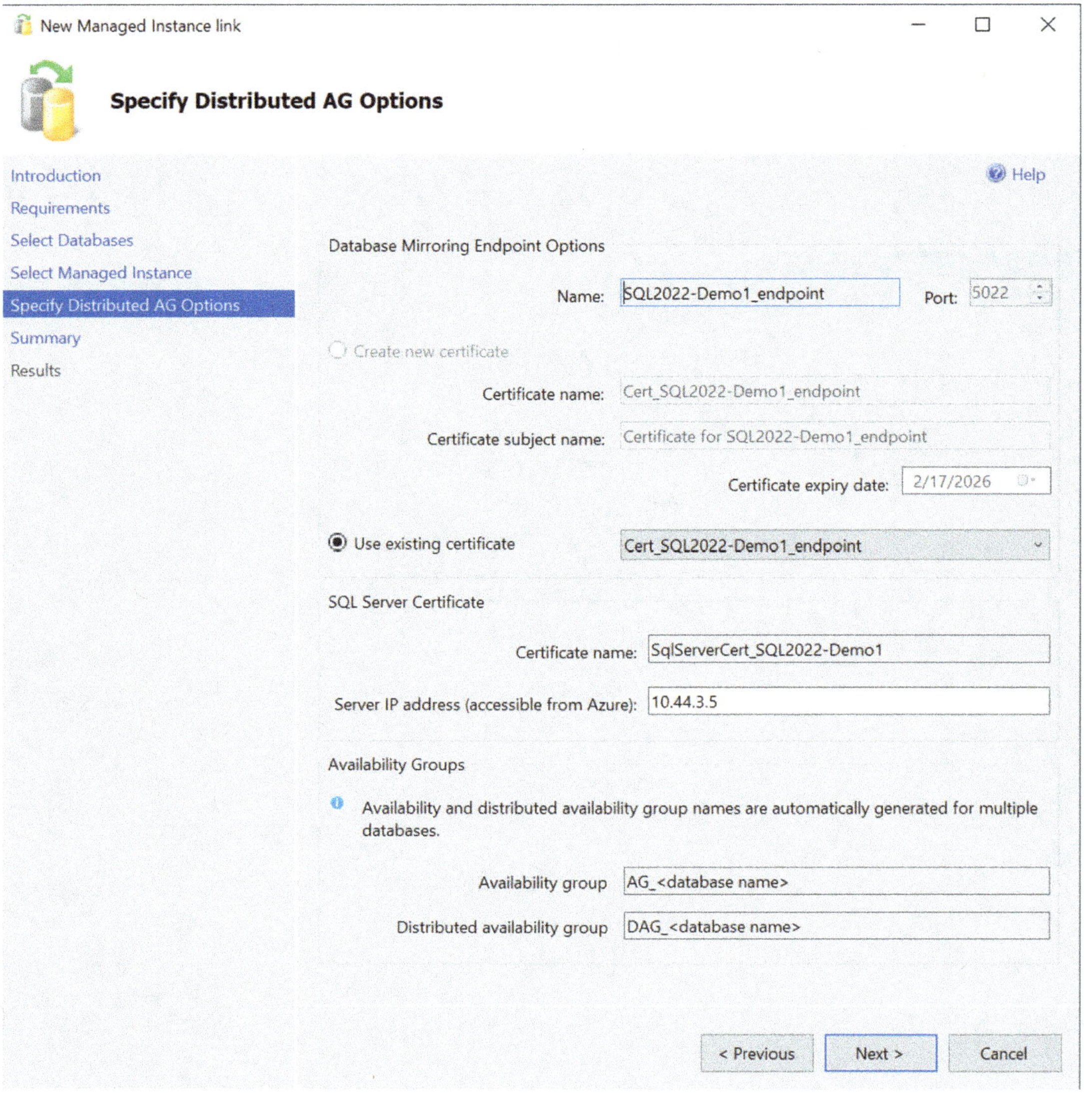

Figure 4-9. *Azure SQL Managed Instance Link Wizard DAG Options*

As with all SSMS wizards, this one generates a summary page with the option to generate a script as we see in Figure 4-10.

Caution   The script generated from this wizard (not shown) is a mix of T-SQL and PowerShell commands and cannot be run "as is" from SSMS. You must cut sections to different script execution engines to successfully automate this process.

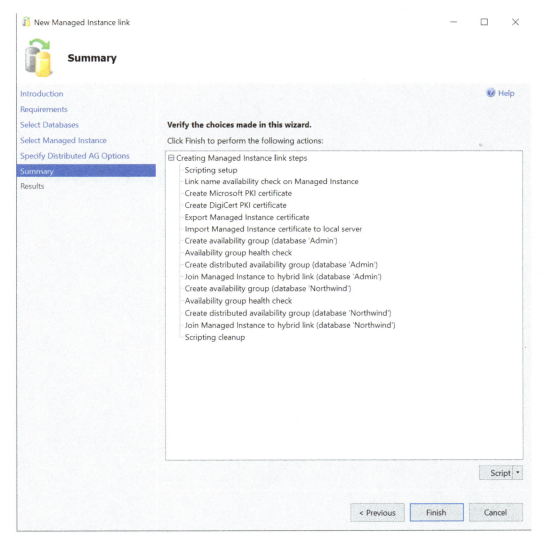

Figure 4-10. *Azure SQL Managed Instance Link Wizard Summary Script*

Selecting "Finish" from the previous page will begin the execution. This may take some time as the *Join Managed Instance to hybrid link (database '<dbname>')* step for each database includes the automatic seeding of that database, which may take some significant time depending on the size of the database. Figure 4-11 shows a successful Azure SQL Managed Instance Link Replication configuration. The wizard helpfully reminds you to back up your transaction logs on the source server to avoid a log full event that will impact the hybrid link.

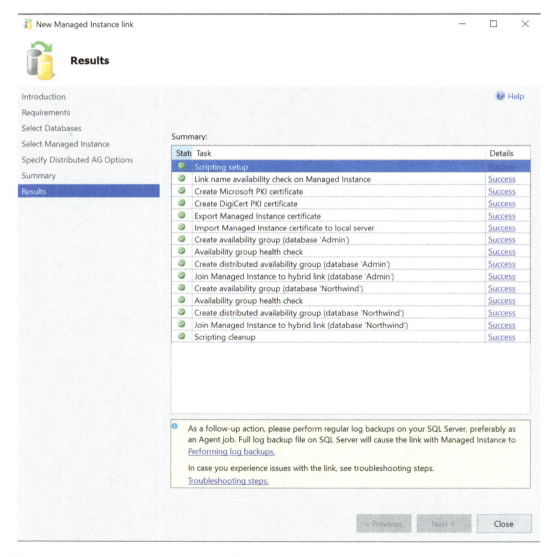

Figure 4-11. *Azure SQL Managed Instance Link Wizard Results*

Just like a SQL Server Distributed Availability Group, the hybrid link can be left
in place indefinitely. It can be used as a migration tool, or it can be used to replicate
data to Azure, landing in Azure SQL Managed Instance. Just like Availability Groups
with on-premises SQL Server, we want to see the status of our link. Figure 4-12 shows
SSMS Object Explorer with the status indicators of the database and Availability
Groups. As with AGs and DAGs, we also have the full suite of DMVs for monitoring.
Note that currently there is no indicator on the Managed Instance side that a database
is a replication target. Figure 4-12 also shows existing databases that were previously
migrated to this Managed Instance.

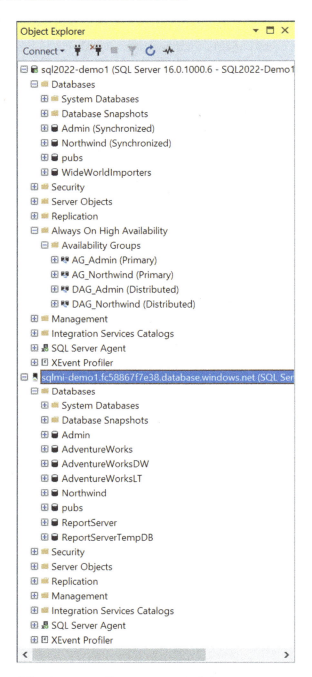

Figure 4-12. *Azure SQL Managed Instance Link Status*

Execute Failover

If we are using Azure SQL Managed Instance Link as a migration tool (after all, this *is* the topic under discussion), at some point we will want to initiate a failover. While I prefer the term *cutover* to *failover*, this book will continue to use the Microsoft terminology to avoid confusion. We start the same way we did with Configuring Replication, only selecting *Failover* database instead of *Replicate* database. (Refer back to Figure 4-2 for reference.) Figure 4-13 shows the introduction to the *Failover database to Managed Instance* Wizard.

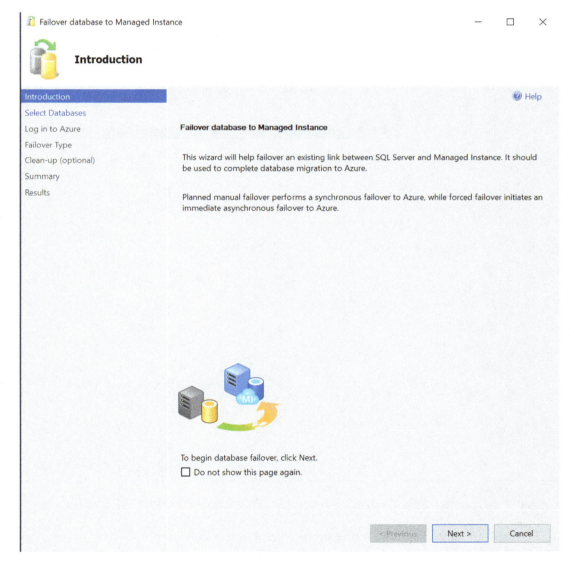

Figure 4-13. *Azure SQL Managed Instance Link Failover Introduction*

As before when we were configuring replication, we have to select one or more databases as we see in Figure 4-14. Note that the *WideWorldImporters* database is not in the list since we excluded it from the initial replication because there was no *Business Critical* tier target Managed Instance available.

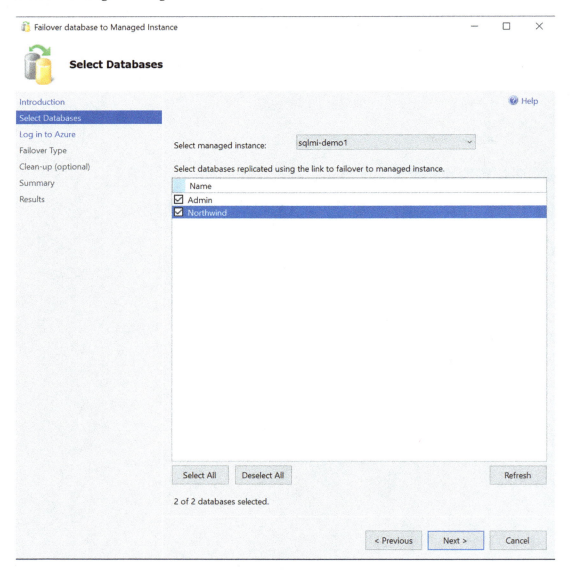

Figure 4-14. *Azure SQL Managed Instance Link Failover Select Databases*

Figure 4-15 has us log in to Azure but does not require us to log in to a target Managed Instance. The DAG knows the target Managed Instance once we selected one or more source databases.

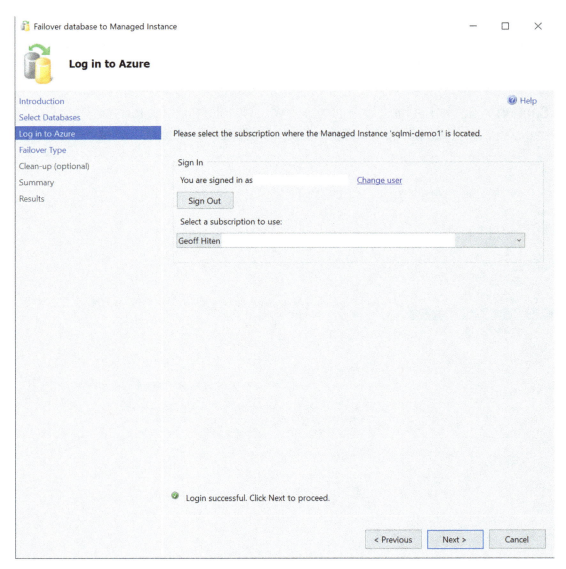

Figure 4-15. *Azure SQL Managed Instance Link Failover Log in to Azure*

Because we are using the Distributed Availability Group feature for SQL data replication, there is no failure detection and management framework like Windows Server Failover Clustering (WSFC) or Pacemaker for Linux. You must decide how to coordinate failover activities to avoid potential data loss. This decision is the core functionality shown in Figure 4-16. For a migration, we would choose the Planned manual failover type and follow the instructions to avoid data loss. If we were using this as a BCDR and the primary system was declared lost, we would force a failover and accept any data loss as inevitable.

Regardless of the choice, we must click a second box and confirm we understand the requirements and limitations as is the general practice for important, irrevocable decisions. For this example, we are choosing the Planned manual failover type.

Caution This is the most critical action you will take during a failover. Data loss can occur if you do not verify all steps are completed prior to accepting.

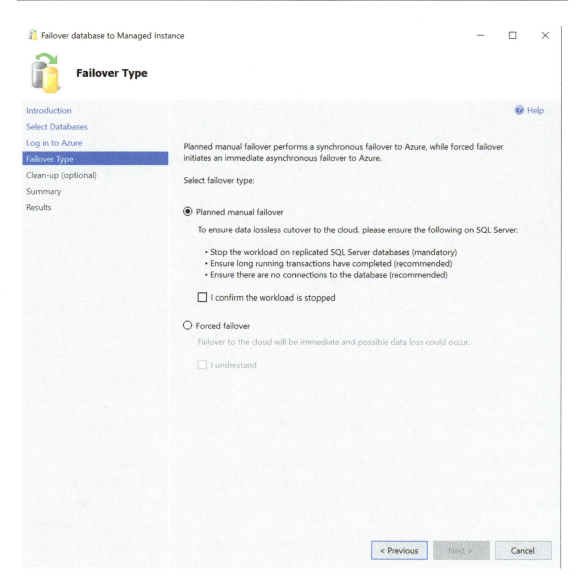

Figure 4-16. Azure SQL Managed Instance Link Failover Type

One final choice is whether to remove the Distributed Availability Group and/or the underlying Availability Group from the systems or not. If these artifacts were created solely for migration purposes, then removing them is the best choice. Choosing to remove the Availability Group will automatically remove the dependent Distributed Availability Group as Figure 4-17 illustrates.

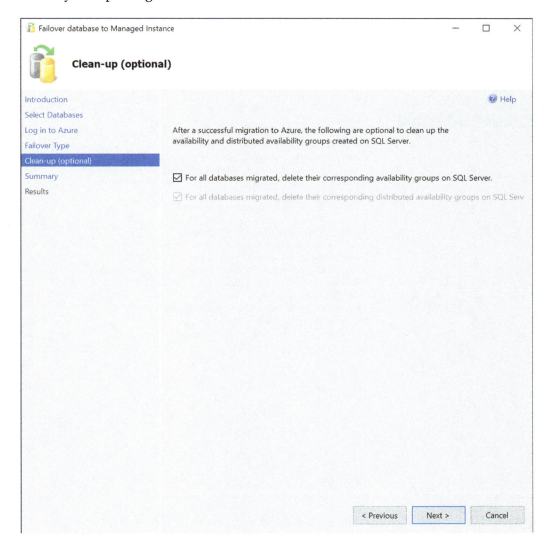

Figure 4-17. *Azure SQL Managed Instance Link Failover Clean-up*

As is the case with all SSMS wizards, we are presented with a summary page shown in Figure 4-18 where we can review and optionally script our choices before selecting a final *Finish* button to execute the failover. As with the *Configure Replication* script, the commands must be split between SSMS and PowerShell to execute.

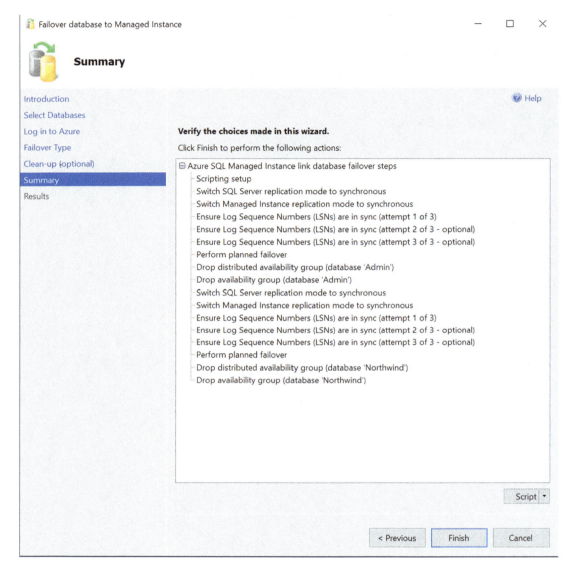

Figure 4-18. *Azure SQL Managed Instance Link Failover Summary*

Finally, we are done. We have successfully migrated two sample databases to Azure SQL Managed Instance. We did not have to copy and restore backups nor wrestle with Azure storage or file system permissions. We just created and extended an Availability Group, using well-proven and tested technology we should be familiar with from our on-premises SQL experience, to an Azure SQL PaaS Service. Figure 4-19 shows the results, including the extra chances the wizard gives us to validate LSN sync, just in case we didn't follow the warnings from Figure 4-16. These were not necessary, hence the *Skipped* designation.

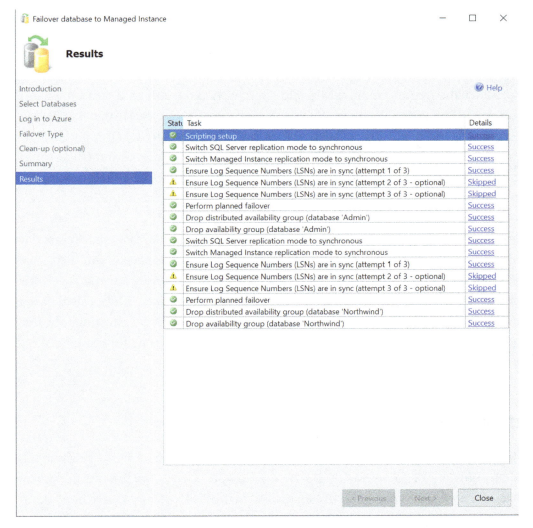

Figure 4-19. Azure SQL Managed Instance Link Failover Results

You can read more about Azure SQL Managed Instance Link in the official Microsoft documentation linked in Example 4-2.

Example 4-2. Azure SQL Managed Instance Link Documentation Landing Page

```
https://learn.microsoft.com/en-us/azure/azure-sql/managed-instance/
managed-instance-link-feature-overview?view=azuresql
```

This link includes a further link to the sign-up page for the public preview of the failback capability of Azure SQL Managed Instance Link.

Online Migrate to Azure SQL Database

Prior to 2020 the Azure Database Migration Service had the ability to perform an online migration to Azure SQL Database. Microsoft had contracted with Attunity to provide drivers that would read SQL transaction logs and push incremental updates via SQL commands to Azure SQL Database, like Transactional Replication. After Qlik acquired Attunity in May 2019, this partnership was allowed to lapse, and the drivers were no longer included in the Database Migration Service, removing the online migration capability to Azure SQL DB.

Alternatives recommended by Microsoft include Azure Data Sync (addressed later in this chapter) and Transactional Replication. Most Azure Database Administrators and Cloud Solution Architects use third-party drivers such as Striim to manage both the initial data load and the ongoing data synchronization tasks. This is a clear case of knowing the "Microsoft answer" vs. what works in the real world. Unfortunately, this is not going to be the last time we see this difference when preparing for both the DP-300 exam and the real-world Azure Database Administrator Role.

Perform Post-migration Validations

During the cutover part of the migration, there are essential checks to perform to ensure the data cutover and the overall migration are ready to accept and process the business workload the system is designed to execute. All of these tests should have been done with test or stale data prior to the start of a final cutover. Validation should cover the following three elements:

- Data integrity

- Completeness

- Connectivity

How much and how deeply to test are solely dependent on your organization's goals and requirements. There is no Microsoft standard, other than to include testing in the process. I strongly recommend getting your QA and Compliance teams involved in defining validation tests that meet your business and technical goals. You will likely have to implement the tests since you are the expert on the systems, but QA teams often have frameworks to automate testing, and Compliance will know if there are legal requirements regarding data migration validations that you are not aware of.

Troubleshoot a Migration

One of the most important lessons learned from practicing a migration is ensuring you aren't troubleshooting anything during the actual cutover. Much like a business continuity/disaster recovery (BCDR) exercise, you will almost certainly fail the first time. Again, much like a BCDR exercise, the odds of success the second time are only 50/50. That is why it is essential to exercise every element of the migration prior to the final data refresh and cutover. Unless the migration is so trivial to be simplistic, you will find complications and failure points. Do not be dismayed; this is part of the process. Be prepared to isolate and remediate these failures.

1. Define exactly what did not meet expectations and how that constitutes a failure.

2. Determine where in the process the fault occurred. Repeat sections or units of the migration and test intermediate stages if necessary.

3. Apply fixes – one at a time – and repeat unit testing until successful.

4. Repeat full migration multiple times to guarantee success.

One quote I heard comes to mind when preparing for a migration: "Amateurs practice until they can do a thing right. Professionals practice until they can't do it wrong." I tried to find a source for this, but its origins are lost to time.

Set Up SQL Data Sync for Azure

Azure Data Sync is another technology that was once useful for migrations but has been surpassed by more modern technologies such as the Azure Database Migration Service. It is the oldest of the migration tools and exists largely as a legacy service. The DP-300 exam still contains questions involving this technology, so it is essential to know the fundamentals and limitations regarding using it as a migration tool. The service documentation can be found linked in Example 4-3.

Example 4-3. Azure SQL Data Sync Documentation Landing Page

```
https://learn.microsoft.com/en-us/azure/azure-sql/database/sql-data-sync-
agent-overview?view=azuresql
```

As far as using Azure SQL Data Sync as a migration tool, the key limitations are that it is not supported with Azure SQL Managed Instance. Any migration targeting SQL MI can be considered "off-limits" for Azure SQL Data Sync. Azure SQL Data Sync relies on immutable Primary Keys to synchronize data. Every table that is synched must have a Primary Key that is immutable. These two factors can eliminate Azure Data Sync as possible answers as a migration technology.

Implement a Migration to Azure

As we discussed before, any SQL database migration is almost always part of an overall migration strategy. Databases have tightly coupled applications that generally run in the same data center or, in Azure, the same region. In the context of the DP-300 exam, the migration is the data refresh and cutover portion. Once you have the business case, executive sponsorship, landing zone, platform selection and deployment, and testing completed, you are finally ready to "pull the trigger" and move your databases to Azure. By this phase of the process, you should have most everything automated or at least written down as a checklist. Migrations often happen inconveniently late at night since they always involve some degree of business disruption, even when using online migration tools. Automation allows you to execute your implementation of the Microsoft Azure Cloud Adoption Framework that you have developed and tested with confidence that the outcome will be successful. The process and tools are proven not only in your environment but in many other SQL shops around the world. I will advance one bit of caution. If something unexpected happens and you do not have a clear solution, do not be afraid to "pull the plug." The most important part of any maintenance or migration outage is not to complete the task but to deliver a working system to the business within the allotted time. This is not to mean give up right away, but to be mindful of the impact that troubleshooting and remediation have on the outage clock. Always have a bailout plan and be prepared to implement it. Missing outage windows is the surest way to not get approved for your next one. Asking for two hours and using six guarantees that management will hear "I need six hours" the next time you ask for a two-hour outage.

Implement a Migration Between Azure SQL Services

Depending on why you are migrating to Azure, you may not make the leap to PaaS services right away. Several migration scenarios have time constraints that require "Right Now" to take precedence over "Right." This is where we divide "migration" from "modernization." Modernization from Azure SQL VM to Azure SQL MI or Azure SQL DB uses the same tools and processes as a migration from on-premises SQL severs directly to a PaaS platform would use, but with connectivity and identity issues already resolved. While it is tempting to shortcut this process, do not yield to this temptation. The process worked to get your systems into Azure, and it will work to help "climb the ladder" into platform-managed services. Make sure you have a solid business case and know why you are modernizing to PaaS and what benefits you expect to get from the new platform.

While it is technically possible to migrate from PaaS to Azure SQL VMs, this is often done as a prelude or part of an Azure exit strategy. In the real world, companies can and do change cloud providers, often for reasons that have nothing to do with the technical merits of Microsoft SQL services. Since helping companies exit Azure is not in Microsoft's business interests, Microsoft has not built tooling to facilitate such migrations, nor does it consider those skills relevant to the DP-300 exam. After all, it is the Administering Microsoft *Azure* SQL Solutions exam.

Chapter and Part Summary

Migrating databases to Azure is one of the scariest parts of journeying to Azure. It is a real leap of faith to execute a cutover and be solely dependent on Microsoft's SLA to provide data services to your organization. Just like putting data on SQL Server in the first place, you are not alone. There is an Azure SQL data community that is the descendant of the Microsoft SQL community that has braved this journey before. It is largely due to their efforts and feedback that you are now the beneficiary in the form of newer and better tools and processes.

Your work is not over after the migration cutover is complete. You may have migrated "like-for-like" into Azure SQL VMs and are now tasked with modernizing your SQL estate to one of the Azure SQL PaaS services. Even if you choose to stay with SQL running on Azure Virtual Machines, there are more steps on the Azure Cloud Adoption Framework, specifically Optimization and Security. We will discuss Optimization in the next three chapters (Chapters 5–7) and Security in the three chapters after that (Chapters 8–10). Welcome to Azure SQL Database Administration. Your adventure is just beginning.

PART II

Implement a Secure Environment

CHAPTER 5

Configure Database Authentication and Authorization

Now that your SQL systems are in Azure, you might think your work is done. After all, Azure just manages everything, doesn't it? That is not how it works. I doubt it ever will. Your job is changing away from routine, automatable, low-value tasks to higher-complexity, higher-value tasks. Data Security is one of the most critical tasks you will perform for your organization. Getting the right data to the right people and preventing unauthorized access are absolute necessities in today's business environment. Failure could lead to catastrophic business consequences and in certain jurisdictions could expose the company to significant legal liability. Most modern compliance regimes focus on Data Security as their number one goal. I cannot emphasize enough the importance of Data Security. Microsoft also considers Security a top priority since the DP-300 exam counts security questions for 20–25% of your total score.

Before we dive into the specific technical tasks involving database authentication and authorization, we need to add some new concepts to our vocabulary and update some others we already know. Our existing world of users and logins still exists, but it has expanded drastically with the addition of Azure technologies.

The first idea we need to discuss is the concept of "Control Planes." Control planes aren't uniquely a cloud computing concept; we had to deal with them on-premises, but likely did not use that name. The Azure portal and associated Resource Manager artifacts represent the Azure Control Plane. This is how you provision and manage resources in Azure. This roughly corresponds to the Virtualization control plane for on-premises systems, but Azure can deploy hundreds of unique services, while Virtualization simply deploys Virtual Machines and a few supporting services like virtual networking.

© Geoff Hiten 2025
G. Hiten, *Administering Microsoft Azure SQL Solutions*, Certification Study Companion Series,
https://doi.org/10.1007/979-8-8688-1585-0_5

Contrasting to the Azure Control Plane is the Azure Data Plane. For SQL PaaS services, this corresponds to Instance or Database access via T-SQL, SSMS, or Azure Data Studio. This is where our existing concepts of Users and Logins come into play. Azure SQL Virtual Machines has an additional Data Plane element in the operating system of the Virtual Machine.

The key concept is that access to various functions of each control plane is managed independently of the other control planes. A SQL login may allow me to query data in an Azure SQL Database, but it won't let me access the Control Plane for that database and change the configuration. An Entra ID login may have rights to both control planes if you have enabled Entra ID logins in your Azure database. Some Control Planes are service-managed and are beyond any user access. Backup file management is an Azure SQL PaaS internal control item and cannot be directly accessed; however, some recoverability configuration controls are exposed in the Azure Control Plane. We will discuss those controls in depth in Chapter 15.

Configure Authentication by Using Active Directory and Microsoft Entra ID

Your on-premises SQL Servers likely are or were members of an Active Directory Domain. This domain provided a central identity management system that you could leverage to reduce password proliferation. This identity was used to log in to your workstation and then was automatically asserted when you connected to any other resource in the Domain, including SQL Servers, unless you specified another identity such as a local SQL login. You could only assert the identity from your system, although you could use jump boxes into isolated domains to "firewall" internal identities from your daily work identity. Even when systems were not part of a domain, you could use Integrated Authentication (also known as Windows Authentication) to connect to local SQL Instances if you were logged directly in to a host system, the servers were configured for Windows Authentication, and your login was mapped to a valid role in the SQL Server.

Entra ID Authentication

Entra ID (formerly Azure Active Directory) is the primary cloud identity manager for Azure. Identities take the form of "*username@contoso.com*" and are often conflated with your email address. While many organizations use this identity as a user's primary email address, that is not a requirement. The *identity* exists whether you associate an *email address* to that identity or not. It is important to keep this separation in mind even though most companies peer the two concepts for convenience. We will be working exclusively with the *identity* component of Entra ID. We will not cover the integration of Active Directory with Entra ID beyond a few basic differences that impact our actions. Any organization that uses M365 for email and applications already has Entra ID integration in place. If this is the case, you likely already have an identity in Azure and can use that to access Azure resources.

Azure PaaS services (Azure SQL DB and Azure SQL MI) both have the option for Entra ID administration for access within the Azure Data Plane. You always use Entra ID authentication on the Azure Control Plane. Entra ID integration begins by defining an Entra ID Administrator for each provisioned Azure SQL Service. This can be done during the initial service deployment or added in later. Without an Entra ID Administrator, the service will only support SQL Authentication. Entra ID Administrator settings for Azure SQL Database services are set at the logical SQL Server level, not at the individual database level.

The Entra ID Administrator is not a member of the sysadmin role on any SQL PaaS system by default. The original SQL Login–Based Administrator is the only initial administrator (sysadmin role member). The Entra ID administrator can create new logins either SQL or Entra ID based and can grant any login permissions or membership in any role. It can grant itself full administrator rights. The Entra ID administrator is the only role that can initially create Entra ID–based logins, although it can grant that ability to other Entra ID–based logins. This concept is somewhat confusing at first as most people expect a login labeled "administrator" to be a member of the sysadmin role.

The process to create an Entra ID Administrator after resource deployment is similar for Azure SQL DB and Azure SQL MI but has slight differences. For Azure SQL DB, start on the SQL Server Overview page and look for the "Entra ID" link in the Settings section on the left "tower" list of sub-pages. There is also an Entra ID Admin tile shown in Figure 5-1 that shows the current status and takes you to the same Entra ID configuration sub-page as the prior link. For SQL MI, the entry is on the Instance Overview page and is labeled "Entra ID Admin." There is no Entra ID Admin tile for Azure SQL Managed Instance.

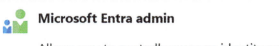

Microsoft Entra admin

Allows you to centrally manage identity and access to your Azure SQL databases.

CONFIGURED ●

Figure 5-1. *Azure SQL DB Entra Admin*

The resulting page is very similar regardless of whether you are configuring an Entra ID Admin for Azure SQL DB or Azure SQL MI. The page shown in Figure 5-2 is from Azure SQL DB and has the additional section on Purview integration that is lacking from the Azure SQL MI page. Otherwise, the pages are identical. If there is an Entra ID Administrator configured, both the name (*username@contoso.com* format) and its Entra object ID will be shown and the "Remove admin" button will be enabled. This page can also be used to disable SQL logins entirely.

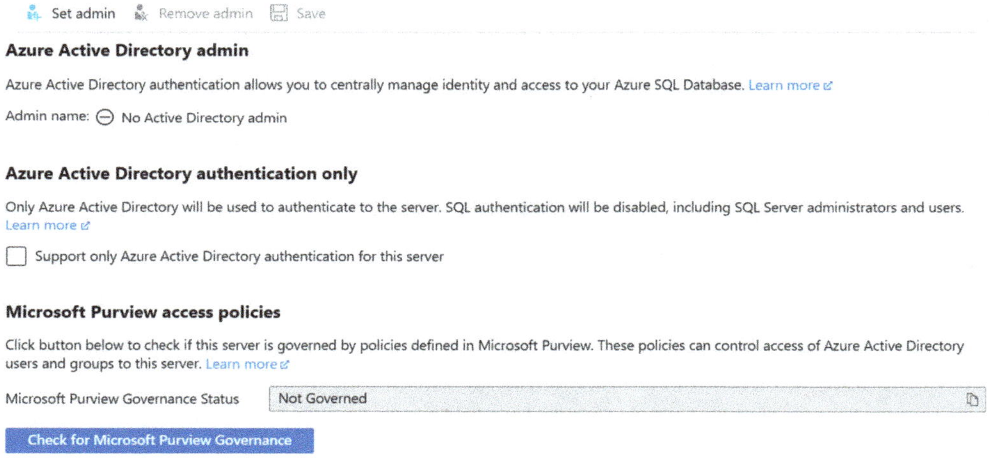

  Set admin   Remove admin   Save

Azure Active Directory admin

Azure Active Directory authentication allows you to centrally manage identity and access to your Azure SQL Database. Learn more ⊠

Admin name: ⊖ No Active Directory admin

Azure Active Directory authentication only

Only Azure Active Directory will be used to authenticate to the server. SQL authentication will be disabled, including SQL Server administrators and users. Learn more ⊠

☐ Support only Azure Active Directory authentication for this server

Microsoft Purview access policies

Click button below to check if this server is governed by policies defined in Microsoft Purview. These policies can control access of Azure Active Directory users and groups to this server. Learn more ⊠

Microsoft Purview Governance Status   Not Governed

Check for Microsoft Purview Governance

Figure 5-2. *Azure SQL DB Entra ID Admin Configuration*

Many of us support hybrid systems – that is, systems that span cloud and on-premises – or systems that depend on legacy identity providers such as Active Directory. Active Directory – the on-premises system based on the LDAP – is often tightly embedded into SQL-based systems and cannot be removed without major refactoring. To avoid confusion due to Microsoft's lack of naming clarity, we will refer to this as "Windows Authentication" going forward.

110

Note   I have personally seen systems that had the original company's domain name embedded into the database code so deeply that it was impossible to remove. This system had changed owners at least three times since the original system was deployed and the original company name was eliminated during the acquisitions. Do not design systems like this.

Create Users from Entra ID Identities

Because the Entra ID Identity Provider is an externally secured entity, we can trust any identities it asserts. We can leverage security policies like geographic boundary or Multi-Factor Authentication (MFA) to enhance security for access to our SQL services, particularly when we are running administrative tasks "inside" the SQL services or, as we describe it now, in the "Data Plane" administrative role. Creating a user from Entra ID must be done by an Entra ID Administrator role member. Without this administrator, you cannot use Entra ID identities in Azure SQL Services.

Best Practices strongly recommend that the Entra ID Administrator identity should be an Entra ID group, not an individual. Roles and permissions should be granted to groups, not individuals. This is a foundational element of modern identity-based security. We will talk about this more later in this chapter.

Configure Security Principals

When we discuss security in the context of SQL Server, including all its Azure manifestations, we need to understand three important concepts, Principals, Permissions, and Securables. Principals have Permissions to access Securables. In some cases, a Securable can be a Principal of its own. Server-level roles are an example of an entity that is both a securable and a principal. This should not be a new concept to an experienced DBA; this is how SQL has worked for decades, only the terminology might be new. In the Data Plane that is still how it works in Azure SQL MI and Azure SQL VMs. However, Azure SQL DB has a slightly different security model between its Server- and Database-level entities.

Previously, we revealed the fact that the *Server* entity in Azure SQL DB is a logical entity, not the physical server the databases connect to. We discussed some of the implications of that and promised more later. Security is one of those areas where things work differently in Azure SQL DB vs. Azure SQL in a VM or Azure SQL Managed Instance due to the difference between a physical and a logical server. One of the roles of the logical server is to manage security to its connected databases.

When Microsoft creates a new way to perform a task and recommends the adoption of the new way over the old one, you can bet the new way will be what is on the test. The new Azure role-based security model is no exception. Azure SQL Server has seven fixed server-level roles to help grant and manage permissions since the logical server permissions do not directly propagate to the connected databases because the server is logical rather than physical. These roles all begin with the prefix "*##MS_*" and end with "*##*". There is no single role in Azure SQL DB that encompasses the *sysadmin* role we find in other SQL Services; rather, the permissions are separated into multiple roles and have specific limitations. Role permissions are more closely aligned with Azure Role-Based Access Control (RBAC) permissions than with the legacy SQL Server roles. The seven Azure SQL-specific database roles are as follows:

- ##MS_DatabaseConnector##

- ##MS_DatabaseManager##

- ##MS_DefinitionReader##

- ##MS_LoginManager##

- ##MS_SecurityDefinitionReader##

- ##MS_ServerStateReader##

- ##MS_ServerStateManager##

The Learning Path and documentation have some exact language to describe these roles and how they work, so I won't duplicate that here. I will discuss some of the unique effects of how these roles work that provide greater security flexibility than the legacy security model. Three of these roles exist simply to provide read-only access to catalog and dynamic management views, greatly simplifying the task of configuring data gathering at scale such as for monitoring, alerting, and auditing systems.

Connecting to an Azure SQL Database using Fixed Server Roles through an Azure SQL Logical Server requires the connecting identity have at least one of three access paths listed below, assuming the Identity is successfully validated:

- The Identity must be the owner of the database.

- Or the Identity must be a member of the *##MS_Database Connector##* role.

- Or the Identity must have a matching username in the target database.

You can also *deny* connectivity for an identity at the database level – overriding any of these except the database owner path. The database owner is always going to have access to every object in the database. Contained Users are an exception in that login and user information is contained in the target database instead of matching a login in the server. In that case, the user does not necessarily have access to the logical server resources and must supply the target database name as part of the connection request.

When a ##MS_DatabaseManager## member creates a database, the member is automatically assigned as the owner, thus getting full access permissions to all objects inside that database. Other members of the ##MS_DatabaseManager## role do not automatically get access to that database. Those identities must follow the rules outlined above to connect to an attached database. This is a significant departure from the behavior of the *dbmanager* fixed database role in the master database where all members had access to all server databases.

Configure Database- and Object-Level Permissions Using Graphical Tools

Configuring database- and object-level permissions for all Azure SQL services works the same way in each service. The same traditional database roles exist along with the same array of permissions. User-defined roles work across all three SQL Services, bearing in mind the cross-database identity restrictions of Azure SQL Database we have already outlined in this chapter.

The DP-300 Learning Path will show running scripts in graphical tools as examples for this objective. This section of the DP-300 study guide will explore a bit more about the two main graphical tools, our old friend SQL Server Management Studio (*SSMS*) and the relative newcomer, Azure Data Studio (*ADS*), which is slated to be retired in 2026.

Figures 5-3 and 5-4 show a slightly expanded Object Explorer view of the same Azure SQL Database, open to the database-level security elements. Note the close similarities.

First, we examine the SSMS Object Explorer view in Figure 5-3.

Figure 5-3. *Azure SQL Database Object Explorer SSMS – Security*

Then we examine the same database in Azure Data Studio.

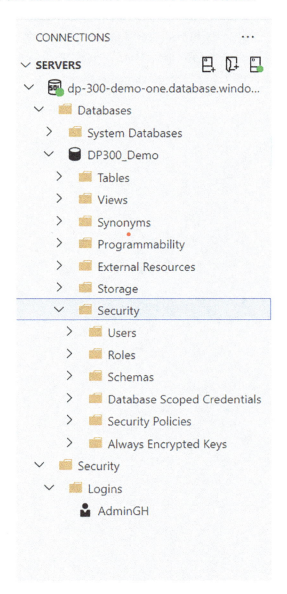

Figure 5-4. *Azure SQL Database Object Explorer ADS – Security*

The ADS version has fewer entries than the SSMS version due to target-specific optimizations to the Object Explorer view. The differences become even more apparent when you right-click the Object Explorer view. Figure 5-5 shows the only option on the entire ADS Object Explorer view is "Refresh," while the SSMS Object Explorer view in Figure 5-6 shows context-sensitive options for right-clicks.

Figure 5-5. *Azure SQL Database Object Explorer ADS – Right-Click*

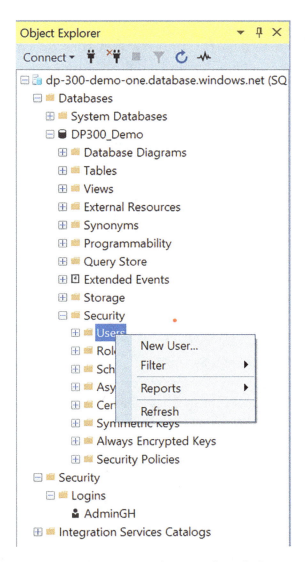

Figure 5-6. *SQL Server Management Studio – Right-Click*

Azure Data Studio is built on the Visual Studio Code platform and enjoys that platform's extensibility options. There are many ADS extensions such as the Azure SQL Migration Extension we mentioned in Chapter 4. These extensions can introduce new right-click menu options. Since the DP-300 exam focuses on Azure SQL Services and not SQL tools, we will use SSMS for future illustrations. The SSMS installer also installs ADS, so you can always choose which one you prefer.

You can use the right-click menus to generate T-SQL Script Templates for creating new users or logins for Azure SQL DB. The Create Login scripts require editing not only for names instead of placeholders, but also require choosing which type of login (SQL or Entra ID) you wish to create. Example 5-1 shows the script generated by SSMS for the right-click context option "New Login."

Example 5-1. New Login T-SQL Script Template from SSMS

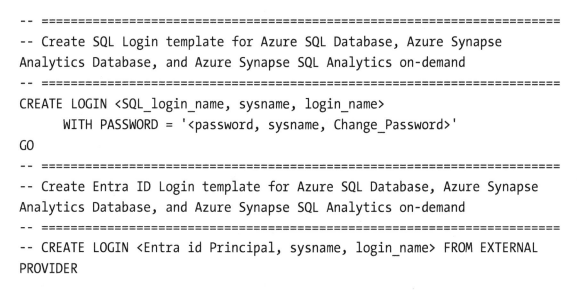

```
-- =========================================================================
-- Create SQL Login template for Azure SQL Database, Azure Synapse
Analytics Database, and Azure Synapse SQL Analytics on-demand
-- =========================================================================
CREATE LOGIN <SQL_login_name, sysname, login_name>
    WITH PASSWORD = '<password, sysname, Change_Password>'
GO
-- =========================================================================
-- Create Entra ID Login template for Azure SQL Database, Azure Synapse
Analytics Database, and Azure Synapse SQL Analytics on-demand
-- =========================================================================
-- CREATE LOGIN <Entra id Principal, sysname, login_name> FROM EXTERNAL
PROVIDER
```

Notice the commented-out option for creating an Entra ID–based login. The only differences are the removal of the password options and the inclusion of the ending "FROM EXTERNAL PROVIDER," indicating this is an Entra ID–based login.

Apply Principle of Least Privilege for All Securables

The Principle of Least Privilege (*PoLP*) is a security component of Zero Trust security, the modern security paradigm that most companies are adopting. Least Privilege prevents applications and individuals from escalating their rights beyond the minimum permissions necessary to perform their role or task. A common example of an *Overprivileged* application would be granting local administrator rights to the SQL Server application or granting sysadmin rights to an application connecting to SQL Server. Overprivileged applications have two types of unnecessary permissions, *unused* permissions and *reducible* permissions.

Unused Permissions happen when giving extra permissions either for expediency or because the application needed it one time during setup and the permission was never revoked. Going back to our example, this would be like giving sysadmin rights to an application that only used them during deployment but never again. Sysadmin rights are rarely needed for ongoing database operations. Some legacy systems require sysadmin rights and cannot be remediated. Those applications should be isolated as much as possible and carefully monitored. Modern applications that constantly require elevated privileges should be carefully vetted for other security compromises as it is clear the developers did not place an emphasis on modern security practices.

Unused permissions allow for Horizontal Privilege Escalation exploits. Horizontal Privilege Escalation allows an entity, either a person or an application, to access resources (APIs, Ports, Services, etc.) that they would not normally be able to access with their native permissions on nearby platforms.

The other type of Privilege Escalation is Reducible Permissions. Unfortunately, this is very common, even among modern SQL applications. Most applications use a single credential to connect from the application to the SQL Service and execute every query under that credential. Often this credential is mapped to the *dbowner* role, giving unrestricted access to every object in the database. This makes any compromise of the application catastrophic. Even simple separation of connection classes into Read–Write, Read-Only, and Restricted connections (for admin-type functions) can greatly reduce the surface area and impact of any attack. Reducible Permissions allow for Vertical Security Escalation exploits. A Vertical attack from a SQL Server would target the host OS or Virtualization platform. Both attacks allow users or applications access to resources they have no legitimate reason to access. While we cannot always reduce permissions down to the minimum that the application *should* need, we must reduce to the minimum the application allows us to.

The PoLP applies to your own access. Do not grant your ordinary login admin rights on systems. Consider implementing your own "just-in-time" role-based administration system by adding and removing yourself to and from admin groups as necessary. Keep those groups relatively small – one admin group for 3,000 logical servers is simply asking for a breach. Think about how much damage could happen if a particular identity was compromised and limit the "blast radius" of an attack as much as possible.

Troubleshoot Authentication and Authorization Issues

Nothing ever works perfectly in the real world. There is always some complication somewhere that prevents systems from connecting perfectly, especially the first time. This requires we simplify the problem to isolate the error and remediate the issue. Sometimes there is more than one issue that needs fixing. This process is called troubleshooting.

General Authentication and Authorization Troubleshooting

The first step in troubleshooting an authentication or authorization issue (shorthanded as "auth" by many) is to make sure it is not a connectivity issue masquerading as an auth issue. Try to establish connectivity using alternate credentials, potentially from alternate sources closer to the target. If you are connecting across a WAN such as from on-premises to Azure, make sure there are other working connections or try a local connection first. Try using SQL authentication with a temporary SQL account just to establish connectivity. SQL auth resides entirely within the SQL system and does not require any other elements such as Entra ID to be correctly configured. Many organizations lock down outbound port 1433 with very specific point-to-point exceptions. Getting the first exception from the security or networking team is often very difficult since it requires a new way of thinking about security.

Once you are sure it is an authentication or authorization issue, then it is time to dig in and find out which one is the culprit. Authentication issues will prevent you from logging in. Authorization issues will prevent you from accessing resources once you are logged in. Sometimes they look alike, but the key is to read the detailed error messages. Dumping the error text, scrubbed of any company-specific information of course, into a search engine or AI bot is the most practical way of getting better information, but that method isn't going to be available during the test.

Most Authentication issues will require the assistance of someone in your organization with administrator privileges into AD or Entra ID to read the exception logs and tell you if your authentication is failing. One of the most common failures for applications using managed identities to connect to SQL services is to hit a Conditional Access Policy. Conditional Access Policies restrict Entra ID logins based on certain conditions such as geographic source, time of day, or Multi-Factor Authentication success. Your Entra ID admin can easily check logs and find exactly which policy or policies caused the authentication failure.

120

Authorization failures are more common inside a resource at the Data Plane level and can happen when implementing Least Privileges. In fact, hitting Authorization errors is a normal part of exploring the boundaries of what permissions an application really needs. It is easier if that was done as part of the application development process, but that depends on how important Security was as a design factor. Software developers and vendors seldom tell exactly what permissions are required in a Least Privileges model. Connection and Query errors will often be your best guide to finding out which privileges are missing when troubleshooting Authorization errors.

Troubleshooting Windows Auth for SQL MI

The most common failures for Windows Authentication to Azure SQL Managed Instance occur where the features of Windows logins and Entra ID logins do not overlap. Entra ID offers Conditional Access Policies such as requiring Multi-Factor Authentication (MFA) or time of day restrictions. Entra ID logins that map to Windows logins for SQL MI must be excluded from conditional access policies that would otherwise block access. This is why it is important to create a dedicated set of logins for SQL MI connectivity in both the Windows and Entra ID Identity Provider spaces to avoid compromising security for existing logins.

To identify blocked logins, run the command in Example 5-2 to find all errors related to Kerberos tickets and your target SQL Managed Instance. You must be a Windows Domain Admin to run the klist command.

Example 5-2. Kerberos Ticket List Command from Entra ID

```
klist get MSSQLSvc/<miname>.<dnszone>.database.windows.net:1433
```

Any ticket containing error 0x52f indicates a valid ticket that was blocked from logging in due to some user account restriction, typically Conditional Access Policies. The Entra ID login log will contain any rejected login attempts along with the exact policy that caused the rejection. There are many other ways for this process to fail, but policy violation is the most common.

Manage Authentication and Authorization by Using T-SQL

Graphical tools are essential to rapidly understand and simplify changes, but scripts are the only way to achieve repeatability and scalability in IT operations. More on that in Chapter 12. For all Azure SQL Services, T-SQL scripts are the scripting language of choice. Another reason to choose T-SQL over graphical tools is sometimes newer or unique features for one SQL Service may not have a full graphical element yet, but it will always have a T-SQL command interface.

One example of code-only control is the "##_<rolename>##" fixed server roles in Azure SQL DB we discussed earlier in this chapter. The graphical tools do not show these roles, nor do they have any controls to create or adjust them. The only interface for inspecting or changing Fixed Server Roles is via T-SQL.

You can see the Fixed Server Roles by running the query in Example 5-3 from any database.

Example 5-3. Listing Fixed Server Roles

```
select * from sys.server_principals
```

Executing the code in Example 5-3 s gives us the list of current security principals, including the fixed server roles. Example 5-4 extends the set of system views to roles and SQL logins to give a list of all SQL logins that are members of any fixed role.

Example 5-4. Listing Fixed Server SQL Login Role Membership

```
SELECT
    sql_logins.principal_id        AS MemberPrincipalID
    ,sql_logins.name               AS MemberPrincipalName
    ,roles.principal_id            AS RolePrincipalID
    ,roles.name                    AS RolePrincipalName
FROM sys.server_role_members       AS server_role_members
INNER JOIN sys.server_principals   AS roles
    ON server_role_members.role_principal_id = roles.principal_id
INNER JOIN sys.sql_logins          AS sql_logins
    ON server_role_members.member_principal_id = sql_logins.principal_id
```

Knowing the relationships between these system views will allow you to easily see and manipulate fixed role membership. Example 5-5 shows how to list all Azure AD logins that are members of the fixed server roles.

Example 5-5. Listing Fixed Server Entra ID Login Role Membership

```
SELECT
    member.principal_id          AS MemberPrincipalID
    ,member.name                 AS MemberPrincipalName
    ,roles.principal_id          AS RolePrincipalID
    ,roles.name                  AS RolePrincipalName
FROM sys.server_role_members     AS server_role_members
INNER JOIN sys.server_principals   AS roles
    ON server_role_members.role_principal_id = roles.principal_id
INNER JOIN sys.server_principals   AS member
    ON server_role_members.member_principal_id = member.principal_id
LEFT OUTER JOIN sys.sql_logins     AS sql_logins
    ON server_role_members.member_principal_id = sql_logins.principal_id
WHERE member.principal_id NOT IN (SELECT principal_id FROM sys.sql_logins
AS sql_logins
            WHERE member.principal_id = sql_logins.principal_id)
```

We included the earlier query from Example 5-4 to remove the SQL logins so we would only see the Entra ID logins. Removing the outer WHERE clause will return all logins that are members of the fixed server roles.

Remember that these are System Views, not tables, and thus cannot be updated. You must *alter* a role and *add* or *remove* a *member* to change membership. I suggest a bit of practice with writing a few queries of your own based on the ones supplied above. You should be able to create both SQL and Entra ID logins, add and remove logins to and from roles, and be able to see which logins and what type of logins are in each role. Writing your own queries to do this is the most effective practice I know.

Chapter Summary

We have covered the first of three chapters on Security on Database Authentication and Authorization. By now you should have the ability to fully control who and what can log in to your systems and what they can do once they are there, at least for normal data access. Chapter 6 will discuss how to keep your data secure at rest and in transit using encryption. The good news is that Azure SQL services inherited much of their encryption capability from SQL Server, so it should be familiar to many of you.

Chapter 7 will discuss specific types of data that require additional compliance steps and how to implement those compliance controls. As always, please follow along the Microsoft recommended Learning Path coursework and especially do the practice labs. Unlike the actual DP-300 exam, those are free.

CHAPTER 6

Implement Security for Data at Rest and Data in Transit

Preventing unauthorized persons from accessing data outside the control of the SQL Server engine is as essential an element of information security as is protecting data while it is under the control of the SQL engine. Such data protection generally focuses on two areas, data at rest and data in transit. Data at rest refers to when data is written to a persisted data store. That includes backups and temporary "scratch" writes such as tempdb. Data in transit, sometimes called data in motion, refers to data communications between the SQL Service and a client application, including communication to other SQL Servers and to administrative tools like SSMS or ADS.

Implement Transparent Data Encryption (TDE)

Transparent Data Encryption (*TDE*) is the fundamental encryption-based protection mechanism for SQL Server data at rest and has been since the feature was introduced in SQL 2008. It is a testament to the robustness of the design that the feature has remained largely unchanged since its introduction. TDE encrypts the data during the page write process as data is written to persistent storage and decrypts the data as it is read from storage. This protects data as it transits any storage networks, including the internal Azure storage network as well as on the storage devices themselves. The TDE mechanisms are the same for all editions, manifestations, and versions of SQL Server including all Azure PaaS SQL services. All Azure SQL Services except Azure SQL VMs have TDE enabled by default. VMs are subject to the defaults set on each instance and

© Geoff Hiten 2025
G. Hiten, *Administering Microsoft Azure SQL Solutions*, Certification Study Companion Series,
https://doi.org/10.1007/979-8-8688-1585-0_6

the TDE capabilities of the SQL Server edition installed on that VM. The differences between Azure and on-premises TDE are how the encryption keys themselves are managed in Azure and the default settings for encryption.

Before we dig into how key management is implemented in Azure, it will help to go over a brief refresher on how TDE works in SQL Server. As I mentioned in the previous paragraph, data is encrypted on write and decrypted on read. This applies to both SQL data and SQL transaction logs. TempDB is encrypted if any database on a physical server is encrypted to avoid any possibility of data disclosure via disk scavenging. The same key is used to encrypt and decrypt the database, meaning SQL uses a *Symmetric Key*. This key is stored in the database, so it is available anywhere the database is restored. Symmetric keys are much simpler and faster to implement than *Asymmetrical Keys* where one key encrypts and another decrypts. Asymmetrical keys are used in Public Key Infrastructure to validate identities and to protect symmetrical keys that are used to encrypt most data and typically stored and transported in the form of a certificate.

In on-premises or Azure VM SQL Server TDE, the internal encryption key is protected by another key called the Key Protector. This *Key Protector* key has the confusing name of Database Encryption Key (*DEK*) and is the key you supply to SQL Server when restoring an encrypted database. Of course, if you are restoring to the same SQL Instance, the server already has the DEK from the original database. If you restore to another server, you must import the key so the SQL Server can use it to "unlock" the physical key and restore or attach the target database. Before you can import a key to a different server that it originated from, you must export the key from the originating server. Microsoft does not support "naked" cryptographic keys. Keys exported from on-premises SQL Server are stored in key files that are password protected. Keys inside SQL are protected by a series of keys at the database and the service level, ultimately protected by the Windows Cryptographic Store.

This process is necessarily complex because both SQL Server and Windows were developed well before the advent of modern encryption protocols. Azure was designed with encryption as a default setting. Encryption is the default for pretty much all data at rest in Azure. This applies to the fundamental storage layer as well as SQL databases. All Azure SQL PaaS Services turn on TDE by default using internally "service-managed" keys. Copying databases across servers, regions, and subscriptions whether using Azure SQL DB or Azure SQL Managed Instance results in the service-managed keys following the database restore and everything working transparently. There is literally no extra planning or work involved with service-managed keys for TDE with Azure SQL PaaS Services; however, it is impossible for users to export service-managed keys.

Transparent Data Encryption in Azure SQL gets complex when customers choose to manage their own encryption keys. This process is called "Bring Your Own Key" (*BYOK*). BYOK is mandatory for Azure customers subject to certain compliance regimes and is highly desired by many other Azure customers.

On-Premises SQL Server has supported Hardware Security Modules (*HSMs*) as part of the Extensible Key Management framework since the introduction of the TDE feature. HSMs were typically only used by organizations requiring very specific levels of security due to the cost and overhead requirements. Most of these customers were required to use HSMs due to regulatory or compliance practices. Azure Key Vault (*AKV*) puts HSMs within the reach of any customer, greatly simplifying the process of managing encryption keys.

TDE with BYOK for Azure SQL PaaS Services is subject to some specific restrictions that differ from using service-managed keys. First and foremost is that all databases on a server share the same default key. This is the same whether your server is virtual as with Azure SQL Database or physical for Azure SQL Managed Instance. If you copy an Azure SQL Database from one logical server to another, you must make sure the new server has access to the DEK via Azure Key Vault.

Deploying Azure Key Vault

Deploying Azure Key Vault is not a topic that will be on the DP-300 exam, but you will need to have one to practice using any form of encryption in Azure SQL. Therefore, we will cover how to deploy a basic tier Azure Key Vault and connect it to your Azure SQL Services using the Azure portal. This example assumes you are deploying AKV using the Private Endpoint networking model, since that is the most popular networking model for companies. This example also assumes you have an Azure private network with a subnet appropriate for an AKV deployment. In most larger deployments, Azure Key Vault will be part of your Application Landing Zone provided for you via automated deployment and configured by your security team.

This example will use a network called Core_Network that has multiple subnets. The subnet we will use for Azure Key Vault is called Base_Subnet and contains endpoints for central services such as Azure Key Vault that will be used by services on all the other subnets. One such subnet is dedicated to Azure SQL Database private endpoints and is called SQLDB_Subnet. The entire network layout is shown in Figure 6-1.

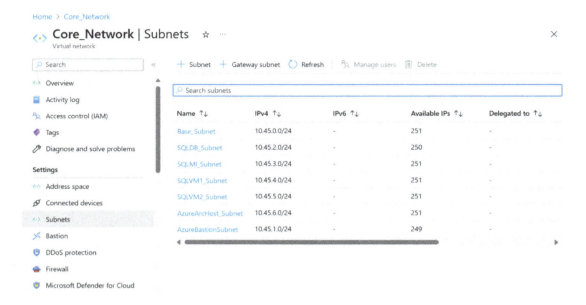

Figure 6-1. *Azure Virtual Network and Subnets*

The above example has seven subnets but does not consume all the Virtual Network address space. Portions of the address space are left for future expansion.

Azure Key Vault (*AKV*) deployment begins with a selection from the marketplace. AKV has no versions, and the SKU is selected during deployment, so there is only one valid choice. Search for "Azure Key Vault" to begin the deployment. Figure 6-2 shows the correct selection.

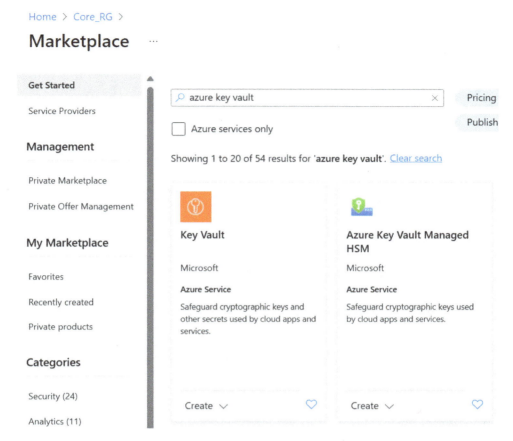

Figure 6-2. *Azure Key Vault – Azure Marketplace*

Choosing "Create" will bring you to the screen shown in Figure 6-3. Note that for this figure and all subsequent figures showing AKV deployment, the subscription ID has been blanked out. You will select a subscription and resource group during an actual deployment as well as entering a name for your key vault. The standard service tier will be sufficient for most learning needs. Premium tier Key Vaults allow for direct on-premises HSM integration and are always managed by an enterprise security team. I recommend sticking with the default options for the remainder of the current deployment page unless you or your organization has other requirements.

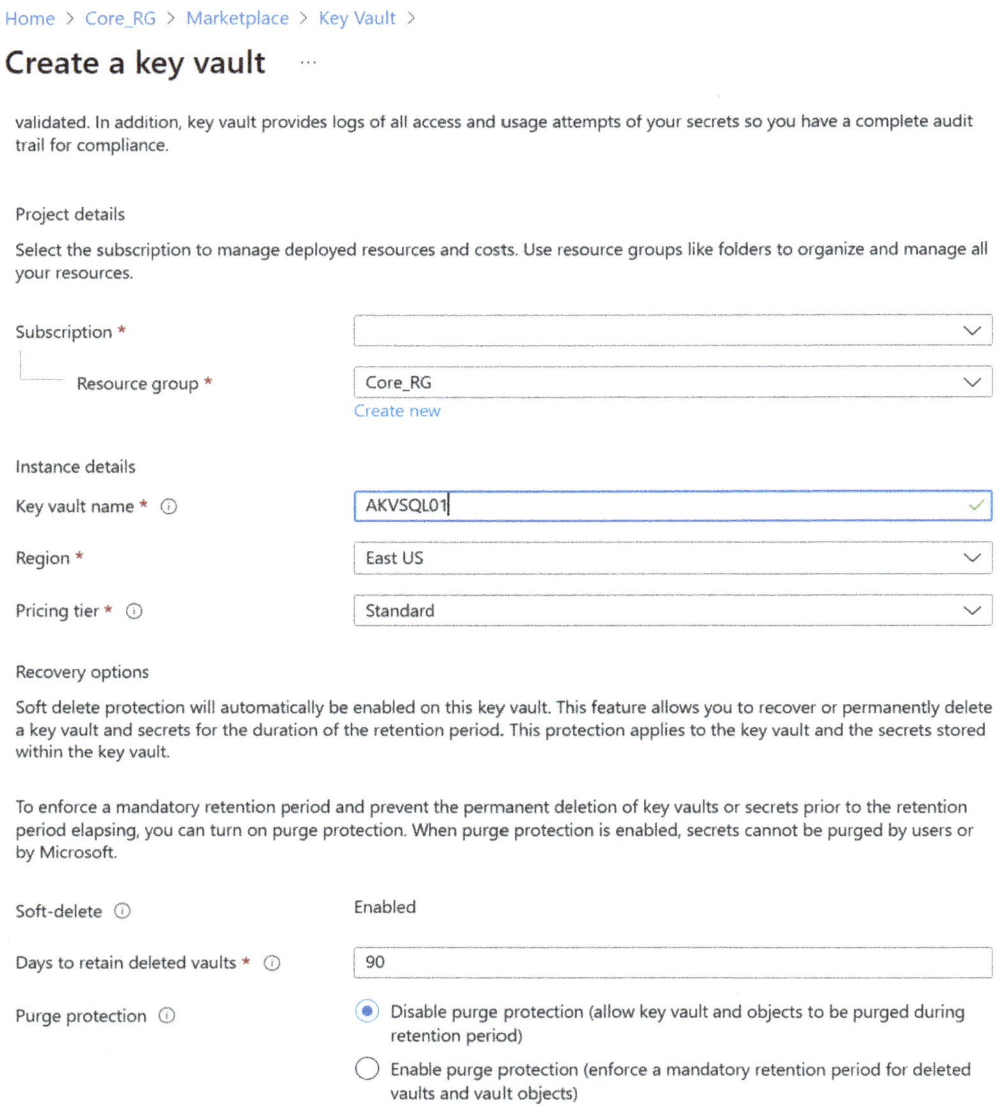

Figure 6-3. *Azure Key Vault Deployment*

Key Vaults are one of the foundational resources in Azure. Encryption keys are required for other Core Azure Services to launch, so AKV must support a direct access method as well as Entra ID–based access. We also need to tell AKV what Azure services can explicitly access resources in this AKV. For now, defaults are fine. We aren't starting Azure from scratch, so we can count on Entra ID to provide identities. Figure 6-4 shows the Access configuration deployment selection page.

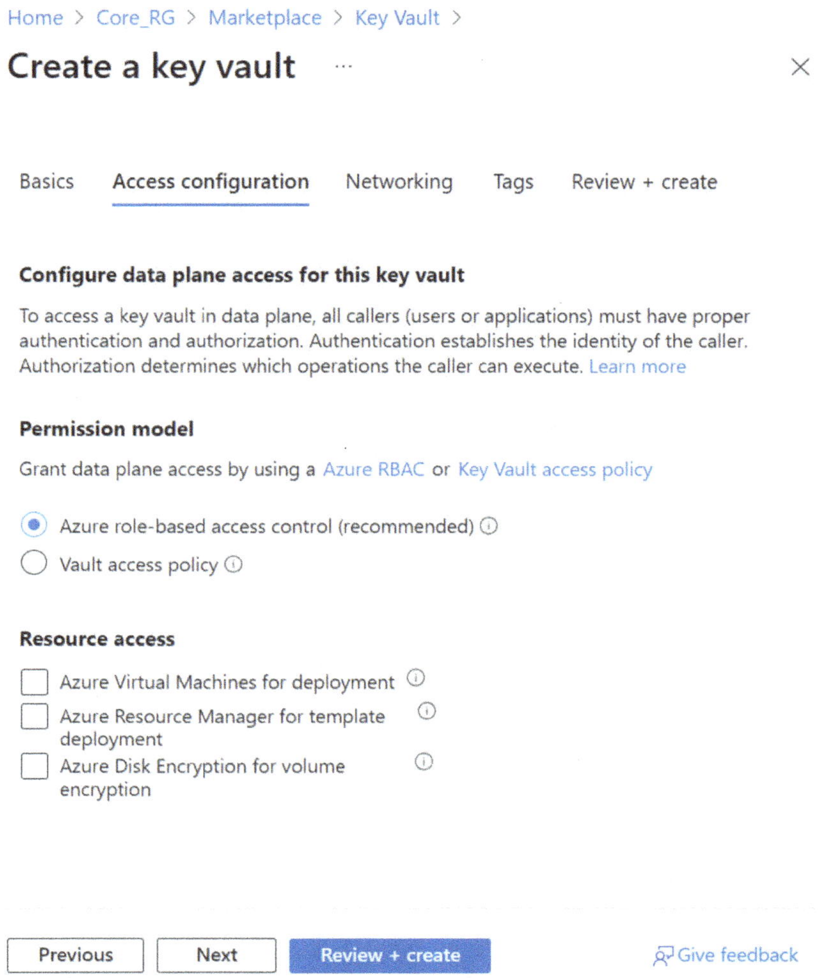

Figure 6-4. *AKV Access Configuration*

For this example, I chose to create a private endpoint on one of the subnets from Figure 6-1. You can have both public and private networking turned on or either one turned on or turn off all access if you wish to archive a vault but not completely delete it. These options can be changed after the key vault is deployed.

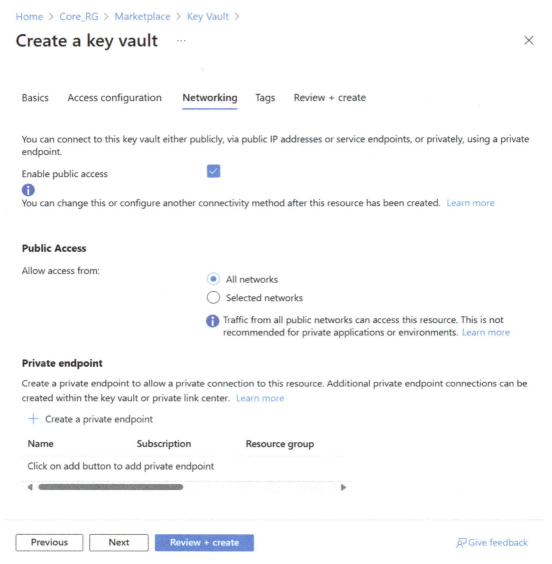

Figure 6-5. *Azure Key Vault Networking 1*

If you click "+ Create a private endpoint" on the blade shown in Figure 6-5, you get a pop-out blade shown in Figure 6-6. This is the same "Create private endpoint" blade used for any service that uses private endpoints. Azure originally was built using only public endpoints, but enterprises want a more controllable abstraction for software-defined networking, so most Azure services now support both Public and Private networking. Azure SQL DB and Azure SQL MI both support Public and Private networking. I chose to put this endpoint on the *Base_Subnet* subnet to signify that it was a shared resource across the entire network and not expected to be used only on one subnet. I also chose to create a private DNS zone for ease of access since I do not have a Windows domain on this network.

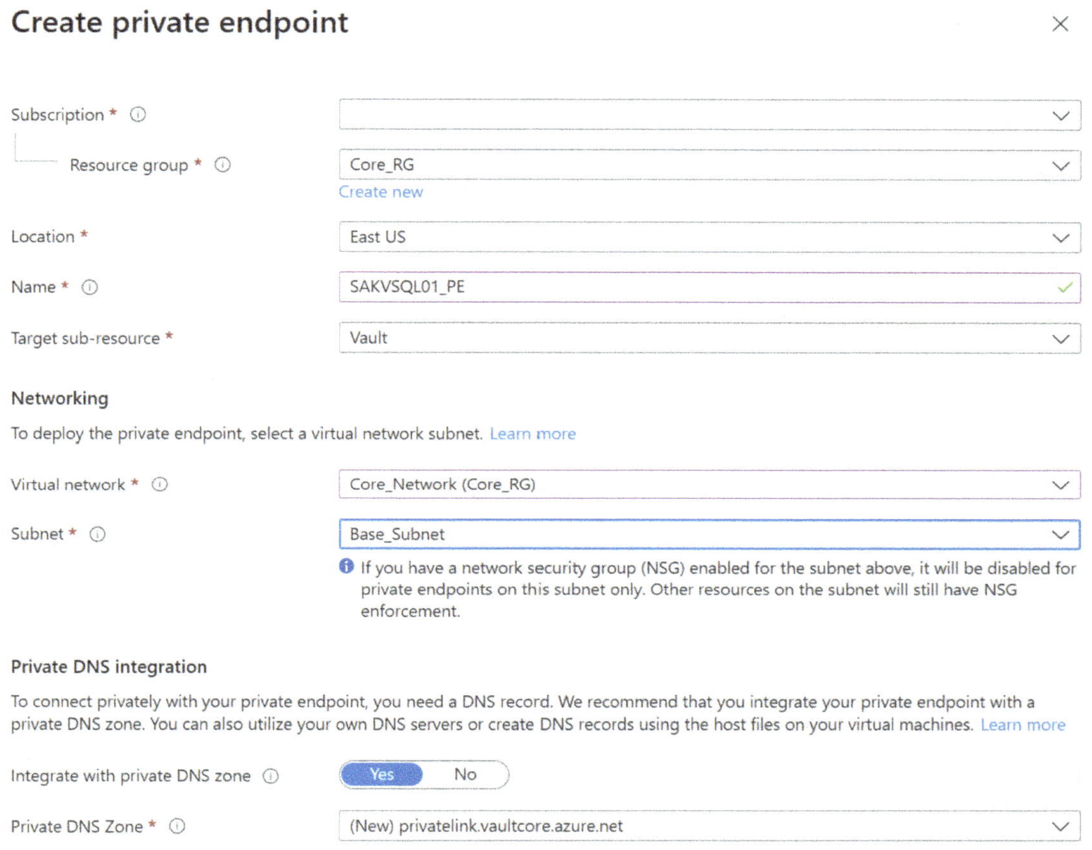

Create private endpoint   ✕

Subscription * ⓘ
[⌄]

   └─── Resource group * ⓘ
[Core_RG   ⌄]
Create new

Location *
[East US   ⌄]

Name * ⓘ
[SAKVSQL01_PE   ✓]

Target sub-resource *
[Vault   ⌄]

Networking

To deploy the private endpoint, select a virtual network subnet. Learn more

Virtual network * ⓘ
[Core_Network (Core_RG)   ⌄]

Subnet * ⓘ
[Base_Subnet   ⌄]

ⓘ If you have a network security group (NSG) enabled for the subnet above, it will be disabled for private endpoints on this subnet only. Other resources on the subnet will still have NSG enforcement.

Private DNS integration

To connect privately with your private endpoint, you need a DNS record. We recommend that you integrate your private endpoint with a private DNS zone. You can also utilize your own DNS servers or create DNS records using the host files on your virtual machines. Learn more

Integrate with private DNS zone ⓘ
[Yes] [No]

Private DNS Zone * ⓘ
[(New) privatelink.vaultcore.azure.net   ⌄]

Figure 6-6. *AKV Deployment Networking Private Endpoint*

When you complete the "Create private endpoint" blade, you will be brought back to the AKV Deployment Networking page as shown in Figure 6-7. Note the addition of the endpoint you created. You should note two important things on this page. One, you can create multiple endpoints if you need the key vault to appear in multiple networks. Two, you can omit the "Create private endpoint" blade entirely if you choose to only use public access. While that is a simpler solution, for purposes of this training exercise, I wanted to show both options as the Private Endpoint option is the one you will most likely encounter as an Enterprise Azure DBA.

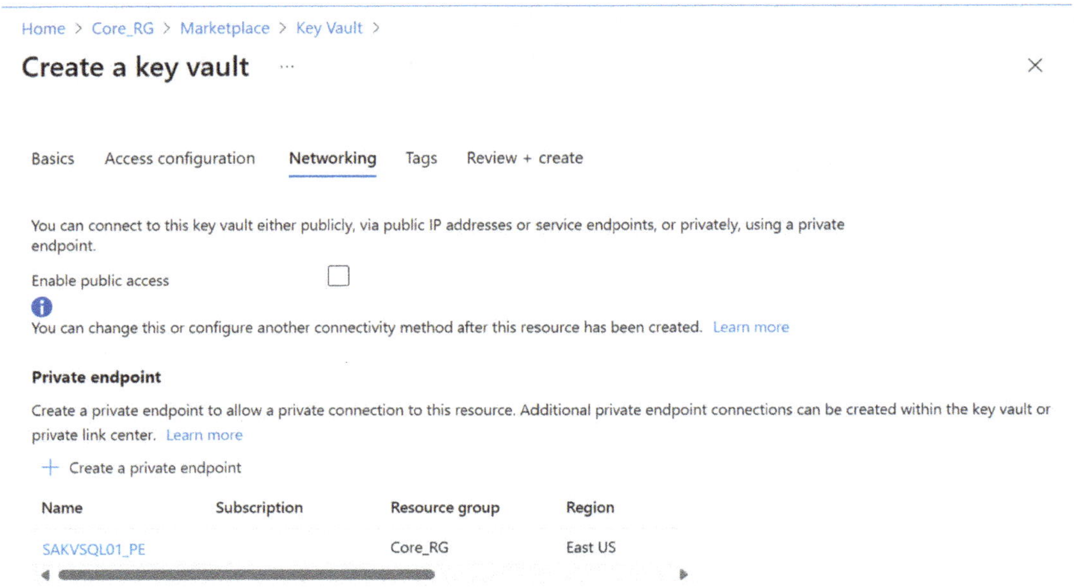

Home > Core_RG > Marketplace > Key Vault >

Create a key vault   ...   ✕

Basics   Access configuration   **Networking**   Tags   Review + create

You can connect to this key vault either publicly, via public IP addresses or service endpoints, or privately, using a private endpoint.

Enable public access   ☐

ⓘ
You can change this or configure another connectivity method after this resource has been created. Learn more

Private endpoint

Create a private endpoint to allow a private connection to this resource. Additional private endpoint connections can be created within the key vault or private link center. Learn more

＋ Create a private endpoint

Name	Subscription	Resource group	Region
SAKVSQL01_PE		Core_RG	East US

Figure 6-7. *AKV Deployment Networking 2*

Finally, the Azure portal presents a summary of our choices and bids us to create this resource. Figure 6-8 shows this helpful recap.

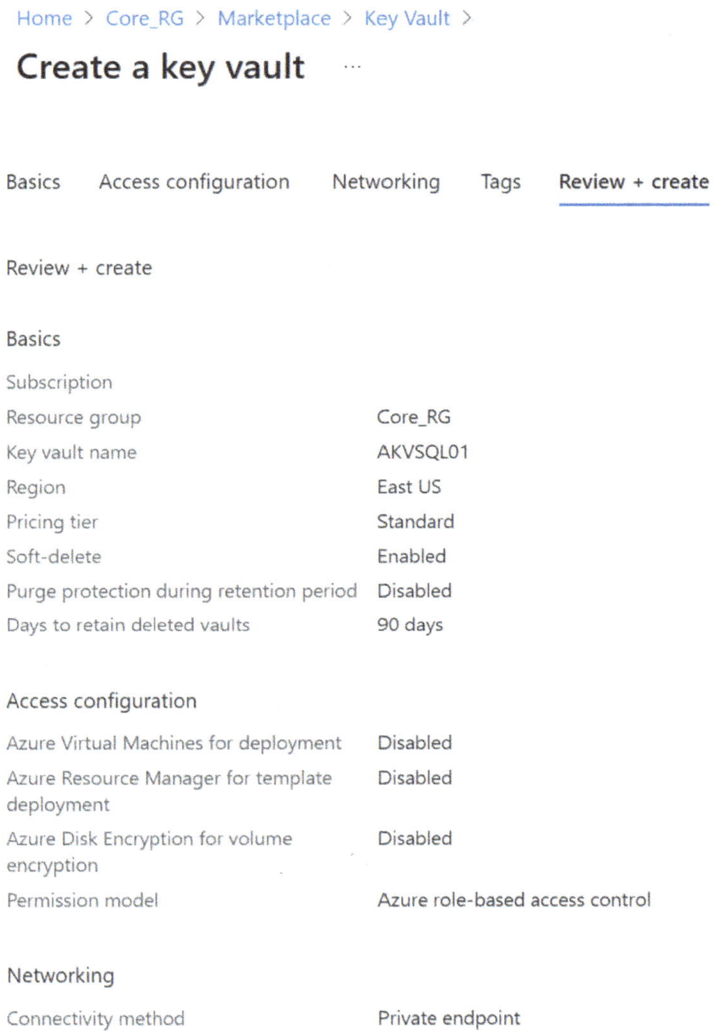

Home > Core_RG > Marketplace > Key Vault >

Create a key vault   ···

Basics   Access configuration   Networking   Tags   **Review + create**

Review + create

Basics

Subscription	
Resource group	Core_RG
Key vault name	AKVSQL01
Region	East US
Pricing tier	Standard
Soft-delete	Enabled
Purge protection during retention period	Disabled
Days to retain deleted vaults	90 days

Access configuration

Azure Virtual Machines for deployment	Disabled
Azure Resource Manager for template deployment	Disabled
Azure Disk Encryption for volume encryption	Disabled
Permission model	Azure role-based access control

Networking

Connectivity method	Private endpoint

Figure 6-8. *AKV Deployment Summary*

Deploying an Azure Key Vault only takes a few moments.

Connecting AKV to Azure SQL PaaS Services

Now that you have a working Azure Key Vault in your subscription, you can generate and/or store encryption keys for any Azure SQL Service. That includes Azure SQL DB, Azure SQL MI, and Azure SQL VM.

Connecting AKV to Azure SQL DB

Connecting each SQL service to an Azure Key Vault begins slightly differently for each service. For Azure SQL DB, you must complete the logical server deployment before you can connect the finished logical server to an Azure Key Vault. All databases on a server will share access rights to the same key vault, so plan your AKV and Logical SQL Server layout accordingly. On the tower menu to the left, choose "Transparent Data Encryption" located under the "Security" section as shown in Figure 6-9.

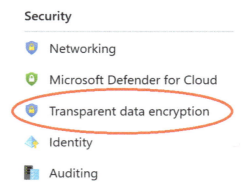

Figure 6-9. Connecting Azure SQL DB to AKV – Start

This will bring you to a deceptively simple screen that can unlock a whole host of choices. Figure 6-10 shows the default "Service-managed key" as the chosen option.

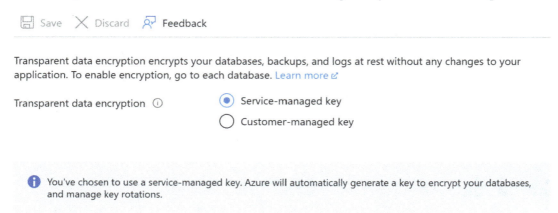

Figure 6-10. Azure SQL TDE Key Selection – Default

If we change the selection to "Customer-managed key," the options expand as shown in Figure 6-11 to let us select a key. Remember, all databases on a logical server share a single key.

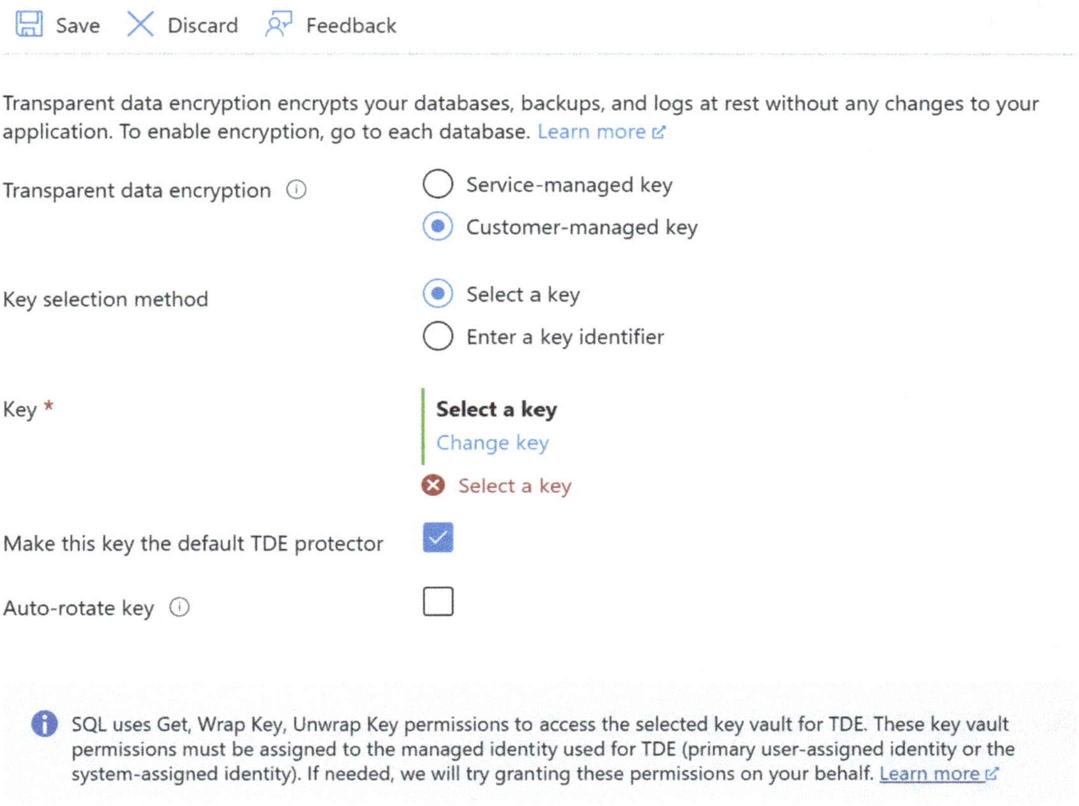

Figure 6-11. *Azure SQL TDE Key Selection – Custom*

You can select a key or key identifier. Take extra care about the note at the bottom. Selecting a key does *not* assign permissions to the Azure Key Vault for the SQL Server Identity. That task must be done independently. Remember, it will be the SQL Server Identity that requests the keys, so that Identity must be granted the listed permissions.

When you click "Change key," this takes you the Key Selection Blade shown in Figure 6-12, which is where you also select the specific Key Vault.

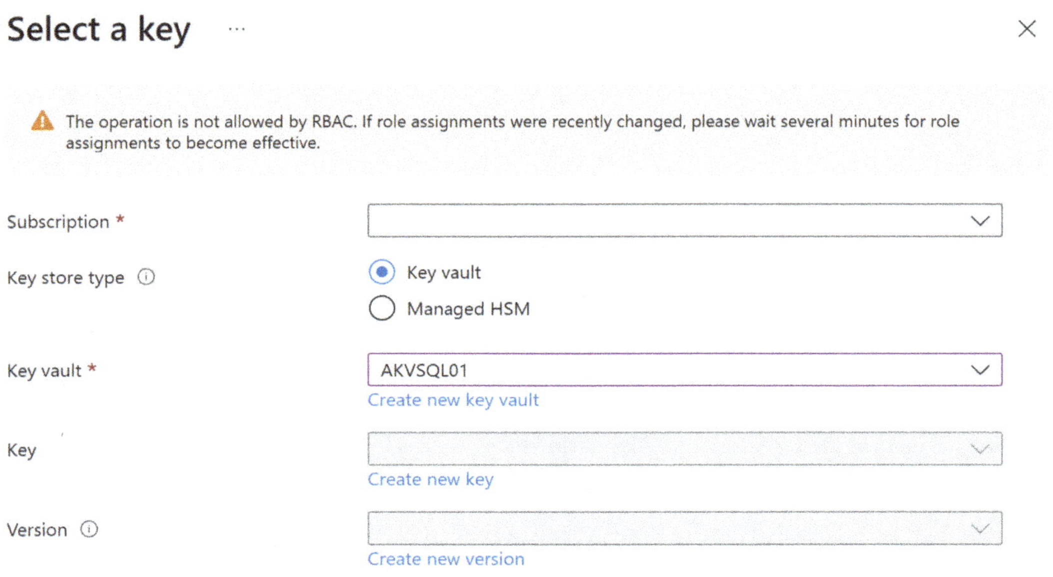

Figure 6-12. *Key and Key Vault Selection*

Notice that all the selections are drop-down menus. You must have all the keys in place and permissions granted before you can choose the key. Unless all the conditions are met, you will not be able to choose the correct key and save this configuration.

Connecting AKV to Azure SQL MI

I am including this as a separate section only to ease searching and reference. The procedure for connecting Azure Key Vault to Azure SQL Managed Instance is nearly identical to the process outlined above to connect Azure Key Vault to Azure SQL Database. Start with the "Security" section and follow the same screens as described above to connect AKV to an existing SQL Managed Instance. In addition, you can also select an Azure Key Vault during the provisioning process, either from the portal or via any of the automation tools we discuss in Chapter 12.

Connecting AKV to Azure SQL VM

One of the reasons Microsoft considers Azure SQL VM as an Azure Service is the SQL Virtual Machine Resource. This resource unlocks many Azure-only features of SQL Server by tightly integrating SQL with specific Azure Services. One of these Services is Azure Key

Vault. If you select an Azure SQL Virtual Machine resource and choose the "Overview" menu item on the left, one of the boxes in the main part of the blade should look something like Figure 6-13, the starting point for Azure Key Vault Integration.

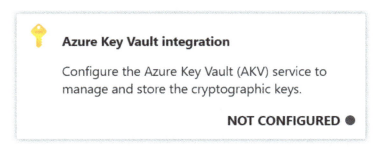

🔑 Azure Key Vault integration

Configure the Azure Key Vault (AKV) service to manage and store the cryptographic keys.

NOT CONFIGURED ●

Figure 6-13. *Azure Key Vault SQL IaaS Integration*

Clicking this button will take you to the Security Configuration blade for that Azure SQL VM. Choosing "Enable" expands the section to add the four fields shown in Figure 6-14.

AZURE KEY VAULT INTEGRATION

Configure your virtual machine to be able to connect to the Azure Key Vault service.

Azure Key Vault integration ⓘ	○ Disable ● Enable
Key Vault URL * ⓘ	_____
Principal name * ⓘ	_____
Principal secret * ⓘ	_____
Credential name * ⓘ	_____

Figure 6-14. *Azure Key Vault SQL IaaS Integration Details*

The Key Vault is accessed by its endpoint URL, available from the Overview page of the Vault Portal resource (not shown). The Principal Name and Secret are the Entra ID artifacts used to access the Key Vault. Finally, the Credential is the name you wish to store this connection under inside SQL Server. Once connected, your SQL Server can access any key the Entra ID account can access.

You can also leverage the Azure SQL IaaS Extension during deployment to connect to an Azure Key Vault. On the "SQL Server settings" tab of the "Create a virtual machine" page as shown in Figure 6-15, you can fill in the exact same four fields as above, and the SQL VM will configure the AKV connection as part of the deployment process.

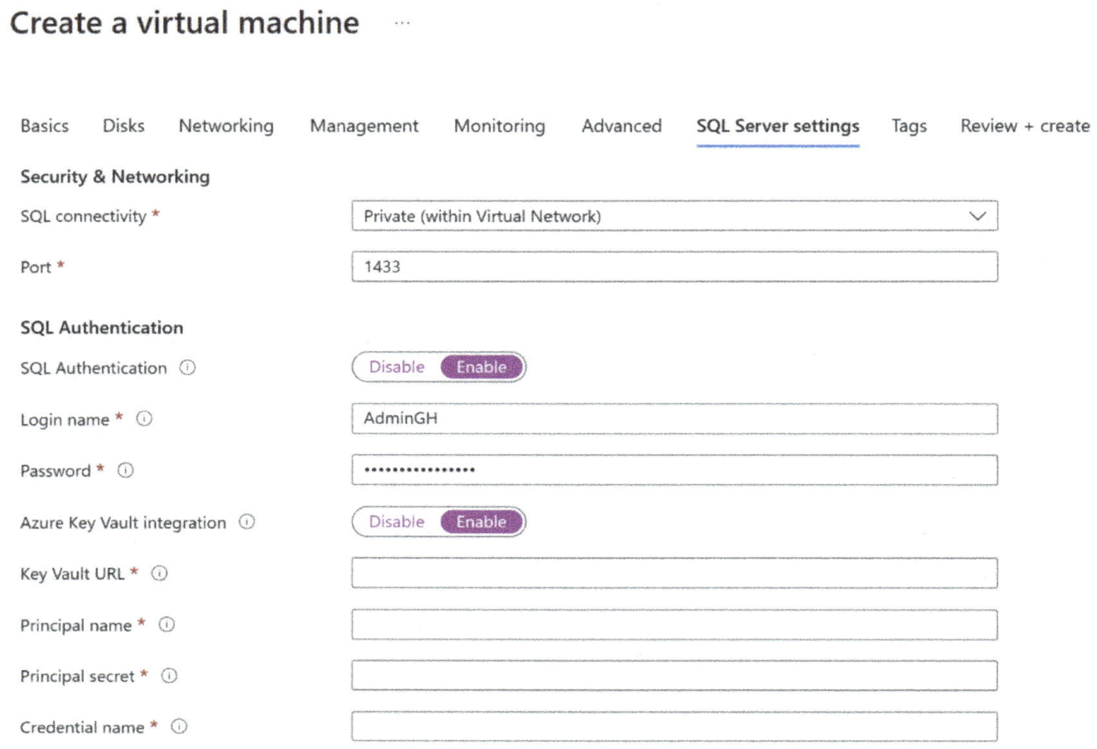

Create a virtual machine   ···

Basics	Disks	Networking	Management	Monitoring	Advanced	**SQL Server settings**	Tags	Review + create

Security & Networking

SQL connectivity *   Private (within Virtual Network)   ⌄

Port *   1433

SQL Authentication

SQL Authentication ⓘ   (Disable **Enable**)

Login name * ⓘ   AdminGH

Password * ⓘ   ●●●●●●●●●●●●●●●●

Azure Key Vault integration ⓘ   (Disable **Enable**)

Key Vault URL * ⓘ

Principal name * ⓘ

Principal secret * ⓘ

Credential name * ⓘ

Figure 6-15. *Deploying a SQL VM with AKV Integration*

Implement Object-Level Encryption

SQL Server can explicitly encrypt various database-level objects. Azure SQL DB and
Azure SQL MI have inherited this capability to ensure compatibility with as many
database features as possible. This section will explore the "other" (non-TDE) SQL
encryption options for data at rest available in Azure. Note that configuring TDE has no
impact on any of the following encryption options.

Column-Level Encryption

SQL Server has long had the ability to encrypt specific columns of data. While the
usefulness of this feature has been superseded by more capable features as the product
has matured, the basic functionality has remained in the SQL engine and is included
in the feature set for both Azure SQL PaaS services. Given the typical past application
authentication model, which did not often implement security granularity beyond the

entire database scope, column-level encryption did not add much value. As applications move to more modern authentication models where the user's identity is managed externally and present throughout all layers of the application stack, encrypting particular data columns may have a renewed focus and utility. Regardless, it's going to be on the test, so we are going to cover it here.

The important factor to remember when using encrypted columns is this is not the same feature as Always Encrypted. Always Encrypted was released many years after Encrypted Columns and has a much more robust and practical feature set. With Encrypted Columns, all encryption happens inside the SQL Server Database Engine, not in the ADO client libraries or as part of a Secure Enclave as with Always Encrypted. Therefore, the Azure SQL Database engine requires access to all encryption keys. As we already learned, encryption keys (or at least external *Key Protector* keys) are stored in Azure Key Vault. In the case of column-level encryption, the Symmetric Key in the database is protected by an Asymmetric key in the Key Vault. Recall from our earlier discussion that symmetric keys are used for actual data encryption and are stored in encrypted form inside the database as part of the column and table definitions. The Key Protector is an Asymmetric key that is protected by AKV in Azure.

Encryption and Decryption are handled explicitly by two T-SQL functions, ENCRYPTBYKEY() and DECRYPTBYKEY(). Given that the encryption is always non-deterministic, you cannot search or join on any encrypted column. Should you try and unencrypt the column inside a JOIN statement or WHERE clause, be aware that SQL will unencrypt all candidate columns and then make any comparisons, essentially using a full scan with a function wrapper to resolve the query. No indexes can be used on encrypted columns, no matter how much you torture T-SQL trying. Due to this shortcoming, I do not recommend implementing Column-Level Encryption; however, you may inherit a database using this feature, so it is an essential Azure DBA skill.

Encrypting Stored Procedures

SQL Server can encrypt stored procedures, including all Azure SQL Database variants. When this feature was first introduced, several companies tried to use it as a form of Digital Restrictions Management to enforce copyrights. This led to a lot of unhappy DBAs, as without visible source code, they could not troubleshoot performance issues. This practice was rapidly abandoned. Encrypted stored procedures also complicated disaster recovery and server migrations, so this feature rapidly fell out of favor with the user community, despite the ease of actual implementation.

Technically, Encrypted Stored Procedures aren't truly encrypted; they are "Obfuscated." *Obfuscated* means the text isn't reported using normal system catalog views. The original text is still stored in the database and can still be viewed via the Dedicated Admin Connection or by inspecting the raw database files. Since the obfuscation was really just an inconvenience to any DBA with moderate skills or access to any major SQL knowledge website, software publishers rapidly stopped using this feature.

In addition, Encrypted Stored procedures could not be published via Transactional Replication, nor could you encrypt (obfuscate) a CLR function. The only way to "unencrypt" a procedure is to *alter* the procedure and remove the WITH ENCRYPTION clause. Of course, this requires access to the original, unencrypted stored procedure text.

Configure Server- and Database-Level Firewall Rules

One of the problems with a long-lived product such as Microsoft SQL Server is when a DBA has to deploy an older version with known security vulnerabilities. There is an unavoidable time between the initial installation and when the systems get patched where the newly deployed SQL Server is highly vulnerable. Microsoft eventually modified the SQL Server Installer to disable all network libraries until the system was patched *or* a DBA explicitly enabled the necessary libraries. Blocking all network access during initial installation and configuration meant that there were no network endpoints to attack while the system was vulnerable. Local connections via Shared Memory were always allowed for administrative and installation purposes.

It is this experience that led to the design of Azure SQL Database networking. Azure SQL DB uses the Public Endpoint networking model by default. The Logical Server has a Fully Qualified Domain Name (FQDN) that can be accessed over the Public Internet via the well-known Microsoft SQL port number 1433. Microsoft Azure SQL Database uses an IP address–based firewall to protect from unwanted connections. Only systems with an allowed IP address may access the server or the database. Allowed addresses can be individually selected or included in a range definition. Multiple individual and disjoint ranges can be chosen, although having too many ranges can lead to security problems. Best Practice is to keep the allowed list as short as necessary. Secure By Default means the initial allowed list is empty. All connections are denied unless explicitly authorized.

There are different firewalls that can be configured, one at the server level and another at the database level. This is yet another reminder that the Logical Server is an endpoint microservice and *not* the actual physical server the database runs on. Understanding how and when you can set these rules as well as how they interact is a major topic on the DP-300 exam. Make sure you know this material thoroughly.

Server-Level Firewall Rules

Server-level firewall rules can only be created post-deployment and only apply to public server endpoints. By default, the "rule" for the Azure SQL Database Server-level Firewall is "Deny All." Addresses can be added either individually or as a CIDR range. Currently the limit is 128 entries at the server level, but as previously mentioned, best practices suggest limiting this to as few entries as necessary. Both the Azure portal and SSMS have an "add this host IP address" capability to allow an administrative user to create an entry for their workstation without having to research their public IP address. As the name implies, server-level rules apply to all databases on a logical server. This reinforces the practice of grouping databases based on common networking and security rather than resource consumption or availability as with non-cloud or IaaS servers and yet another way that having a logical endpoint rather than a physical server host for a database collection changes how systems are best architected.

Note   The first firewall rule must be created from the Azure portal, PowerShell, Azure CLI, or Azure REST API. Once you have established connectivity allowed by one or more rules, additional rules can be created via Transact-SQL commands.

Database-Level Firewall Rules

While best practice has PaaS databases grouped into logical servers, real-world deployments do not always conform to best practices. Azure PaaS SQL Databases can inherit legacy IaaS or on-premises groupings or have commonality determined by other considerations. In such cases we can deploy database-level firewall rules allowing custom access to each database.

Database-level firewall rules can only be created post-deployment via Transact-SQL commands after connectivity has been established through creation and application of a Server-level rule. Database firewall rules are limited to a maximum of 256 rules.

Firewall Rules Interaction

When a connection attempt is made to an Azure SQL Database or Azure SQL Managed Instance Public Endpoint, the originating IP address is checked against the Database-level firewall rules if any exist. If a matching rule is found, the connection is established. If there is no database-level rule that allows a connection, then the Server-level firewall is checked. If a rule allowing connections is present, a connection is established. There is no "DENY" rule type in the Azure SQL Database firewall set, only "ALLOW." If either firewall allows connection, then a connection will be established. Connections are only allowed on port 1433, the well-known SQL port. Take care to make sure that there are no other firewall rules blocking outbound connections from your originating system. Many organizations block outbound traffic on port 1433 as a default.

Connections originating from Azure, either from native Azure services or from applications hosted in Azure, are a special case. The Firewall Rules page on the Azure portal has a checkbox labeled "Allow Azure services and resources to access this server." This creates a special rule starting and ending with "0.0.0.0" and named "AllowAllWIndowsAzureIps". You can create a rule with "0.0.0.0" starting and ending values using PowerShell, Azure CLI, or Azure REST API to enable Azure connectivity. The exact name does not matter. Be aware that this is a global allow switch for all of Azure, including services hosted in other Azure tenants.

Implement Always Encrypted

Always Encrypted is the latest data security measure to be added to Microsoft SQL Server. Always Encrypted was introduced in Azure SQL DB in 2015 and included in the SQL Server 2016 retail product. Always Encrypted stores individually encrypted columns of data and does not decrypt the columns until they are in the client application. All encryption and decryption are handled in the SQL Server client libraries, requiring minimal adjustment to existing applications to implement. To maximize security, SQL Server itself never decrypts the encrypted columns. With the addition of Secure Enclaves, decryption can happen inside SQL. We will first explore Always Encrypted and then examine the extra capabilities that Secure Enclaves offer.

Prior to Always Encrypted, it was impossible to use encrypted data as a search argument (SARG) in a query. Most modern encryption is intentionally non-deterministic, meaning that encrypting the same value will yield multiple different encrypted values.

144

Always Encrypted offers an option to force deterministic encryption so limited searches can be performed on encrypted data without access to the decryption key. Care must be taken when choosing deterministic encryption for a column. The likelihood of using the column as a SARG in a query must be high. Always Encrypted is often used for Personally Identifying Information (PII) such as Social Security numbers (SSNs) in the United States or other National Identification numbers in other nations. Since those are often quasi-unique identifiers, they act as record locaters for persons and are often Search Arguments. These are good candidates for Deterministic Encryption. Always Encrypted deterministic encryption is a poor candidate for low-cardinality columns with few unique values. If there are only a few unique raw values (low cardinality), there will be correspondingly few encrypted values.

SQL Server itself does not have access to the encryption key for a specific Always Encrypted Column absent Secure Enclaves; however, it knows what the key is and where it can be obtained. This is so authorized client applications can obtain the keys and encrypt/decrypt the target column(s) while ensuring that anyone accessing the SQL Service directly cannot read the protected data. One of the basic requirements to successfully implement Always Encrypted is to have Separation of Duties between DBAs who configure Always Encrypted and security engineers who manage and authorize access to encryption keys. One person with access to everything defeats the whole purpose of Always Encrypted.

It is possible for different columns to have different keys, so each encryption key has an identifier that is transmitted to the client application SQL libraries. The appropriate key is selected, the data decrypted, and the column(s) presented to the application. The reverse happens on write where the data is encrypted and transmitted to the SQL Server.

Always Encrypted with Secure Enclaves

Always Encrypted with Secure Enclaves extends the capability of Always Encrypted by securely decrypting data within the SQL Server inside a specific section known as a Secure Enclave. This secure enclave exists as a hardware-protected memory within SQL Server. This Secure Enclave is only available to the SQL engine itself for operations such as comparisons on non-deterministic columns, range queries, initial data encryption, key rotation, and other data functionality that is unavailable without access to the decrypted data. It is important to note that nothing outside the SQL engine can access this data. Not the SA login, not the system administrator, not even a debugger attached to the SQL engine can access this protected data.

This feature was introduced in SQL 2019 and is available on specific hardware platforms. Intel SGX–based systems support Always Encrypted with Secure Enclaves. The Windows Hypervisor also can create a Secure Enclave in virtual guest systems called a VBS enclave. Azure SQL Database uses Intel SGX hardware for the DC series–based databases that are available via the vCore purchasing model. VBS enclaves are currently in preview.

As with most SQL technologies, the best way to learn is hands-on. Fortunately, Microsoft has provided a public repo with a fully developed Always Encrypted with Secure Enclaves solution that is ready to deploy. This repo includes both HGX and VBS scenarios. Follow the link in Example 6-1 to deploy Always Encrypted with Secure Enclaves to your chosen Azure SQL Service.

Example 6-1. Always Encrypted with Secure Enclaves GitHub Repo

```
https://github.com/microsoft/sql-server-samples/tree/master/samples/
features/security/always-encrypted-with-secure-enclaves
```

Configure Transport Layer Security (TLS)

Transport Layer Security (*TLS*) is a widely used network protocol designed to protect data in transit across networks, particularly TCP-IP networks. TLS is designed to protect against message tampering, message interception, and message forgery. We need not be concerned about the internal workings of the TLS protocol; rather, we need to know how the protocol has evolved over time and how that impacts our security decisions around SQL Server in Azure.

Azure Standards currently state that all networking communications to or from Azure services require TLS 1.2 as the minimum default data-in-transit protection mechanism. All Azure SQL PaaS Services follow this guideline. No intervention or change is required to deploy TLS 1.2 for Azure PaaS Services. Some legacy applications require much older drivers that do not support TLS 1.2. For that reason, TLS 1.0 and 1.1 are still available, but use of these protocols is highly discouraged due to widely known security flaws.

You can set the minimum supported TLS level during service deployment or change it at any time. Allowing TLS 1.0 or 1.1 as the minimum does not impact client applications using TLS 1.2. When a connection is established to a SQL Service, the TLS level is negotiated between the application tier and the database service. This negotiation includes finding the maximum TLS level that both ends support. If a client application uses TLS 1.2, any SQL PaaS service will still support that level. Changing the minimum TLS level only enables earlier protocols; it does not disable current ones.

Since TLS is a network security option, this choice must be made at the server level, either for Azure SLQ DB or Azure SQL MI. Generally, if an Azure SQL DB client requires TLS 1.0 or 1.1, that database should be segmented off as a higher-security risk and not mixed on the same logical server as other databases that do not require compromised security protocols.

When deploying Azure SQL DB Logical Server or Azure SQL MI, you have an option to choose a different minimum TLS level (Figure 6-16).

You can also change the level at any time via the portal, PowerShell, or Azure CLI as shown in Figure 6-16. To change the TLS level via the Azure portal, access the Networking blade from the target Azure SQL DB Logical Server. Select the Connectivity tab, scroll to the bottom, and select the minimum TLS level required from the drop-down box as shown in Figure 6-16.

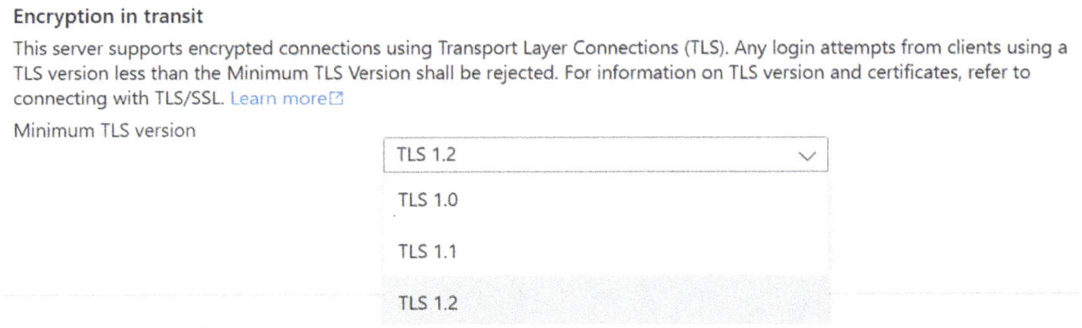

Encryption in transit

This server supports encrypted connections using Transport Layer Connections (TLS). Any login attempts from clients using a TLS version less than the Minimum TLS Version shall be rejected. For information on TLS version and certificates, refer to connecting with TLS/SSL. Learn more

Minimum TLS version

TLS 1.2	∨
TLS 1.0	
TLS 1.1	
TLS 1.2	

Figure 6-16. *Azure SQL Database TLS Selection*

Chapter Summary

Data Security is an essential job task for an Azure SQL Database Administrator. The General Data Protection Regulation (GDPR) – the European Union law regarding data security and privacy – has severe civil and criminal penalties for data mismanagement, including failure to protect Personally Identifying Information (PII). While the Chief Information Security Officer is the individual legally responsible for data security, your role is essential to preventing unauthorized data disclosure. Companies have lost tens of millions of dollars and some have gone out of business after data breaches. It is impossible to overstate the requirements for data security in our profession. Securing Data at Rest and Data in Transit is a foundational element of an overall data security strategy.

CHAPTER 7

Implement Compliance Controls for Sensitive Data

Not all data is the same. It just makes sense to apply more stringent data security to the CEO's Personally Identifiable Information (PII) than you would to the purchase history of cleaning supplies for the Company Headquarters building. Those two data sets are about as different as possible, yet they are both data sets that potentially can reside in a SQL service that you are responsible for. One of the key security responsibilities for an Azure SQL Database Administrator is to connect the people with the data they need while also keeping out anyone who does not need access to that specific data.

Fortunately, our job is not to figure out who should have access to what data; our task is to implement technologies that enable compliance with whatever rules and standards apply to our data. Those standards can come from within your organization or from an external compliance regime. Regardless of where your standards come from, implementing those standards is an essential part of an Azure Database Administrator role.

The good news is you are not alone in this quest. Microsoft considers compliance and security to be a shared responsibility. Microsoft provides platforms that are secure by design and tools to help maintain that compliance. Your implementation of these tools and platforms should conform to both Microsoft and your company's policies and procedures. Microsoft provides guidance for many external compliance regimes such as HIPAA, FERPA, PCI-3DS, and others via the Trust Center located at `https://Microsoft.com/Trust`.

© Geoff Hiten 2025
G. Hiten, *Administering Microsoft Azure SQL Solutions*, Certification Study Companion Series,
https://doi.org/10.1007/979-8-8688-1585-0_7

Apply a Data Classification Strategy

Data Classification is the process of identifying, labeling, and reporting the sensitive data that resides in your Azure SQL databases. You can't just say "everything's sensitive and we treat it all with maximum care." Different people need access to different data for different reasons. You don't disclose everything to everyone all the time. Likewise, you can't keep all data from all people. You must maintain a balance. Azure provides data classification tools for Azure SQL Database services, both Azure SQL DB and Azure SQL MI, to help classify data.

SQL Server first introduced data classification support in SQL 2012 using column metadata to store classification labels. All currently supported releases of SQL Server and all Azure SQL Server products as well as Azure Synapse Data Warehouse support storing labels; however, starting with SQL 2019, the data is stored in the catalog view `sys.sensitivity_classifications` instead of column metadata. As with most Azure tools, the included tools work well to administer a resource directly, but you may require an enterprise-scale tool such as Microsoft Purview to handle this task for a large number of databases. For this section, we will focus on the built-in classification tools for Azure SQL DB and Azure SQL MI.

Before we look at how classification tools work, we need to understand exactly what we mean when we talk about data discovery and classification. According to Microsoft, data discovery and classification consists of four capabilities. First is Discovery and Recommendations. This identifies columns that may contain sensitive data along with recommendations as to what classification to apply. The second part labels those columns, applying sensitivity classification information obtained during discovery. Once these labels are applied, Query Sensitivity results are calculated in real time for auditing purposes. Finally, Discovery and Classification provides visibility to these classification labels through an Azure dashboard portal. Sensitivity is applied per column of data, not per row. Going back to our initial example of your CEO's Personally Identifiable Information, discovery and classification will treat every employee's Personally Identifiable Information with equal sensitivity and all Purchasing Records (cleaning supplies or otherwise) with a different sensitivity.

To use the Azure SQL Database built-in Discovery and Classification tools, start on the home blade of your Azure SQL Database. On the left column in the section labeled "Security," there's an entry named Data discovery and classification. Choosing this option will display a dashboard overview of the labels and the information types contained in this database. Until you configure Data Discovery and Classification, this dashboard will show 0 in all columns and graphs. At the top of the page is a button for configuring data discovery and classification. This button will take you to a page labeled "Information protection." The first choice you need to make is selecting which protection policy mode you wish to use. The SQL Information Protection Policy has a predefined set of sensitivity labels that are generally used for SQL Server databases. The Microsoft Information Protection Policy for your Azure Tenant is derived from sensitivity labels defined in your Microsoft 365 Tenant. For this discussion we will be using the default Microsoft SQL Information Protection Policy. The SQL Information Protection Policy has six levels of sensitivity labels, two of which are related to the specific privacy legislation known as GDPR. These follow in order from least to most sensitive:

1. Public

2. General

3. Confidential

4. Confidential GDPR

5. Highly confidential

6. Highly confidential GDPR

Information Protection Policies are often set at the tenant root or at the subscription/ management group level. You may not have the authority or Azure permission to change this policy. With the correct permissions you can add additional policy labels using the *Create label* control at the top of the blade.

The "magic" that ties all this together is the definition of the various information types. Selecting "Manage information types" at the top of the page brings you to a list of predefined information types. The SQL Information Protection Policy includes 12 specific information types, all of which are associated with either the Confidential or Confidential GDPR sensitivity level. These definitions are what allow the Data Discovery and Classification Service to identify specific column headings indicating certain types of data.

Let's use the SSN field as an example. For my non-US readers, SSN stands for Social Security Number, a de facto US ID number. Go to Manage information types, and when you get to the SSN field, go to the right, hit the three dots, and then select *Configure.* This will bring up a mini-blade labeled "Configure information type." Figures 7-1 and 7-2 show the complete "Configure information type" mini-blade for SSN, broken into two parts for legibility. You can enable or disable this information type, but you cannot change the display name or description since these were based on built-in ones from the SQL Information Protection Policy set at the subscription policy level. You can change the associated Information Protection Policy label with this tool. In the SQL Information Protection Policy, a Social Security number is a confidential GDPR type of data. If you have a different classification system, perhaps a different sovereign policy regarding a national ID number you must comply with, you can choose another label that matches your policy.

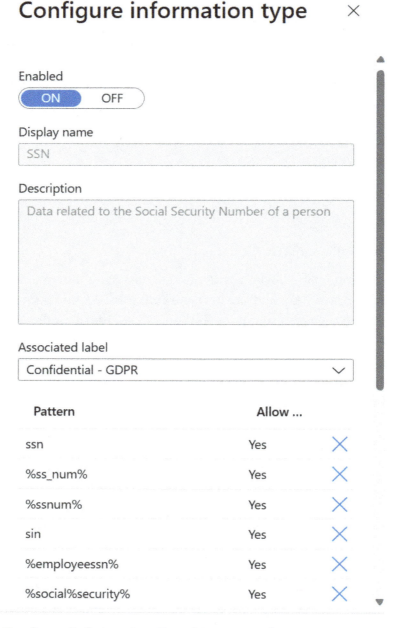

Figure 7-1. *Configure Information Type SSN Example 1*

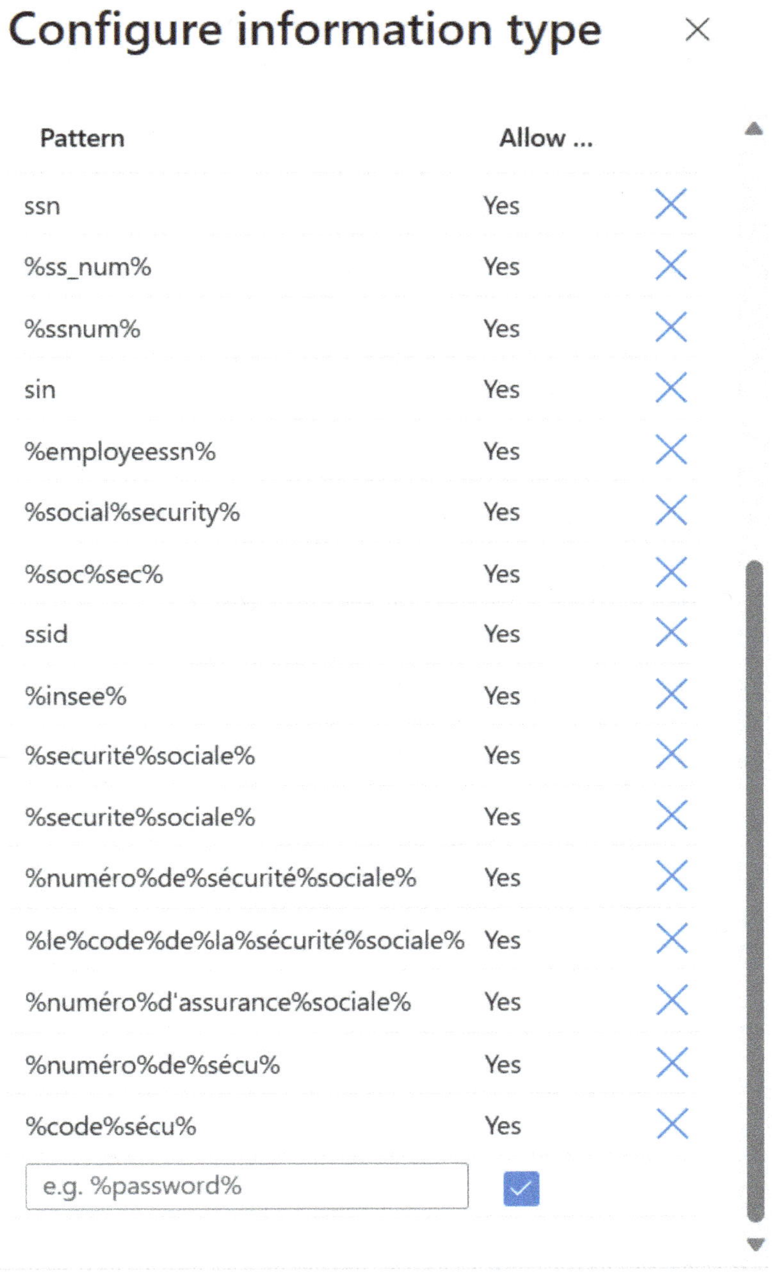

Configure information type   ✕

Pattern	Allow ...	
ssn	Yes	✕
%ss_num%	Yes	✕
%ssnum%	Yes	✕
sin	Yes	✕
%employeessn%	Yes	✕
%social%security%	Yes	✕
%soc%sec%	Yes	✕
ssid	Yes	✕
%insee%	Yes	✕
%securité%sociale%	Yes	✕
%securite%sociale%	Yes	✕
%numéro%de%sécurité%sociale%	Yes	✕
%le%code%de%la%sécurité%sociale%	Yes	✕
%numéro%d'assurance%sociale%	Yes	✕
%numéro%de%sécu%	Yes	✕
%code%sécu%	Yes	✕
e.g. %password%	✓	

Figure 7-2. *Configure Information Type SSN Example 1 Continued*

Examining the patterns, none of them match what would be considered the Social Security Number itself. In the United States, a SSN is composed of three numeric characters followed by a dash, which is followed by two numeric characters followed by a dash, which is followed by four numeric characters (NNN-NN-NNNN). Other nations have their own distinct patterns for a SSN equivalent. This list does not contain any data patterns. We are not looking at data patterns for discovery; we are looking at column heading patterns for discovery. This implies that Azure SQL Database Data Discovery and Classification doesn't actually look at data; it only looks at column headings. That is a correct assumption that Data Discovery and Classification uses column headings and not actual data patterns to identify and classify information types.

Now that we have a solid understanding of how information policy classification labels and information types all work together to power Azure SQL Data Discovery and Classification, we can begin to use this tool to apply a policy to a database. Choose a target database and then Data Discovery and Classification on the left menu under Security. You will start off with a blank report showing an overview with no label distributions, no information types, no classified columns, nothing. Up at the top it will show the current Information Policy to be applied, in our case the SQL Information Protection Policy. As Figure 7-3 shows using the AdventureWorksLT sample database, Azure SQL Data Discovery and Classification has found 15 recommendations.

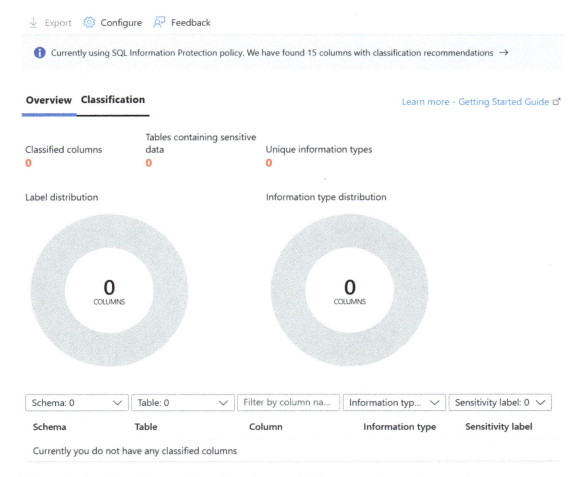

Figure 7-3. *Blank Data Classification and Discovery Overview with Recommendation Count*

Following the recommendations banner link brings us to Figure 7-4 showing the Schema, Table, Column, Information type, and Sensitivity label associated with the candidate data element.

155

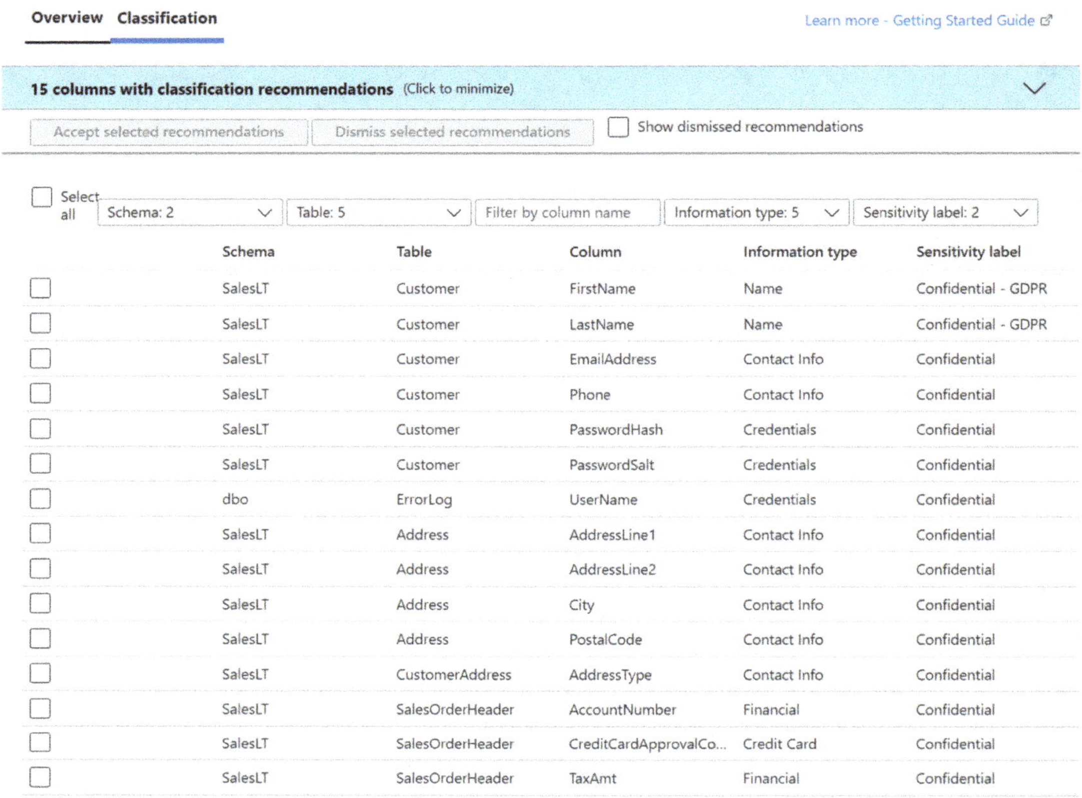

Schema	Table	Column	Information type	Sensitivity label
SalesLT	Customer	FirstName	Name	Confidential - GDPR
SalesLT	Customer	LastName	Name	Confidential - GDPR
SalesLT	Customer	EmailAddress	Contact Info	Confidential
SalesLT	Customer	Phone	Contact Info	Confidential
SalesLT	Customer	PasswordHash	Credentials	Confidential
SalesLT	Customer	PasswordSalt	Credentials	Confidential
dbo	ErrorLog	UserName	Credentials	Confidential
SalesLT	Address	AddressLine1	Contact Info	Confidential
SalesLT	Address	AddressLine2	Contact Info	Confidential
SalesLT	Address	City	Contact Info	Confidential
SalesLT	Address	PostalCode	Contact Info	Confidential
SalesLT	CustomerAddress	AddressType	Contact Info	Confidential
SalesLT	SalesOrderHeader	AccountNumber	Financial	Confidential
SalesLT	SalesOrderHeader	CreditCardApprovalCo...	Credit Card	Confidential
SalesLT	SalesOrderHeader	TaxAmt	Financial	Confidential

***Figure 7-4.** Azure SQL DB Data Discovery and Classification Recommendations Detail*

Selecting all columns, choosing "Accept selected recommendations," and saving changes immediately update the dashboard. You can choose to accept any, all, or none of the recommendations or reclassify any data element or even manually add entries for classification from this blade. Any changes are immediately reflected in the Overview page as shown in Figure 7-5.

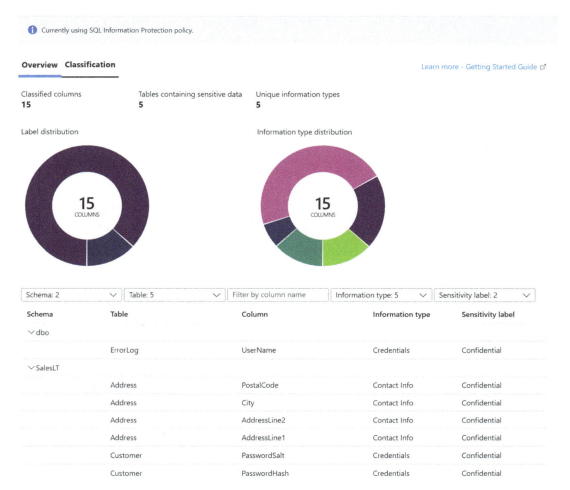

Figure 7-5. *Azure SQL DB Data Discovery and Classification Overview –*
Populated

Data Discovery and Classification is an essential first step in most policy or
compliance regimes. You must know what data you have and where it resides before you
can institute appropriate controls over that data.

Configure Server and Database Audits

Auditing on SQL Server has long been an important feature for compliance. A record
of who wrote, changed, or read certain data is fundamental for particular compliance
regimes. Prior to Azure, auditing SQL Server was always a complex endeavor, requiring

detailed configuration and laborious audit file management along with separation of duties that make auditing meaningful. Azure simplifies this process greatly. You only need to decide which level to audit, a server, a database, or both, and then decide where the audit data should land. Once again, we see a difference between the Azure Logical SQL Database Server and a traditional physical SQL instance with separate, independent audit configurations for server and database.

Auditing Azure SQL DB

Let's start with a Server Audit. Server Audits include all databases attached to a Logical Server. This includes databases created after the Audit is defined. If you define a separate Database Audit for one or more databases on a Logical Server, Microsoft recommends you use separate landing spaces for the audit from each database.

Azure SQL Database Audits can land in Azure Storage, a Log Analytics Workspace, or an Event Hub. These are the three standard streaming data landing zones in Azure. For this exercise, just accept that we will use Azure Log Analytics. A detailed explanation of Azure Monitor and Log Analytics workspaces as well as the other data landing options will be provided in Chapter 8 when we see more streaming data sources.

Both Server and Database auditing have a blade that is accessed under the Security section of the left menu labeled "Auditing." Enabling either Azure SQL Auditing or Auditing of Microsoft Support Operations will open up additional menu options to describe where the audit data will land. You do not see any audit event configuration options – everything is predefined except for enable/disable and where the data should land as shown in Figure 7-6.

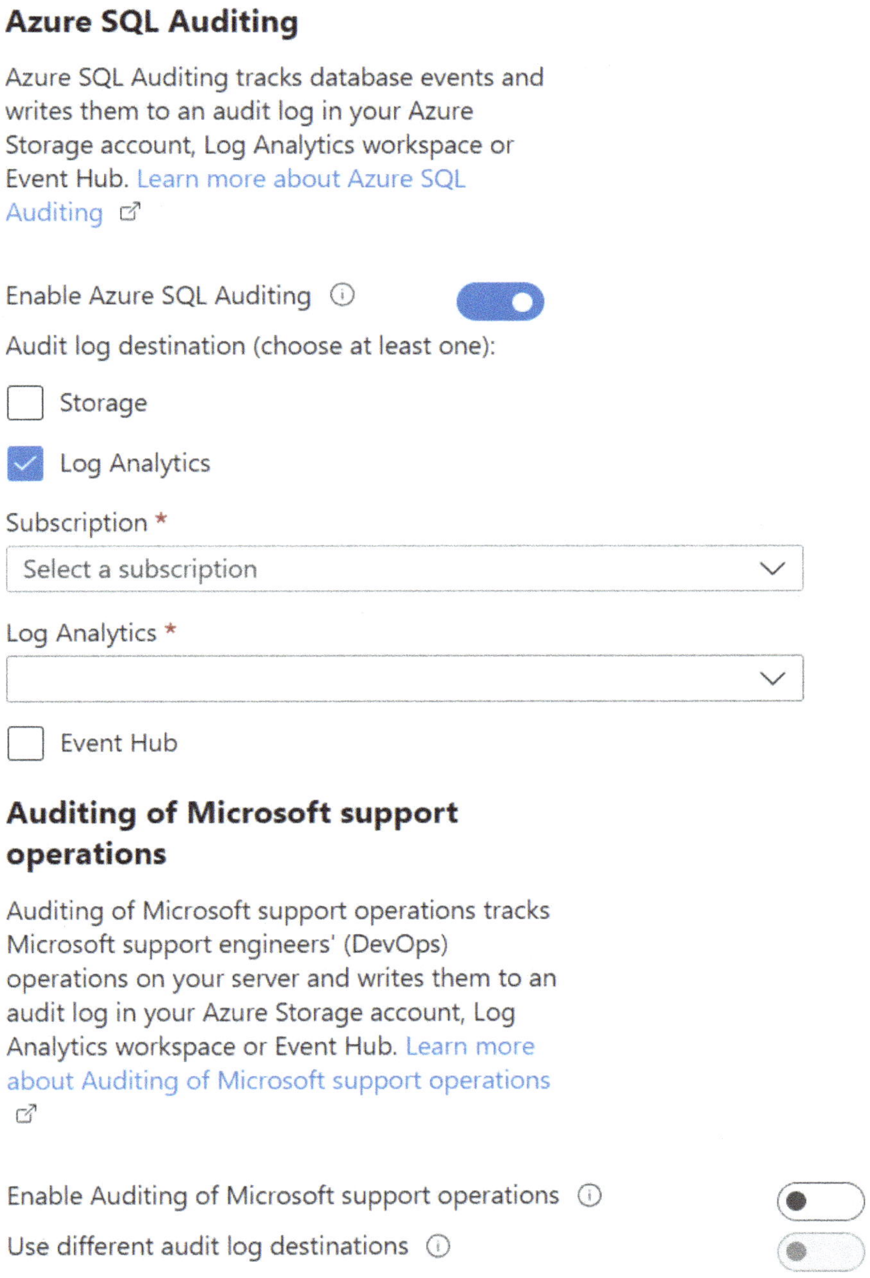

Azure SQL Auditing

Azure SQL Auditing tracks database events and writes them to an audit log in your Azure Storage account, Log Analytics workspace or Event Hub. Learn more about Azure SQL Auditing ☐

Enable Azure SQL Auditing ⓘ

Audit log destination (choose at least one):

☐ Storage

☑ Log Analytics

Subscription *

| Select a subscription | ⌄ |

Log Analytics *

| | ⌄ |

☐ Event Hub

Auditing of Microsoft support operations

Auditing of Microsoft support operations tracks Microsoft support engineers' (DevOps) operations on your server and writes them to an audit log in your Azure Storage account, Log Analytics workspace or Event Hub. Learn more about Auditing of Microsoft support operations ☐

Enable Auditing of Microsoft support operations ⓘ

Use different audit log destinations ⓘ

Figure 7-6. *Azure SQL DB Auditing Configuration Options*

You should pay close attention to a couple of options here. First, notice the ability to send the audit data to a separate subscription. Enterprise-level Azure customers often have complex Azure Landing Zone configurations set up with a hierarchy of subscriptions for different purposes. One or more subscriptions are often set up for auditing and tracking with separate roles and permissions than the workload landing zones. Since the basic functioning of auditing requires clear separation of duties, this model simplifies implementation for new workloads.

Second, notice you can send audits of Microsoft Support Operations to a separate destination. Again, this is so the team responsible for managing and responding to such events has a clearly separate set of data and does not have to disentangle other data that would obscure events they care about.

Auditing Azure SQL Managed Instance

Azure SQL Managed Instance configures auditing slightly differently. For this service, Auditing is configured from the Monitoring ➤ Diagnostic Settings menu option. Audit data is included in the diagnostic and event data stream. The audit landing spaces are the same three options – Azure Storage, Log Analytics, and Event Hubs. Auditing is only available as a Server-level configuration option and automatically includes all databases, including ones created after the audit is enabled. We will go deeper into configuring Diagnostic Settings in Chapter 8.

Implement Data Change Tracking

By nature, SQL Server is concerned with the current state of whatever data it is tracking. Transactions exist so that the system can accurately keep track of whatever it is asked to track, whether that is a running total or a current address. While this fulfils the primary function of a database, we often need to track how we got to the current totals. The most common reason is to stream these changes to another system for downstream consumption. Streaming changes is often much less intrusive than copying the entire database any time the downstream system needs an update.

With VM or on-premises-based SQL Servers, this was often accomplished by reading the transaction log and replaying relevant transactions to other data systems. SQL Server Transactional Replication is one such system, but third-party vendors have also built systems using this technology.

Unfortunately for us, Azure SQL DB has incorporated all recovery options into its service framework and does not expose the transaction log to external view. While this provides a well-defined recovery service, it does eliminate the option of low-impact Change Tracking in Azure SQL DB.

Fortunately, Microsoft recognized this and provides an alternative method to track and view database changes without inspecting the transaction log. Change Tracking is an Azure SQL feature that tracks internal database changes (transactions) for specific tables and will keep such history for a specified period of time. Change Tracking must be enabled at the database and the object (table) level. This can be done with SSMS or via T-SQL commands. Be aware that SSMS has an upper practical limit on the number of tables the tool can readily handle. If you want to track a large number of tables, you should use T-SQL scripts.

Example 7-1 shows a typical Change Tracking Code snippet to enable database-level Change Tracking. You would still need to enable specific tables to capture data.

Example 7-1. Enable Change Tracking

```
ALTER DATABASE AdventureWorksLT
SET CHANGE_TRACKING = ON
(CHANGE_RETENTION = 3 DAYS, AUTO_CLEANUP = ON)
```

While Microsoft documentation calls Change Tracking a low-impact solution, that does not mean it is a *zero-impact* solution. There is a bit of overhead just for enabling the feature, plus extra overhead as you add each table. Finally, the cleanup task can cause blocking, particularly on high-volume tables. Like any SQL feature, there are trade-offs when using Change Tracking that you must be aware of. Knowing the impact and watching for performance changes are essential to successfully deploying Change Tracking in Azure SQL Database.

Implement Dynamic Data Masking

Dynamic Data Masking (DDM) is another Azure SQL feature that partially obfuscates sensitive data for non-privileged users. If your app or users connect using privileged accounts (DBO, sysadmin, etc.), then you will likely have more security issues than Dynamic Data Masking (DDM) can help with.

The classic use case for DDM is masking part of a user's credit card or phone number for identity verification without displaying the entire number to a non-privileged user. Showing the last four digits of a credit card or US-based phone number allows a call center employee to "verify" a caller's ID without providing an opportunity for identity theft by showing the full ID element.

Dynamic Data Masking is applied at the database level and works the same for all types of Azure SQL, including Azure SQL VMs 2016 SP2 or later. Only Azure SQL DB has an Azure Portal Blade to configure DDM. All others must be configured directly via T-SQL commands, which is what the Portal Blade is actually building as you fill in the blade. Figure 7-7 and Example 7-2 show the exact same mask rule creation through the Azure portal and via T-SQL.

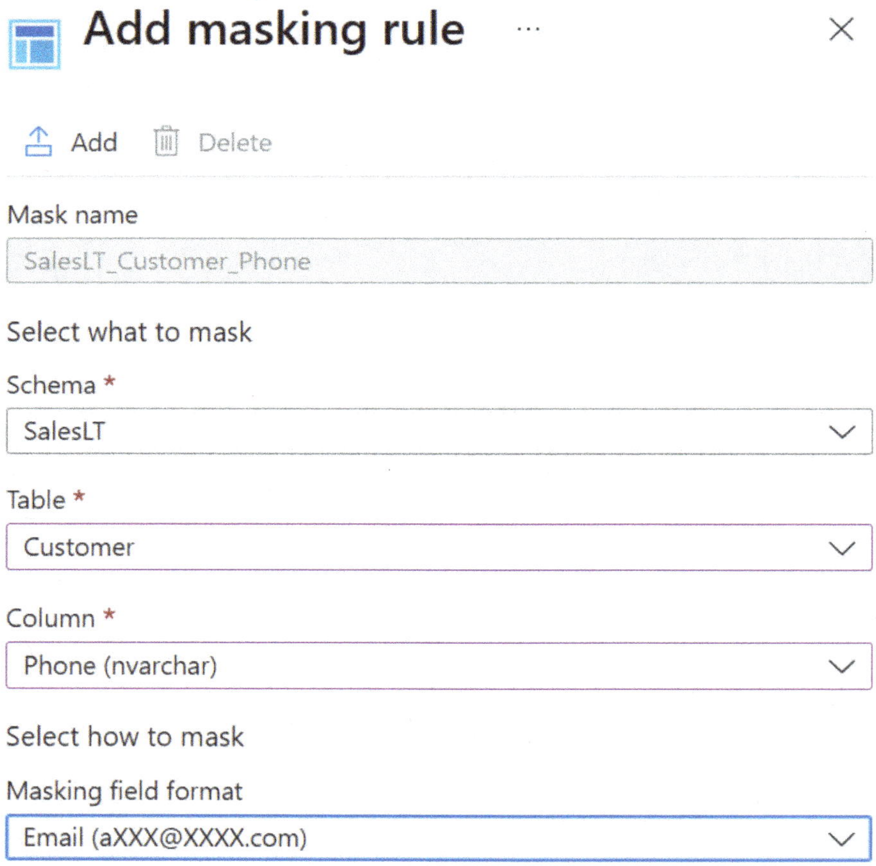

Add masking rule   ⋯   ✕

⬆ Add   🗑 Delete

Mask name

SalesLT_Customer_Phone

Select what to mask

Schema *

SalesLT   ⌄

Table *

Customer   ⌄

Column *

Phone (nvarchar)   ⌄

Select how to mask

Masking field format

Email (aXXX@XXXX.com)   ⌄

Figure 7-7. *Create a Dynamic Data Mask – Azure Portal*

Example 7-2. Create a Dynamic Data Mask – T-SQL

```
ALTER TABLE [SalesLT].[Customer] ALTER COLUMN [EmailAddress] ADD MASKED
WITH (FUNCTION = 'email()')
```

The function 'email()' is a predefined pattern provided by SQL Server along with Credit Card, Default Value (shows the default value for columns or MinDate for date types), and Number (shows a random number). You can define custom string patterns as well.

Users with *unmask* rights can explicitly request complete data as can users with sufficient privileges.

Be very careful when deploying Dynamic Data Masking. DDM only applies to the *display* of the data. The complete underlying data element is still available for comparison. Users that can run ad hoc queries can infer the whole underlying data element using joins to "guess" patterns or brute-forcing comparisons to the entire data range.

Masking recommendations in Azure SQL DBs are unrelated to Data Discovery and Classification data. The two features do not interact with each other and use completely different definition sets.

Manage Database Resources by Using Azure Purview

Earlier in this chapter we discussed Data Discovery and Classification. I noted that one shortcoming of the feature was it existed in isolation and did not scale well to Enterprise Data Governance. Azure Purview is that exact service. At first glance, it would appear that Microsoft has fallen back into the bad habit of Marketing by Certification by emphasizing what appears to be an Azure Data Engineering Service in the Azure Database Administrator certification path. That would be a wrong impression. Azure Purview is an end-to-end Data Governance service that impacts every one of the Azure Data Professional roles we discussed back in Chapter 1.

Data Governance goes well beyond mere Data Discovery and Classification. Data Governance tracks the origin and use of all data elements in an enterprise. It allows end users to discover data they need and track where this data came from. It allows Data Curators to control access to sensitive data via policy.

One of the persistent issues with linked systems and downstream data consumption is data correctness. Data is extracted from primary systems like SQL Server and is then "cleansed" for further use or presentation. Data is often hand-patched as it moves through systems to prevent downstream problems. With Purview, data engineers can track data through connected systems and request that originating systems of record update data so one-off fixes become less necessary. Downstream data is self-corrected when the updated source data is reprocessed.

Given the cross-role functionality of Azure Purview, it is important to our responsibilities as data professionals to understand how it works and interacts with the Azure SQL Systems we are responsible for. The good news is that the Microsoft Learning Path has a very good walkthrough of the various steps to implement Purview and exercise its various components. The other good news (at least in the long term) is that you are going to stretch your Azure skills by provisioning and operating many non-SQL services.

I won't be duplicating the excellent walkthrough in the Learning Path module. I will be guiding you through the parts that may cause Azure novices some trouble. Azure SQL services are only one type of data input available to Purview. Let's start by opening the "Implement Azure Purview" module located here: `https://learn.microsoft.com/en-us/training/modules/implement-compliance-controls-sensitive-data/8-implement-azure-purview`.

The second illustration (copyright prevents me from showing it here) gives a good idea of the scope of Azure Purview's data connection capability. The list includes on-premises data sources, Azure and third-party cloud services, SAP data sets, and multiple SQL Servers/services. While access to non-SQL data sources will provide you a richer learning experience, you can learn all you need for the test with only Azure SQL data sources.

Azure Purview is now configured as a Tenant-Wide resource. Unless you are an Azure Purview Administrator *or* you have an isolated tenant (not just a subscription), you won't be able to provision Azure Purview in your company's tenant. If you can provision Azure Purview, the experience is fairly basic. The option to provision Purview to process messages is beyond the scope of the test and this book. For our purposes, this option can be ignored.

Purview's minimum pricing is non-trivial (currently about $450/month in the United States), and the service *cannot* be paused. You must delete the service to stop billing.

Azure Purview works via Connections, Scans, and Scan Rule Sets. A Connection in Purview is exactly what a Connection is in any database context – the endpoint location and Identity to establish a query connection. In this case, the query is going execute a Scan. Selecting the service is the simple part. Making sure Purview has the correct elements to connect and execute the scan is the more complex part. The Training Module has clear instructions on how to allow connectivity from Purview to your Azure SQL Database or Managed Instance. The fastest way is to simply allow Azure connections through the Server firewall if you are using Public Networking. Most enterprises will use a Private Network configuration, so that won't be an option for most of us. If that is the case, you will need to establish connectivity between the Purview Runtime and the SQL Service Private Endpoint, wherever those are located within your network.

Authentication is likewise clearly defined. If you are unsure about the various authentication methods, you can refer back to Chapter 5 where these are described in detail. If you choose to use any of the Azure Entra ID–based options, you will need to enable Entra ID authentication for your Azure SQL Service. The recommended method is to use the Purview Managed Identity to connect to target systems where supported. All Azure SQL Services support Azure Purview Managed Identity.

One area where Purview can impact authentication in your SQL Services is via Data Governance Policies. As I mentioned in the Purview feature overview earlier, Azure Purview can control access to data resources across the enterprise. Back in Chapter 5, we ignored the "Microsoft Purview access policies" option on the Entra ID blade of the logical SQL Server resources because this is an information-only element, not a changeable field. You can use this element to see whether a SQL resource is governed by Azure Purview access policies. Azure Purview access policies apply to Entra ID users and roles only. SQL authentication remains unaffected by Azure Purview access policies.

Once you have established a connection with appropriate permissions, you can create a Scan. Scans have four elements. Scans operate through a Connection. Scans have a Scope that defines which databases within a Connection are to be scanned. Scans have a Rule Set that defines which classification rules to apply. Finally, Scans have a Trigger that determines when and at what frequency the scan is applied. The trigger is like a SQL Agent Job Schedule but executed natively in Azure.

Scans report data to a Collection. Collections are the fundamental elements of the Purview Enterprise Metadata Map. It is this map that Enterprise Data Administrators use to manage all data sources, assets, and scans into a custom hierarchical map. This map is used to implement data governance. The full scope of Purview is well beyond the requirements of the DP-300 exam or the Azure SQL Database Administrator role. For our purposes, understanding what Purview does and how it interacts with our Azure SQL Services is sufficient.

Implement Azure SQL Database Ledger

One of the critical differences between SQL Server databases and traditional accounting practices is that many accounting practices date back centuries to pen and paper ledgers. Such ledgers were hard to alter as every transaction was added sequentially to a page, leading to bad actors keeping a complete second set of "books" to hide shady activities. SQL Server does updates logically "in place," changing values to match the current state of whatever SQL Server is tracking. Modern accounting still needs the tamper-proof capability of the old paper ledgers with the modern transaction volume processing and precision of SQL Server. Azure SQL Database Ledger uses cryptographic and blockchain technology to create tamper-evident ledger tables inside SQL Server. While the underlying data in a ledger table can be altered, it cannot be altered without leaving evidence it has been altered.

The technological proof of exactly how blockchain technology creates a tamper-evident ledger is beyond the scope of this book and could likely be enough material for a book of its own. Fortunately, like any other computer technology, we can implement blockchain functionality without understanding how the internal math works. Microsoft has extensive documentation on the implementation of Cryptographic Blockchain if you want a little light bedtime reading. For purposes of the DP-300 exam, we need only know how to enable Azure SQL DB Ledger and connect it to other Azure services.

Ledger tables come in two forms, Updatable and Append-Only. Updatable tables keep complete history of all changes, while the Append-Only tables block inserts and deletes at the API layer. Both ledger table types are self-certifying as to the accuracy of the data. No completed transactions are ever lost or altered without detection, including by directly writing data blocks to the underlying storage layer while bypassing SQL Server. Blockchain cryptographically entangles immediate past transactions and the current transaction to create a sequence of encrypted data that will fail validation if any previous data is altered. SQL Server aggregates multiple transactions into blocks to prevent complex blockchain calculations from slowing SQL Server transaction throughput.

Note that Ledger doesn't prevent all forms of data tampering. It prevents such tampering from being undetected. That is a subtle but important difference.

Azure SQL Database Ledger can be enabled for all tables during database deployment. Ledger falls under the Security page of options as you deploy an Azure SQL Database as we see in Figure 7-8. For Azure SQL Managed Instance, Ledger is the only option on the new database Security tab.

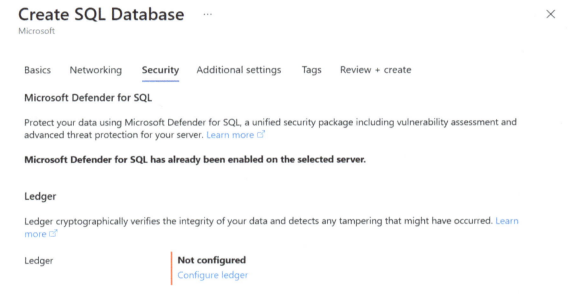

Figure 7-8. *Enable Azure SQL DB Ledger*

Azure SQL DB Ledger enablement makes *all* future tables updatable ledger tables. Once set, this option *cannot* be removed from the database. You can still create individual ledger tables without enabling this option. Regardless of whether you create ledger tables, you need to decide how to manage the digest. The digest is an export of the current block cryptographic hash. It serves the temporary function of the "next" block in the chain until the current block is completed and calculated. This digest should be stored somewhere with appropriate data protection such as Azure Immutable Storage or Azure Ledger.

Figure 7-9 shows the options for configuring Ledger for Azure SQL Managed Instance as you deploy a database. The option is the same for deploying a new Azure SQL Database. I intentionally switched illustrating between service types (Azure SQL DB and Azure SQL MI) during this section to show this similarity.

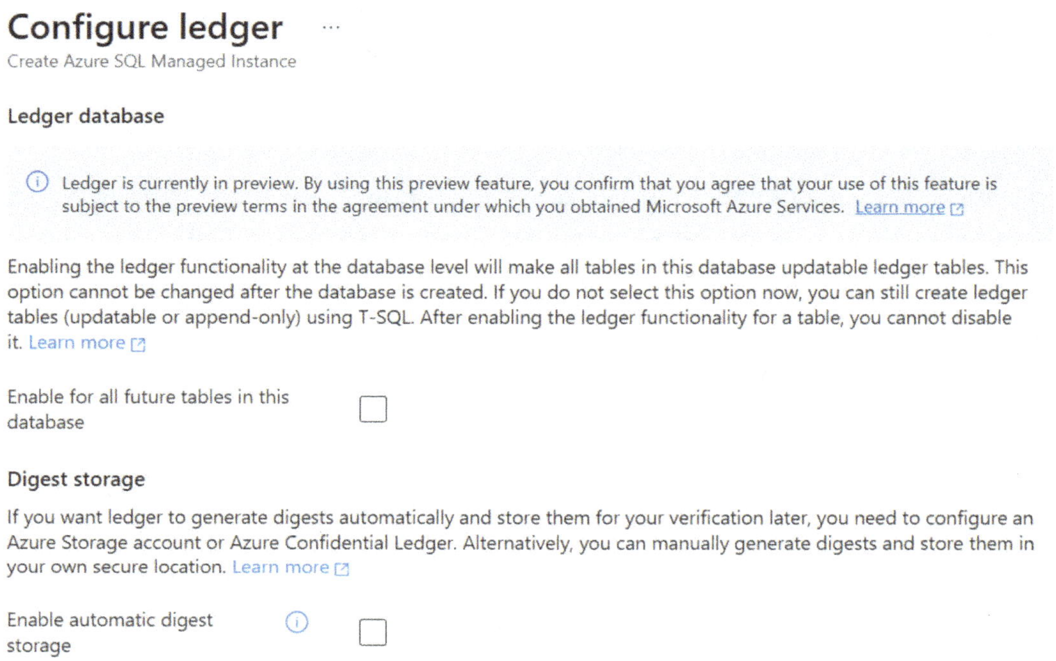

Configure ledger ···
Create Azure SQL Managed Instance

Ledger database

ⓘ Ledger is currently in preview. By using this preview feature, you confirm that you agree that your use of this feature is subject to the preview terms in the agreement under which you obtained Microsoft Azure Services. Learn more ↗

Enabling the ledger functionality at the database level will make all tables in this database updatable ledger tables. This option cannot be changed after the database is created. If you do not select this option now, you can still create ledger tables (updatable or append-only) using T-SQL. After enabling the ledger functionality for a table, you cannot disable it. Learn more ↗

Enable for all future tables in this database ☐

Digest storage

If you want ledger to generate digests automatically and store them for your verification later, you need to configure an Azure Storage account or Azure Confidential Ledger. Alternatively, you can manually generate digests and store them in your own secure location. Learn more ↗

Enable automatic digest storage   ⓘ   ☐

Figure 7-9. Azure SQL Managed Instance Configure Ledger

SQL Ledger is also available in SQL 2022 and higher in Azure SQL VMs.

Implement Row-Level Security

Row-Level Security is another method to restrict data for non-privileged users. Since the Table-Valued Function (TVF) that implements the Security Predicate depends on unique identified users with role membership, a single-connection application using a high-privilege connection will not be able to effectively use Row-Level Security. Privileged users such as object or schema owners can also alter the elements of row-level security or data that row-level security depends on.

Row-Level Security uses a Table-Valued Function (TVF) that implements a Security Predicate on a table. The TVF typically implements a Join between the username and a column or function in the table. Without a valid match, the row is invisible to unauthorized users. This is functionally equivalent to an Inner Join in a "WHERE" clause added to all queries to the underlying table.

Due to the known vulnerabilities and shortcomings, including Side Channel Attacks using crafted WHERE clause queries to force error conditions like Divide-By-Zero and the known performance shortcomings of Table-Valued Functions, this feature is one of the "know for the test but never use" features of SQL Server.

Configure Microsoft Defender for SQL

Microsoft Defender for SQL is the SQL-specific facet of Microsoft Defender for Cloud. Enabling Microsoft Defender for SQL is one of the simpler tasks in Azure. Microsoft Defender for SQL is available for all Azure SQL Services, including Azure SQL Virtual Machines, provided these machines are running the SQL Virtual Machine IaaS Extension. For all services, simply go to the server-level resource (Azure SQL Managed Instance, Azure SQL Logical Server, Azure SQL Virtual Machine) and select "Microsoft Defender for Cloud" under the "Security" section. You can also turn on Defender at the Subscription or Management Group (set of subscriptions) level. All existing and any new Azure SQL resources will have Microsoft Defender for SQL automatically enabled as they are provisioned. Microsoft requires Defender for SQL for *all* SQL Services in its Azure Tenant or any Employee External Tenant as a security best (and required) practice.

Defender has two facets, proactive and reactive. Proactive Defender runs a security best practices scan. Defender will execute a regular proactive best security practices scan for each database that is covered by the enabled server. These scans are unique for each service type but do contain common elements. For example, VM-based scans may contain alerts for backup configurations. Those are unnecessary for Azure PaaS SQL Services since those are managed by the service.

The reactive scan generates alerts based on events discovered by monitoring the incoming TDS stream. These include brute-force password attacks, login attempts from recently disabled logins, and ML-powered SQL Injection Detection. These alerts are reported to the main Microsoft Defender for Cloud dashboard and must be dealt with according to your organization's security policy.

As a sidenote, I once intentionally triggered a SQL Injection attack alert for an Azure SQL Database running in the Microsoft.com main tenant as part of a customer demonstration. I was strongly informed that I need not ever do that again.

Chapter and Part Summary

Security is an ongoing challenge in the modern IT world. Database systems in particular require extra vigilance. The data in our SQL Services are often the "crown jewels" of the enterprise. This data is what bad actors are trying to collect and exfiltrate. We must use all the tools at our disposal to prevent such bad actors from succeeding. Those tools include knowledge and experience from our peers both inside and outside the organization. Security policies based on external compliance regimes represent constantly updated best practices for thwarting bad actors and protecting our organization's data and its legal liability. Modern security requirements have added immense complexity to the SQL Database Administrator role, both in and outside of Azure. This has also made the role much more valuable as it requires more skills than in the past. These past three chapters provide both a good foundation for the DP-300 exam and a practical basis for securing your Azure SQL Services.

PART III

Monitor, Configure, and Optimize Database Resources

Monitor Resource Activity and Performance

This chapter begins not only a new chapter in our study guide; it begins a new part on optimizing Azure SQL database activity and performance. Per the Microsoft Azure DP-300 Learning Path, this part is worth between 20% and 25% of your total score. Many people make the mistake of believing that "Azure takes care of that" when talking about Resource usage and Performance. While Azure offers many tools to help monitor Resource Consumption and SQL Performance, the ultimate responsibility for both falls to you, the Azure SQL Database Administrator.

Over the next three chapters, we will look at Activity and Performance Metrics for Azure SQL (Chapter 8), Query performance (Chapter 9), and Performance-related Operations and Tasks (Chapter 10). These three chapters are tightly related – what you do (or do not do) to tune query performance will have an impact on resource consumption. The same goes for Performance-related configurations and operations. All three elements are necessary for a well-performing and cost-effective Azure SQL deployment. The good news is that Azure provides a plethora of tools to help with these responsibilities.

Prepare an Operational Performance Baseline

Sometimes I tell uncomfortable truths to customers to jolt them out of comfortable ways of thinking. Changing how you think about problems is just as important to success in Azure as is learning about new technologies. Yet some of the classic unpleasant truths remain. One of those is that any system you do not have a measured performance baseline for is *by definition* out of control. While ignoring performance questions until

© Geoff Hiten 2025
G. Hiten, *Administering Microsoft Azure SQL Solutions*, Certification Study Companion Series, https://doi.org/10.1007/979-8-8688-1585-0_8

they become performance problems may be comfortable in the beginning of your Azure journey, the extreme discomfort that comes when a minor performance question becomes a major performance issue can be easily avoided.

Every SQL Server is constantly changing. Users are adding, updating, and deleting data. Tracking and reporting data change transactions is literally the whole reason SQL exists. While most of the time individual changes are not significant enough to alter the fundamental operations of a system, eventually there is the proverbial "straw that broke the camel's back" when enough changes reach a previously unknown limit, often with catastrophic results. Eventually, SQL will grow and consume more resources than you have provisioned. That could be storage, CPU, memory, or some combination of the three. Telling your organization that they need a larger server or bigger provisioned SQL system isn't necessarily a bad thing. Giving them time to put it in next year's budget is good. Telling them it is needed now to fix a performance growth issue is very bad. Performance baselining and monitoring will give you the lead time to present good information to your management in a timely manner.

The first step in monitoring performance in SQL Server is to understand what "normal" looks like for your systems. This is called "establishing a baseline." Knowing the baseline resource consumption of your systems from a typical workload is fundamental to managing performance. CPU Consumption, Page Life Expectancy, Processor Queue Length, Storage Latency, Storage IOPS, Storage Throughput, and Batch Requests/Second are the "Vital Signs" of your SQL Service. Just like a medical doctor checks your vital signs during a checkup to see if they need to look deeper, you need to monitor the vital signs of your server. Since SQL Servers and Databases come in all sizes, you must establish a baseline for each one.

The definition of "healthy" in Azure is a bit different than on-premises. Back in Chapter 3 we discussed Capacity Planning for migrating workloads to Azure SQL Services. Just like when we recommended hardware for our on-premises SQL Servers, we always added a little extra. For on-premises, we had to account for SQL resource consumption growth for the lifecycle of the hardware. For an Azure Migration, we made a safety factor to prevent resource starvation on an unfamiliar platform. Once a migration is completed and the workload stabilized on the new SQL platform, we can optimize the server settings and run much closer to maximum capacity. We do not need to provision for growth or seasonality until the need is immediate. Azure is elastic. However, we absolutely must monitor our baseline usage over time to predict when we do need to grow our systems or correct a performance anomaly.

Determine Sources for Performance Metrics

Knowing about the resource consumption and performance of your Azure SQL Services is not difficult. The "vital signs" metrics that we just discussed are the same metrics that we use on-premises, in Azure VMs, and with Azure SQL DB and Azure SQL MI PaaS Services. The only difference is where we gather those metrics from for each service.

I often tell my customers that everything in Azure has a meter. A very few of those meters have price tags. Worldwide, Azure generates and ingests more than ten petabytes of performance data each day. This all lands into a platform designed from the ground up for Performance and Event management called Azure Monitor. There are multiple ways to access and use this data, but this system is at the heart of all performance monitoring and alerting in Azure.

If you have a small SQL footprint or are just learning Azure SQL, your best source for SQL Performance metrics is going to be the Azure portal itself. All the key metrics for your Azure SQL Service are going to be available right there – based on the normal data collected by Azure to operate Azure. Let's explore performance metrics via the Azure portal for Azure SQL DB.

Azure SQL PaaS Performance Metrics

The Overview page for your Azure SQL Database shows two essential metrics, storage and CPU consumption. These metrics are essential because they are the two meters that generate billing data. Other metrics can show performance characteristics, but these first two represent resources you are paying for.

Storage consumption is the first metric we see as shown in Figure 8-1. The "Max storage" value is the same as the Data max size value configured under Compute + Storage.

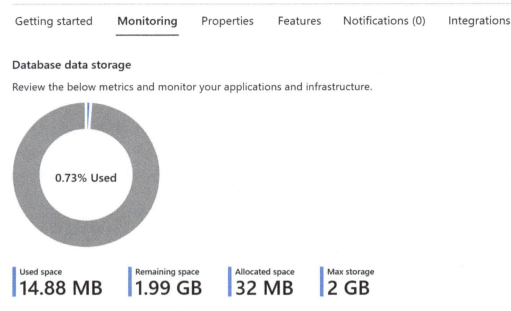

Getting started   **Monitoring**   Properties   Features   Notifications (0)   Integrations   ...

Database data storage

Review the below metrics and monitor your applications and infrastructure.

0.73% Used

Used space	Remaining space	Allocated space	Max storage
14.88 MB	**1.99 GB**	**32 MB**	**2 GB**

Figure 8-1. *Azure SQL DB Storage Consumption Overview*

The second metric, CPU consumption, is expressed in percentages of your allocated CPU capacity – also shown and changed on the Compute + Storage blade. Figure 8-2 shows CPU consumption for an example Azure SQL DB. The scale and metric (DTU/vCore) will be dependent on the actual consumption and your Azure SQL DB billing model.

Key metrics

Review the below metrics and monitor your applications and infrastructure or See all metrics ☒

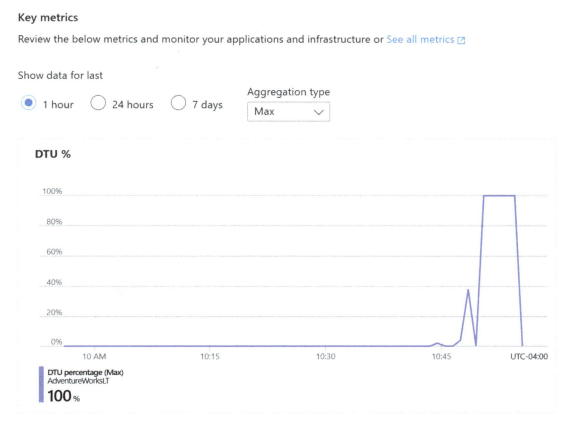

Figure 8-2. *Aure SQL DB CPU Consumption Overview*

You can change the Aggregation type between Max, Min, and Average to help identify specific consumption patterns. You can also use the "See all metrics" link in the upper-right corner to open the Metrics Explorer blade. Metrics Explorer will let you examine the standard SQL metrics or combination of metrics. You can even examine metrics from multiple resources, provided they are of the same type and in the same geographic region. Figure 8-3 shows CPU consumption on the Azure Metrics Explorer blade.

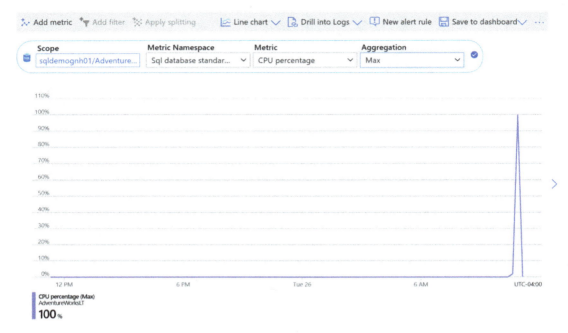

Figure 8-3. *Azure SQL DB CPU Consumption in Metrics Explorer*

The Azure Metrics Explorer blade can also be accessed via the Metrics option on the left tower menu under Monitoring. Azure SQL Managed Instance has nearly identical content on the Overview and Metrics blades; however, Azure SQL Managed Instance metrics include instance-level as well as database-level metrics.

Azure SQL IaaS Metrics

Data gathering for Azure SQL IaaS (SQL on Azure Virtual Machines) is a bit fragmented in the native Azure experience. The first step to collect performance metrics is to configure *Monitoring Insights* for the Virtual Machine. Do not confuse Azure Virtual Machine Monitoring Insights with Azure SQL Database SQL Insights. Those are different services with different capabilities and purposes. Once again, Microsoft names are often confusing.

Any Azure VM provisioned via the Azure Resource Manager (portal, CLI, or PowerShell) has basic external performance metrics visible on the portal page. These metrics are from the virtualization layer, not from instrumentation inside the Virtual Machine. To access those internally collected metrics, you have to configure Azure Virtual Machine Monitoring Insights. Choosing "Insights" under "Monitoring" on the Azure SQL VM Portal home blade brings up the blade shown in Figure 8-4.

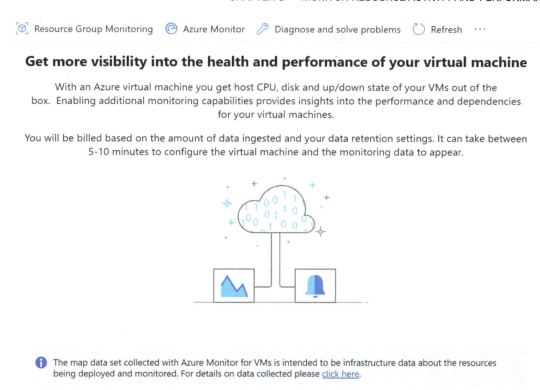

⬡ Resource Group Monitoring   ⊕ Azure Monitor   ✎ Diagnose and solve problems   ⟳ Refresh   ⋯

Get more visibility into the health and performance of your virtual machine

With an Azure virtual machine you get host CPU, disk and up/down state of your VMs out of the box. Enabling additional monitoring capabilities provides insights into the performance and dependencies for your virtual machines.

You will be billed based on the amount of data ingested and your data retention settings. It can take between 5-10 minutes to configure the virtual machine and the monitoring data to appear.

ⓘ The map data set collected with Azure Monitor for VMs is intended to be infrastructure data about the resources being deployed and monitored. For details on data collected please click here.

Enable

Figure 8-4. *Azure SQL VM – Enable Monitoring Insights*

Selecting "Enable" brings you to the Monitoring Configuration blade. The two choices at the top are the key elements of this page. Figures 8-5 and 8-6 show the two choices and their corresponding blade configurations. Both options land the data in a Log Analytics Workspace as is normal for Azure Performance data. We will discuss Azure Monitor and Log Analytics Workspaces in greater detail in the upcoming section "Configure and Monitor Activity and Performance" later in this chapter.

The Azure Monitor Agent option allows Azure to build a process and dependency map in addition to collecting and alerting on performance data. Neither option enables SQL Performance Metrics. Those must be gathered directly from each VM. Monitoring Insights provides fundamental metric-based resource consumption insights on operating VMs and is not a SQL-specific tool.

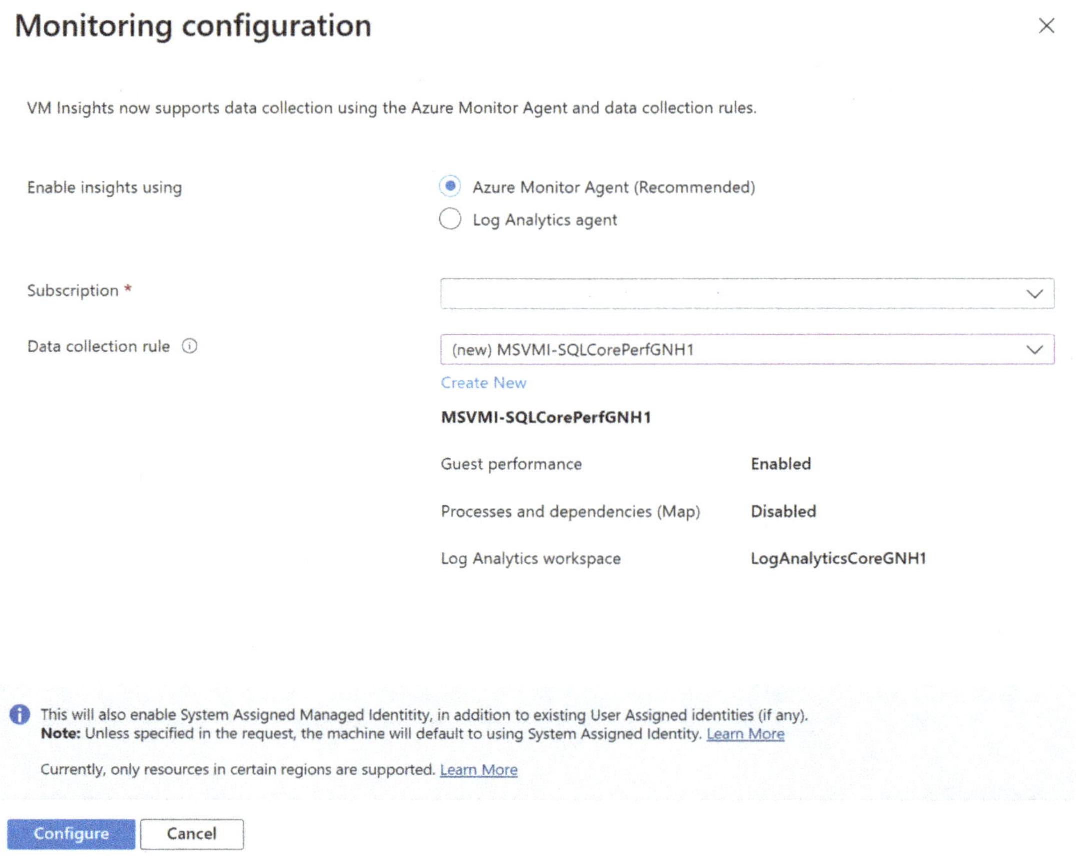

Monitoring configuration   ✕

VM Insights now supports data collection using the Azure Monitor Agent and data collection rules.

Enable insights using   ⦿ Azure Monitor Agent (Recommended)
                                          ◯ Log Analytics agent

Subscription *   [⌄]

Data collection rule ⓘ   [(new) MSVMI-SQLCorePerfGNH1   ⌄]
                                          Create New
                                          MSVMI-SQLCorePerfGNH1

                                          Guest performance   **Enabled**

                                          Processes and dependencies (Map)   **Disabled**

                                          Log Analytics workspace   **LogAnalyticsCoreGNH1**

ⓘ This will also enable System Assigned Managed Identity, in addition to existing User Assigned identities (if any).
   Note: Unless specified in the request, the machine will default to using System Assigned Identity. Learn More

   Currently, only resources in certain regions are supported. Learn More

[Configure] [Cancel]

Figure 8-5. *Azure SQL VM Monitoring Insights Azure Monitor Agent*

Azure Monitor Agent collection requires a rule to control actions prior to the data
landing. This is an Azure Monitor data collection rule that can be configured from
a blade linked from this Monitoring configuration page. If you are not going to use
Azure Monitor to create a process and dependency map, then saving data directly to
a Log Analytics workspace is a simpler configuration option. An Azure Log Analytics
Workspace is also the most functional landing zone for performance metrics as it is the
native Azure repository for most all performance metrics.

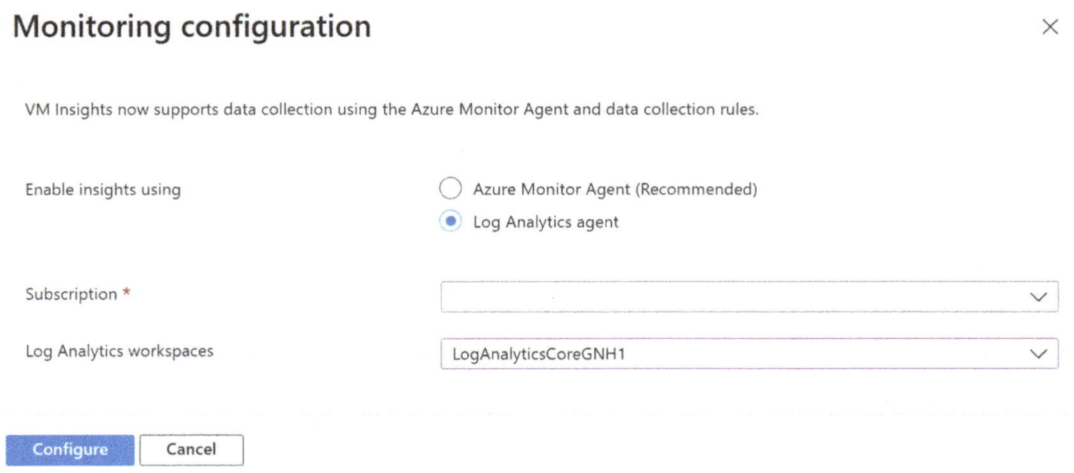

Monitoring configuration ✕

VM Insights now supports data collection using the Azure Monitor Agent and data collection rules.

Enable insights using	○ Azure Monitor Agent (Recommended)
	● Log Analytics agent
Subscription *	[⌄]
Log Analytics workspaces	[LogAnalyticsCoreGNH1 ⌄]

[**Configure**] [Cancel]

Figure 8-6. *Azure SQL VM Monitoring Insights Log Analytics agent*

Interpret Performance Metrics

Performance metrics are an essential part of troubleshooting SQL services, but do not provide a complete solution. They can and will point to problem areas that may need code or schema design remediation to correct an overall performance issue, especially when you have a known baseline performance to compare to. A well-crafted monitoring and alerting solution will alert you to a problem well before it becomes a user-facing issue, at least most of the time. Certain unforeseeable catastrophic events will become known to everyone at the same time.

Troubleshooting Azure SQL problems starting with performance metrics works very similar to on-premises troubleshooting. Start with "vital signs" metrics like CPU, IO, and memory. These may not tell you the problem, but will focus your attention toward the root cause. Back to our "vital signs" analogy, a high fever starts a doctor down a particular diagnostic path. You also have one advantage in the cloud – you can easily increase these primary resources temporarily or permanently to solve problems. Of course, bad code and design will always overwhelm good hardware, so you should identify problems and determine if they can be remediated or simply adjusted for.

Cloud services also have an advantage in storage troubleshooting. In Azure, you know what the upper end of the scale is. Unless you established a baseline for your IOPS and throughout for your storage system when you installed your SQL Server, you are not sure exactly what the maximum capacity is for either of these metrics. For Azure storage, there is a chart showing exactly how many IOPS and how much throughput you get with each provisioned amount of storage. We discussed this extensively in Chapter 3 if you need to review how storage capacity works in Azure. Knowing whether a resource is at its provisioned capacity limit is extremely useful information for Azure SQL performance troubleshooting. If none of the provisioned resources is at its limit, then additional resources will not help. You then need to look elsewhere to resolve performance issues.

You also need to look at multiple metrics to see the entire picture. Consider the following example. You may see very high IO consumption and believe you have a storage problem. A look at memory velocity (Page Life Expectancy) shows it to be very low, indicating high memory pressure or inadequate memory provisioning. Subsequent examination shows a new analytic aggregation query is pushing the OLTP data out of memory, forcing the system to reload that data from storage time and time again, ultimately causing the IO bottleneck.

While you may not run into this exact scenario, it is common enough that you should recognize not only the problem but that examining only one metric in isolation will not lead you to a correct resolution of a performance problem. Only when you look at all relevant metrics, their deviation from the baseline normal metrics you established when you migrated or became responsible for the SQL workload, and how much of your provisioned capacity is consumed will you have the full picture of a performance issue.

You may still need more information to completely diagnose all issues. In the previous example, I waved my hands with the "Subsequent examination shows …" conclusion. We will discuss more about that in Chapter 9 and identify some prevention and remediation strategies in Chapter 10. Only when you can see what the workload is requesting the SQL engine to do *and* how the engine responds will you have a complete troubleshooting toolkit.

Configure and Monitor Activity and Performance

At the beginning of this chapter, I alluded to an Azure-wide comprehensive metric collection repository that every service in Azure could use to manage performance and log data. We have looked at a few facets of this system that do not require additional configuration. Now we get to the heart of performance management in Azure by configuring our own place to land and manage performance data in Azure.

Azure Monitor is the name for the overall performance management system in Azure. This includes ingesting, storing, and deleting data, firing alerts, dashboard presentation, and ad hoc performance querying to identify trends or optimization opportunities. Some systems like the Azure VM Insights are just branded facets of this system. Given that Azure Monitor is one of the fundamental, original Azure systems, it has undergone many changes as it has evolved over time to meet changing customer and internal Azure needs. This can lead to some confusing names as people use older names or use the name of a subsystem in place of the entire system name. The part of Azure Monitor we care the most about is the Log Analytics Workspace. We have used Log Analytics workspaces in some examples prior to now but have not really defined or described what that service does nor how to interact with it properly. Let's explore what these systems do and how they are related.

When you configure an Azure resource to save log and performance data to a private repository, you generally have three choices:

- Archive to an Azure Storage account.

- Send to a Log Analytics workspace.

- Stream to an Event Hub.

Some services have an additional option to send to a partner solution. We will not explore that option here as it is not on the exam. The choices are not exclusive. You can send data to more than one destination. Let's take a detailed look at what each choice offers.

Azure Storage Account

Azure storage is the least expensive option to save performance data. Correspondingly, it also offers the least functionality. Azure storage simply writes the data in blob or table format, depending on the source of the data (event logs, performance data, audit logs, IIS logs, etc.). It has no active analysis capability. You cannot alert on Azure Storage data without some external processing mechanism. It doesn't support any native query capability – you have read the data into some type of data compute like Azure Data Factory, Synapse External Tables, or Azure Databricks to execute any queries. This is why it is labeled as an archive solution. Much of the time Azure customers use this option to store log data long-term for legal compliance reasons. Azure Storage offers low-activity tiers with extreme discounts in exchange for delayed access to archived data. The one caution that applies is that due to the high volume of data, you should not cross region boundaries either when writing data or saving to a geo-redundant storage account as those charges can add up unexpectedly.

Event Hub

Event Hub is Microsoft Azure's streaming data ingestion solution. It is often used as an Internet-of-Things (IoT) data landing zone. It is similar to Kafka in that it can ingest data from many different connections at high rates and perform quick analysis and dispatch actions based on that data. Prior to SQL 2014 and the introduction of the In-Memory OLTP feature, this was something that SQL Server simply could not do at scale.

Customers use Event Hubs to build custom real-time alerting solutions based on the incoming data stream. The trade-off of highly scaled data ingestion is a very short retention period of one to seven days. Event Hubs have a very short view of the world. While it provides an exceptional alerting framework, it does not provide any long-term baseline or trending capacity. Customers often send data to both Event Hub and Azure Storage to cover short- and long-term needs.

Log Analytics Workspace

Log Analytics workspaces provide a complete performance and logging data solution across all Azure resources. Azure Log Analytics also enables alerting and dashboards on data it ingests and retains. This section is going to be a bit deeper than the test will likely cover, but the knowledge is going to be essential for success as an Azure SQL Database Administrator.

Provision Log Analytics

Provisioning an Azure Log Analytics Workspace is as simple a process as provisioning any resource in Azure. All you need is a subscription, resource group, name, and region. It's so simple an illustration would be pointless. However, there should be some planning based on how Log Analytics works. First and foremost, due to the volume of data, you should always plan to write data from any service to a Log Analytics workspace in the same region. Diagnostic data (performance and event logs) is one of the ways you can easily spend far more than you expect on region data egress charges even with small-scale infrastructure deployments.

Log Analytics Workspaces are often configured as part of a Workload or Enterprise landing zone to facilitate full-stack diagnostics. Since Log Analytics can ingest data from every Azure service, including user-generated events, you can use it to view errors or events across the full stack. This native Azure capability is typically available outside of Azure only as a component of high-end enterprise Security Information and Event Management (SIEM) software.

One more caution about provisioning Log Analytics Workspaces: Once data is in the workspace, anyone with access to the workspace can see everything in the workspace. In short, the workspace boundary is the only security boundary for data collected inside a workspace. For security segregation, plan for multiple workspaces to accept data from sources having different security requirements. This is particularly important for Log Analytics workspaces ingesting SQL Audit logs, since the logs will contain sensitive end user data.

Once the service is provisioned, you can change many options including pricing plans, data retention (and the associated costs), and network isolation (private link networking) as well as configure data sources, alerts, and solutions (dashboards). Much of the time, you will be connecting and using existing Log Analytics workspaces rather than managing workspaces yourself, but it is important to know how it all works to use it effectively or to know what access to request.

Configure SQL Services for Log Analytics

You can manually direct data from an Azure SQL PaaS Service (Database or Managed Instance) from the Portal blade. Choose "Diagnostic Settings" under "Monitoring" to bring up the Diagnostic Settings blade where you select what data to save and where to save it. The Diagnostic Settings blade will show any existing configurations along with the type and name of each destination. As was noted before, you can have multiple destinations of similar or different types enabled. You can send the same data sets to multiple destinations using multiple settings. Figure 8-7 shows the Diagnostic Settings blade without any destinations configured.

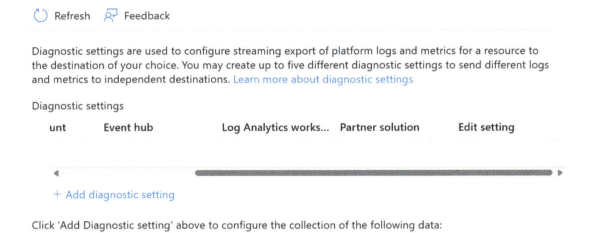

Figure 8-7. *Azure SQL MI Empty Diagnostic Settings*

Selecting "+ Add diagnostic setting" takes you to the Diagnostic setting page shown in Figure 8-8. This page, with a few minor variations, is the same for nearly every Azure service, including all the Azure SQL Database Services. The differences are in what data sets you can send to the Log Analytics Workspace, so naturally, those differ depending on the specific service involved. Again, the technical process to configure this is one of the simplest processes in Azure. The challenge comes in designing the Log Analytics workspace architecture to support multiple needs within your organization while maintaining security and containing costs. In larger organizations, this is typically handled by a dedicated enterprise monitoring team, and the configuration is enforced via Azure Policy.

Diagnostic setting   ...   ✕

🖫 Save   ✕ Discard   🗑 Delete   ⯗ Feedback

A diagnostic setting specifies a list of categories of platform logs and/or metrics that you want to collect from a   JSON View
resource, and one or more destinations that you would stream them to. Normal usage charges for the destination will
occur. Learn more about the different log categories and contents of those logs

Diagnostic setting name *

[   ]

Logs   **Destination details**

Category groups ⓘ   ☑ Send to Log Analytics workspace

☐ audit

☑ allLogs   Subscription

                                                      [⌄]
Categories

☑ Audit   Log Analytics workspace

                                                      [LogAnalyticsCoreGNH1 (eastus)   ⌄]

Metrics

☐ AllMetrics   ☐ Archive to a storage account

                                                      ☐ Stream to an event hub

                                                      ☐ Send to partner solution

Figure 8-8. *Azure SQL MI New Diagnostics Setting (Subscription ID Redacted)*

Configuring data destinations for Azure Diagnostics is exactly the same for all the
destinations. This blade lets you select from predefined destinations, not create new
destinations. Whether you send data to Azure Storage, Azure Event Hub, Azure Log
Analytics, or a partner solution, you simply select the solution. Creating and defining
these solutions is normally well outside the scope of an Azure Database Administrator
role, so this is as far as we will take this subject in this study guide.

Alerting and Reporting with Azure Log Analytics

Now that you have diagnostic or audit data flowing onto Azure Log Analytics, we can
explore the real power of this service. Log Analytics has a built-in query language called
"Kusto." Queries are written in the Kusto Query Language (KQL). Many experienced
DBAs, myself included, immediately wondered why they didn't just use SQL since
there is a large body of knowledge about how to write SQL queries as well as quite a
few experienced query writers "in the wild." The answer is the nature of the data we are

exploring and the native capabilities of the language. KQL was developed exclusively to query time-series data to identify patterns, trends, and exceptions. It is trivial to write a KQL query to find the peak activity for a counter (say CPU percentage as an example) averaged over an arbitrary five-minute period for the last 24 hours. Now try and write that query in T-SQL. Did you account for possible missing data elements? How about changing data collection frequencies?

Alerts and dashboards both have a KQL query at their heart. In the case of the alert, the query is executed at a specific frequency, and the result determines whether an action is required or not. For a dashboard, the resulting data set is displayed to the end user. There are many query repositories on GitHub containing queries for various purposes – they are far too numerous and dynamic to list here. Azure also provides a query builder to go from a counter to an alert condition or dashboard that bypasses the need to learn to write KQL queries from scratch. Personally, I like to examine the underlying queries to expand my knowledge of KQL. You never know when you need to go exploring in the diagnostic data to deal with a very complex Azure SQL troubleshooting issue.

Cost Management with Azure Log Analytics

Alert rules run on a specific frequency, typical no more often than every five minutes. While you can run alerts on a higher frequency, Microsoft strongly discourages alerts more often than one minute and defaults to five minutes for typical alerts. While Azure Log Analytics data ingestion is near real time, Log Analytics is not a "fire alarm." Alerts are intended to pick up patterns, not single data point anomalies. For example, a typical CPU Percentage High Alert sets a threshold that the system remains above for a specific period of time such as five minutes. Momentary peaks do not concern us as much as steady CPU saturation. With the dwell time (duration above the alert threshold) for the alert at five minutes, it does not make sense to run such an alert query more often than every minute.

Azure Log Analytics bills based on two major axis – data ingestion/retention and query execution. Log Analytics' first billing dimension is the amount of data ingested multiplied by how long such data is retained. The rate is a little more than raw Azure Storage due to enabling KQL functionality. The second dimension is the cost per query executed. Most simple alert queries like we discussed in this chapter cost maybe 0.10 USD per month. While this sounds inexpensive, it can rapidly get out of control by running queries at artificially high frequencies, having a large number of high-frequency alert queries, and constantly aggregating across large sets of data. If you find yourself in this situation, you can change your billing plan to include a larger set of queries and data, sort of a volume discount.

Monitor by Using SQL Insights

Azure SQL Insights is one of those perpetual "preview" features that never got finished but also never quite made it to General Availability. Azure SQL Insights was an early attempt to provide monitoring capability for Azure SQL Database. It is also a feature that Microsoft will ask about on the DP-300 exam, so we will go over it here.

Azure SQL Insights is a VM-based solution that uses SQL Dynamic Management Views and Azure Monitor's Log Analytics Workspaces to provide SQL service monitoring and Alerting. Unlike most of the Azure monitoring solutions, Azure SQL Insights uses VM-based agents to collect data to send to Log Analytics workspaces for ingestion and alerting. Pricing is a combination of the VM costs, the Log Analytics costs, and the Azure Monitor Alert costs. All access and control for Azure SQL Insights is from the Azure Monitor control blades, not from any SQL service blade.

Azure SQL Insights has some important limitations you need to consider before deploying. One of the biggest is it only works with some of the Azure SQL DB tiers. Specifically, it excludes elastic pools, Serverless, and low DTU-based service tiers S0, S1, and S2. Azure SQL Insights does not collect any data on secondary replica use. Azure SQL Insights only supports SQL authentication, rendering it unacceptable to many security policies. Since Azure SQL Insights runs on user-provisioned and managed Virtual Machines, it is a step back for organizations that have modernized to Azure SQL PaaS services.

Azure SQL Insights contains some excellent rule templates for default SQL Monitoring. These templates should be examined and deployed after careful consideration and adjusted to your specific environment. Use the baseline data you learned about early in this chapter to decide what is "normal" and what exceptions need alerting. Like any predefined alerting system, enabling everything will result in a cacophony of false alerts, drowning out any meaningful data.

Azure SQL Insights uses the concept of a Profile to group individual SQL Service or VM connections and route data to a specific Log Analytics workspace. Azure SQL Insights profiles allow customized settings for each Azure SQL Service (Azure SQL DB, Azure SQL MI, and Azure SQL VM). Azure Monitor's strength is it is the only solution that natively provides performance monitoring support for all three Azure SQL Services. Individual service connections are stored in the Profile. Microsoft strongly recommends saving SQL connection information in Azure Key Vault – slightly mitigating the risk of unmanaged SQL logins.

Monitor by Using Extended Events

Profiler is dead. Long live Extended Events. Seriously, if you are still using Profiler and Trace (the command-line version of Profiler), stop. Just stop. Profiler is an original SQL capability going back to the beginnings of the engine. Extended Events was created specifically to replace Profiler/Trace due to the shortcomings of Profiler. While some of the earliest iterations of Extended Events were not quite feature complete, the system we have today works exceptionally well, largely thanks to community feedback. Even when Profiler was the only tool for the job, Microsoft and the SQL community issued dire warnings about the risks of running Profiler on production systems.

Microsoft uses Extended Events extensively to manage Azure SQL PaaS Services. Maybe you should do likewise. Figure 8-9 shows the default extended event sessions created by Azure SQL Managed Instance that allow Azure to monitor how certain aspects of the service are functioning. You can use these same tools to gather information about what is happening inside your SQL Server.

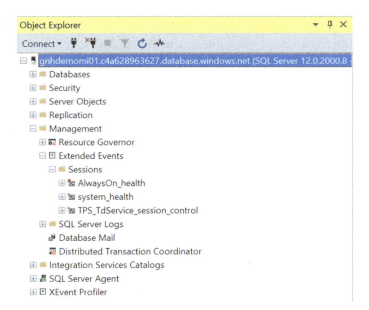

Figure 8-9. *Azure SQL Managed Instance Default Extended Event Sessions*

Extended Events is more than just a Profiler replacement. Extended Events allows you visibility inside your SQL Server to see what is happening – without having to go into debug mode and halt the SQL engine. Extended Events instructs a SQL Server to export a data packet when certain conditions are met – more precisely when exact sections of code are executed. The data export is extremely fast and non-invasive, but like any user-configurable system, it is possible to configure in a way that will negatively impact performance.

Entire books have been written on Extended Events. It would be impossible to cover anything more than the basic concepts here in one section of one chapter. Fortunately, you just need to be familiar with some high-level concepts to get started with Extended Events. Knowing what they do, how they work, and how to configure them is enough to answer the exam questions correctly. I do suggest you study this subject deeper if you are going to be troubleshooting Azure SQL Performance issues.

Extended Events is a comprehensive system designed to extract and export key data to help troubleshoot SQL Server. To manage this better, Extended Events is divided into four channels, each with an intended audience who will use the event data for a specific purpose. The four channels are as follows:

- *Admin* – Admin events are intended to provide specific, actionable information to an administrator to resolve an issue that the SQL engine cannot resolve itself. The classic example is a deadlock graph to let the administrator know what code needs to be remediated.

- *Operational* – SQL System State Changes that operators need to be aware of. An availability group replica latency exceeding a target threshold would be this type of event.

- *Analytic* – These are typically high-volume events related to specific T-SQL code execution such as a stored procedure.

- *Debug* – Specific code breakpoints and variable dumps, often enabled by Support to troubleshoot suspected SQL Server code issues. Do not try these at home – only use with Microsoft support guidance.

Extended Events are created in Sessions via T-SQL commands. SQL Server Management Studio provides an Extended Event Session Wizard to help create sessions. Templates for many common tasks are provided as part of this wizard. Templates are grouped into the following categories:

- Locks and Blocks

- Profiler Equivalents

- Query Execution

- System Monitoring

These templates cover the most common use cases for Extended Events. Figure 8-10 shows a partial list of ready-to-use templates in SSMS.

Figure 8-10. *Extended Event Templates*

You are not limited to the Event Session templates when creating an Extended Event Session. You can search for the specific event you need if you choose not to use a Template. When searching for an event, you can use both the Category and the Channel to find the correct event to trap the action you are interested in. Figure 8-11 shows an example event with both the event and data field descriptions.

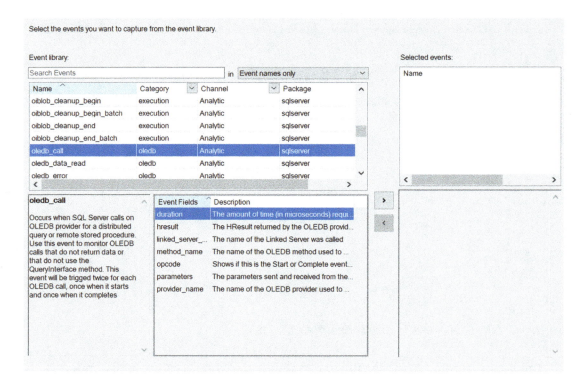

Figure 8-11. *Extended Event Selection*

After selecting one or more event for the session, you can choose to add global data fields. Data elements like database ID, logical server name, query plan hash, and session ID are all available to provide context to the data exported by the actual event. Figure 8-12 shows a partial list of these global fields.

You can capture global fields (also called actions), which are common to all events. Select the global fields you want to capture in this event session.

Name	Description
numa_node_id	Collect current NUMA node ID
plan_handle	Collect plan handle
pool_id	{MetricDimension} -- Collect current pool id.
process_id	Collect the Windows process ID
query_hash	Collect query hash. Use this to identify queries with similar logic. You can use the query hash to determine the aggregat...
query_hash_signed	Collect query hash. Use this to identify queries with similar logic. You can use the query hash to determine the aggregat...
query_plan_hash	Collect query plan hash. Use this to identify similar query execution plans. You can use query plan hash to find the cum...
query_plan_hash_signed	Collect query plan hash. Use this to identify similar query execution plans. You can use query plan hash to find the cum...
request_id	Collect current request ID
ResourceGroup	{MetricDimension} -- Collect current resource group
ResourceId	{MetricDimension} -- Collect current resource id
ResourcePoolName	Collect current resource pool name.
scheduler_address	Collect current scheduler address
scheduler_id	Collect current scheduler ID
server_instance_name	Collects the name of the Server instance
server_principal_name	Collects the name of the Server Principal in whose context the event is being fired
server_principal_sid	Collects the SID of the Server Principal in whose context the event is being fired
ServerName	{MetricDimension} -- Collect current server name. Alias for logical_server_name.
session_id	Collect session ID
session_nt_username	Collect session's NT username
session_resource_group_id	Collect current session resource group ID
session_resource_pool_id	Collect current session resource pool ID

Figure 8-12. *Extended Events Global Fields*

One of the features that makes Extended Events so efficient is the ability to define filters that are applied as the event "fires" inside SQL Server. If the filters do not match, the data grab and export never occurs. This allows us to focus on actual problems without having to wade through mountains of irrelevant records while bogging down the service creating those irrelevant records. Figure 8-13 shows an example filter where the Event Session only applies if I am the SQL user and the service is Azure SQL Managed Instance.

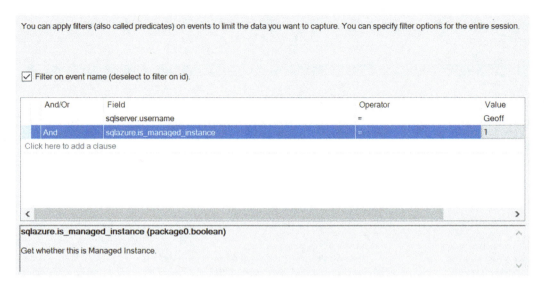

Figure 8-13. *Extended Events Filter Example*

We need to make one last decision on our Extended Event Session. We need to choose how to store the data. Extended Events has six targets to land the data, which are as follows:

- Event Counter

- Event File

- Event Pairing

- Event Tracing for Windows (ETW)

- Histogram

- Ring Buffer

The Event Counter and ETW are both synchronous; all the others are asynchronous to avoid blocking the SQL engine. The Event File was originally only to a local disk but can be configured for Azure Storage if you are collecting data from Azure SQL PaaS services since managed services have no locally accessible disk.

The most common target is the internal ring buffer. The ring buffer is local to the session, so when the session ends, the memory is returned to SQL. A ring buffer is automatically created when you choose this target. All other target types require external creation and configuration.

Chapter Summary

At first glance, there appears to be almost too many options for gathering and reporting performance data for Azure SQL Services. Many of these options were early attempts to provide performance management capability since some of the fundamental elements of Azure that we take for granted were not yet developed and deployed. Upon deeper examination, most of them have a common element – the Log Analytics Workspace. Regardless of where the data originates, how it is gathered, or how it is delivered, the Log Analytics workspace in Azure Monitor is the heart of Azure SQL Resource Performance monitoring. Most of the performance metrics are the same as we use on-premises such as CPU Percentage, Page Life Expectancy, IOPS, etc. We just need to understand and apply what those metrics mean in the context of a provisioned service or VM.

CHAPTER 9

Monitor and Optimize Query Performance

This second chapter of the part on Azure SQL Performance and Optimization focuses on the actual queries executed by the SQL engine sent from the external workload. Knowing what queries consume the most resources and take the most time to execute allows us to focus improvement efforts on queries that have significant impact on the overall system performance. Most SQL Systems exhibit performance skew with a few queries consuming the most resources. This pattern stays consistent, but the exact "top consumer" queries can change over time as data sizes grow and users use the system in new and different ways. This skew helps us with performance management. We can focus on a small number of queries that will maximize our impact rather than having to make improvements to many queries with little impact for each.

As with resource consumption, it is important to gather baseline data. Know your current resource-intense queries so you can recognize when a new query rises to the level you need to pay attention to and possibly take action.

Like other topics in this study guide, entire books have been written on SQL Query performance tuning and optimization. This chapter will focus on tools and techniques available or introduced first in Azure SQL that help monitor and optimize query performance. I will not attempt to teach in-depth SQL Query performance tuning. You will not need that level of skill to pass the DP-300 exam, but it is an important skill to master as an Azure SQL Database Administrator for long-term success.

You may not be able to implement some of these techniques depending on the source of the workload. If your application is internally written with a current, robust development process, you may have the opportunity to provide performance information to the development team to be included in future releases. If your application is a "Common-Off-The-Shelf" (COTS) package, you may only be able to

© Geoff Hiten 2025

G. Hiten, *Administering Microsoft Azure SQL Solutions*, Certification Study Companion Series, https://doi.org/10.1007/979-8-8688-1585-0_9

make minimal adjustments to how the system responds; the actual queries may not be changeable. If your system hosts SharePoint databases, you have few or no options as SharePoint almost eliminates user data tier query changes.

Query Plans

Query plans are not going to be a specific topic on the DB-300 exam. Understanding what query plans are and how they are used in SQL Server is a fundamental skill for Query Performance Tuning either in Azure on on-premises. It will do you little good to identify a problem query and notify a developer unless you suggest an improved version. If the developer knew how to write a better query, they would have done it the first time.

T-SQL is an unusual language. It is a Declarative language, not an Imperative language. T-SQL describes the result set you are looking for but generally offers the SQL engine little or no direction on how to obtain that result. An Imperative language describes the exact steps to obtain a result.

Let's take an abstract example. We have a list of items, and we would like to determine which are duplicates. In most languages this list would be called an Array. SQL refers to this as a table. Rather than choosing a particular imperative language like C++ or Java, we will use pseudo-code to describe the steps in Example 9-1.

Example 9-1. Duplicate Check Pseudo-code

```
Sort the array
Read the first item
BEGIN LOOP
      Increment Loop Index
      IF End_of_List THEN BREAK LOOP
      Read Current from ARRAY
      IF Current = Previous
             THEN Duplicate Found - add to output list
      Set Previous = Current
REPEAT LOOP
Print Output List
```

We simply loop through a sorted array comparing the current to the previous item and note the duplicates. Nothing complicated here. Now let's contrast that with T-SQL code that does the equivalent in Example 9-2.

Example 9-2. Duplicate Check T-SQL

```
Select Column1, COUNT(*) from Table1
      Group By Column1
      Having COUNT(*) > 1
```

This tells the SQL engine nothing about *how* to execute the command; it only describes the desired outcome. Unfortunately, many developers have thought patterns rooted in Imperative model languages and thus write code more suited to Imperative model languages. More on this later.

Even with trivial queries like our example above, there are multiple ways to implement the query. Should the SQL engine use an index or simply scan the data? More complex queries joining multiple tables on various filter conditions offer even more choices. Does SQL filter before or after joining tables? Which type of join implementation should be used? The problem gets very complex very fast.

The Microsoft SQL engine resolves this problem by using a cost-based optimizer. The process begins with a parser reading the query, validating the syntax, and tokenizing the query into an internal representation called a query tree. This query tree is fed to the Optimizer, which does some basic token algebra to clean up the representation by folding constants and evaluating expressions that resolve to constants. The optimizer can then use this query tree to start looking at possible ways to provide the results. The optimizer starts searching the solution space of all possible plans that would yield the correct result, estimates the cost of each operation, and compares the total cost. In general, the lowest-cost query will be the one that returns the fastest *and* has the least resource impact on the SQL Server.

"Cost" is used here as a relative weighting term to compare queries. It does not relate to any specific resource usage, only to convert each query operation to a common metric so that plans can be readily compared.

The optimizer typically does not search all possible plans, especially when the underlying query is very long and complex. The general idea is to get a plan that is "good enough" without spending excessive time searching plans that are not "better" enough to justify the time and compute cost spent searching for them. The SQL Optimizer has internal checkpoints to balance expected query performance with the cost of the optimization process itself.

It is important to note that any query parameters or constants are used during this optimization process. This is called "parameter sniffing" and can lead to some Query Plans that only work for specific parameter combinations. The cost of an operation is highly dependent on the number of rows input and output from an operation as well as the type of operation. An index lookup may have a lower cost for a small number of rows, but a scan may be more efficient if more rows are involved.

This often happens when the optimizer doesn't have a proper understanding of the data patterns of joins or filter columns in tables. SQL Server uses Index Statistics to estimate the number of rows that go into and come out of individual operations in a Query Plan. Bad statistics lead to bad query row count estimates, which lead to bad query plans. This is especially likely when tables have high rates of change where statistics may lag behind actual value distributions.

The output of the Optimizer is a pair of Query Plans. One plan uses parallel operators, and one plan is single threaded. The actual degree of parallelism is determined when the query is executed based on runtime options. Query Plans are executed over data tables to create result sets that are returned to the application that issued the query. These result sets can and will differ depending on the runtime parameters used to call a particular procedure.

Given all the work that goes into creating an optimized query plan, the SQL engine caches these plans in the obviously named SQL Plan Cache. Plans are marked with their optimization cost – the CPU resource used to create the optimized plan – which is used to determine how long they should stay in cache. The more expensive the optimization costs, the longer the time a plan stays. Using a plan resets the "stay" timer so that frequently used plans aren't dropped. Plans are identified either by their Stored Procedure identifier *or* a simple checksum on incoming ad hoc queries. SQL does not want to spend any unnecessary time on a complex lookup algorithm to pull a plan from cache for use. Stored Procedure plans can have multiple sequential steps that represent individual statements in the procedure and are what the whole process is targeted at. Ad hoc query plans should be one-off and short-lived in cache in most transaction-processing SQL Server environments.

The SQL Server Plan Cache generally works well but has some limitations that can lead to performance problems. The SQL Plan Cache is in-memory only. Restarting the SQL service drops everything and requires SQL to recompile every plan as each query comes in. I mentioned earlier that sometimes plans only work for specific sets of parameters. If the parameters used to create the cached plan do not represent the most common use case, the resulting plan may perform poorly until it is forced out of the Query Plan Cache. This is referred to as a Poisoned Plan. Since the Query Plan Cache can only store a single plan at a time, this poisoned plan may impact performance for a considerable time until it is forced out of cache.

Starting with SQL 2022 and the corresponding Azure SQL Server internal version deployed around that time, SQL can now hold multiple plans in Cache for *Parameter-Sensitive Plans (PSPs)*. I expect this feature to grow and become more complex in subsequent releases.

There are also two types of plans – Estimated and Actual. Sometimes the Query Plan changes or gets re-optimized during execution, particularly if the plan is for a multi-step procedure. More common is when the plan does not change. Then the Actual plan will contain the actual costs and row counts for each operation, while the estimated plan remains with the values calculated at optimization time. Plans with significant differences between Actual and Estimated values are good candidates for Query Performance Optimization.

Caution   The behavior I just described is the default Query Optimizer and Plan Cache behavior. You can use query hints, T-SQL commands, and trace flags to override specific query optimizer and plan cache behaviors. Always test such changes in non-production environments before trying them in production. You can easily anti-optimize a query and bring an active SQL Server to a virtual halt.

Configure the Query Store

The Query Store was first introduced to Azure SQL DB and eventually made its way to all versions/editions of SQL Server. The Query Store records execution plans and metadata in tables inside each database. Queries executed in the context of a database are stored in that database's Query Store making the Query Store a Database-Scoped entity. Since data is stored in persistent tables, the Query Store survives service restarts and is included when a database is backed up or copied to another server. The Query Store holds a historical record of query plans.

The Query Store consists of three internal data stores:

- *Plan Store* – Stores the Query Text and Estimated Plans

- *Runtime Stats Store* – Stores a record of resources consumed by specific plans

- *Wait Stats Store* – Stores Wait Statistics collected during query plan execution

The Query Store solves the issue of *Persistence* for Query Plans. Without persistence, the optimizer has no feedback mechanism to know the effectiveness of any particular query plan after the service restarts. The plan *should* be effective if the estimated row counts (called *Cardinality* in set theory) for each plan correspond to the actual rows processed by each query operator. Since sequential cardinality estimates in query operations build on each other – the later operation inputs are the outputs of earlier operations – an early "miss" on estimates can destroy the entire query optimization. Persistence allows SQL to compare the accuracy of various cardinality estimates over a longer period of time and thus the efficiency of multiple query plans for a specific query or stored procedure.

The Query Store is on by default for all databases created on Azure SQL DB and Azure SQL Managed Instance. The Query Store status on Azure SQL VMs depends on the version of SQL Server installed on that VM. The Query Store is only available on Azure SQL VM for SQL 2016 or later and is on by default starting with SQL Server 2022. Databases restored to Azure SQL Managed Instance inherit the Query Store status (on/off) from their origin databases.

The Query Store can be enabled or disabled with simple T-SQL commands shown in Examples 9-3 and 9-4.

Example 9-3. Enable the SQL Query Store

```
ALTER DATABASE <database_name>
SET QUERY_STORE = ON (OPERATION_MODE = READ_WRITE);
```

Example 9-4. Disable the Query Store

```
ALTER DATABASE <database_name>
SET QUERY_STORE = OFF
```

I cannot emphasize this enough. Do not disable the Query Store except as a very last resort. If it causes problems, try reconfiguring it first.

Do not disable the Query Store except as a very last resort.

You cannot disable the Query Store in Azure SQL Database Single Database or Elastic Pool mode. The query will return a warning that this operation is not supported. Azure relies on the Query Store to properly manage Azure SQL DB.

Story time. One customer had disabled the Query Store in Azure SQL Managed Instance to "save" costs. Their workload was growing, and they did not use any of the Azure SQL MI cost optimization tools we discussed in this book, nor did they properly tune the Query Store for their workload. Their sole remedy was to disable core functionality, specifically the Query Store, to "free up" compute resources. As with most SQL workloads, when their main database hit saturation, performance for everything took a dive. The system did not degrade gracefully.

To "fix" the issue, the customer would force a failover to the internal HA replica, wiping all collected data and making troubleshooting impossible. To be fair, since the system was largely unresponsive, they couldn't troubleshoot effectively before the failover. They were not happy.

To fully resolve this issue, they had to temporarily increase their provisioned size, enable the Query Store, collect data, and find where their resources were going. Since they started at 32 vCores, the next "stop" was at 40 vCores, so they had to provision the equivalent cost of an eight-vCore Business Critical SQL Managed Instance. Not an inexpensive proposition. After gathering data, the cause of both the growth and slowdowns was attributed to one user writing ad hoc analytic-type queries against the operating Transactional database – not the built-in read replica. Redirecting and improving the poorly written queries resolved the issue, and the customer was able to reduce their provisioned system back to its budgeted level – with the Query Store still enabled. The entire situation with its cost and business disruption could have been avoided by using data that the Query Store routinely kept and reported.

The default settings for the Query Store are like many SQL settings – good for somewhere around 70–90% of SQL Server systems. Some systems will feel an impact from Query Store operations beyond the expected 3–5% overall Server/Database impact. You may need to adjust some Query Store parameters if the impact exceeds those levels. Again, *do not turn off the Query Store* unless you cannot tune its impact below the 3–5% threshold even after opening a support ticket with Microsoft. Data from the Query Store powers most of the query optimization improvement strategies implemented in Azure and for SQL Server since its release in SQL 2016.

Figure 9-1 shows the Query Store page on the Database Properties pop-up from SQL Server Management Studio. This example comes from Azure SQL Managed Instance, but it is identical to the Query Store properties for all Azure SQL Services, including VMs running SQL 2016 or higher. These settings control the collection and retention of data in the Query Store and are the "knobs" you adjust to tune the Query Store.

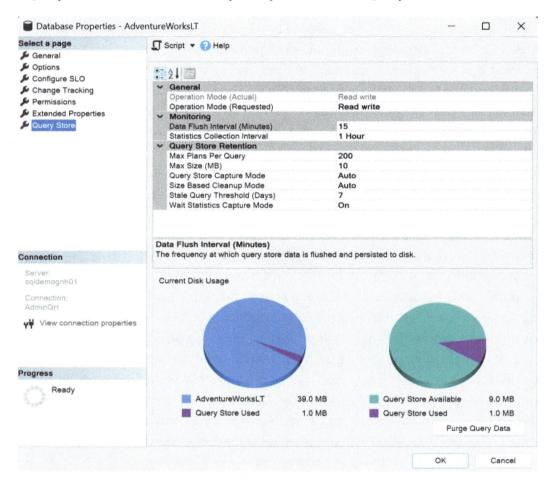

Figure 9-1. *Database Properties – Query Store*

These Query Store configuration options can also be changed via ALTER DATABASE SET options. Most of you will never need to tune the Query Store for it to stay under the 3–5% impact threshold. If you do need to do so, I strongly suggest engaging with Microsoft directly for guidance. Of course, the systems are ultimately yours to manage as you see fit.

Monitor by Using the Query Store

SQL Server Management Studio provides seven specific reports based on data captured in the Query store. These reports present query-centric diagnostic data that can help identify specific queries that impact overall SQL Server Database performance. Figure 9-2 shows the list of Query Store reports in the Explorer pane of SQL Server Management Studio.

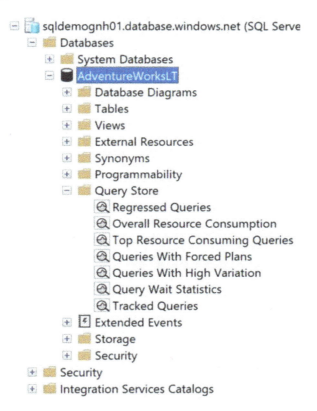

Figure 9-2. *Query Store Reports*

Before we dive into query and plan analysis, we need to understand something important about the Query Store. The Query Store needs time to collect data. We started this section discussing the need to collect a baseline of performance data to be able to perform meaningful performance analysis. It is equally important to collect a baseline of query plans and activity to analyze query performance. The Query Store is not a magic flashlight that you can point at a SQL database and the problem "lights up." The Query Store needs data to work well, preferably data from a well-performing system so it can have a "good" to compare with a "bad." In the previous story it took time to collect baseline query performance and catch the outliers before identifying and resolving the root cause. Unless you can predict which systems will need query performance optimization, it is best to leave the Query Store running so you have that baseline ready if the need occurs.

One more item before we dig into query optimization, and that is a specific recommendation for the practicing Azure SQL DBA. If you are going to examine query plans, do yourself a favor and download the SolarWinds SQL Sentry Plan Explorer tool. It is a free tool that does a much better job than the Showplan tool built into SQL Server Management Studio. If you prefer to use Azure Data Studio, there is a Plan Explorer Extension for that tool. Microsoft will not include or mention a third-party tool in its exams, but I have found SQL Sentry Plan Explorer to be one of my core DBA tools since it was introduced many years ago.

Regressed Queries

The definition of a Regressed query is a query that has changed plans where the new plan performs poorer than an earlier plan. Prior to the inclusion of the Query Store, SQL Server had no mechanism to compare query plan effectiveness over time as all query play data was lost whenever the server restarted. SQL could not even tell when a plan changed; it only had data on the current plan and the last execution – assuming that the plan even was still in cache. The Query Store's collected data easily lets us identify Regressed Queries and force SQL to use an earlier, more effective plan. This can help the situation where a query occasionally gets a poisoned plan that destabilizes the whole server. The plan may be less than ideal for the infrequent case that generated the poison plan, but it helps overall stability and buys time while the underlying query is improved or refactored to eliminate the narrow problem case. The Regressed Queries report lets you explore the top 25 impactful regressed queries on the Query Store.

Overall Resource Consumption

Since the Query Store collects resource consumption for each query, it makes sense that aggregating across all queries will yield the total resource consumption for the Database. This is distinct from the resources used by the Server (Aure SQL MI and VM) or by an elastic pool (Azure SQL DB). You can use this data to determine if this database is the actual resource consumption problem *and* which resource is running at its limit without having to use one of the tools we discussed in Chapter 8 to examine performance metrics. Like many resource-focused tools, it may not solve the problem, but it can help eliminate options that are not causing issues and help focus on the actual cause.

Top Resource Consuming Queries

Earlier in this chapter we discussed query impact skew – the concept that only a few queries consumed the most resources in any particular SQL Server. Focusing on those queries will gain the most performance improvement for the effort expended. This is the idea behind the Top Resource Consuming Queries report. Older versions of SQL Server Management Studio had similar reports, but those were based on the Query Plan Cache. As we have noted before, the plan cache has limited visibility and does not survive a SQL Service restart.

Using the previous report to find the overall resource that is constrained, you would select the same resource from the list in Figure 9-3.

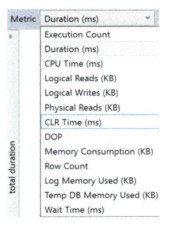

Figure 9-3. *Top Query Resource Metric Choices*

Sometimes a single query execution can consume too many resources; other times the individual query execution may not be significant, but as the query is repeated more and more, it exhausts a critical underlying resource. Using the "Statistics" option (not shown) and switching between the choices will help identify both types of impactful queries.

Queries With Forced Plans

One of the options to resolve poor plan choice by the optimizer or to prevent plan cache poisoning is to force a plan for a specific query. This is useful when you cannot alter the application code or for short-term mitigation while the code is refactored since this is purely a data tier operation. We do not have to change the underlying query to force a plan. Forced plans require heightened scrutiny since the normal optimizer checks no longer apply. This report allows you to see forced plans and their impact on resource consumption within a SQL Database.

Queries With High Variation

Parameter-Sensitive Queries – queries that have high variation in cardinality depending on the calling parameters – are of particular concern. In my experience, these are generally written using Imperative code modes or implement correlated subqueries that make incorrect assumptions about how the SQL Optimizer works, limiting the range of possible plans that would efficiently resolve the query. In some cases, the query is overloaded (another Imperative model concept) to do multiple functions and is unable to do multiple tasks efficiently. In these cases, the query may need to be split into multiple queries, each targeted to a specific task and corresponding parameter range. This report identifies High-Variation queries and notes them for your attention.

Query Wait Statistics

Wait Statistics is a useful methodology for SQL Database Performance Optimization. SQL Server operates on an internal SQL Operating System (SQLOS) that is a cooperative multitasking system. Unlike Windows or Linux, which are preemptive multitasking systems, SQL threads do not interrupt each other; they voluntarily yield to other threads. One of the cases where threads yield is when they are waiting for a resource to become available. These resources could be a lock to protect a row of data, a latch to manage writes to a page, a different latch to indicate a page that needs to be read into memory, or almost any resource. The time spent waiting for resources is the Resource Wait Time and can be used to indicate where resource contention is slowing queries.

The Query Wait Statistics report lets you select the wait category and drill into the queries generating the most wait time. One performance area I have found this useful is in tuning the degree of parallelism by comparing parallelism wait times across different settings.

Tracked Queries

There are multiple reasons to track the performance of specific queries. That query may enable an application feature with a very specific performance SLA. It may be a query you "fixed," and you want to compare before and after – especially if it no longer surfaces as an impactful query on another report. It may be one that is newly introduced to the system in a feature deployment. Regardless of why, you can tag specific queries for data gathering, even if they would not normally be tracked based on the normal data capturing and retention rules configured for the Query Store.

Identify Sessions That Cause Blocking

Blocking in SQL is defined as query contention over the same data elements. Blocking is a side effect of how SQL Server implements its lock-based transaction-processing system. Locks are a logical flag that indicates some degree of data stability is required for a query to execute successfully. There are many types, categories, and purposes of locks in SQL. An exhaustive examination of each would be yet another complete tome. The reason for the wide variety of locks is so SQL can use the least restrictive lock (and thus the least impactful lock) possible to protect transactional integrity.

A block is when one query cannot access a resource locked by a different query. SQL Server can have lock chains (not to be confused with blockchain – the cryptocurrency technology) where queries are blocked by another query, which is in turn blocked by another query. The query at the bottom of the chain that holds the first lock is called the Lead Blocker. Transient Blocking is perfectly normal for a SQL Server operating at scale. When the blocks become excessive and start to impact performance is when we need to pay attention to them.

Deadlocks

A special case of blocking is called a Deadlock. This is where the sequence of locks and blocks forms a loop, having no specific lead blocker as you explore down the lock chain. The only way to resolve a deadlock is to abort one query and roll back its changes, releasing its locks in the process. All SQL Services automatically detect deadlocks and will select a Deadlock Victim – quickly choosing the query that has spent the least resources up to the point of the deadlock. Occasional Deadlocks are mostly benign and can be ignored unless the resulting errors cannot be resolved by the client application using retry logic.

SQL Server will always raise alerts when a Deadlock Occurs. The victim query client receives a 1205 error that is also recorded in the SQL Error Log. Older versions of SQL (prior to SQL 2012) relied on Trace Flags 1204 and 1222 to add extra deadlock diagnostic information to the SQL Error Log. This may cause a major impact on systems with significant DeadLock activity and is no longer a recommended DeadlLock troubleshooting technique. The `xml_deadlock_report` Extended Event captures all Deadlock Diagnostic information starting with SQL Server 2012 and including Azure SQL Managed Instance. The xml_deadlock_report Extended Event is enabled by default as part of the system_health Extended Event Session. No additional action is required.

You can view recorded DeadLock Data using SQL Server Management Studio by examining the Event File or Ring Buffer in Object Explorer as shown in Figure 9-4.

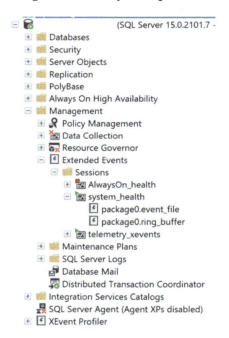

Figure 9-4. *Extended Events Explorer – Session Health*

You must create a database-scoped Extended Event session in Azure SQL Database to capture and view DeadLocks. The `system_health` Extended Event Session is not available in Azure SQL Database as it is a server-scoped Extended Event.

Data Normalization

Deadlocks are almost always due to a fundamental data architecture design flaw. Sometimes query construction can help, but most of the time it is due to the database not having a fully realized Third Normal Form (3NF).

Third Normal Form follows three rules:

- Each set of related data belongs in its own tables.

- Individual tables cannot contain repeating groups.

- All tables have a Primary Key to uniquely identify each row.

Data models conforming closely to 3NF tend to perform better in transaction-processing applications than other data architectures Most Transactional databases are designed around 3NF to minimize locking collisions in highly transactional systems – you only have to protect the smallest data element such as an address, not the entire customer account and transaction history records.

In reality, most SQL transactional databases are "mostly" 3NF with various compromises thrown in. Sometimes these compromises are part of the original design; sometimes they are a result of later additions that have grown beyond the original design requirements. Deadlocks are often a symptom of poor database and query design.

Transaction Isolation Levels

Locking and blocking is inextricably linked to Transaction Isolation Levels in SQL Server. Different Transaction Isolation Levels determine how long transaction locks are held and how read locks interact with transaction locks. The SQL Transaction Isolation Levels are ranked from least strict to most strict as follows:

1. *Read Uncommitted: Least Strict* – "Dirty reads" – reads of transaction data that has not been committed (in flight) – can be read by another query. May result in incorrect data. Useful when "close enough" works – such as a preliminary report that needs to be generated quickly but does not need financially exact totals.

2. *Read Committed* – Read locks are released after data is consumed into a query execution. In-Flight data is not read, and the query blocks until those rows are released. Read locks only block write locks, not other read locks. Multiple reads across the same data may obtain different results if the row is changed between reads.

3. *Repeatable Read* – All rows read or written are locked until the transaction completes. Multiple reads across the same rows will always yield the same results. Ranges of rows can have data inserted between reads.

4. *Serializable* – The most strict isolation level. All data read or written, including range locks, are kept for the duration of the transaction. Prevents any data interaction to the affected data even if rows for that data do not exist for the duration of the transaction.

SQL Server also has two additional Transaction Isolation Levels available if the database is enabled for row versioning:

1. *Snapshot* – Snapshot Isolation mimics Oracle's default transaction isolation level. Snapshot Isolation level is dependent on row versioning. Read locks no longer block on write locks; they merely reference the previous row and continue on, resulting in transactionally consistent data. This is particularly useful on large aggregation queries across highly transactional systems, but can have a measurable impact on TempDB usage.

2. *Read Committed Snapshot* – Read Committed Snapshot Isolation is a way to allow Snapshot Isolation behavior for queries that explicitly request Read Uncommitted transaction isolation level. This most commonly occurs in legacy code where the author may have routinely used "dirty read" logic without exploring the consequences. Whenever the Optimizer sees a Read Uncommitted hint or setting, it is replaced with Snapshot Isolation. Read Committed Snapshot isolation also is dependent on Row Versioning enabled for the database.

Identify Performance Issues Using Dynamic Management Views (DMVs)

Edgar F. Codd is the grandfather of modern relational database design. Back in the 1970s, Codd formulated his set of 12 rules (there are actually 13 rules numbered 0–12 because all real computer scientists start counting at zero) of database design. Every single modern relational database is derived from an implementation of these design rules (sometimes more guidelines than rules in practice). The relevant one here is Rule 0, called the Foundational Rule:

> *For any system that is advertised as, or claimed to be, a relational data base management system, that system must be able to manage data bases entirely through its relational capabilities.*

> —Edgar F. Codd

And Rule 1 is called the Information Rule:

> *All information in a relational data base is represented explicitly at the logical level and in exactly one way – by values in tables.*

> —Edgar F. Codd

Original written sources of the rules are disputed, but the exact text of the rules is agreed upon by the relational database community and was verified repeatedly by Codd prior to his passing in 2003. These rules were interpreted by the original authors of SQL Server who were largely following Codd's design principles to mean that all actions within SQL Server had to respond to be initiated by a relational query and responded to with a table. This included all administrative and diagnostic actions.

SQL Server originally exposed internal *System Tables* as a means of complying with these rules while providing diagnostic information to SQL Database Administrators. That rapidly became problematic when administrators would often directly update those system tables without understanding all the consequences, sometimes rendering SQL Server unresponsive or even unusable without reinstalling the software or rebuilding the master database. Microsoft introduced an abstract, read-only set of views called Dynamic Management Views (DMVs) in SQL Server 2005. DMVs still comply with Codd's rules by displaying administrative information via a virtual table (view) while protecting the underlying system tables from user-induced mayhem. The set of DMVs has grown over time since it has proved a very useful capability in SQL Server. New DMVS have been introduced to provide visibility into new features as well as expanded visibility into existing SQL capabilities. DMVs are now the primary method to extract diagnostic data about the internal state of a SQL Server or Database.

DMVs are generally broken into two categories: Server-scoped DMVs and Database-scoped DMVs. Given the different surface areas of the various Azure SQL Services, the set of DMVs is not universal across all SQL Services. Particularly, the set of Server-scoped DMVs in Azure SQL Database is more limited than in the other two services since the Server object is a logical endpoint and not the physical host server. Allowing access to true Server-scoped DMVs would be a major security violation. Some Server-scoped DMVs have been rewritten to be meaningful at the database level and reintroduced at that level for Azure SQL Database.

DMVs all start with "sys.dm_" followed by the name of the DMV. The names tend to be descriptive; the first part of the name may indicate the feature that the DMV supports. For example, all DMVs related to Always-On Availability Groups save for one begin with "sys.dm_hadr_". The exception is sys.dm_tcp_listener_states.

DMVs are further classified into the following three categories:

- Database-related dynamic management objects

- Query execution–related dynamic management objects

- Transaction-related dynamic management objects

There are a few DMVs that return very similar information that exist in a Database-scoped form and a Server-scoped form. The name of the specific DMV will include information about the scope.

Just about anything you want to know about the current internal state of an active SQL Server or Service can be queried via one or more DMVs. Like any other view on SQL Server, you can join DMVs to provide meaningful, actionable diagnostic data. Stack Overflow, GitHub, and Microsoft documentation are rife with example queries on how to glean specific information on nearly any system within SQL Server. This is yet another area you will need to go "hands-on" and practice to truly understand.

Identify and Implement Index Changes for Queries

One of the most powerful actions we can take as Azure SQL Database Administrators to improve query performance is to optimize the table indexes for a database. Indexes enable SQL Server to rapidly access just the data necessary to resolve a query without having to wade through large quantities of data that do not satisfy the current query. Indexes are the foundation of SQL Server performance. Almost all query tuning is focused on getting to and using the proper indexes in the optimal order to most efficiently resolve that query.

Row-Version Indexes

What we think of as ordinary SQL data is stored in row-version indexes. Indexes are b-tree structures that optimize data lookups. Clustered Indexes store the row data in the leaf level of the index, while non-clustered indexes point to clustered index entries. Indexes are internally unique – a uniquifier (yes, that is what the Microsoft documentation calls it) is added to non-unique indexes to make every index value unique. The next paragraphs discussing index optimization will focus on Row-Version Indexes.

Caution   It is possible to run out of uniquifiers. Microsoft implements uniquifiers as signed 32-bit integers that reset for each unique column value, yielding about two billion usable values. If you add more than ~two billion identical values to an index, you will generate SQL Error 666 with the following text: The maximum system-generated unique value for a duplicate group was exceeded for index with partition ID <partition ID>. Dropping and re-creating the index may resolve this; otherwise, use another clustering key.

Index optimization is not an exact science. If it were, Microsoft would have long ago built a perfect index tuning wizard into SQL Server. The repeated failures of such attempts over the years simply illustrate just how challenging it is to write a "perfect" query. The challenge is that index tuning is not about achieving one single goal; there are multiple competing goals that may carry different weights in achieving overall performance. A few examples will illustrate my point.

For our first example, imagine a complex report that joins several tables to produce a critical report. This report takes three hours to run. One particular table is very large, but if you create a specific index on that table, the report runs in ten minutes. Obvious answer is to create the index, right? But what if the report is only run as part of year-end closing and the index is so complex that it measurably slows the normal transactional operation of any transaction writing to that table? Perhaps the best optimization is to only create the index during year-end closing period and drop it for the rest of the year.

Another consideration is multiple, similar queries that are "slightly" different. Do you create separate indexes to optimize each query or attempt to create a composite index that satisfies all the queries? This leads to what columns, what order the columns are in, and what columns are included in an index. The possibilities can quickly explode beyond what a reasonable algorithm can explore but can be managed by a human with experience and intuition.

Finally, we have the possibility that certain indexes just aren't being used by the optimizer, despite what looks like it would be an obvious solution at first glance. Imagine a single table with a WHERE clause identifying a single column value. That column is indexed, yet the index never shows up on the query plan. There are at least two circumstances where that is the correct optimizer choice. Even more important, we cannot fix it with a simple index.

One reason would be that the index is poorly selective. Imagine an index on a 100K-row table that has six unique values. All but 12 rows are a single value – "CLOSED." The other rows represent various states for requests. You query for "EMERGENCY." The statistics may not have that value recorded since it is a rare event. Given the poor selectivity, the optimizer may elect to scan the table. If an index lookup returns more than 20% of the underlying row values, the optimizer will correctly decide that a scan is more efficient. The optimizer always estimates the effectiveness of an index before choosing one. SQL also may be using a cached plan that was optimized with "CLOSED" as a parameter. This would be an example of a parameter-sensitive query.

These are only three examples of possible scenarios that affect Index optimization. As you practice and grow your index tuning skills, you will start to recognize effective indexing patterns. Regardless, always test in non-production first. As my colleague Andy Leonard has remarked, *"All Software is tested, some intentionally."* Be intentional.

ColumnStore Indexes

A ColumnStore index stores data in compressed column format rather than in rows. Instead of 10,000 rows with the same value in a column, the data is recorded as Beginning Row ID, Ending Row ID, Value. While this is a gross oversimplification of the actual storage engine, you can readily see that this saves a great deal of storage space for duplicate column values. It also saves computation time in that the range of rows can be treated as a batch by the query optimizer rather than dealt with on a row-by-row basis as with Row-Version Indexes.

To accommodate transactional workloads, ColumnStore indexes have an internal row-version store–based Delta table where changes are recorded. Compressed rowgroups are combined with the Delta table during query execution to provide up-to-date transactionally consistent data. Background processes migrate data from the Delta table to Compressed ColumnStore rowgroups based on data size thresholds. This happens automatically and seldom requires any user intervention. More recent versions of SQL Server and all Azure PaaS Services have improved the logic for managing these indexes.

ColumnStore indexes work poorly on data schemas based on Third Normal Form (3NF) architecture. ColumnStore data is primarily used for Analytics workloads and is the native index type in Azure Synapse Analytics pools.

ColumnStore technology was first introduced in SQL 2008R2 as an add-in to Excel called PowerPivot. This fundamental technology has evolved into multiple manifestations over the years. These include the SQL Server ColumnStore storage engine, SQL Server Analysis Services Tabular Mode, Azure Analysis Services, and the VertiPaq engine behind Power BI.

Choosing a ColumnStore index transforms the entire table into a Clustered ColumnStore table. The "Clustered" moniker is used to remind everyone that this is the physical representation of the table, not just an abstraction.

Recommend Query Construct Modifications Based on Resource Usage

There are several query design patterns, largely derived from Imperative mode programming, that will reduce the effectiveness of the optimizer. The resulting queries will often end up in the Top Resource Consuming Queries list. They also tend to cause excessive locking and blocking. An effective Azure SQL Database Administrator will not only be able to identify these poorly performing queries but will also be able to provide recommendations on alternative query constructions that are mathematically equivalent. That is, they will produce the exact same results. The key is to focus your effort on the most impactful queries to achieve the most meaningful results. Here are a few common query constructions that can cause performance issues. This is not a comprehensive list but is intended to be a starting collection for your query improvement skills.

Subqueries vs. Joins

One persistent pattern I find in analytic queries is unnecessary use of correlated subqueries. Not only are they hard to read, but they cannot always be easily refactored by the optimizer. Consider the query in Example 9-5. You can execute the query against any AdventureWorks database to see for yourself.

Example 9-5. Correlated Subquery

```
select
distinct
        CU.CustomerID
        ,(SELECT SUM(TotalDue) from Sales.SalesOrderHeader SOH
                where SOH.CustomerID = CU.CustomerID) as Totals
        ,(SELECT SUM(TaxAmt) from Sales.SalesOrderHeader SOH
                where SOH.CustomerID = CU.CustomerID) As Tax
        ,(SELECT SUM(Freight) from Sales.SalesOrderHeader SOH
                where SOH.CustomerID = CU.CustomerID) As Freight
        ,SP.CommissionPct
        ,PS.FirstName
from
        Sales.Customer CU
        inner join Person.Person  PS
                on PS.BusinessEntityID = CU.PersonID
        INNER JOIN Sales.SalesPerson SP
                ON SP.TerritoryID = CU.TerritoryID
        left join Sales.SalesOrderHeader SH
                on SH.CustomerID= CU.CustomerID
```

```
            left join Sales.SalesOrderDetail SD
                    on SD.SalesOrderID = SH.SalesOrderID
where CU.CustomerID = 30114
order by CU.CustomerID desc
```

The excessive use of parentheses forces the optimizer to execute the joins in a specific order, eliminating more efficient query resolution paths. Example 9-6 shows a Declarative mode version of the same query.

Example 9-6. Refactored Query

```
select CU.CustomerID
        ,SUM(SH.TotalDue) as Totals
        ,SUM(SH.TaxAmt) as Tax
        ,SUM(SH.Freight) as Freight
        ,SP.CommissionPct
        ,PS.FirstName

from
        Sales.Customer CU
        inner join Sales.SalesOrderHeader SH
                on CU.CustomerID = SH.CustomerID
        INNER JOIN Sales.SalesPerson SP
                ON SP.TerritoryID = CU.TerritoryID

        inner join Person.Person  PS
                on PS.BusinessEntityID = CU.PersonID
where CU.CustomerID = 30114

                group by CU.CustomerID ,SP.CommissionPct ,PS.FirstName
                order by CU.CustomerID desc
```

Not only is the query easier to read without all the parentheses cluttering it up, but it requires approximately half the resources the original query did. While this is a simplistic example, the differences will quickly multiply based on the complexity and number of correlated subqueries. Use the Query Store to track changes in resource usage between different versions of the same query when making query improvements.

Shrouded SARGs

Another poorly performing design paradigm is when a column value in a query is wrapped in a function. We refer to the Search Argument (SARG) as having been "shrouded" when the column value must be run through a function before comparison. WHERE (Column_Date +3) > GetDate() is a simple example. The optimizer cannot extract the constant +3 and algebraically apply it to the GetDate() function due to the parentheses. The query plan must read each value from the column, execute the +3 function, and compare it to the constant output from GetDate(). GetDate() is only run a single time and the result reused as a constant in the query. Again we have a simple example, but this effect can be devastating at scale.

Sometimes you can shroud a SARG unintentionally. I once was responsible for an automotive database where the application looked up factory automobile configurations by Vehicle Identification Number (VIN). The procedure in question was several hundred lines long and had a lot of procedural logic surrounding this particular query. The query was consuming almost 25% of the entire server capacity and was performing very slowly. I identified the specific query in the procedure that was causing the problem. It was a single-row lookup on an exact string match to an indexed column. SQL refused to use the index – even with a hint it insisted on scanning the ~350K-row table.

By legal definition, a VIN in North America consists of a 17-digit string using only uppercase letters and numbers. It is an externally defined data type that the lookup database provider stored as char(17). The procedure extracted a substring from the supplied VIN that represented the manufacturer-coded build list called a trim level. This value was compared to the externally provided lookup database. Up at the very beginning of the procedure, around 600 lines before the problem line, the parameter for this query was defined as an NVarChar string, not a varchar or char string. SQL is polymorphic so the value was accepted and executed successfully. However, comparing a VarChar to an NVarChar requires a one-way transformation. SQL "promotes" the VarChar to an NVarChar to make the comparison. I removed the "N" from the code definition, and the query disappeared from the most impactful resource consumers. It was the equivalent of adding a full core to the server. The procedure coder had implicitly created a shrouded SARG due to not following an externally defined data standard, rendering all indexes useless on that column.

These examples are only a beginning. The key to improving query performance via query construction is to methodically search what elements of a query are consuming the most resources. Is the same data getting read multiple times inside a query? Are joins working to reduce the total result set as fast as possible? Do certain operations block parallelism? Do not try and fix everything at once. Make controlled changes and measure the improvements. Always, test in non-production if you have that capability.

Assess the Use of Query Hints for Query Performance

At the beginning of this chapter, I described at a very high level the operation of the query optimizer. Sometimes you cannot significantly change a poorly performing data architecture but do have access to rewrite specific queries. Ideally you would not need to use query hints as they tend to be overused to attempt to compensate for poor data architecture design, but sometimes you must exert some control over the optimizer to achieve the best results. The optimizer uses a greedy algorithm; it wants to optimize the specific query under consideration. It does not balance the needs of the entire server.

Query hints can control things like Maximum Degree of Parallelism (MAXDOP), Parameter Optimization Choice, Join Methodology, Forced Recompile, and Transaction Isolation Level or even force a specific plan. Note that any forced plan must still be a valid plan according to the optimizer. As with any query optimization process, compare plans and resource consumption before and after changes. Don't make the problem worse.

Review Execution Plans

Up until now, we have talked about plans as single entities. In reality a plan can have multiple steps, each of which is an individual query. Each query plan consists of nodes that represent specific computational building blocks with one or more input sets and a single output set. The size and complexity of these intermediate result sets generally determine the resource consumption of the individual query along with the computational costs of the individual nodes within a query. Let's compare two query plans using the queries from Examples 9-5 and 9-6. The Actual Plan from Example 9-5 is shown in Figure 9-5.

Figures 9-5 and 9-6 were generated using the SQL Sentry Plan Explorer tool from SolarWinds. The SHOWPLAN_XML component of SSMS creates visual plan representations that do not easily fit on a page.

Figure 9-5. *Imperative Mode Query Plan*

The three nodes with their percentages highlighted in red (only in Plan Explorer) are the most resource-intensive (highest cost) nodes in the query. They show the same data lookup repeated from the SalesOrderHeader table due to the correlated subquery construction.

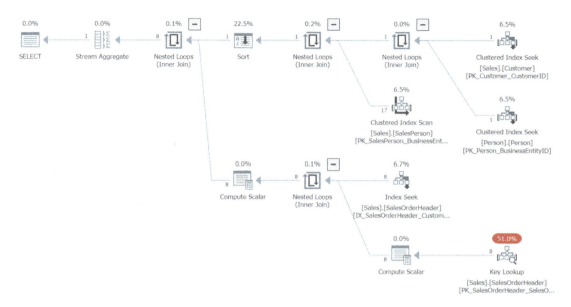

Figure 9-6. *Declarative Mode Query Plan*

You can easily see the plan for this query is much simpler, representing the simpler construction of the underlying query. While the two queries are mathematically the same, the execution plan is simpler and corresponding resource consumption is much lower.

One feature of both SSMS and Plan Explorer is to create wider node interconnect lines to represent larger intermediate result sets. One pattern (not shown) that tends to perform extremely poor is when you have a query with many very wide lines that lead to a final node or two that filter or aggregate the results to a small number of rows. If that filtering can be pushed to earlier in the query, then the intermediate result sets will be smaller, resulting in much lower resource consumption.

Chapter Summary

This chapter has presented the bare bones of query plan optimization – just enough along with the Learning Path materials to get you through the test and firmly ground your future exploration of this specialized skill set in the Azure SQL Database Administrator toolkit. As with any skill, it will only develop with practice and further study. Something you might want to look into – after you pass the exam.

CHAPTER 10

Configure Database Solutions for Optimal Performance

In Chapters 8 and 9 we explored how to diagnose and troubleshoot performance challenges at the Platform and the query level, respectively. This chapter will focus on how to configure the Azure Platform itself to improve performance. Some of these concepts we first explored in Part 1 (Chapters 2–4) along with some basic Azure SQL concepts. Here we will focus on maximizing performance, emphasizing features that are exclusive to Azure SQL or were first developed and introduced in Azure SQL.

Implement Index Maintenance Tasks

One of the biggest misconceptions prospective Azure SQL Database Administrators have is exactly where the dividing line lies between what Azure takes care of and what the DBA is responsible for. Let us be absolutely clear on this subject. Azure SQL does not automatically rebuild or reorganize Indexes. Index Maintenance is the sole responsibility of the DBA, regardless of your SQL platform. The only question becomes how to implement automatic Index Maintenance tasks in Azure vs. on-premises.

The topic of Index Maintenance is a well-known topic for a SQL Server Database Administrator. Right after verifying and testing backups, index maintenance is one of the first tasks a DBA will perform when deploying or inheriting a SQL Server. The concepts of rebuilding and reorganizing indexes are ones we should all be comfortable with. These concepts and requirements do not change in Azure.

© Geoff Hiten 2025
G. Hiten, *Administering Microsoft Azure SQL Solutions*, Certification Study Companion Series,
https://doi.org/10.1007/979-8-8688-1585-0_10

Implement Statistics Maintenance Tasks

The Azure SQL Database Administrator Learning Path insists on separating the topic of Index Maintenance from Statistics maintenance, despite the deep connection between the two topics. Chapter 9 detailed why statistics must be kept up to date – the optimizer depends on current, accurate statistics. Bad Statistics leads to inaccurate plans that often perform poorly.

An index rebuild will force a statistics update, while an index reorganization will not. Many DBAs ignore the implicit statistics rebuild from the index rebuild and simply schedule an automatic statistics rebuild on a fixed schedule. The extra "cost" of this operation is negligible as long as you have sufficient maintenance window time to complete all tasks. Further optimization on statistics rebuilding is seldom worth the effort.

Many of us are familiar with the fantastic work done by Ola Hallengren and his SQL Server Maintenance Solution. Ola's work is the gold standard for Index and Statistics maintenance scripts and is used nearly universally except where a central backup solution has been mandated by an organization. Azure SQL Managed Instance and Azure SQL Virtual Machines both support Ola's scripts or any T-SQL script scheduled by a SQL Agent. Ola has written specific, automatic optimizations for Azure SQL VM backup to URL. Unfortunately, Microsoft only includes Microsoft-native solutions on the exam, but you really need to be aware of these tools.

Azure SQL Database does not have any native scheduling tools. Azure SQL Database relies on external scheduling agents. The three most commonly used scheduling Agents are as follows:

- Azure Runbooks

- SQL Agent via Remote SQL Server

- Azure SQL Elastic Jobs

Azure Runbooks are an automated PowerShell environment that can connect to Azure SQL DB and run scripts. SQL Agent can run reindex commands to a remote SQL Database as well as its own host. Azure SQL Elastic Jobs was described in Chapter 2.

Implement Database Integrity Checks

The subject of database integrity checks in Azure SQL Database and Azure SQL Managed Instance is somewhat contentious. While some Azure SQL DBAs let the internal Microsoft integrity checks stand, others prefer to perform their own checks. Let's explore exactly why and how Microsoft implements integrity checks (DBCC CHECKDB) so you can decide if this is "good enough" for your purposes. No Integrity Checks are automatically performed for Azure SQL Virtual Machines and are the sole responsibility of the DBA. This discussion focuses on Azure SQL DB and Azure SQL MI.

A long history of SQL Server shows that database corruption – outside extremely rare code bugs – is typically caused by a malfunction in the storage stack. The storage stack consists of everything involved in persistently writing data to storage, including all interfaces, connections, and software. Somewhere along the write or read path the data changed. That unwanted change is called corruption.

Microsoft tests Azure SQL (both DB and MI) attempting to identify and correct such corruption before it becomes irrecoverable. Azure performs an integrity check on a statistically meaningful sample of databases. This sample covers all possible combinations of host, network devices, and storage arrays used in a particular service. Your databases may or may not get tested on a particular test run. They may never be automatically tested. Even if corruption is detected, the system will attempt to recover it silently – you do not receive any notification. Having said that, the potential for actual corruption is still minimized by the background testing done in Azure as well as Azure's storage-level redundancy.

As a DBA, I am confident that any actual database corruption will be caught and corrected by Azure. I still have the responsibility to do my best to protect my organization from losing data. As such, I always set an Integrity Check as part of my normal maintenance tasks. Implementation options for DBCC CHECKDB are exactly the same as for Index and Statistics Maintenance for the corresponding Azure SQL platform.

Configure Database Automatic Tuning

Experienced SQL Database Administrators, both on-premises and Azure-based, are highly skeptical. It's a necessary job trait. Microsoft has touted new "self-tuning" features in many SQL Server releases for a couple of decades now, often with mixed results. These efforts represented the best capabilities of the SQL engineers at the time but lacked two key elements. First, there was no mechanism for SQL to observe query performance improvements over time. Every time SQL Server restarted, the tuning wizard had to start from zero. It did not know what it had tried before, much less whether any of those attempts were successful or not. The Query Store has resolved that issue, allowing SQL to observe long-term performance improvement efforts. Second, SQL Server had no built-in consistent, comprehensive performance capturing capabilities. Various Microsoft and third-party tools existed to monitor and alert for SQL Server performance, but none were wired back into the SQL engine to accurately measure overall system performance.

Given these two missing elements, the SQL Engineering team had very little information on whether their efforts to improve SQL Query performance automatically worked or not. Even if things worked, the multi-year development and release cycle of SQL Server meant that there was no consistency for long-term improvement.

For Microsoft to successfully host Azure SQL Database as a Platform Service, they had to be able to measure long-term query performance *and* track database performance in detail over time. As we learned from Chapter 8, Azure has a meter for everything. That includes Azure SQL DB Performance. With these foundational elements in place, Microsoft finally had all the pieces to build an effective automatic query performance tuning service.

Before we talk about how to configure Azure SQL Automatic Database Tuning, we need to outline the basic design principles Microsoft developers followed when creating Azure SQL Automatic Database Tuning. The first and most important principle is "do no harm." This means any changes must have a net positive impact on query performance or they are quickly reverted. Changes that do not show immediate benefit are rolled back and marked as unsuccessful. The second principle is to make changes one at a time. This protects the stability of the system while also helping measure the impact of specific changes in isolation.

There are only three areas where Azure will work to automatically improve performance. These three areas are as follows: Forcing Plans, Creating an Index, and Dropping an Index.

Force Plans

Forcing Plans simply automates the regressed query fix in the Query Store. Queries that exhibit degraded behavior over time will be forced to use an earlier plan that provided better results. Such queries are marked as forced and are tracked as such. If this action does not improve query performance under current operating conditions and parameters, the plan is "un-forced," and the particular forced plan attempt is marked as unsuccessful. Forcing Plans is the only Automatic Tuning option available for Azure SQL Managed Instance.

Create an Index

Index Creation in SQL has always been a little art and a little science. SQL can easily see which columns should be in an index that will benefit a specific query. Combining these into a more generally applicable index is challenging. Microsoft uses the entirety of Azure SQL Database to train its algorithms (horizontal learning) on how to create effective indexes. Microsoft chose to implement a slowly changing algorithm to improve index usage in measurable increments over time rather than a single "big bet" fix attempt. Microsoft simply creates a new index based on the combination of temporary indexes created during query optimization and execution, using patterns learned across Azure SQL Database. These new indexes are then considered by the optimizer alongside the existing indexes during query optimization.

Indexes are only created during low-activity times so as not to disrupt ongoing operations. Available space is also checked prior to deploying a new index, which is blocked if the result brings available space below 10% free. Note that these protections are *not* checked if you choose to manually deploy the index recommendations. These checks only exist in the fully automatic mode.

Drop an Index

Automatic Index improvement would be incomplete without a way of removing unused indexes. Over time, the index creation process should create better index choices for the optimizer, resulting in unused indexes. Since the Query Store tracks which indexes are used, it is relatively easy to decide on an appropriate interval to determine when an index is not used. Microsoft has settled on 93 days as the appropriate interval. If an index is not used by a query in 93 days *and* automatic index drop tuning is enabled, that index will be removed.

Enable Automatic Query Tuning

Automatic Query tuning can be controlled at multiple levels from Subscription on down to the database. Settings are inherited by all Servers/Databases unless specifically overridden. Figure 10-1 shows a Database-Level option setting. Default values (as shown) are "Inherit from Server" for all three options.

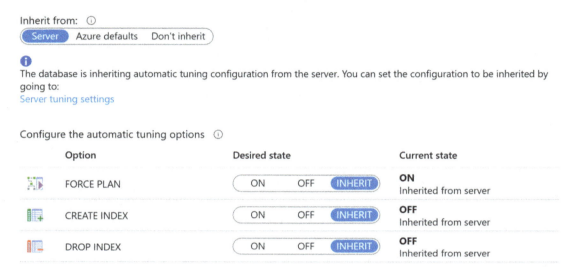

Figure 10-1. *Azure SQL Database Automatic Tuning Settings*

The Settings blade also shows the current settings as well as where they are inherited from if applicable. Turning *off* the automatic tuning options does not stop Azure SQL Database from calculating performance optimizations. It merely stops the system from automatically deploying them. You can see manual performance optimization recommendations on the Performance Recommendations blade under Intelligent Performance. The blade has two sections, Recommendations and Tuning history, as shown in Figure 10-2

Figure 10-2. *Azure SQL Database Performance Recommendations*

Recommendations are sorted by estimated impact (low, medium, high) and include a link to a T-SQL script to manually deploy the recommendation. As noted above, this is considered a manual code deployment. Azure SQL Database hands off the responsibility to the DBA for making sure the change does no harm. Tuning history is kept for 21 days and only shows automatically deployed tuning actions. In practice, I have seen many Azure SQL DBAs run on a "recommendations-only" configuration for several months, only to realize they are implementing all recommendations and should just let Azure SQL Database manage tuning automatically.

Given the "do no harm" mandate, the tuning process is necessarily slow. Azure SQL Database must gather a baseline of "good"-performing queries to learn what "normal" looks like. This is particularly challenging when the workload varies periodically. Then Azure SQL Database needs to identify areas for improvement. This means poorly performing queries must run "bad" for a while so Azure SQL Database can learn to fix it. Changes are going to be slow and incremental, but they do happen. Overall, the process works as intended. A DBA should only need to intervene if performance has degraded to the point that it is impacting the business.

Configure Server Settings for Performance

One of the most important resources impacting SQL Server is Storage. Entire products have been developed for on-premises SQL Server to maximize IOPS and throughput while minimizing latency. Solid-State Storage has eliminated rotational latency issues, but storage is still orders of magnitude slower than memory.

Azure has options for very fast storage for almost any SQL workload. The economics of Cloud Computing means Azure SQL DBAs now must determine how much is "enough." Given the large array of options and corresponding costs for Azure SQL Storage, we need to balance cost and performance. Once again, we are back to knowing our baseline performance metrics, resource consumption needs, and our user expectations.

We have previously discussed the fundamentals of Azure Storage for SQL Server in Chapter 3. Please review that material before continuing with this section if you have not done so yet.

Azure SQL Storage for SQL Server on Azure Virtual Machines is generally implemented using Azure Managed Disks. Managed Disks are an Azure Storage abstraction that is presented to an Azure Virtual Machine in a format that looks like a classic, block-addressable storage device, much in the same way a SAN presents an abstracted "slice" of the underlying storage array to a physical or virtual machine on-premises. It is important to know that the virtual data connection to the storage system is different than the virtual network connection. As such, there are different throughput and IOPS limitations for networking vs. storage in Azure SQL VMs. Each VM series and size has different storage IOPS capabilities. The possible combinations are more extensive than can be listed here. Any such printed list would be obsolete before I finished writing this chapter, certainly by the time you are reading it. The types of Azure Managed Disks stay relatively small, with the addition of Premium SSD V2 in 2025.

Azure Managed Disks are divided into four categories. Each disk type has different capabilities:

- *Ultra Disk* – Fastest current native storage disks in Azure with sub-millisecond latency guaranteed 99.99% of the time. Also the most expensive. Cannot be resized after deployment. Other manageability features may be limited. Only usable for data, not OS.

- *Premium SSD V2* – Offers many of the capabilities of Ultra disks but much closer to the cost of Premium SSD. Should be seriously considered as an alternative to Ultra for new SQL deployments.

- *Premium SSD Disk* – Most common for Production SQL Virtual Machines in Azure. Economical balance of size, IOPS, throughput, and cost. All manageability and availability features supported.

- *Standard SSD* – Used for dev/test workloads where predictable latency is important but not overall throughput and IOPS.

- *Standard HDD* – Used for backups and infrequently accessed file storage.

Premium SSD V2 disks have configurable IOPS and throughput, subject to limits per GiB like Ultra disks. Pricing is also complex, counting each provisioned capacity element (size, IOPS, throughput) in a formula to determine the actual price. Ultra disks, while generally available, are subject to specific region availability as well as functional and size limits according to region.

VM Support for Storage Types

Only certain series VMs support Premium, Premium V2, and Ultra Disks. Any VM with a lowercase "s" in the name will support Premium disks. The throughput and IOPS limits will still depend on the VM series and size (vCore count). While this generally also indicates Ultra disk compatibility, it is not definitive. You must check your desired VM for Ultra and Premium V2 compatibility; there is no naming convention letter to indicate availability or compatibility for either. Ultra and Premium V2 disks default to 4K sector sizes but can be configured with 512-byte sectors. 4K is best for SQL data. SQL has specific issues with AOAG that may require trace flag configuration to mitigate if the log devices on different nodes have dissimilar block sizes.

Host Caching

Microsoft recommends enabling Host Read Caching for Azure SQL Data Disks and No Caching for Log Disks. If your Virtual Machine type supports write acceleration, it should be enabled. Only a few VM types support this feature, specifically the Storage-Optimized machines.

Striping Disks for Performance

It is possible for very large VMs that are Bandwidth Optimized (we go over this concept later in this chapter) to have higher IOPS and throughput capability than a single disk pair (Data + Log) can support. For these cases, Microsoft recommends provisioning multiple Ultra or Premium/Premium V2 disks and striping the disks at the OS level using

Storage Spaces. Do not stripe using any degree of redundancy; simple striping is best here. Redundancy is provided by the Azure Storage system, and the overhead for local redundancy will more than cancel any speed improvements you would obtain from multiple disks.

Configure Resource Governor for Performance

Resource Governor is one of the most misunderstood features of SQL Server. Many DBAs are baffled by unexpected outcomes after configuring Resource Governor. Here we will dive into Resource Governor and explain exactly what it does and how to use it.

Resource Governor exists to protect one set of queries from another set of queries by guaranteeing certain groups of queries priority access to specific resources such as CPU time. Originally, Resource Governor only protected CPU resources, but was later expanded to include Physical I/O and Memory. Resource Governor exists in all forms of Azure SQL, but Azure SQL Database blocks any user configuration of Resource Governor. Resource Governor along with other features is used internally by the Azure SQL Database service to provision and isolate CPU and Memory for each Azure SQL Database on a physical host.

Before we examine how Resource Governor works with each resource, let's explore how Resource Governor is configured and set some terminology. The first concept is a Resource Pool. A Resource Pool represents a portion of the total resource available in the SQL instance, expressed in percentages. By default, SQL has two pools named Internal and Default. The Internal pool is unalterable and has no limits. The Internal pool runs the SQL engine itself and cannot be altered in any way. The Default Pool runs all user queries. You can create additional User Pools but cannot remove the Default Pool or the Internal Pool. Starting with SQL Server 2016, there is an External pool for features like the "R" language server in addition to the Default and Internal Pools.

Pools have a MIN% and a MAX% setting. These interact in ways that may yield unexpected results but are entirely predictable if you understand how Resource Governor calculates Effective MAX%. The first rule is that the sum of all MIN% values in all pools cannot exceed 100%. You cannot guarantee more than 100% of any resource in a system. You can have the Pools' MIN% sum to less than 100%, and there is no harm. The MIN% value is a Protected amount, not a Reserved amount. A Reserved MIN%

setting of 20% would prevent any other pool from using 20% of the target resource. A Protected MIN% setting of 20% will allow other resource pools to use that CPU unless the designated pool is using that resource to that capacity.

One common Resource Governor scenario is to create an Analytics pool to isolate Analytics queries on an OLTP system with the goal to protect the OLTP queries remaining in the Default Pool. The DBA sets a CPU MIN% of 75% for the Default Pool and 25% for the Analytics Pool. MAX% is set for 100% for the OLTP and 25% for the Analytics pool. After configuring, the OLTP workload still consumes 90% of the CPU and the Analytics workload only 10%, just as it did prior to deploying Resource Governor. This is entirely normal and predictable. If you removed the Analytics workload, the OLTP workload would still consume only 10% of the CPU. Other pools can always use unused CPU and IOPS resources, regardless of their MAX%. MAX% only matters if there is contention for resources. If a MIN% target has not been reached, the protected resources are released for other pools to use.

A DBA can set a hard limit on CPU consumption with the CAP_CPU_PERCENT Resource pool setting. This acts as an internal Provisioned capacity for a particular pool.

MIN% and MAX% work differently for memory than for CPU. First, Memory means query execution memory, not buffer pool memory. Buffer Pool memory is a global resource. Query Execution Memory is allocated to a pool and will remain there as long as the MIN% is not exceeded *and* no other pool is requesting memory. Memory is not deallocated immediately after use unless the server is under memory pressure. CPU and IOPS are ephemeral resources; allocations for one slice of time do not carry over to the next time slice. Memory may stay persistently allocated and prevent future memory allocations for other pools.

The previous paragraphs used the non-specific term "workload" to differentiate sets of queries. The actual object for this is called a Workload Group. Workload Groups are assigned to Resource Pools. Workload Groups have a many-to-one relationship with Resource Pools. A Resource Pool can have many Workload Groups. A Workload Group is technically a collection of sessions expressed as Server Process IDs (SPIDs). Any query executed on a session uses resources from the assigned pool.

The final piece of the puzzle is the Classifier Function. This is a user-defined function that executes against every newly created session to determine which Workload Group the session belongs to. That assignment is immutable during the lifetime of the session. Connection pooling has no effect on the classifier function. It still runs for every new session even if the underlying connection is pooled. The classifier function can refer to SQL Tables, other functions, or anything that is known about the session at the time of connection. The Classifier function runs immediately after login authentication and after login triggers (if they exist) are run. The Classifier function returns the name of the Workload Group the session is to be assigned to. Any session generating an error, a NULL, or a value that does not match a Workload Group name is assigned to the default Workload Group. Dedicated Admin Connection (DAC) queries execute in the context of the Internal Resource Group and are not subjected to the Classifier Function.

You can examine the Resource Pools and Workload Groups using the following System DMVs in Example 10-1.

Example 10-1. Resource Governor DMVs

```
sys.resource_governor_resource_pools
sys.resource_governor__workload_groups
```

While it is possible to use a lookup table in a Classifier function, such as to implement schedule-based resource management, it is highly discouraged. Lookup table contention could cause a classifier function timeout resulting in a terminated connection. Exercise extreme caution and test thoroughly before implementing any complex logic in a Resource Governor Classifier function. These functions need to execute extremely rapidly.

Before we wrap up discussion about user-defined Resource Pools and Workload Groups, we need to examine the special characteristics of the Internal Pool. The Internal Pool exists to isolate internal SQL operations from user-defined Resource Governor pool limitations. There are no limits on any resource for any session assigned to the Internal Workload Group. Percentages for the remaining pools are calculated *after* the Internal Pool usage is deducted. For all practical purposes, the Internal Pool and its corresponding Internal Workload Group exist outside of Resource Governor.

Implement Database-Scoped Configuration

Azure SQL Database presents some unique challenges by using a Logical Server instead of a Physical Server. We have addressed some of those in prior chapters and will continue to find new implications as we continue. Obviously, there is a physical host server somewhere behind the scenes. Equally obviously, the actual server is a resource no user should ever have visibility or access to. Since there is no actual server object a user can use to change server-scoped configurations, this puts those server-scoped configuration options out of reach. Microsoft has responded to this challenge by creating Database-Scoped configuration options. These options are in addition to the database-level options that existed prior to introducing this feature.

Many options are set naturally at the database level. The database is the scope for transactional consistency and recoverability, so the Recovery Model is naturally a database setting. Other settings are also database level by default. These natural database settings are accessed using the `ALTER DATABASE` command. These settings include the following:

- `Database Recovery Model`

- `Automatic Tuning Settings`

- `Automatic Statistics Creation and Update`

- `Query Store options`

- `Snapshot Isolation`

- `Database Compatibility Level`

These do not have any impact on other databases on a server, regardless of whether it is a logical or physical server.

Database-Scoped changes are the only way to apply certain changes in Azure SQL Database, given the lack of a physical server for server-scoped configuration settings. These settings also exist in Azure SQL Managed Instance and Azure SQL VMs – depending on version. In Azure SQL Managed Instance and Azure SQL VMs, the server-scoped settings still exist at the server level but can be overridden at the database level. The settings exist across the platform for consistency and use the `ALTER DATABASE SCOPED CONFIGURATION` command. You can use the `ALTER CONFIGURATION` command to change the corresponding server-scoped configuration setting on supported platforms. The list of database-scoped configuration changes includes the following:

- Maximum Degree of Parallelism (MAXDOP)

- Legacy Cardinality Estimation

- Last Query Plan Stats

- Optimizing for Ad Hoc Workloads

Note that some of these settings can be further overridden at the individual query level.

Configure Compute and Storage Resources for Scaling

Back in Chapter 1 when we described the fundamental characteristics of cloud computing, we discussed *Elasticity* – the ability to expand and contract resources as your workload varies. Sometimes the only way to improve performance is to provision more resources. Conversely, sometimes you overprovision resources and need to reduce costs. This is a common occurrence for seasonal workloads. For Azure SQL DB and Azure SQL MI, this is a seamless process. Select the new compute size and Azure does all the work. Worst case, your resizing options may be limited due to the amount of storage you have allocated and consumed. For SQL on Azure VMs, this process is a bit more complicated.

The first restriction is that resizing Azure SQL VMs usually requires a reboot. You can mitigate the impact of a reboot if you have High-Availability technology deployed such as Always-On Availability Groups or Failover Clustered Instances (FCIs). We will cover these technologies in Part 5, Chapters 14–16. Resize/reboot a passive node, fail over the workload, and resize/reboot the remaining node. More nodes can be managed by "walking" the nodes one at a time for resizing/rebooting.

The second restriction is that it is very difficult to change the Series of a Virtual Machine once it is configured and deployed. You can change the Size within a series easily, but changing series is much more complex. We discussed the naming conventions and purposes of various VM series in Chapter 3. You may want to refresh your understanding by reviewing that chapter before we continue.

To change the series of a VM, you have to completely turn off the VM. Only certain changes to/from are supported even with a full power cycle. The biggest constraint is that you cannot change to a VM series that does not support all the current configuration options. For example, if you are currently using Azure Premium Storage for your SQL Data and Logs, the new VM Series must support premium storage as well. It also must support at least as many disks as you have attached. Azure will not check operational limitations and Storage Bandwidth since the lowest constraint (VM or storage) becomes the actual constraint. Figure 10-3 shows a partial list of machine types available to change to for a particular Azure SQL Virtual Machine.

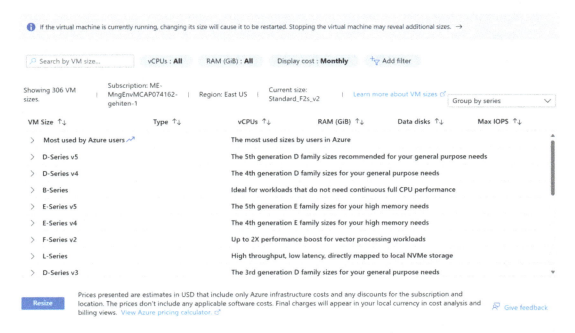

Figure 10-3. *Azure SQL Virtual Machine Types (Partial)*

Constrained Cores

One of the key concepts of cloud computing is proportionality. You can think of a virtual machine as a share of a physical machine. Each VM has a share of cores, memory, and IOPS/throughput. Each resource is provisioned in proportion to the other resources. If you have one quarter of the cores, you likely have one quarter of the memory and storage bandwidth as well. Most of the time this is fine. All workloads hit some resource limit at some point, but each workload may find a different resource to be its limiting factor. You almost never find a perfect balance of all three resources in a system for any workload.

The complication comes from SQL License costs. SQL Server on Azure SQL VMs is licensed per vCPU (cores in Azure-speak), exactly like it is on-premises. In Azure, you can pay for a License "up front" or rent a license along with the Virtual Machine. Either way, you need a license for each vCPU. Disabling certain SQL schedulers does not eliminate the need to license the vCPUs managed by those schedulers. All cores/vCPUs in an Operating System Environment (OSE) in Azure or On-Premises must be licensed for SQL Server. To save SQL License costs, it would be advantageous to have that same proportion of memory and IO capacity but with fewer vCPUs.

In Azure this is accomplished by creating VMs with Constrained Cores. Certain cores are disabled at the virtualization layer, so they are not present in the Operating System Environment (OSE) and therefore do not require SQL licenses. Figure 10-4 shows several Virtual Machine Sizes with eight vCPUs but different memory and storage capacities.

VM Size ↑↓	Type ↑↓	vCPUs ↑↓	RAM (GiB) ↑↓	Data disks ↑↓	Max IOPS ↑↓
E8ads_v5	Memory optimized	8	64	16	12800
E8bds_v5	Memory optimized	8	64	16	22000
E8ds_v5	Memory optimized	8	64	16	12800
E16-8ads_v5	Memory optimized	8	128	32	25600
E16-8ds_v5	Memory optimized	8	128	32	25600
E32-8ads_v5	Memory optimized	8	256	32	51200
E32-8ds_v5	Memory optimized	8	256	32	51200

Figure 10-4. *Constrained Core Sizes*

The E16 and E32 machines have the memory and storage capacity resources that 16- and 32-vCPU systems would normally have, hence the designation, but only present eight vCPUs to the OSE, requiring only eight cores of SQL Licensing. The actual cost of the hardware is still what the 16- or 32-vCPU machine would cost since you are still provisioning the same share of the host computer; it is just the vCPU presentation is altered to optimize SQL licensing costs.

General Purpose

Another fundamental tenet of cloud computing is that *compute* resources are commodities. Web, Application, or Data hardware is fundamentally the same and is interchangeable for most purposes. As with any commodity, the more common the use, the better the pricing. For most Azure SQL Virtual Machine workloads, General-Purpose Virtual Machines are going to be the most cost-effective solution. First explore General-Purpose VM series and sizes before trying to find something custom that exactly matches what you currently use. Remember, your current system was based on either hardware availability in the past *or* Virtual Machine provisioning rules not created by DBAs. That's why it is essential to know what resources your workload consumes in order to find the most cost-effective solution that meets your performance needs.

Bandwidth Full

Starting with the E*nn*-V5 series of Virtual Machines in 2022, Microsoft created a series of machines specifically for high-bandwidth (IOPS/throughput) SQL Servers. These machines have a greater storage bandwidth than the E*nn*-V4 series machines without constrained cores. These are based on newer Intel CPU and Chipset Architectures with overall greater throughput capacities. These VMs are a way to increase storage bandwidth without increasing core or constraining core capacity for storage bandwidth–intensive workloads. Microsoft designates these with a lowercase "b" in the size name.

Configure Intelligent Query Processing (IQP)

Prior to SQL 2017, Microsoft had largely focused on adding features to SQL Server rather than improving its core Query Processor (QP) functionality. Starting with SQL 2017, Microsoft began applying lessons learned from Azure SQL to expanding the capabilities of the Query Processor itself. These improvements are collectively known as Intelligent Query Processing (IQP).

These improvements were largely created and tested in Azure, so Azure SQL (DB and MI) has these same improvements. Many of these changes targeted specific anti-patterns commonly found in queries across multiple workloads – often coming from Imperative-style programming techniques. Due to the significance of the changes, they are "locked" behind compatibility mode switches. Some of these features were upgraded from version to version, requiring you to test and select which version of the feature you want by choosing a database compatibility level. The intent of this section is to give you basic familiarity with the most common IQP improvements along with how to select which ones work best for your workload. This is not a comprehensive discussion or description of all IQP improvements to date. No such comprehensive knowledge is required for the DP-300 exam.

Adaptive Query Processing

Adaptive Query Processing is one of the first and most comprehensive changes in Intelligent Query Processing. Adaptive Query Processing was first introduced in SQL 2017 and made use of the Query Store introduced in the previous version, SQL 2016. Each successive release has added new features to Adaptive Query Processing and improved existing features. Most of the improvements have been in utilizing various feedback mechanisms powered by the Query Store to improve estimates. Memory Grand Feedback (SQL 2017, SQL 2019, SQL 2022), Cardinality Estimate Feedback (SQL 2022), and Degree of Parallelism Feedback (SQL 2022) are all part of the Adaptive Query Processing feature set.

Table Variable Deferred Compilation

As we covered in Chapter 9, SQL Server uses a *cost-based optimizer*. Poor cardinality estimates give skewed costs, which lead to poorly performing query plans. One seemingly insurmountable challenge was estimating costs for objects that do not exist at compilation time. One such object is a Table Variable. Until the Table Variable is created and populated, the Query Processor has no idea what the size or count of the table will be. This same problem exists for Table-Valued Functions, but that is not part of this solution. Microsoft arbitrarily chose to use one row as the count for a Table Variable for the optimizer, more to act as a placeholder value than any meaningful guess. Starting with SQL 2019 (compatibility level 150), SQL will defer optimization of plan elements referencing table variables until the first execution of a query line that populates the variable. At that time, the remaining portion of the query is optimized. Note that any subsequent changes are not accounted for; only the first change is counted for optimization purposes. The table is not re-optimized if it changes row counts.

Parameter-Sensitive Optimization

Prior to SQL 2022, SQL Server could only have one active plan in cache (technically two plans existed, but they were the same plan with and without parallelism). Forcing a plan would replace all occurrences of the plan. Parameter-Sensitive Plans (PSPs) are plans that behave significantly differently depending on the exact set of parameters. Parameter-Sensitive Optimizations allow for multiple plans to be kept in cache. Selecting which plan is executed depends on the actual parameter values supplied to the query at runtime.

One example of a Parameter-Sensitive Plan is the "If @parameter1 = ColumnValue OR @Parameter1 IS NULL" construction. This is intended to implement Optional Parameters but in reality generates plans that fit a particular combination of parameters and perform poorly for others. This works for Imperative languages like C# where all branches are realized and optimized during compilation but not for a Declarative language like T-SQL where only the parameter-based branch is optimized.

There are two important limitations to be aware of with Parameter-Sensitive Optimization. First, it takes multiple plan executions to detect the PSP pattern and which parameter(s) the plan is sensitive to. This may mean suffering through less than ideal performance while the system learns. Second, there are limits to how many plans/parameter combinations the system can adapt to. If there are too many parameter combinations, the system will not be able to accommodate all combinations.

Enabling Intelligent Query Processing

Intelligent Query Processing options are enabled and disabled by compatibility mode settings. You get the complete set of all features created and updated for the current compatibility mode as well as the ones inherited from prior versions. Changing compatibility mode can be done from SQL Server Management Studio Database Properties as seen in Figure 10-5.

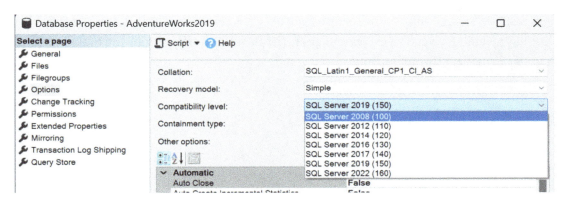

Figure 10-5. *Change Compatibility Mode via SSMS*

Compatibility mode can also be set via a T-SQL command as shown in Example 10-2.

Example 10-2. Change Compatibility Mode via T-SQL

```
USE [master]
GO
ALTER DATABASE [AdventureWorks2019] SET COMPATIBILITY_LEVEL = 160
GO
```

Microsoft strongly recommends leaving any workload migrated to Azure on its original compatibility mode for at least 30 days to provide the Query Store a performance baseline unless you have a compelling reason to advance the compatibility mode to enable a specific feature. While it is tempting to immediately turn on the shiny, cool, new feature, it is safest to let SQL Server work the way you are used to before making any drastic changes.

Chapter and Part Summary

This chapter ends our journey into Azure SQL Performance Management. We learned the importance of understanding our workloads and how they impacted resource consumption. We learned about tools to measure and persist performance data so we could spot exceptions and predict future growth. We deeply explored the Query Optimizer and how we could enable it to find and keep the "best" plan. Finally, we looked at how to optimize our Azure SQL platform for the most cost-effective performance. As with most topics, we covered enough for you to understand the topic and pass the exam. Many of these topics have a great deal of training material available should you feel the need to explore further. Think of this as the beginning of your Azure SQL Performance Tuning journey.

PART IV

Configure and Manage Automation

CHAPTER 11

Create and Manage SQL Agent Jobs

This chapter begins Part 4 of this study guide, corresponding to the fourth section of the DP-300 exam Learning Path. This part is on Automation, an essential skill for any Cloud Database or Systems Administrator. One of the oft-repeated phrases cloud advocates say is "cattle, not pets." We need to be able to manage a large group of SQL Instances across multiple SQL Services without expending additional effort per server. Automation is how we make that transition from taking care of a small number of beloved pets (Servers) to the care, feeding, and maintenance of many profitable herd assets (SQL fleets or farms).

In this part, we will explore the full range of tools for automating processes in Azure, both for building and for operating Azure SQL Services. We will start in this chapter with a deep review of SQL Agent jobs in Azure SQL Managed Instance and Azure SQL Virtual Machines.

SQL Agent

SQL Agent is the companion service to the SQL Server Engine. SQL Agent goes back to the beginnings of SQL Server before tools such as Enterprise Scheduling or Enterprise Alerting were built into the Windows Server Operating System or available from third parties. SQL Agent originally had two functions. First, it monitored the SQL Server Service, alerted operators, and restarted SQL when the service crashed. This was necessary on early versions of SQL Server and Windows Server as the platform and services lacked the robustness and maturity of modern enterprise-class software.

The second job of SQL Agent is the one we typically associate with the service, managing scheduled tasks associated with SQL Server. SQL Agent is a robust task scheduling platform with a direct, implicit connection to its corresponding SQL Server

© Geoff Hiten 2025
G. Hiten, *Administering Microsoft Azure SQL Solutions*, Certification Study Companion Series,
https://doi.org/10.1007/979-8-8688-1585-0_11

service. SQL Agent uses a Job/Job Step/Job schedule model to manage specific tasks. SQL Agent is often used to trigger SQL Server Integration Services (SSIS) jobs, export data on a schedule, and – most importantly for our consideration here – execute maintenance tasks.

Since this book is primarily targeted at data professionals, I will present the SQL Agent structure in terms of its underlying tables. The SQL Agent job system is controlled via the contents of nine tables in the msdb database. These tables are as follows:

- sysjobactivity
- sysjobhistory
- sysjobs
- sysjobschedules
- sysjobservers
- sysjobsteps
- sysjobstepslogs
- sysschedules
- syssessions

These entities are represented in the Entity-Relationship (E-R) diagram shown in Figure 11-1.

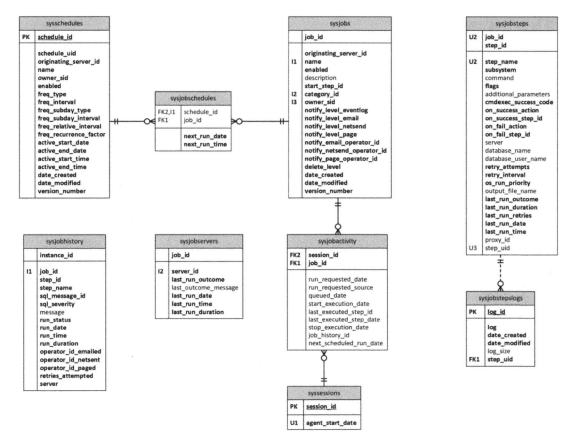

Figure 11-1. *SQL Agent Job System E-R Diagram*

The diagram shown in Figure 11-1 exactly matches the table definitions as extracted from SQL 2022 RTM, but is completely unchanged since at least SQL 2000 and possibly further back. There are application tier parent–child relationships between sysjobs and three other tables (sysjobsteps, sysjobhistory, and sysjobservers) that are not implemented via declarative referential integrity constraints in SQL Server, so they do not show on this diagram. The SQL Agent job system data model has two top-level entities, sysjobs and sysschedules.

SQL Agent can be administered by any member of the sysadmin fixed server role or any member of the SQLAgentOperatorRole fixed database role in the *msdb* database.

SQL Agent Jobs

The first top-level entity of SQL Agent is the Job. A SQL Agent job is a collection of individual job steps. Jobs implement step ordering and completion notification with success/failure and support basic flow control between steps. Job definitions are stored in the sysjobs table. You can create, read, update, and delete records directly in the sysjobs tables with the correct permissions; however, it is more practical to use the SQL Agent controls in SQL Server Management Studio.

The sysjobservers table is used for multi-server job administration, a feature that is not supported in Azure SQL Managed Instance. From a practical perspective, very few environments use multi-server job administration since it introduces many more complexities than it solves. Most organizations use newer tools to accomplish cross-server job administration. Multi-server job administration is not a covered topic for the DP-300 exam, so we will not explore its details here.

sysjobhistory is used to track completed jobs, while sysjobactivity and syssessions are used by SQL Agent to track current Job and Agent Execution status.

SQL Agent Job Steps

The actual work in a SQL Agent job is done by individual job steps. Each job step is an independent execution task and is represented by an individual row in the sysjobsteps table. Job steps execute tasks in specific *subsystems*. Each subsystem is a unique execution environment. Due to security restrictions of a PaaS platform, not all subsystems are supported in Azure SQL Managed Instance. The complete list of SQL Server Job Step subsystems available on Azure SQL VMs is as follows:

- Operating System (CmdExec)
- PowerShell
- Replication Distributor
- Replication Merge
- Replication Queue Reader
- Replication Snapshot

- Replication Transaction Log Reader

- SQL Server Analysis Services Command

- SQL Server Analysis Services Query

- SQL Server Integration Services Package

- Transact-SQL (T-SQL) Command

Prior versions of SQL Server had an ActiveX subsystem, but that has been deprecated and removed.

Job steps control the next step action on success or failure, providing a basic flow control mechanism. The sysjobsteps table also tracks basic run information (last times, duration, success/failure) to help diagnose problems. These tables, like many production database tables, do not exactly align with Third Normal Form, but they work very well as evidenced by the fact they have remained unchanged for many versions across more than two decades.

SQL Agent Schedules

The existence of the top-level tables sysjobs and sysschedules along with the bridge table sysjobschedules implies that schedules exist outside the context of an individual job. This would be a correct assumption. Schedules are named entities that can be associated with multiple jobs. Schedules exist independently of jobs or job steps. SQL Server includes eight predefined schedules to match common use scenarios as shown in Figure 11-2. Each Schedule is persisted by a matching row in the sysschedules table.

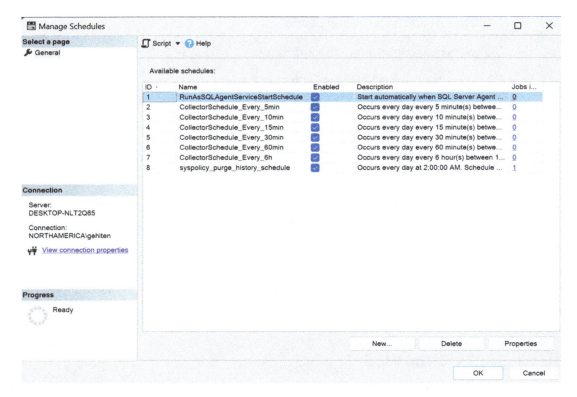

Figure 11-2. *SQL Agent Predefined Schedules*

Schedules are complex entities with multiple options. Let's examine one of the predefined SQL Agent Schedules using the SQL Agent Schedule control in SSMS, shown in Figure 11-3, and explore what options it provides.

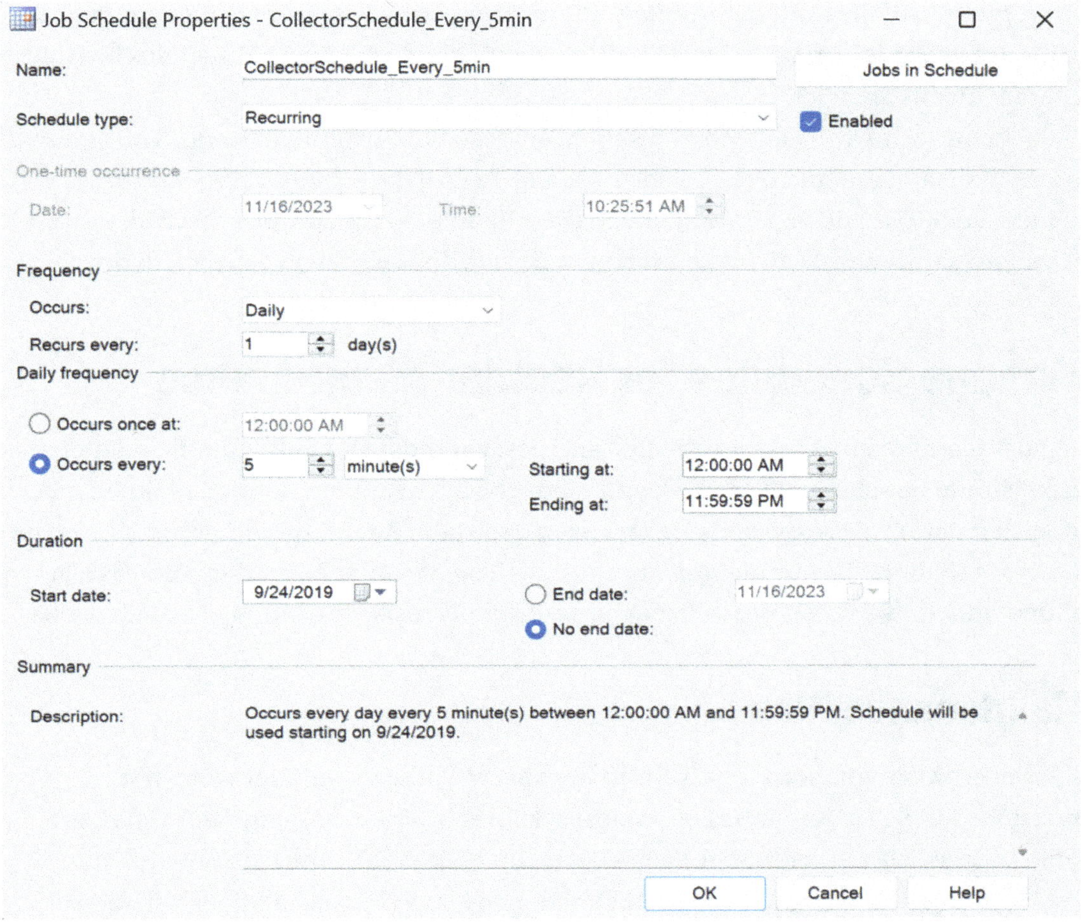

Figure 11-3. *SQL Agent Schedule Details*

The *Name* is cosmetic but should be unique and identify the key characteristics of the schedule. The *Schedule type* shows as "Recurring," which is what most people think of when the word "schedule" comes up. However, a schedule can also be set to run once. This is useful for a long-running query where you do not want to leave a client application such as SSMS running on a console somewhere. The One-time occurrence section is only enabled for the one-time schedule type and is self-explanatory. If the one-time occurrence is enabled, the remaining scheduling options are disabled, and the corresponding column values in the sysschedules table are disregarded. Schedules can also run at Agent startup or when the system CPU has idle time. *Frequency* uses multiple columns in the row to determine exactly how often the schedule recurs. *Occurs* options are Daily, Weekly, or Monthly. Each option changes the schedule page as well as the interpretation of the underlying data column. This is why it is strongly recommended to always use SSMS or Azure Data Studio to manipulate SQL Agent Schedules to avoid internal inconsistencies.

Schedules are also enabled or disabled and can have expiration times. The Summary is automatically generated to provide a second view of the schedule. It is very easy to misread the UI and generate an incorrect schedule, so the summary provides an excellent "sanity check" to make sure the schedule does what you expect it to do.

Manage Schedules for Regular Maintenance

Regular maintenance tasks are the first and best candidate for automation. Maintenance tasks should be scheduled, alerted, and managed by exception. Routine maintenance tasks that perform as expected need no extra oversight. A DBA should only get involved if there is a failure. If your maintenance tasks fail on a regular basis, then there is a larger, underlying problem that needs fixing beyond simply restarting the specific failed jobs.

Maintenance Plans

SQL Server Maintenance Plans were an unexpected boon when they were first introduced in SQL 2008 alongside its host platform SQL Server Integration Services (SSIS). Since SQL Server Maintenance Plans run as SSIS jobs, they are not available for Azure SQL DB or Azure SQL MI. Maintenance Plans are part of Microsoft's effort to provide a "comprehensive solution" with native services for SQL Server. Prior to maintenance plans, SQL Server DBAs had to write their own scripts to handle all maintenance tasks, including backups. Because of the multiple technical elements of handling backups, including file naming, retention, and alerting, most solutions focused on creating valid backups rather than on overall system point-in-time recoverability for a specified history window. Many backup solutions did not use differential backups to optimize both space usage and recovery times. Indexing was generally a "roll your own" or community-shared mishmash of scripts with varying degrees of effectiveness.

SQL Server Maintenance Plans provide a built-in, readily deployed, standard solution for database maintenance tasks including backup scheduling and management. Best of all, the plans are easily created by a SQL Server Management Studio Wizard.

The SQL Server Maintenance Plan Wizard can be started from the Object Explorer Tree under Management ➤ Maintenance Plans. Right-click and select "Maintenance Plan Wizard." You can also manually build a Maintenance Plan by choosing "New Maintenance Plan," but most of the time the wizard does exactly what you need. The first page has you name the plan and decide on a schedule. You can make a new schedule, select an existing one, or have no schedule at all. Recall that Schedules and Jobs are independent top-level entities in the SQL Agent data model. If you choose to schedule the plan, you can have each task run under a separate schedule or just run everything all at once. This is convenient when setting up a new server as you can make sure the basic tasks are all covered until you have time to optimize.

Figure 11-4 shows the second page of the Maintenance Plan Wizard with the list of tasks you can select.

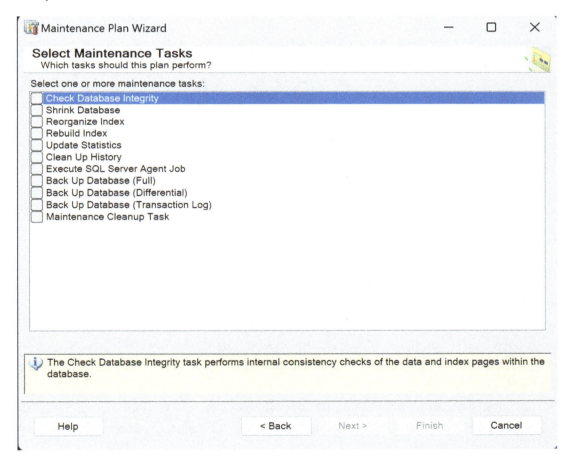

Figure 11-4. *Maintenance Plan Wizard Task List*

The Execute SQL Server Agent Job allows you to include other tools and tasks into maintenance plans or to combine existing tasks into a sequence. If you choose multiple tasks, the next page (not shown) will allow you to select the order in which the tasks are executed. At this point, the "next" page to configure the specific task is entirely dependent on the task(s) you selected. The order presented is the order from the selection list, not the order you choose to have the tasks executed.

Figure 11-5 shows one of the most powerful elements of Maintenance Plans, the database selection dialog box. This allows you to select all databases, user databases, system databases, all except a list of databases, or just a specific list of databases. The database sets, excluding the exact list, are evaluated at runtime, not when the schedule is saved. New databases are automatically added to the set each time the job is executed if they meet the list criteria. This selection option applies to any maintenance plan task that targets *databases*.

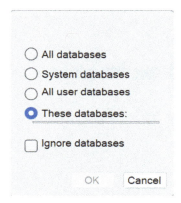

Figure 11-5. *Maintenance Plan Database Selection*

From here, each page offers tuning parameters for each task. While the defaults will work as a baseline, make sure the choices are applicable to your specific system. Your best bet for learning this is to get in and exercise the system. Build a maintenance plan around each task, execute it, and check the logs for the output. See how various options and target choices change the output and interactions. There are far too many options to illustrate here.

As noted at the beginning of this section, Microsoft considers Maintenance Plans an essential element of a comprehensive native solution. Therefore, Maintenance Plans are fair game for the DP-300 exam.

Maintenance Scripts

Maintenance tasks for Azure SQL DB and Azure SQL MI are generally better done via T-SQL or PowerShell scripts. Most maintenance tasks can be done via T-SQL Scripts, the exception being file management for backups. That step generally requires file system access to clear out old backups. Fortunately for us, backups are internally managed by Azure SQL PaaS services as a part of Point-in-Time Recovery (PiTR). We no longer need to manage the process; we simply configure the retention times. We still need to manage index and statistics maintenance tasks ourselves. We can use SQL Agent on Azure SQL Managed Instance to schedule T-SQL scripts such as those written by Ola Hallengren to keep our indexes and statistics fresh. Since these scripts are not provided or supported by Microsoft, they will not be on the exam, but are an essential item in any SQL Server DBA's toolkit. You can use SQL Agent from Azure SQL Managed Instance to target databases on Azure SQL Database for maintenance script operations.

We still need a tool to manage maintenance tasks for Azure SQL Database in the absence of Azure SQL Managed Instance. We will discuss the various options for automating maintenance tasks for Azure SQL DB in Chapter 13.

Configure Job Alerts and Notifications

Management by Exception requires that a responsible person, the *Operator*, be notified of exceptions so they can take appropriate action. SQL Agent handles this via two entities, *Alerts* and *Operators*.

Alerts

Alerts are a SQL Server Agent–specific way to surface error and alert conditions to a DBA for further action. As we noted at the beginning of this chapter, one of the original tasks of SQL Agent was to monitor SQL Server. In the absence of any other tools, SQL Server Agent can fire alerts to take actions. SQL Agent has limited options for actions. It can notify an operator and/or run a SQL Agent job. Alerts can be raised on three conditions:

- An Alert can be raised on an error set by the SQL Server engine, filtered by database, error number, or error severity.

- An Alert can be raised by a Performance Counter threshold crossing.

- An Alert can be raised by a WMI event (Azure SQL VM only).

259

A DBA can create a comprehensive alerting system using SQL Agent. Most choose not to due to two major limitations. First, each instance of SQL has a completely independent and isolated SQL Agent. All alerts must be manually configured for each SQL Instance. This is not too bad when you only have a handful of "pets" to take care of, but when you scale to hundreds of "cattle" servers, generating an alert framework for each server is not practical. The second limitation is that the Agent cannot see outside the host computer. It cannot alert if the host is "down." SQL Agent Alerts were essential in the earlier days of SQL Server but are less important now that enterprise-wide alerting and monitoring systems are now commonly available. For Azure SQL Managed Instance, Azure itself monitors the service and initiates any failover or recovery activity directly.

Operators

A SQL Agent Operator is simply a collection of contact information used to send alert or job completion notifications to. SQL can send email or pager alerts via the Database Mail connector. Each operator has an email address, an optional pager contact, and an optional pager schedule. Operators can be disabled so alerts and notifications will no longer flow to them. Operators, like Agents, are unique to each server, making large-scale administration challenging. Figure 11-6 shows the choices available for creating a new SQL Agent Operator.

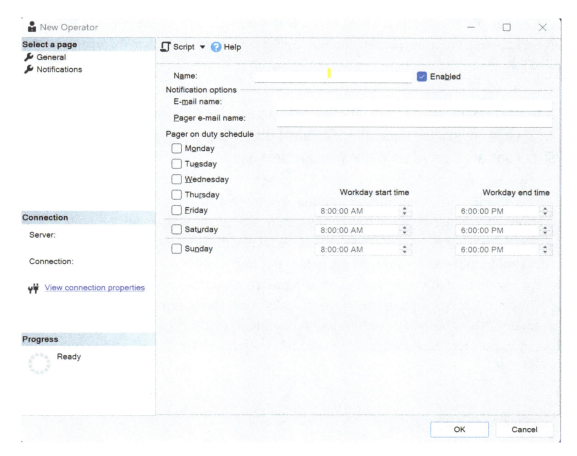

Figure 11-6. *SQL Agent New Operator Choices*

Many customers use third-party tools to generate alerts, create tickets, and notify on-call personnel should the alert require human intervention. Smaller SQL shops still use the built-in alert and notification system for SQL Server.

Troubleshoot SQL Agent Jobs

As with any computer system, eventually a human being will need to intervene and troubleshoot a failed job. SQL Agent provides two native tools to help identify the specific job step that failed. Beyond that, you have to look at the specific subsystem and task the job step executes to identify the exact cause of failure. The first tool is the Job Activity monitor. This is available directly from SSMS Object Explorer below the Jobs entry under SQL Server Agent. This is a good starting point. From here or from SSMS Object Explorer, you can examine the SQL Agent Error Log and look at the history of the failed job.

Note   The SQL Agent Error Log is not the same as the SQL Server Log. SQL Agent Error Logs are located under the SQL Agent Object Explorer entry, while the SQL Error Logs are located under the Management entry.

One specific issue that confounds initial troubleshooting due to extremely non-descriptive error messages is a legacy of the multi-server administration capability that was never removed. A job is designated as local if the originating_job_server field in the sysjobs table is set to zero. If the field is not zero, the job is considered "owned" by another server. Only the other server, designated as the "master" server, can edit or delete this job. Attempting to change it locally results in an error and a rolled-back transaction. This is one of the few times I recommend writing to a SQL Agent table directly in order to force set a job to "local." After that, the job can be "cleaned up" using SSMS.

Chapter Summary

SQL Agent has been a part of SQL Server for most of its history. SQL Agent Scheduled Jobs are still a major part of most SQL Server deployments and are the easiest way to create automated maintenance tasks for SQL Server on Virtual Machines and Managed Instances. *Alerts* and *Operators* round out the capabilities of SQL Agent as it continues to provide many of the essential elements of a comprehensive SQL Management solution. Some of these elements have been superseded by more modern, enterprise-wide tools, but are still important to understand what tasks these tools should perform relative to a SQL Server.

CHAPTER 12

Automate Deployment of Database Resources

This second chapter in our Azure SQL Automation journey is all about how to deploy Azure SQL Services via automated tools. I often joke that the Azure portal is the Fisher-Price version of Azure. It is a visual tool useful for learning, illustrating, and exploring Azure, but it is not the "real" interface. The grown-up version of Azure is accessed via the automation interfaces. When you deploy a resource using the Azure portal, you are simply filling in a form and submitting an automation task. This chapter shows you how to skip the portal "helper" form filler.

Automated Azure deployment brings to life the cloud concept that "infrastructure is code." We will be discussing specific automated tools used to deploy Azure resources. We will not be exploring code lifecycle management tools beyond simple mentions. You will not be tested on that material for the DP-300 exam, nor is it a skill you will likely use often. I am also not going to try and teach the entirety of any automation language. I am not going to provide any working code samples. I will tell you where to find good, working Azure SQL Automation examples.

Many larger organizations have a designated "DevOps" team using Enterprise Code management tools and practices to create automated Azure deployment solutions. You need to be able to understand their work and communicate with them using their terms and definitions to be an effective Azure SQL DBA.

Azure Resource Manager

The Azure Resource Manager is the framework Azure operates on. Every service in Azure is enabled by a Resource Provider with the Azure Resource Manager coordinating the actions of all the individual Resource Providers. Figure 12-1 shows a partial list of resource providers, which can be found on the menu list on the "Subscriptions" blade.

© Geoff Hiten 2025
G. Hiten, *Administering Microsoft Azure SQL Solutions*, Certification Study Companion Series,
https://doi.org/10.1007/979-8-8688-1585-0_12

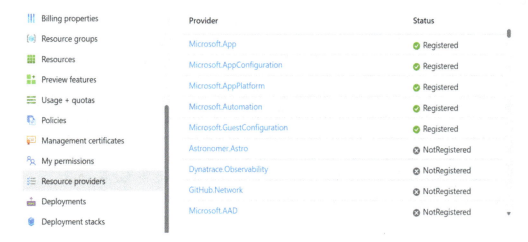

Figure 12-1. *Azure Resource Providers (Partial)*

Note the very small size of the slider bar to the far right. There are hundreds of Resource Providers in Azure. As the figure shows, not all of them are *Registered* – enabled – for every subscription. There are some standard Resource Providers that are enabled for every subscription, but most are only enabled when required. Either *Owner* or *Contributor* role membership at the *Subscription* level is required to register a Resource Provider. Once a provider is registered, then lesser permissions are necessary to deploy individual resources created and managed by that provider.

If you filter the provider list by the keyword "SQL," you get the five results in Figure 12-2.

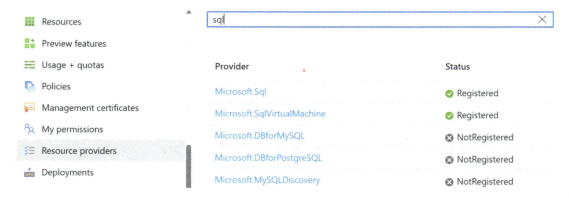

Figure 12-2. *Azure SQL Resource Providers*

The *Microsoft.SQL* provider does the management work for Azure SQL Database and Azure SQL Managed Instance, while the *Microsoft.SQLVirtualMachine* provider does the back-end work for the Azure SQL IaaS Extension we discussed back in Chapter 2.

One key to understanding Azure is that one Azure Resource Provider can call other Azure Resource Providers. Azure SQL Managed Instance General Purpose tier uses Azure Premium Storage to persist the databases and Azure Blob Storage to store backups. Both resources are accessed via the *Microsoft.Storage* Resource Provider. This resource provider is not seen in the portal as part of Azure SQL Managed Instance since the underlying resource is completely managed by the *Microsoft.SQL* provider calling the *Microsoft.Storage* resource provider directly. This is how most resource providers in Azure function. Just like in Windows where one DLL can depend on and thus call another DLL, Resource Providers can depend on and call each other. Unless a Resource Provider is controlling hardware directly, it almost always builds on the basic compute, storage, and networking resource providers in Azure. These resources are the same ones you can provision directly; there are no "hidden" resource providers in Azure. For example, when a Resource requires one or more "captive" virtual machines, the machines allocated are the exact same size, configuration, and names you can allocate directly from the portal or the Resource Provider API.

Tools

If "Infrastructure Is Code," then we must put down our screwdrivers and cable crimpers and pick up our code development tools if we want to deploy Azure resources. Unfortunately, the Azure Resource Manager does not understand the T-SQL language, so SQL Server Management Studio or Azure Data Studio isn't going to be able to help us with this task. We are going to have to learn some new tools.

The objective here is merely surface familiarity and comprehension, not deep understanding. As with any topic we only lightly touch, feel free to dive deeper with other resources if that is something that interests you or is something your job requires.

GitHub

GitHub (`www.github.com`) is a cloud-based platform for code development, management, and sharing. It is the de facto world standard repository for the majority of open source projects while also supporting enterprise closed source development.

Microsoft uses GitHub extensively for sharing non-proprietary solutions with its customers and community, including many templates and examples for both SQL and Azure. Many organizations use GitHub as their enterprise software development repository. As with many topics in this book, entire volumes can be and have been written about GitHub. However, we aren't going to delve very deeply into GitHub. For our purposes, GitHub is an open source repository where we can find Azure SQL examples to leverage for our own use, but that is a small fraction of its capability.

One of the notable repositories within GitHub is the SQL Server Sample repository located at `https://github.com/microsoft/sql-server-samples/`. Here you can find all the SQL Server samples created by Microsoft going back to SQL 2000. New samples are added as new versions and features are released. Items include sample databases in .bak, script, and .bacpac format as appropriate, T-SQL scripts, and even application code to illustrate specific features where necessary. The general rule is every folder in the repository, as well as the top-level folder for the repository itself, has a README. md file to describe the folder contents and how to use and deploy those contents. I suggest browsing the sample folders and deploying any solutions you find interesting. Some repositories include their own automation whereby you fill in a few variables (subscription IDs and resource group names primarily) and the code deploys the example for you automatically.

The SQL Server Sample repository is by no means the only useful repository on GitHub. Many individuals place collections of code and examples on GitHub that are free to share. Some groups welcome new contributors to various projects. As I mentioned earlier, GitHub is *the* core platform for any developer community and can easily provide many rewarding hours of learning.

If you don't want to interact with GitHub any more than necessary, you can simply download a ZIP file copy of any public repository and deploy that in your local system. It will be a completely disconnected copy that has none of GitHub's version management and branch/merge capabilities. That will be enough to follow along with the examples in the rest of this chapter.

If you do not have an account on GitHub, I urge you to create one now. You don't have to fill in any information but the basics (email, password), and it doesn't cost anything. This will allow you to better follow along with the examples we will work through in the rest of the chapter. Many employers ask for a link to your public GitHub repository during an interview process, especially for code-centric positions.

One GitHub repository we will be using is the Azure Quickstart Templates located at `https://github.com/Azure/azure-quickstart-templates`. We will be using examples from this Community-Sourced repository in this chapter. Let's look at the landing page for the repository in Figure 12-3.

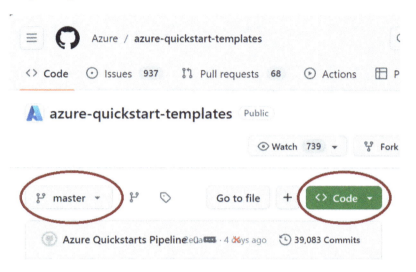

Figure 12-3. *GitHub Repository Controls*

The control on the left determines which *Branch* you are working in. This is almost always "Master" when you are downloading or deploying code from somebody else, but may be a different branch if you are creating the code. Be careful as any actions you take are targeted to this branch. The left control is one we will use a lot, at least when interacting with GitHub directly and not via Visual Studio Code or another tool. Clicking this control shows us Figure 12-4.

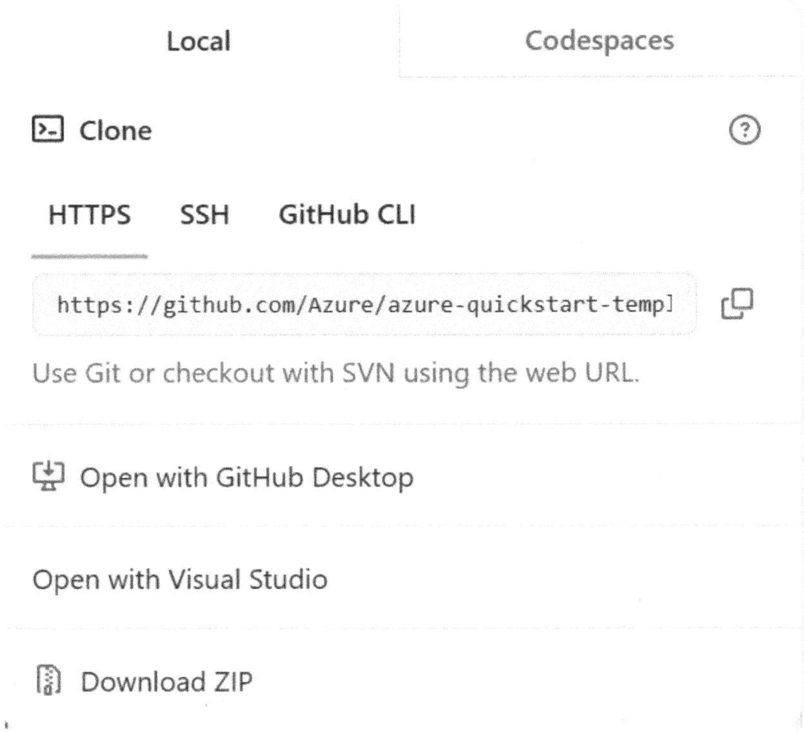

Figure 12-4. *GitHub Code Options*

These are all options on how to interact and use GitHub hosted code. Many times we will simply copy the code and use it. Other times we want to start with GitHub code and extend and modify it ourselves. Either option is fine; just be sure and choose which way suits your current goals.

Visual Studio Code

While it's true that Notepad can be used as a code editor, that doesn't mean it is the best tool for writing Azure Automation code. Notepad skill is not going to be a tested competency in any case. Just like we use SSMS or Azure Data Studio to write and deploy T-SQL code, we should use a purpose-built tool that is optimized for writing Azure Automation.

For most of us, this tool is going to be Visual Studio Code (VS Code). You have already explored one derivative of VS Code called Azure Data Studio. Azure Data Studio is based on Visual Studio Code and inherits many of its capabilities including a comprehensive extension mechanism. A very few of you will be dedicated Azure Infrastructure Developers and will live in Visual Studio. Visual Studio and Visual Studio Code are very different platforms that serve similar purposes. Visual Studio is generally part of an Enterprise Development process, while VS Code is geared more toward an individual worker or small team. The majority of us will use VS Code as our primary Azure deployment automation development tool, so all our examples will continue on that platform.

VS Code can also interact directly with GitHub – managing many of the GitHub activities directly in the tool by leveraging extensions.

Automate Deployment by Using Azure Resource Manager Templates (ARM Templates) and Bicep

We have already discussed the Azure Resource Manager and ARM templates, but Bicep is likely a new term. We haven't discussed it yet in this text. Bicep is a domain-specific language to automate the deployment of Azure resources. Terraform is a more well-known language that is cross-cloud compatible, but since it is not a Microsoft product, it is not going to be on the DP-300 exam. Bicep will be.

Azure Resource Manager Templates

An Azure Resource Manager (ARM) template is a reusable code fragment that will deploy a defined set of resources into an Azure subscription. An ARM template has *Parameters* that can be substituted at runtime to create repeated copies of the resource in different subscriptions or resource groups. Almost every resource in Azure is able to export an automation template based on its current configuration. The template will include the entire scope of the resource in question, including an entire Resource Group. Not everything is configurable directly from ARM. Any such shortcomings will be identified and noted during template creation. Figure 12-5 shows the beginnings of a template derived from an Azure SQL Server with a single database using the AdventureWorksLT image. The template is a .JSON file opened using VS Code.

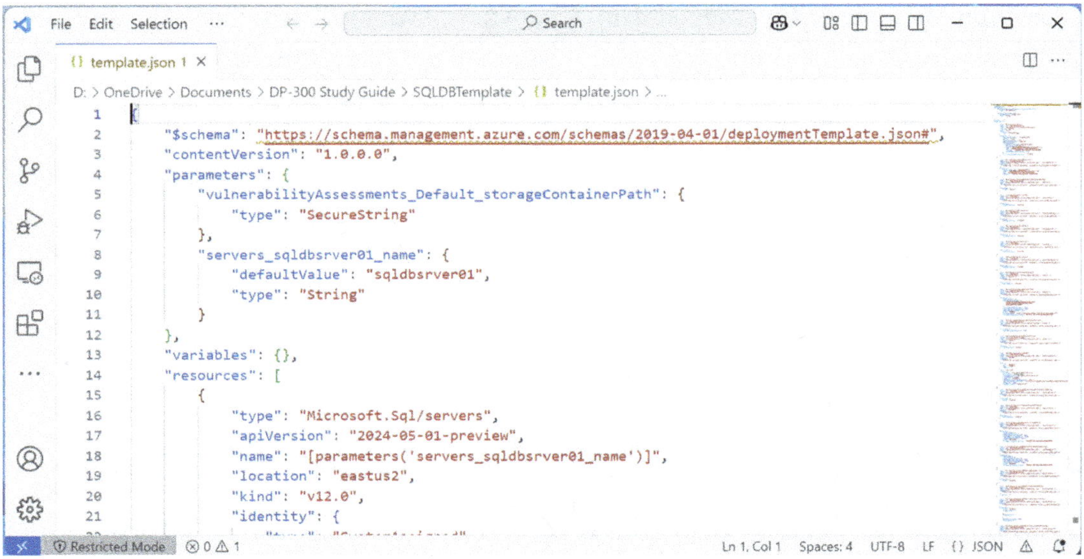

Figure 12-5. *Azure SQL Database ARM Template (Visual Studio Code)*

A quick glance at the left-hand side shows the template for even a simple, basic resource such as a SQL Server and Database is very complex. If I attempted to show the entire template, it would run to several pages. The reason is that an ARM template assumes no default values. ARM templates include *every* possible value exportable by the Azure Resource Providers in use, including provider versions. This particular example runs to 664 lines of code, making direct ARM templates a very precise but largely impractical code platform for automated deployment.

ARM templates aren't targeted toward human developers. When you deploy a resource from the Azure portal, the portal UI creates and fills out the ARM template. That template, which is a JSON format document, is then submitted to the Azure Resource Manager for deployment. You can also export the template prior to deployment, using the Azure portal as an ARM template generator.

In general, JSON documents aren't intended for human consumption; ARM templates are no exception. Most of the time, ARM templates are used to copy or redeploy a resource or resource group within Azure. The template is generated and consumed directly in the portal. You never see nor edit any code. You just supply new parameters.

Bicep

Bicep is a declarative language specifically created for deploying Azure Resources. Terraform is a similar language that can target multiple clouds. Having a language specifically designed to create and manipulate Azure Resources is incredibly useful. Bicep supports all native services, including preview and GA versions. Bicep is also much easier to read and edit than ARM templates. Figure 12-6 shows a sample Bicep code fragment to deploy the same Azure SQL Server and Database.

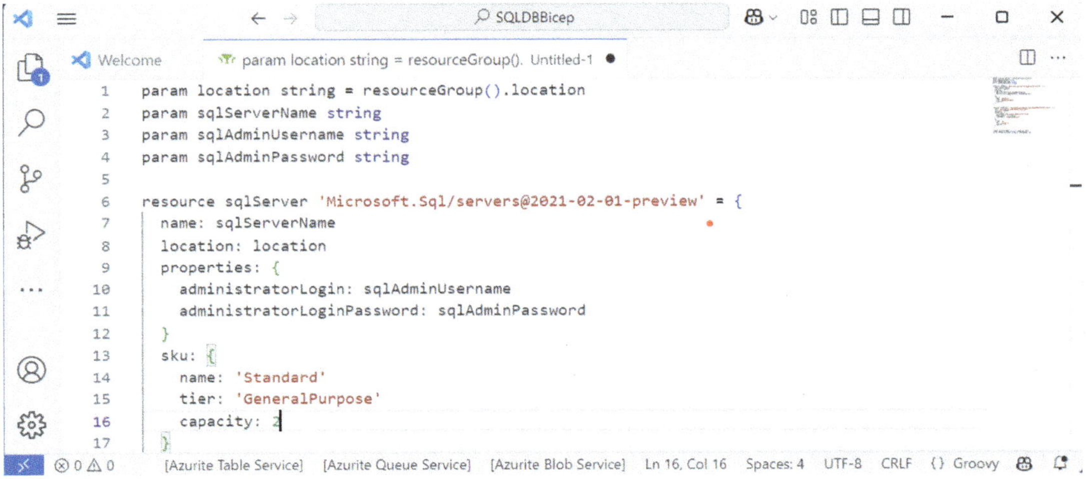

```
1    param location string = resourceGroup().location
2    param sqlServerName string
3    param sqlAdminUsername string
4    param sqlAdminPassword string
5
6    resource sqlServer 'Microsoft.Sql/servers@2021-02-01-preview' = {
7      name: sqlServerName
8      location: location
9      properties: {
10       administratorLogin: sqlAdminUsername
11       administratorLoginPassword: sqlAdminPassword
12     }
13     sku: {
14       name: 'Standard'
15       tier: 'GeneralPurpose'
16       capacity: 2
17   }
```

Figure 12-6. *5 Azure SQL Database Bicep Code*

These 17 lines of code do the exact same job as the 664-line ARM template. You can edit in any parameters such Resource Provider versions or any details you require, but the language assumes default values where possible without a need to expressly create a value.

Bicep can also incorporate ARM templates via the USING command, thus leveraging any existing code you may have. Bicep can be deployed via the PowerShell or CLI or from within Visual Studio Code. Bicep supports the PowerShell What-If syntax.

Automate Deployment by Using PowerShell

PowerShell scripts are the foundation of automation in Azure and in the entire Microsoft software ecosystem. Azure SQL is no exception. When using PowerShell you have two choices – run from your local system or run from the Cloud Shell. To run Azure deployment commands from your local system, you need to install the Azure (AZ) PowerShell module and connect it to your Azure subscription.

Microsoft provides an excellent script at the link in Example 12-1.

Example 12-1. PowerShell Automation Script

```
https://learn.microsoft.com/en-us/azure/azure-sql/database/scripts/create-
and-configure-database-powershell
```

I recommend running this first in the Azure Cloud Shell since that removes the need to install the AZ PowerShell module and connect it to your Azure subscription. The example even has the ability to deploy directly from the web page, although I would suggest downloading it to your environment and editing it before deploying.

Automate Deployment by Using Azure CLI

Those of you coming from the Linux/Unix world often prefer some variation of a Bash CLI shell environment. Microsoft provides exactly such an interface in its Azure CLI environment, also available in local and cloud varieties. "Local" in this case includes Bash shell in Linux, if that is where you are more comfortable.

The exact same script functionality from the "Automate Deployment by Using PowerShell" section is available at the link in Example 12-2.

Example 12-2. Azure CLI Automation Script

```
https://learn.microsoft.com/en-us/azure/azure-sql/database/scripts/create-
and-configure-database-cli
```

As before, I suggest running this in your Cloud Shell directly from the Azure portal, at least for the initial runs.

Automate Scaling Up or Scaling Down

One of the more common requests I hear from customers is why don't we provide a mechanism to automatically scale up or down Database Provisioning on a schedule or in response to increased/decreased workload. The Serverless tier is a partial answer to that, allowing for dynamic billing by the second on highly variable workloads, preferably with long, inactive periods. This helps one scenario, but does not address the most common request. Our customers even remark how easy it is to build and deploy a Workbook that executes a PowerShell script on a fixed schedule to change Database Provisioning.

The reason Microsoft does not provide Dynamic Database Provisioning is because our customers do not support any automation that can change their billing without their approval. Creating and deploying such a mechanism has a huge reputational risk and is counter to the general principle that the customer always has the final say in making changes that would alter the Azure bill. In that vein, Microsoft does provide step-by-step instructions on how to build an auto-scale solution at the link shown in Example 12-3.

Example 12-3. Azure SQL Database Auto-scale

```
https://techcommunity.microsoft.com/blog/azuredbsupport/how-to-auto-scale-
azure-sql-databases/2235441
```

Monitor and Troubleshoot Deployments

One key element to know about Azure Deployments is that your bill does not start accumulating until the resource is provisioned and fully available. This also means that deployment is not a billable service itself; therefore, deployment has no Service-Level Agreement. Deployments may take more or less time than expected, but that is not a billable or actionable issue unless the deployment gets "stuck." All Azure deployments are intentionally throttled in aggregate to not impact the provisioned services running in Azure. Most of the time this does not matter, but it may have an impact on recoverability after a region loss when there will be a "land rush" of people deploying new resources in a failover region.

When you submit an Azure Deployment job via the portal, the portal switches to a "Deployment is in progress" status page shown in Figure 12-7.

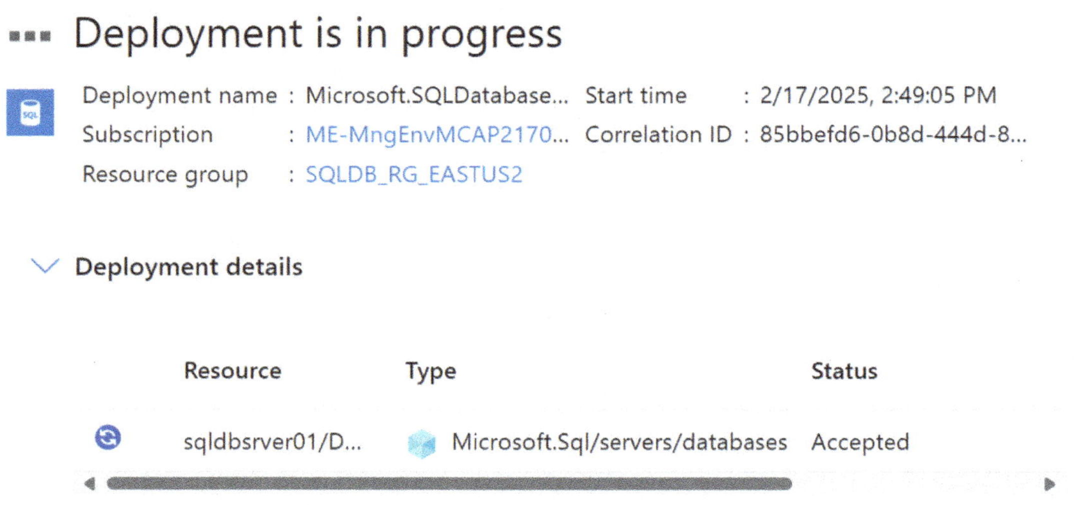

▪▪▪ Deployment is in progress

Deployment name : Microsoft.SQLDatabase...   Start time   : 2/17/2025, 2:49:05 PM

Subscription   : ME-MngEnvMCAP2170... Correlation ID : 85bbefd6-0b8d-444d-8...

Resource group   : SQLDB_RG_EASTUS2

∨ **Deployment details**

Resource	Type	Status
🔄 sqldbsrver01/D...	🔷 Microsoft.Sql/servers/databases	Accepted

◀ ▬▬▬▬▬▬▬▬▬▬▬▬▬▬▬▬▬▬▬▬▬▬▬▬▬▬▬ ▶

Figure 12-7. *Deployment Is in Progress*

With automated (script-based) deployments, you will only receive an error message if the deployment fails. This may be a top-level error message and often conceals the underlying low-level fault that is the real reason for failure.

The Azure Activity Log page, accessible from the Subscription or Resource Group page Tower Menu (left side of screen), shows all Azure activity, including detailed steps for each deployment. Figure 12-8 shows the steps for a new Database Deployment on an existing Server.

Operation name	Status	Time
∨ ⓘ Create Deployment	Succeeded	2 minutes a...
ⓘ Create Deployment	Started	3 minutes a...
ⓘ Create Deployment	Succeeded	3 minutes a...
ⓘ Create Deployment	Accepted	3 minutes a...
ⓘ Update SQL database	Started	3 minutes a...
ⓘ 'auditIfNotExists' Policy action.	Started	3 minutes a...
ⓘ Update SQL database	Accepted	3 minutes a...
ⓘ Get Azure SQL Database(s) List	Running	3 minutes a...
ⓘ Get Azure SQL Database(s) List	Running	3 minutes a...
ⓘ Get Azure SQL Database(s) List	Running	3 minutes a...
ⓘ Get Azure SQL Database(s) List	Running	2 minutes a...
ⓘ Update SQL database	Succeeded	2 minutes a...

Figure 12-8. Deployment Activity Log

Clicking any single line goes to the detail page showing the complete operation name, the resource affected, and the JSON ARM Template that the Azure Resource Manager consumed to implement that step. Additional columns showing Resource Groups, who submitted the deployment, the target subscription, and other elements are available. Results can be filtered by any of these columns.

Azure Verified Modules

One of the greatest challenges in the modern code development world is finding code sources that you can trust. Azure is no exception. The problem is not so much avoiding bad actors, but in finding code that reflects current best design and security practices, is clear and concise, is aligned with the Microsoft Well-Architected Framework, has been thoroughly tested, and accomplishes the desired task. GitHub SQL Examples is a good source for learning, but the code examples are often contrived and severely limited to illustrate a particular language element or product feature. None of them contain production-ready code.

Azure Verified Modules (AVM) is Microsoft's attempt to provide standardized code modules that deploy specific Azure resources in a way that meets all the above criteria. These modules are presented for both Bicep and Terraform and are ready to be included in any larger infrastructure project. Modules are divided into three types, Resource, Pattern, and Utility. In addition to providing "good" code, AVM is fully supported by Microsoft and has been approved by the relevant Product Groups. Rather than reprint the introductory web page here, I recommend you go to `https://azure.github.io/Azure-Verified-Modules/` and read the introduction page.

Chapter Summary

Infrastructure as Code certainly has some interesting implications. No longer do we physically wire up hardware or insert extra disk drives into chassis. We describe what we need within structured documents and languages and then issue a single command that can deploy an entire data center's worth of systems and services. Most of that is not our daily task, but we need to understand that world and how it has changed with cloud computing. Most importantly we need to understand how to ask for new and updated resources from the teams that do manage infrastructure via code.

CHAPTER 13

Create and Manage Database Tasks in Azure

The third and final chapter of our Azure SQL Automation journey will focus on automating tasks using Azure-native resources. The first chapter in this part focused on using the familiar SQL Agent tool to automate tasks in Azure SQL. While SQL Agent is a powerful tool, its design goes back multiple decades, so it does not integrate well with modern, cloud-native systems. In this chapter we will explore Azure-native automation services, some of which are specifically designed for SQL services and some automation services that are not targeted specifically at SQL workloads but designed and built for all of Azure.

Create and Configure Elastic Jobs

Elastic Jobs is an Azure-native service designed to replace much of the functionality of the SQL Agent service for Azure SQL VMs. Azure SQL Elastic Jobs predates both Azure SQL VMs and Azure SQL Managed Instance and goes back to some of the earliest days of Azure. While it was not possible to exactly mimic all the functionality of SQL Agent due to the differences in platforms, there is considerable overlap and even a few extra capabilities that Azure SQL Elastic Jobs gives us.

Elastic Jobs Use Cases

Modern software design revolves around functional use cases. Developers ask what tasks this software service should perform. Azure SQL Elastic Jobs is no exception. While it is easy to say "just like SQL Agent," that isn't a very good use case or specification. Microsoft engineers decided on four main use cases.

© Geoff Hiten 2025
G. Hiten, *Administering Microsoft Azure SQL Solutions*, Certification Study Companion Series,
https://doi.org/10.1007/979-8-8688-1585-0_13

The first use case covers the majority of the workload for SQL Agent – scheduling and automating database management tasks to run at specific times or intervals. While backups are handled by the Azure SQL Database service, other management tasks such as index maintenance, data collection, or data import are still under the control of the DBA and are not automatically scheduled.

The next use case is an expansion of the SQL Agent capability, but is somewhat obvious in the context of how Azure SQL Database operates, specifically the use of a logical Server entity. Azure SQL Elastic Jobs can easily coordinate jobs across multiple Azure SQL Databases and Servers, something that SQL Server Agent struggled with.

Data Collection management is a use case that leverages both the scheduling capability and the ability to execute tasks across multiple databases and servers. You can easily aggregate user and performance data from multiple databases into a single landing database for further processing, analysis, or presentation.

The final intended use case is for small-scale data movement. Users can schedule external or custom solutions for Data Engineering and data platform communication. Microsoft still recommends Azure Data Factory, which uses its own scheduling and execution engine, for large-scale Data Engineering ETL or ELT operations, but Azure SQL Elastic Jobs is a handy way to quickly deploy a simple data movement solution.

For Azure SQL Elastic Jobs as with any software system, the user community will always find additional use cases. Most of them will be at least adjacent to or a subset of one of the design use cases, but if it works, is manageable, and is cost effective, it isn't wrong.

One of the biggest challenges users see in using Azure-specific tools like Azure SQL Elastic Jobs is they are almost too similar to their on-premises legacy counterparts. We expect the new tool to work exactly the same as the old one even though the fundamental environment (Azure Cloud) is completely different from a PC operating system. When we do see something different, we tend to think there is something broken or that we did something wrong. While using Azure SQL Elastic Jobs is not the only time you will experience this dissonance, you should be particularly aware of it here. Of course, if you do not have familiarity and practice with SQL Server Agent, then this will all be new to you.

Next, let's look at the components that make up Azure SQL Elastic Jobs and what each component does.

Elastic Jobs Components

Azure SQL Elastic Jobs has four identifiable components that work together to deliver the descried functionality. These four are as follows and are discussed further below:

- Elastic Job Agent
- Jobs Database
- Job
- Target Group

The Elastic Job Agent is the actual resource provisioned by the Azure Resource Manager. Azure SQL Elastic Jobs uses the *Microsoft.SQL* resource provider. The Azure Marketplace uses the name "Elastic Job Agent" as shown in Figure 13-1.

Figure 13-1. *Azure Elastic Job Agent Marketplace Entry*

Elastic Job Agent

The Azure SQL Elastic Job Agent is anchored to a particular Azure SQL Virtual Server. This can be the same server that hosts the Jobs Database but does not have to be. Most users use the same server for convenience. The Elastic Job Agent is the most complex of the four components of Azure SQL Elastic Jobs.

When provisioning an Azure SQL Elastic Job Agent, the first set of required information on the *Basics* tab is the standard Name, Subscription, and Resource Group, along with the host Virtual SQL Server as we see in Figure 13-2.

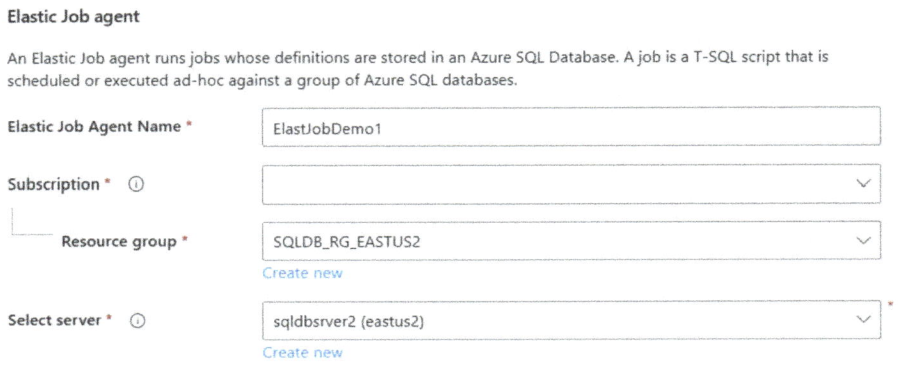

Elastic Job agent

An Elastic Job agent runs jobs whose definitions are stored in an Azure SQL Database. A job is a T-SQL script that is scheduled or executed ad-hoc against a group of Azure SQL databases.

Elastic Job Agent Name *   ElastJobDemo1

Subscription *   ⓘ

Resource group *   SQLDB_RG_EASTUS2
                                 Create new

Select server *   ⓘ   sqldbsrver2 (eastus2)
                                 Create new

Figure 13-2. *Azure Elastic Job Agent Provisioning (Part 1)*

Pricing for Azure SQL Elastic Jobs is based on provisioned capacity expressed in number of concurrent jobs. Note that the Elastic Jobs Database must be provisioned to at least an S1 capacity. Basic tier and S0 databases are not sufficient to support an Azure SQL Elastic Job Agent. Figure 13-3 shows the Jobs Database and Service Tier selection.

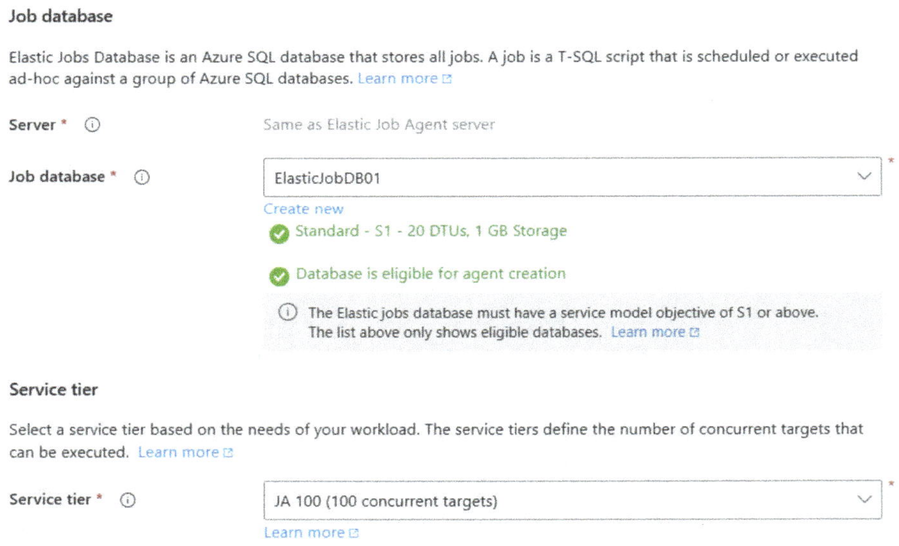

Job database

Elastic Jobs Database is an Azure SQL database that stores all jobs. A job is a T-SQL script that is scheduled or executed ad-hoc against a group of Azure SQL databases. Learn more ⊡

Server *   ⓘ   Same as Elastic Job Agent server

Job database *   ⓘ   ElasticJobDB01
                                 Create new
                                 ✔ Standard - S1 - 20 DTUs, 1 GB Storage

                                 ✔ Database is eligible for agent creation

                                 ⓘ The Elastic jobs database must have a service model objective of S1 or above.
                                   The list above only shows eligible databases. Learn more ⊡

Service tier

Select a service tier based on the needs of your workload. The service tiers define the number of concurrent targets that can be executed. Learn more ⊡

Service tier *   ⓘ   JA 100 (100 concurrent targets)
                                 Learn more ⊡

Figure 13-3. *Azure Elastic Job Agent Provisioning (Part 2)*

The minimum service tier for Azure SQL Elastic Jobs is JA 100, provisioning up to 100 concurrent jobs. There are also JA 200, JA400, and JA 800 service tiers representing 200, 400, and 800 concurrent jobs, respectively.

The only remaining item to decide on when provisioning an Azure SQL Elastic Job Agent is whether or not to create and assign a User-Assigned Managed Identity to the Agent. Microsoft Azure highly recommends assigning a managed identity to the Agent. We will discuss why in further detail in the section "Elastic Jobs Security," but for now we will take the recommendation and assign an identity. Note that the identity must already exist in your Azure tenant before it can be assigned. Creating a Managed Identity can be done via the portal by typing "Managed Identities" in the search box, clicking the "Create Identity" button, and filling in the required information. Select the same Resource Group and Region as the SQL Elastic Job Agent.

Elastic Jobs Database

The Elastic Jobs Database is the persistent component of Azure SQL Elastic Jobs. It roughly corresponds to the subset of the SQL Server *MSDB* database that persists and manages the SQL Agent job data. All job definition, activity, history, and security information are stored in the Elastic Jobs Database. Unlike the *MSDB* database, all the objects in the Elastic Jobs Database are dedicated to Elastic Jobs. No other functionality is supported. You can see the list of tables in Figure 13-4.

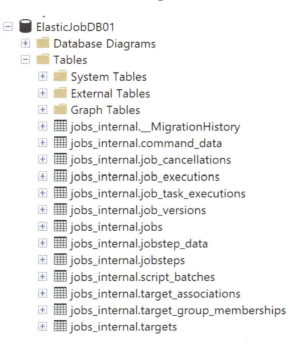

Figure 13-4. Azure SQL Database Elastic Jobs Tables

Notice the tables are all in the *jobs_internal* schema. You should not manipulate the contents of these tables directly. Microsoft does not guarantee the structure of these tables and may alter the contents at any time. Internal table and procedure definitions are not Application Programming Interfaces.

The correct way to manage Azure SQL Elastic Jobs is to use the stored procedures in the *jobs* schema. The complete list of stored procedures is shown in Figure 13-5.

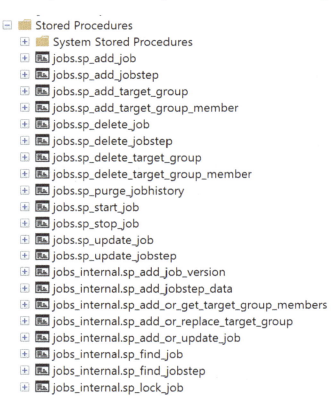

Figure 13-5. *Azure SQL Database Elastic Jobs Stored Procedures*

Notice that there are two schemas used for stored procedures, *jobs* and *jobs_internal*. Microsoft considers the *jobs* schema objects public-facing interfaces and will not update them without proper warning. Like the tables in *jobs_internal*, stored procedures are internal and may change without notice. We will discuss some of the key procedures below in the section "Managing Elastic Jobs."

One departure from how SQL Agent Jobs work is the Azure SQL Elastic Jobs Database also stores optional *database-scoped credentials*. A *Credential* is a database object that stores identity and security information to connect to a resource outside of the SQL Server. Credentials were originally Server-scoped objects, but like many other SQL Objects such as DMVs, database-scoped credentials were created to implement necessary functions in Azure SQL Database where the Server object is a logical server and the *master* database is a virtual database. The most common use for credentials, server- or database-scoped, is to access file storage locations for backup/restore/import/export. We will discuss credentials in more depth in Chapter 15.

Jobs

The *Job* entity is the basic task element of Azure SQL Elastic Jobs and is almost exactly analogous to a SQL Agent Job. Like jobs in SQL Agent, Jobs have job steps containing a T-SQL Script to execute and one or more target groups to execute the script against. Unlike SQL Agent, Azure SQL Elastic Jobs can only execute T-SQL Script job steps. None of the other types of jobs that SQL Server Agent can execute are available in Azure SQL Elastic Jobs.

Jobs also have *schedules* to control how and when to execute. Unlike SQL Agent, Azure SQL Elastic Job Schedules are not independent entities. Schedules are part of the job definition and cannot be shared between jobs.

Target Groups

A Target Group is a set of one or more databases that the job step's T-SQL Script will be executed against. A target group can be one or more of the following items:

- Databases
- Servers
- Elastic pools

Targets can contain any combination of Databases, Servers, or Elastic Pools. Target Groups are enumerated at job execution time so they are always up to date. This means that the current database collection of a server or pool is targeted for execution. Target Group definitions can contain both inclusion and exclusion logic. This means that you can create logic like "all databases on these three listed servers that aren't named Admin" to create complex Target Groups.

Elastic Jobs Security

Security is where Azure SQL Elastic Jobs diverges the most from the SQL Server Agent template. With SQL Server Agent, we generally were executing on a server environment using a trusted connection to one local target SQL Server. While it was possible for SQL Server Agent to use proxy accounts, most local jobs did not use this feature as it added unneeded complexity. The practical result is that we really didn't consider security at all when using SQL Agent. We created jobs on the local server and everything just worked.

In Azure, we are in a low-trust environment that is secure by default, design, and operation. The only database that an Elastic Job Agent has access to by default is its own Jobs Database using certificate-based authentication between the Job Agent and the Jobs Database. This means that to connect to any database, we need to establish an identity so the database will know the agent is authorized to perform work in the database.

A few pages back when we provisioned an Azure Elastic Job Agent, we accepted the default recommendation of a user-assigned managed identity but did not explain why that was our choice. With a managed identity, the Azure SQL Elastic Job Agent becomes a "user" in Entra ID. You can assign various roles to the user, grant specific rights to the user, and manage it exactly as you would any other Entra ID user. This means you simply grant the Agent Identity the rights to access whichever Azure SQL Database or other Azure resource it may need to connect to. As with any Entra ID identity, you can assign it to any role within a database or grant it explicit rights to objects. The identity exists in Entra ID and is outside the context of both Azure SQL Elastic Jobs and whatever databases it connects to.

The alternative is to create and manage explicit *Credentials* in the Azure SQL Elastic Jobs Database. You can create and manage these credentials via the Azure portal, PowerShell scripts, or T-SQL commands. Credential creation involves two steps. First, you create the credentials (username and password) in the target database, and then you store them in the Azure SQL Elastic Jobs Database.

Managing Elastic Jobs

Now that we have all the building blocks defined, we can look at how to manage Azure SQL Elastic Jobs. For several years, Azure SQL Elastic Jobs languished in preview status – incomplete and unloved. Eventually, in Calendar Year 2024 one Azure Program Manager picked up the feature and pushed it across the finish line. The major missing piece was a portal interface to manage jobs. Prior to the completed and deployed Portal Management interface, you could only manage Azure SQL Elastic Jobs via PowerShell or T-SQL.

Note   Most Azure features begin life with PowerShell or CLI interfaces only. Portal pages and blades are only built in the last stages of development. Azure SQL Elastic Jobs is in a very small set of services where one of its command-line management interfaces is T-SQL.

Portal

The Azure portal provides all the options necessary to create and manage Azure SQL Elastic Jobs. Figure 13-6 shows the standard portal menu items as well as the resource-specific items for Azure SQL Elastic Jobs. We are only going to focus on the Jobs and Security items for this discussion. Everything else is common across resources and should be familiar to anyone with basic Azure portal operation skills.

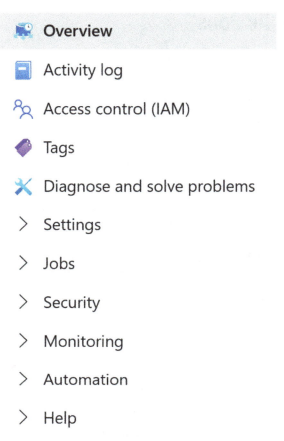

Figure 13-6. *Azure SQL Elastic Job Agent Portal Menu*

Jobs

Expanding the *Jobs* menu item lists three more menu choices as shown in Figure 13-7.

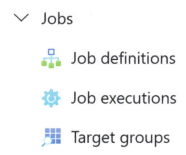

Figure 13-7. *Azure SQL Elastic Job Agent Jobs Menu*

Job Definitions takes you to a blade with a list of job definitions. Each job definition will show currently defined jobs and data such as schedule type, last execution date and status, and the job start time. Each job name is a clickable link that takes you to the job detail blade. This blade allows you to look at past job executions, edit the job – with yet another blade to edit each job step – and edit the job schedule. You can also enable or disable a job from here.

Job Executions shows currently running jobs only.

Target Groups opens a fairly complex blade set that allows you to create and manipulate Target Groups and members. This is necessarily complex in that Target Groups can contain multiple types of set definitions and both inclusive and exclusive logic. This is so complex the designers gave two options to view this – Grid View and Card View. I suggest you explore creating and managing Target Groups using both views and multiple complex logic settings to familiarize yourself with this capability. The visual representation will help cement the concepts you will use if you choose to manage Target Groups via PowerShell or T-SQL Scripts.

Security

The Security menu item has three sub-menu items as shown in Figure 13-8.

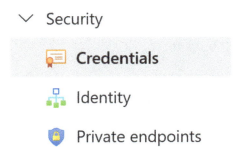

Figure 13-8. *Azure SQL Elastic Job Agent Security Menu*

Selecting *Credentials* allows you to view credentials stored in the Azure SQL Elastic Job Agent Jobs Database, but does not allow you to create, alter, or delete those credentials. You must use T-SQL or PowerShell to manage SQL Database Credentials. Again, the blade reminds you that the preferred method for securing access to target resources is via a Managed Identity.

The *Identity* blade allows you to view or change the Managed Identity associated with the Azure SQL Elastic Job Agent. As per our earlier discussion, you can only have one Managed Identity associated with an Agent at a time. Changing the Agent Identity does not impact access to the Jobs Database or any of its contents as that uses certificate-based security.

The final Menu item under *Security* is *Private Endpoints*. This is often listed under a *Networking* menu item in other resources, but since this is the only related item and the choice of public or private networking model is generally a security-driven option, it was placed here for convenience. This blade will allow you to create a private endpoint to an existing SQL Server anywhere in your tenant. This private endpoint must be approved at the SQL Server resource by someone with the correct authorization.

PowerShell

You can create and manage Azure SQL Elastic Jobs via PowerShell using the *Az.SQL* PowerShell module. As with most PowerShell commands, the cmdlets can be grouped into four sets, Get-, New-, Set-, and Remove-, with the expected functionality of each leading verb.

Here are the Get-AzSqlElasticJob cmdlets:

- Get-AzSqlElasticJob

- Get-AzSqlElasticJobAgent

- Get-AzSqlElasticJobCredential

- Get-AzSqlElasticJobExecution

- Get-AzSqlElasticJobPrivateEndpoint

- Get-AzSqlElasticJobStep

- Get-AzSqlElasticJobStepExecution

- Get-AzSqlElasticJobTargetExecution

- Get-AzSqlElasticJobTargetGroup

Here are the New-AzSqlElasticJob cmdlets:

- New-AzSqlElasticJob

- New-AzSqlElasticJobAgent

- New-AzSqlElasticJobCredential

- New-AzSqlElasticJobPrivateEndpoint

- New-AzSqlElasticJobTargetGroup

Here are the Set-AzSqlElasticJob cmdlets:

- Set-AzSqlElasticJob

- Set-AzSqlElasticJobAgent

- Set-AzSqlElasticJobCredential

- Set-AzSqlElasticJobStep

Here are the Remove-AzSqlElasticJob cmdlets:

- Remove-AzSqlElasticJob

- Remove-AzSqlElasticJobAgent

- Remove-AzSqlElasticJobCredential

- Remove-AzSqlElasticJobPrivateEndpoint

- Remove-AzSqlElasticJobStep

- Remove-AzSqlElasticJobTarget

- Remove-AzSqlElasticJobTargetGroup

Microsoft has more than adequately documented each of these commands in detail with examples as well as having written a Learning Path document on the overall use of these together. My suggestion is to create several practical scenarios, perhaps duplicating some existing on-premises SQL Agent use cases, and create the PowerShell script to deploy and manage such scenarios. The PowerShell interpreter is a harsh taskmaster and will not accept intent, only correct actions.

T-SQL

As I noted earlier in this chapter, Azure SQL Elastic Jobs is somewhat unique in that one of its script interfaces is T-SQL. Normally, resource configuration is handled at the script level via PowerShell or Azure CLI. Since the Azure SQL Elastic Job Agent is inextricably tied to the Azure SQL Elastic Jobs Database, it makes sense to use a database manipulation language such as T-SQL to manage the Azure SQL Elastic Job Agent.

Recall our discussion of the Azure SQL Elastic Jobs Database earlier in this chapter and the list of tables and stored procedures. The tables were all labeled "internal," but the stored procedures had both "internal" notation and no notations. The "no notations" are public and constitute the public T-SQL interface for Azure SQL Elastic Jobs.

As a quick reminder, here is the list of Azure SQL Elastic Jobs public stored procedures in the Azure SQL Elastic Jobs Database:

- jobs.sp_add_job
- jobs.sp_add_job_step
- jobs.sp_add_target_group
- jobs.sp_add_target_group_member
- jobs.sp_delete_job
- jobs.sp_delete_jobstep
- jobs.sp_delete_target_group
- jobs.sp_delete_target_group_member
- jobs_sp.purge_jobhistory
- jobs.sp_start_job
- jobs.sp_stop_job
- jobs.sp_update_job
- jobs.sp_update_jobstep

There are no Azure SQL Elastic Job Agent–specific commands for credentials. T-SQL already has CREATE, ALTER, and DROP Credential commands. Wrapping them in a stored procedure specific to Elastic Jobs would only add unnecessary complexity.

Again, there are documentation pages for each of these stored procedures online. As with PowerShell, create scenarios and practice if you wish to understand this material fully.

Create and Configure Database Tasks by Using Automation

One of the characteristics of Azure is that services focus on very specific tasks. The Elastic Jobs Service is separate from the SQL Database Service, which is separate from the SSIS Runtime in Azure Data Factory/Synapse/Fabric. Each is provisioned, metered, and billed as separate services. Contrast that with licensed products such as SQL Server where all three services, or their on-premises counterparts, are sold under a common license and the consumer decides how much functionality to implement and use.

Azure SQL Elastic Jobs almost replaces SQL Agent for most circumstances. Its biggest constraint is it can only connect to SQL Databases, including those hosted on Azure SQL MI and Azure SQL VMs, and can only execute T-SQL commands. Sometimes we need to enroll multiple resource types into an automation workflow. Another way to state this is we sometimes need to perform tasks outside of SQL Server in a workflow. In SQL Agent, we could invoke a command-line or PowerShell script to interact with another application to perform work outside of SQL Server. One example would be to execute a T-SQL command to BCP data out to a file and then issue an external command such as a PowerShell script to FTP it to a specific destination. Azure SQL Elastic Jobs cannot do that. There is no underlying operating system visible to Azure SQL PaaS Services. In Azure, we use Azure Automation to accomplish tasks across heterogeneous resources.

I will not try and teach all about Azure Automation or PowerShell here. Both of those topics are well beyond the scope of this book and the DP-300 exam. However, a brief overview to establish context and familiarity is appropriate.

Azure Automation is a fundamental Azure service and is the common service to perform automated tasks across all of Azure. PowerShell is a common scripting language used in Azure and the entire Microsoft ecosystem. Azure Automation relies on *Runbooks* to store and execute scripts including Python and PowerShell scripts.

What we will focus on here is how to use the Azure Automation service to connect and manage SQL Server resources. While you can use Python scripts in Azure Automation, we are going to focus on PowerShell only for this chapter, since the DP-300 exam does not use Python. Feel free to explore that subject on your own.

In order to connect an Azure Automation account to SQL, you need to enable two modules in the automation account. *Az.SQL* is the module used to manipulate Azure SQL PaaS Services. All the Az.xxxx modules are available by default in Azure Automation for obvious reasons. Az.SQL lets you affect the configuration and provisioning of Azure

SQL PaaS resources managed by the Microsoft.SQL Azure Resource Provider. You can use this resource provider to alter existing SQL PaaS resources or provision new ones. You can even automate the creation and management of Azure SQL Elastic Jobs by referencing the Az.SQL PowerShell functions we discussed earlier in this chapter should you wish to explore that somewhat redundant and recursive rabbit hole.

There is an Az-SQLVirtualMachine module to control aspects of the SQL IaaS Extension resource to control SQL services on Azure Virtual Machines. For more information on the Azure SQL IaaS extension, you can familiarize yourself with the documentation here: `https://learn.microsoft.com/en-us/azure/azure-sql/virtual-machines/windows/sql-server-iaas-agent-extension-automate-management`.

The other PowerShell module you will likely use is not provided by default and will need to be manually enabled. This is the SQLServer module. Fortunately, it is in the PowerShell gallery, which means you don't have to track down and download a file or manage versions. Simply go to the Shared Resources ➤ Modules blade from the left tower menu as shown in Figure 13-9.

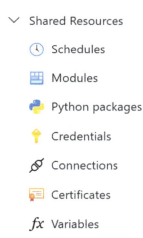

Figure 13-9. *Azure Automation Shared Resources*

This will bring you to a page showing all currently available modules (not shown). An available module is one that is installed and ready to use. No "import-module" cmdlet required, just reference the desired function and go. Let's add SQLServer by selecting "Add a module" at the top. This brings you to the page shown in Figure 13-10 where you should select "Brows from gallery."

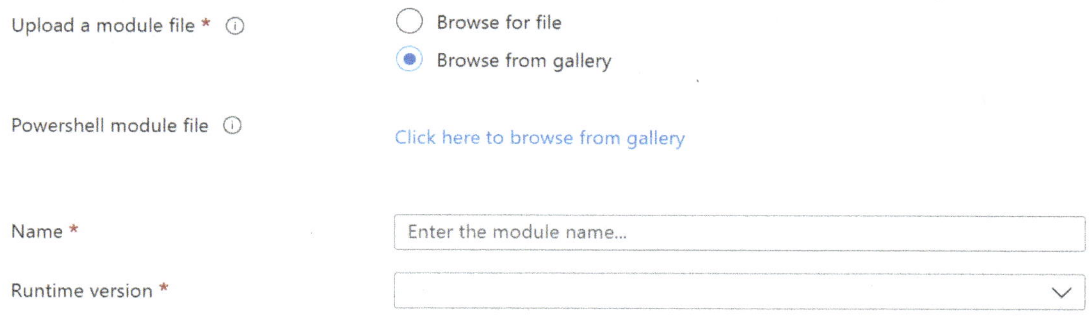

Upload a module file * ⓘ
- ◯ Browse for file
- ⦿ Browse from gallery

Powershell module file ⓘ

Click here to browse from gallery

Name *

Enter the module name...

Runtime version *

Figure 13-10. *Azure Automation – Add a Module*

Click the "Click here to browse from gallery" to open the Gallery blade (not shown). Type "SQLServer" in the search box and hit enter or click the search icon. Selecting the SQLServer module will take you to a detail blade (also not shown) listing a description, properties, and the cmdlets of the SQLServer module. Once you select the module, you will be taken back to the "Add a module" page where you will select the version of the module.

This brings us to the number one challenge with Azure Automation – version compatibility. While the Az.xxx series and SQLServer modules are core Microsoft PowerShell modules and are always kept up to the current supported version of PowerShell, not all modules are so fortunate. Finding a common, supported version of all necessary modules, especially when using third-party PowerShell modules to support external software, can be challenging. Dealing with updates as various modules roll out newly supported versions is equally challenging. The rapidly changing module list and versions is why I chose not to show an example of either during this section. The information changes so rapidly as to render a printed example obsolete long before you would ever see it.

The other challenges people face when using Azure Automation, whether with SQL Server or not, are connectivity and identity, the same challenges we faced with Azure SQL Elastic Jobs. Unlike Azure SQL Elastic Jobs, Azure Automation always has a Managed Identity. The only question regarding the Managed Identity is whether it's a System-Managed Identity or a User-Managed Identity. Either way, you can have that identity provide the connection credential. For services that do not support Entra ID identities, Azure Automation securely stores *Credentials* – name/password pairs. You do not store actual names and passwords in scripts; you access the stored credential information at runtime to establish an identity.

Once you have the Azure Automation environment configured with the appropriate modules Active and Available, you simply schedule PowerShell scripts. You can write these scripts yourself or obtain them from GitHub or other sources. As I mentioned earlier, the biggest challenge with PowerShell is coordinating compatible versions across various sources.

Automate Database Workflows by Using Azure Logic Apps

Logic Apps is an Azure-specific low-code/no-code development environment using a visual workflow to accomplish simple automation tasks. Like the previous section on Azure Automation, Logic Apps is far too deep and complex a topic to cover completely. Again, we will focus on SQL-specific elements of Logic Apps.

For this example, we will use the Multi-Tenant Consumption Workflow Service plan. While it is not the most common configuration, it is the easiest and least expensive for learning since you only pay for what you consume. Most companies use a private networking model, which requires a Standard Tier plan that allows VNET integration. These plans are also provisioned so you pay for the capacity rather than the actual workflow consumption. Your organization may mandate a specific Service Plan or conversely forbid certain plans. Do not get wrapped up with choosing a specific plan. For our purposes they will all work.

Logic Apps workflow is much closer to SQL Server Integration Services or Azure Data Factory than either Azure SQL Elastic Jobs or Azure Automation. You choose *Triggers* to initiate a workflow and *Actions* to implement work.

The simplest trigger is Schedule – Recurrence. This executes the task on a fixed interval between starts, regardless of the prior run duration. Once you create a Trigger, you can create a sequence of Actions. The SQL Server Action has multiple specific tasks it can perform.

Any result sets that are returned are persisted and can flow to the next action item. Subsequent actions can alter these rows and update or delete them from SQL. There are two catch-all tasks for Execute SQL Query and Execute SQL Stored Procedure to expand the capability beyond the row-specific tasks built into an Action.

When you first select a SQL Server Action, you are prompted to create a *Connection*. In Azure Logic Apps, a Connection encompasses both a defined Target SQL Server and the identity information used to connect to that Target. The SQL Connector supports all SQL login authentication methods. Once a Connection has been defined, it can be used by subsequent Actions just by selecting it.

You can create Logic Apps directly in the Azure portal or in Visual Studio Code designers. There are separate designers for consumption-based and provision-based (standard) Workflow Hosting Plans, so you will need to know which plan you intend to use. You can actually write fairly complex workflows using Azure Logic Apps with connectivity SQL Server as part of the workflow.

Configure Alerts and Notifications on Database Tasks

Each of the three Automation platforms for SQL (Azure SQL Elastic Jobs, Azure Automation, Logic Apps) has built-in alerting and notification capabilities. Azure SQL Elastic Jobs has automatic retry logic, which covers most of the failures right off the bat. You can examine the Jobs.JobExecutions view (note the lack of the "internal" flag in the name – it's a public interface) to examine and troubleshoot job execution issues. You can even create an automated tasks to watch for a "Failed" status in the "Lifecycle" column and fire an alert.

Azure Automation has built-in monitoring and alerting for job runs – you only need to configure it. Be aware that a script can execute successfully yet still not accomplish its intended tasks. You must write scripts that return or log a failure if you want the host platform to be able to act on that failure.

Home-grown monitoring and alerting is practically a cottage industry in the SQL community, largely because we were the first to need such capability or because the monitoring team is not willing to work with us to provide meaningful, actionable alerts. Fortunately, Azure offers a centralized monitoring repository with individually configurable alerting. We discussed Azure Monitor in the context of monitoring and alerting for SQL Services in Chapter 8. That same Azure Monitor can collect operational metrics and logs for any of the automation platforms we discussed in this chapter. As with the SQL Performance Metrics and Logs, we can craft alerts on the various services we use to automate SQL tasks.

Chapter and Part Summary

Automation is one of the core features of Azure. Everything is scriptable and can be managed via scripting. When Infrastructure is Code, then we can easily automate the creation and configuration of SQL Services. We no longer need "click-next" checklists to deploy or update any SQL Service. We can choose from multiple automation languages and platforms to create, manage, and maintain SQL Services. Automation tools can be SQL specific or completely SQL agnostic. T-SQL is now just one well-integrated element of our automation toolkit. We now have the power to truly manage SQL Server at a scale we never could in an on-premises environment. You are starting to see the real capabilities of the Azure SQL Platform.

PART V

Plan and Configure a High Availability and Disaster Recovery (HA/DR) Environment

CHAPTER 14

Recommend a HA/DR Strategy for Database Solutions

Welcome to the final part of this study guide. If you are reading this cover to cover, thank you and congratulations on making it this far. If not, well, I suggest reviewing all the topics prior to here. Everything we have worked on and discussed so far goes into creating and operating a Highly Available Azure SQL Database platform. Steady, predictable performance, alerting and monitoring, security, and maintenance are "table stakes" that prevent most SQL Database service disruptions. What we have left are "external" factors like hardware, power, and data center failures. Problems with the platform or the environment that stop the host services from operating are what we need to anticipate and mitigate. Either way, we are starting my favorite topic – High Availability/Disaster Resilience. This part is about how we plan for and react to such disruptions.

This chapter will help you decide between various options for HA/DR, using non-technical or light technical terms that senior company management can easily understand and compare. Chapter 15 will walk through the technical elements of the most basic function of a database administrator – putting things back the way they were. We refer to that as "Backup and Restore." Finally, Chapter 16 will walk through the various technical configurations available for Azure SQL services.

Before we discuss exactly what our options are for dealing with service disruptions, we must first establish some common vocabulary terms and definitions. The terms we use to describe the various elements and concepts of BCDR (Business Continuity/ Disaster Recovery) are not necessarily standardized across the industry. There is a lot of

© Geoff Hiten 2025
G. Hiten, *Administering Microsoft Azure SQL Solutions*, Certification Study Companion Series,
https://doi.org/10.1007/979-8-8688-1585-0_14

ambiguity with most of the terms we use to talk about system resilience. Without a set of common definitions, we can easily find ourselves reading the same words but thinking about very different concepts.

Notice that many of the subheadings in this chapter start with "Recommend" or "Evaluate." All the exam questions referring to this material will ask you to choose between alternatives. Many of the lesser alternatives (*distractors* in test-speak) will accomplish the task, but not as well as the "correct" answer *given the stated goals for the question*. Some will clearly not meet the desired goals at all and can be quickly discarded. Others are good solutions but do not provide the most desired outcome as measured by the stated goals. This chapter will be less interactive and more theoretical than most chapters up to now have been. A successful HA/DR strategy requires looking at SQL operations through a specific mental lens, understanding exactly what certain terms mean, and evaluating solutions according to some very strict criteria. It's important we get this right. BCDR (Business Continuity/Disaster Recovery) discussions often begin and end in corporate boardrooms. I have had many customers come to me with a mandate from their Board of Directors to create a DR Strategy. We must be clear and accurate with our assessments and recommendations for that audience.

Let's begin defining what we mean when we talk about Highly Available Infrastructure so we can move on to learning how to evaluate the different alternatives available in Azure for SQL Services. Many of the terms we will use apply to any Azure technology, not just SQL Services, so they are good to know in any event. We will get into SQL-specific terminology when we discuss technology options for the various Azure SQL Services.

Let us first discuss the meaning of "High Availability" – the HA part of HA/DR – as Microsoft sees it. High Availability refers to hardware redundancy within a single location. For Application or Web tier systems, this is achieved by scaling out redundant, identical servers and load balancing the incoming work requests. This works well for systems that do not persist data internally. Any single machine in a tier can readily substitute for any failed system in that tier. The incoming work requests are rerouted by the load handler. Failed requests are resent from the prior tier. While this works well for stateless web and app servers, SQL Server systems require a significantly different approach.

For HA evaluation purposes, think of SQL Server as a sequential transaction-processing engine operating over a defined data set. The transaction log is the timeline of stateful changes to the database. Operating and preserving that timeline and data set is the core of what SQL Server does. Each SQL Server is the primary source of truth for the databases it owns and manages. Without the existing database state, you cannot meaningfully process additional transactions and achieve consistent outcomes to the next state. SQL failover partner systems "follow" the primary system's transaction changes in a manner that allows the redundant hardware to take over and become the primary SQL processing engine should the initial SQL System fail for some reason.

All the various supporting HA technologies for SQL Server exist to manage the redundant copies (called *failover replicas*), detect failures automatically, and switch any connected workloads over to use the newly promoted primary replica. How the replica is created and maintained, what technology decides to execute a failover, what failover process does it use, and how connection redirection happens are all implementation details specific to each technology. We will discuss implementations in detail in Chapter 16. For now, we need to see how it all works as a whole. To do that we must define proper ways of measuring the system.

Recommend a HA/DR Strategy Based on Recovery Point Objective/Recovery Time Objective (RPO/ RTO) Requirements

We begin our in-depth discussion of HA/DR by looking at two very common measures for HA/DR systems. Time is a simple measurement we are all familiar with. Even C-suite executives understand time as a concept. Microsoft, as well as most companies in the IT industry, uses two time-based metrics to measure the effectiveness of a HA/DR strategy. *RPO* (Recovery Point Objective) measures how much data loss is expected during an outage. Using time as a metric removes all technical aspects of the problem, allowing all parts of the business to understand and participate in planning, implementing, and executing a HA/DR strategy. *RTO* (Recovery Time Objective) measures how long an outage should continue until service is restored.

RPO and RTO are one of the key differences between High Availability and Disaster Recovery implementations. In the Azure world, we prefer the term geo-redundancy to the term Disaster Recovery. This clearly delineates the difference between local failover within an Azure region (HA) from failover across different regions (DR).

High Availability

A local replica generally has an RPO of zero. That is, no data loss for committed transactions is expected should a failure situation occur in any single compute or storage component. This is accomplished by writing redundant copies of the transaction log prior to reporting a successfully committed transaction, either to redundant storage that is transparent to the host or to storage on a SQL Service that is separate from the primary server. Since all Azure Storage is minimally triply redundant – that is, it takes at least *two* storage tier failures to lose data – all SQL Services that use Azure Storage for their database and transaction log files inherit this minimum HA standard. Not all SQL Services use Azure Storage, however.

For a more detailed discussion of Azure Storage Redundancy, refer to Chapter 1, section "Azure Storage Basics."

Some Service Tiers use local storage for SQL data files. "Local" in this context means storage that is built into the compute host node, generally SSD (Solid-State Drive) technology. Local SSD storage offers some of the highest throughput and lowest latency available in Azure and is a common choice for SQL Services. Even if the storage is configured redundantly on the host computer, that can only protect against a local storage failure, not a compute node failure, so it does not contribute to the overall SQL availability.

Availability Sets

Availability Sets were Microsoft's first attempt to expose some physical attributes of Azure Virtual Machine hosting to customers needing to put separation between virtual machines for High Availability planning. In this case, the separation was to make sure Virtual Machines never landed on the same physical host. You may be more familiar with the VMWare term "anti-aliasing" to refer to the same thing. Availability Sets are part of the Azure architecture in every region. You must choose to make a VM part of an Availability Set when it is provisioned. You cannot go back and change it later.

Availability Sets prevent a single host failure from taking out both nodes in a High-Availability Windows Server Failover Cluster, but do not protect from multiple physical host machines shutting down due to a power issue or other environmental issues or even from undergoing maintenance at the same time.

Availability Zones

The solution is to create a replica using SQL-native technology on a different physical compute host than the Primary node – "more separation." While this sounds easy, it can be challenging in an abstract cloud computing environment to create just the right amount of separation. Too little separation and a power or network failure could take out both nodes. Too much separation and latency can creep in between the nodes, affecting performance or recoverability.

Microsoft's solution is to create *Availability Zones* in certain Azure regions. A region with Availability Zones divides the physical infrastructure into three parts, generally kept in different physical buildings. Power distribution, cooling, networking, and maintenance schedules are all defined per zone with only a single zone undergoing any changes at one time. In regions that support Availability Zones, Azure SQL PaaS Services that use internal replicas can choose replicas to be zone redundant. Existing deployments can choose to upgrade to zone-redundant deployments, but it is not an automatic selection. SQL VMs also can be deployed to a specific zone when the VM is provisioned. You cannot retrofit a VM into a specific Availability Zone after it has been deployed. Availability Zones are numbered 1, 2, and 3 for easy reference.

Disaster Recovery

Azure regions were originally deployed in matched pairs with extra dedicated communication links dedicated to storage replication between the two regions. Each region is a minimum of 600 miles (rounded to 1,000 km) from its peer. Microsoft's original advice was to put all DR infrastructure in the peer of whatever region you chose as your primary. This kept any GRS (Geographically Redundant Storage) data in the same region as your DR infrastructure. As Azure infrastructure evolved, certain regions were not built with every possible hardware combination, and therefore some services were not offered in those regions or became available only under heavy capacity restrictions. Microsoft has updated its guidance so that GRS is still strongly recommended for backups, but the choice of DR regions is no longer bound to that choice. In fact, the recommendation is to make your applications as region-independent as possible.

Because Azure regions are spaced widely apart to prevent one physical event from affecting both sides of a paired region set, there is considerable latency in communications between regions. This latency means that all communication between the regions is always set to be asynchronous. From a SQL transaction log perspective, this means that the primary system does not wait on a successful transaction log write signal from a geographic failover replica to report a transaction is committed. Data is sent *asynchronously* between regions. In an asynchronous system, it is possible to commit a transaction on the primary system but not on a secondary replica. By definition, this can lead to possible data loss. RPO for all SQL DR implementations is therefore always greater than zero. This is one of the primary differences between High Availability (HA) and Disaster Recovery (DR) for Azure SQL. Let's examine RTO and RPO for both HA and DR.

RPO and RTO are both target metrics for a projected failure event. This is what your design, implementation, and practice should determine – the expected length of both metrics. Calculating these metrics can be extremely complex. Fortunately, Microsoft has done much of the heavy lifting for you. Combine that with some basic "rules," and you can come up with some reasonable estimates.

Any time a human is involved in a HA/DR step, the minimum time impact is four hours for planning purposes. Exceptions are when there is a 24/7/365 operating staff trained and empowered to implement any projected solution. If you have to call someone, expect to plan for a minimum of four hours to get them connected to the problem when projecting RPO/RTO.

Evaluate HA/DR for Hybrid Deployments

Large enterprises often choose more than one cloud provider and use public cloud in addition to private compute resources. Smaller companies may not have the will or the resources to migrate everything to Azure at one time. Legacy workloads, including SQL Server–centric applications, may remain in on-premises data centers for various technical and business reasons. These multi-location environments are referred to by Microsoft as Hybrid infrastructure.

Hybrid solutions are by nature IaaS (Infrastructure as a Service) solutions. PaaS (Platform as a Service) solutions are typically proprietary to each cloud provider, but we do have some interesting options with SQL Server. IaaS serves as a "least common denominator" that every cloud provider supports as well as being available to on-premises SQL Server operators. There is one notable exception in the SQL Server world that we will discuss shortly.

Azure Site Recovery

Azure Site Recovery (ASR) is a storage-based recovery service that allows you to create a replica of each of your on-premises servers in Azure. ASR takes periodic snapshots of your virtual machines and saves those images in Azure. These images, along with their corresponding Azure Virtual Machine configurations, are used to "hydrate" a complete site in Azure for Disaster Recovery Purposes.

ASR was designed to mimic on-premises storage snapshot solutions, including the ability to build and populate an isolated "sandbox" for testing DR solutions. ASR allows for failover and failback to most popular virtualization solutions including Hyper-V and VMWare. ASR also can protect machines running in Azure with the replica targeted to a different Azure region.

ASR recognizes SQL Server and will create crash-consistent snapshots using the Volume Shadow Service storage system interface to properly quiesce IO. This does not mean that ASR is an ideal solution for SQL Server. There are two potential drawbacks for using ASR as a DR solution.

The first is the snapshot interval. ASR has a minimum snapshot interval of 15 minutes. With the need to subsequently copy the results to Azure, a 15-minute snapshot yields an RPO of greater than 15 minutes. For simplicity, the snapshot interval is typically doubled get the actual RPO of 30 minutes. It is essential to identify this shortcoming and get management sign-off if you choose (or have imposed on you) ASR as your SQL DR solution.

The second potential shortcoming is when you have a large and/or very active database. The size of the initial seed files or the differential files (not to be confused with SQL Differential backups – we will discuss that in Chapter 15) may exceed the allowed copy time window. Simply put, your network connection to Azure or your ASR Infrastructure may not be able to keep up with the storage changes created by large, busy SQL Servers. In this situation, many people choose to use ASR to protect the operating system image only and use another technique to protect the SQL Server data. Other times, the SQL Server is completely removed from the ASR collection, and the entire server is protected using another technology.

Another option is to use a non-ASR technology such as pre-building your DR VM in Azure and keeping it in sync with Log Shipping or enrolling it into an Always-On Availability Group while still using ASR for your non-SQL VMs. Most customers that use ASR for on-premises or Azure VM protection use ASR for some SQL Servers but not always every one. They recognize that some SQL Systems are too highly scaled for ASR to be an effective DR solution.

SQL Server Always-On Availability Groups

SQL Server Always-On Availability Groups are probably the most common method of creating a Disaster Recovery replica in Azure, either from on-premises or from within Azure. SQL Server Availability Groups were first introduced in SQL Server 2012, and Microsoft has incrementally improved the feature in every subsequent release. It is well-proven technology that most of the SQL Server Administrator community is familiar with. The only question many DBAs have is should they build a "normal" multi-site cluster and Availability Group or should they use a Distributed Availability Group (DAG). The answer used to be much more complex due to limited cluster quorum management options. In older versions of Windows, it was difficult or even impossible to limit the impact of failed or disconnected remote nodes on the primary site machines. The entire point of a DR solution is lost if it can destabilize the primary system and cause a HA failover.

Fortunately, the Microsoft Windows team has answered the challenge. By carefully selecting a quorum model and cluster node weights, you can isolate the local system from anything that happens on the Azure side of the cluster. That leaves only one criteria for AG vs. DAG. If you have the same Active Directory forest on-premises and in Azure, you can and should use an ordinary Availability Group. A Distributed Availability Group only manages data synchronization, not failover redirection. There is no Listener in a DAG. In the event of DAG failover, your application servers will need to identify and connect to a new SQL Server endpoint in Azure.

If you have a single security context – a common AD infrastructure – between on-premises and Azure, you should not implement a Distributed Availability Group. The original Availability Group will provide much better functionality.

Automatic Failover for DR is not an issue as it is not available. It is almost impossible to operate a multi-site SQL Server Availability Group replica in Synchronous mode. The simple physics of distance and signal propagation time – even at the speed of light – is enough to add more latency than almost any SQL workload can tolerate. DR replicas are Asynchronous. You may be able to bring them into a Synchronous mode briefly at low activity times for a no-loss failover test, but this often requires extreme workload throttling. SQL Server Availability Groups do not allow for automatic failover to Asynchronous replicas. Microsoft requires a human actively choose a course of action that might lead to data loss. HA is automatic and quick. DR is a mindful action that requires thoughtful human action.

Azure SQL Managed Instance Link

In Chapter 4 we introduced the concept of Azure SQL Managed Instance Link, a service that creates a Distributed Availability Group with a SQL Server on one end and an Azure SQL Managed Instance on the other as a means of migrating to Azure. This technology can also be used as a Disaster Recovery technology.

A Disaster Recovery failover to Azure is almost exactly like a Migration to Azure. The two differences are (1) you don't get to pick the cutover time and (2) you need a failback plan. In order to fail back, the internal version of each database must match between the SQL Server and Azure SQL Managed Instance. This version is locked for SQL Server at each major version release and is unchanged through any patches including Service Packs. This version is based solely on the actual running SQL Server engine and is independent of the database compatibility mode. If you have ever restored a SQL Server database to a newer version than it was created on, you will see messages where SQL Server updates the database to a new internal version after the restore completes but before the database is opened for connections.

SQL Server 2022 on-disk database version is 957 and is the lowest supported version SQL Managed Instance can match.

Evaluate Azure-Specific HA/DR Solutions

One well-used format for questions on all Microsoft exams including the DP-300 exam is to rank or select the "best" option among several similar choices. I discussed the overall strategy on these questions back in Chapter 1, but it is time to be much more specific here. Ranking HA/DR solutions or selecting the "best" is how many of the HA/DR questions are formed. You will almost certainly encounter such a question during your exam. The key to this question is knowing the pros and cons of each solution and what it is optimized to achieve and what are its shortcomings. The question will give you an indication of what axis to use to measure "best." It may be cost, downtime, simplicity, or some other criteria or combination of criteria. The question may also eliminate a distractor by saying a particular capability is required.

Knowing the structure and intent of the questions is helpful; knowing the actual information they will be measuring is essential. Let's explore the pros and cons of each SQL offering and its associated HA/DR configuration with the pros and cons of each.

PaaS SQL

PaaS SQL includes both Azure SQL Database and Azure SQL Managed Instance. The HA/DR solutions available for both are almost identical, including using the same terminology. The only significant difference goes back to the Azure SQL Database Services themselves and whether the service is an instance or a database. Chapter 16 explores the actual configuration of each service's HA/DR technologies and serves as an excellent basis for comparisons.

Azure SQL Disaster Recovery Solutions

Geo-redundant Backups

Geo-redundant backups (writing backups to Azure GRS) are the default recovery protection level for Azure SQL PaaS services. You can change this at provisioning time to LRS, ZRS, or RA-GRS.

LRS and ZRS do not offer any DR capability as all backups are in-region. The advantage of LRS and ZRS is they are cheaper than GRS. This is best used for "pass-through" databases used to land or aggregate data into Azure where the contents stay in the database for a relatively short time (days or weeks at most). The entire database can be reloaded from external sources so very little backup is needed.

Sticking with the default GRS surfaces an endpoint in the Azure Paired Region based on the Primary region, but only when a region-level failure occurs. Microsoft will determine if that happens and open the endpoint automatically. That endpoint can be accessed by any Azure region for a database restore. GRS does not have a guaranteed SLA for replication, but it is almost always less than one hour behind. Be aware that a question may use words like "desired" or "required" to describe how to choose and rank outcomes.

The advantage of geo-redundant backups is they are built into the service and offer the lowest cost of any DR solution. One downside is they have a significant RPO lag and the largest RTO of any solution. Another downside is the servers and databases will need to be recreated with new names since the old names still exist in the Azure SQL Namespace, even if the region supporting them does not. Therefore, all the client applications will need to update their connection information.

Geo-redundant backups are the Azure equivalent of having an offsite tape archive but with less rollback. You still must deploy the Azure databases to restore the backups, although that can be done in a single step. That leads us to the next evolutionary step in HA/DR solutions, Automation Scripts for database deployment and recovery.

Automation Scripts

As we noted in Chapter 12, Infrastructure definitions in Azure are actually code fragments. With Automation Scripts, you can define the characteristics of your Azure PaaS SQL databases and servers for deployment in a recovery region. You can even do some smart interrogation of the Azure SQL Database resource provider and find the latest recovery point for a specific database and then encode that point in time as your desired recovery point.

Of course, this means that having a backup available outside the region using geo-redundant storage is a prerequisite for useful automation scripts. Saving the automation scripts outside of the primary region, either on-premises or in Azure Storage, is also a requirement.

You can start with just the resource group, network, and server definitions for automated deployment and build on that as you have time. Regardless of whether you write automation scripts, you need to document what your Azure SQL PaaS Infrastructure looks like so you can recreate it in a secondary region after a failure.

Geo-replication and SQL Failover Groups

Active Geo-Replication is the foundation of an Azure SQL Active DR Solution. Geo-replication is the synchronization component for a DR Replica that we discussed earlier during the HA/DR theory discussion in this chapter. Azure SQL Active Geo-Replication is available only for Azure SQL DB, not for Azure SQL MI.

Azure SQL Geo-replicas are continuously synchronized via log streaming, exactly like on-premises SQL Server Availability Groups. Each geo-replicated database is separate from any others. You can have different databases targeted to replicas in different regions from the primary or other secondaries, just like with availability groups. Geo-replicas are more than the name implies; you can create a replica in the same region, although this would not protect in the event of a region-level failure.

Azure SQL Failover Groups are the pinnacle of Azure SQL PaaS Disaster Resilience. Failover Groups are essentially fully managed Availability Groups, only with some Azure-specific functionality and terminology. We will go through configuring an Azure SQL Failover Group in Chapter 16.

Recall our discussion earlier in this chapter about the elements of a successful DR solution. Geo-replication creates the up-to-date replica of a single database, within the limits of asynchronous communication. Due to the distance between regions, especially paired regions, the signal latency would add too much time to log write operations, thus forcing the log streaming mechanism to send data asynchronously. Asynchronous communication implies the possibility of data loss, giving a non-zero RPO. Currently there is no SQL Server technology, PaaS, IaaS, or On-Premises, that can provide zero RPO for committed transactions at transaction throughput speeds typically required by SQL Server applications. The speed of light and electrical signals are hard limits that physics imposes on our world.

Technically, an Azure SQL Failover Group is a declarative framework on top of the data synchronization provided by Azure SQL Active geo-replication. Like Availability Groups, SQL Failover Groups provide an abstract SQL endpoint functionally equivalent to a Listener that follows to the current primary server on a planned or unplanned failover. Azure SQL Failover Groups provide the connection redirection and failover activation that Azure SQL Active Geo-Replication needs to become a complete DR solution. However, the two technologies are deployed independently. You do not need to deploy Active geo-replication in order to use Azure SQL Failover Groups.

When you create an Azure SQL Failover Group, you will get two new endpoints. The original Azure SQL Server endpoints will remain and can be used, again just like with on-premises Always-On Availability Groups. These endpoints are the Global Read–Write endpoint and the Global Read-Only endpoint. The Read–Write endpoint is pointed at the Primary server, and the Read-Only one is pointed at the secondary server. There is a cost-saving option that reduces the price of the secondary if you turn off the read-only capability. This is done by designating the secondary as a "failover-only" secondary.

Azure SQL Failover Groups also fail over databases as a set rather than individually, completing the functionality provided by Always-On Availability Groups for IaaS or On-Premises SQL. An Azure SQL Failover Group must contain databases that share both a primary and a secondary SQL Server, implying that all databases in a group must use the same primary and secondary regions.

Failover Groups interact properly with local HA or patching to eliminate triggering a false failover. Failover can be manual or automatic. As we will see in Chapter 16, there is a dashboard and a control interface to visualize and manage all your SQL PaaS Failover Groups in one place. Failover can be set to trigger as completely manual or manual + automatic. Microsoft will only trigger an automatic failover after at least one hour of regional service loss. Microsoft strongly suggests configuring for manual failover and creating a strong process around triggering such a failover. Do not rely on Microsoft to trigger an Azure SQL Failover Group failover that will likely meet your Service-Level Agreements.

SQL Failover Groups offer the lowest RPO and RTO of any Disaster Recovery solution in Azure. They are also the simplest to implement from an application standpoint. The global read–write endpoint (the Listener equivalent) does not change its name on a failover, requiring zero application changes regardless of which server is acting as primary. The trade-off is that SQL Failover Groups have the highest cost of any Azure Disaster Recovery Solution. An entire secondary server and database set must be running at all times to receive the transaction log stream. Neither the Primary nor the Secondary server can be Serverless or paused for any reason. Microsoft does allow the Secondary Server for Azure SQL Managed Instance to be flagged as a "DR replica," reducing license costs, but you still must pay for the compute and storage of that instance and databases. If you flag the replica as "DR-Only," it is not available as a *read-only* replica.

Azure SQL Managed Instance imposes additional restrictions on Azure SQL Failover Groups. First, there is no need to establish geo-replication before adding in Failover Groups. The two are configured all at once at the Server level. You create an ordinary Azure SQL Managed Instance and designate the instance as a secondary to an existing Managed Instance. All databases are included in a single failover group. If a new database is created on the primary, it will automatically be extended to the secondary.

IaaS SQL

Cloud computing, Azure included, is built on the premise that all compute nodes have a measurable, predictable level of statistical reliability. That level is not 100%. In fact, cloud computing replaces individual machine reliability with failure mitigation. In the case of IaaS SQL, we use the same technologies we used for on-premises HA/DR with a few minor enhancements for Azure.

Let's review our HA and DR solution choices for Azure SQL Virtual Machines.

SQL Always-On Availability Groups

Since its introduction in SQL 2012, SQL Server Always-On Availability Groups (AOAGs) have been the strongest HA and DR solution platform for SQL Server. Properly configured, an AOAG can protect from both local disruption (HA) and data center–level loss (DR) with the lowest RPO and RTO possible. However, it can be complicated to configure and maintain, and the multiple active virtual machines required make it the costliest solution. This will be a factor both on the test and in real life.

SQL Server Failover Clusters

SQL Server has an older HA technology based on shared, arbitrated storage that goes back to SQL 2000. The technology is called SQL Server Failover Clustering, and a deployed configuration is referred to as a SQL Server Failover Clustered Instance (FCI). While you can use Azure Storage or third-party storage such as NetApp to create an FCI, it is not as common in Azure since Azure Storage did not always support multiple hosts. There are some SQL workloads that do not work with AOAG technology, leaving FCIs as the only effective HA solution possible. In the on-premises world, storage costs were also a deciding factor for FCI vs. AOG clusters. Each node in an Availability Group requires local storage for the entire database, potentially doubling or tripling storage costs. This is less of a concern in Azure since bandwidth is often the cost driver for SQL storage and storage is the cheapest resource available for SQL.

Recommend a Testing Procedure for a HA/DR Solution

No HA/DR deployment is complete without a successfully executed test. Regular testing is required to guarantee continued protection.

Warning   An untested recovery process is a recovery hope, not a recovery plan. Your job may be at risk if your recovery process fails.

If you think that sounds harsh, try this.

Warning   You will fail your first DR attempt. Do not make it the one your company depends on.

Now that I have your attention, let's talk about taking your DR hopes and converting them into effective recovery plans. The key to that transformation is testing. Start with isolated unit testing of HA failover and grow from there. Testing should never be a "one and done" exercise either. Some companies mandate regular disaster recovery drills with failover and failback enabled. During the drill, the company actually runs on its alternate infrastructure. Obviously, this only happens after all lesser testing has been completed successfully and the company is confident it can either abort the test or run on alternate infrastructure successfully.

Every Azure SQL Service that has HA replicas, including IaaS FCIs and AOAGs, has the ability to trigger an internal, local failover. This will disrupt long-running queries but will validate two important application tier technologies that are necessary to implement any SQL HA or DR solution. Applications must include Query and Connection retry logic in order to take advantage of a failover to a local or remote replica. Without connection and query retry logic, the data will move, the endpoint will update, but the application will not recognize the change and fail.

You also need an infrastructure test environment separate from your DevOps testing stack. The DevOps stack is all about validating code, not infrastructure. You can think of it as "production" for the development and QA teams. Without it operating normally, they can't do their jobs. You need a place to test infrastructure changes and failover processes. The good news is that in Azure, your infrastructure testing environment can be ephemeral. You can deploy the resources only as needed and for only as long as you need. You can even leverage automated infrastructure deployment tooling like we discussed in Chapter 12 to manage such an environment.

Once you have validated local failover, you can move on to DR testing. For this type of testing, I like to borrow from the Migration processes we discussed in Chapter 4. Create an "offline" copy to populate the DR site while it is being tested. Only when it is complete do you replace it with a synchronized copy of your data and exercise a complete "end-to-end" failover and failback test. After all, a Failover is just an unscheduled migration you can return from.

Azure Site Recovery

ASR allows for a test recovery in an isolated "sandbox" without breaking the ongoing replication or switching the full workload to the testbed. This greatly simplifies testing, provided you haven't run into the exceptions we discussed earlier in this chapter that require additional post-failover work. Be aware that the recovered server will be an exact clone, name and Active Directory ID included, of the original server. Don't try and re-integrate any data from your failover test databases back into your production environment.

Chapter Summary

As I mentioned at the beginning of this chapter, SQL Server HA/DR is complicated. Creating and implementing a successful HA and DR strategy is going to be one of the most detailed projects you will work on in your career. It is also one of the most professionally rewarding endeavors a DBA can accomplish. Clarity of definitions, understanding the desired outcomes, thoroughly mastering the technology, and successfully testing a HA/DR solution can be a game changer in your career. This ability will differentiate you from your peers and bring positive attention from company management. At least, it has for me.

CHAPTER 15

Perform Backup and Restore of a Database

Recovering a database from backup is a fundamental Database Administrator function. In the past, when I started a new job, the first thing I did was check that I could restore every database I was responsible for. Notice I did not say I "checked backups." Backups are a necessary but not sufficient element to successfully restore a database. In addition to the backups, you need a place to restore the database and some command or tool to initiate the restore. In some cases, you may need Encryption Keys to unlock the backup or the restored database.

Nobody in a serious IT or company management position cares about your database backups. They care that you can recover the systems you are responsible for within a specified time frame and with no more than an expected amount of data loss. In addition, there may be regulatory or other compliance requirements that specify Long-Term Retention of data, which is typically implemented via retention of backup files. If you cannot meet the stated goals, you should document exactly what you did to verify the shortfall, what resources you need to meet the goals, and how long it will take you to be able to provably meet the goals when provided with the necessary resources.

Business does not care about the mechanical elements of database recovery. We certainly do care about how we provide the database continuity services when we need to restore a database to an earlier point in time. That is what this chapter is all about. Most of you come from a SQL Database Administrator background and should understand the basics of SQL Server database backup and restore. Azure SQL extends and automates that same on-premises SQL backup and restore mechanism we have used for decades. Some of you have no SQL Server experience. I am intentionally adjusting the technical level of this chapter to help those who do not have SQL Server Administration experience. If this comes across as a bit basic for those with SQL Server administrator experience, remember, we all started out knowing nothing.

© Geoff Hiten 2025
G. Hiten, *Administering Microsoft Azure SQL Solutions*, Certification Study Companion Series, https://doi.org/10.1007/979-8-8688-1585-0_15

SQL Server can be thought of as a transaction-processing engine operating over a defined data set. The Transaction Log is the chronological sequence of the transactions, and the database file(s) are the data set. If this sounds familiar, it is because I wrote the exact same thing in Chapter 14. I am repeating it here because (a) people skip around this book and may not read it cover to cover and (b) it is important to look at SQL data as changing over time. Restoring to a particular point in time is far more important to SQL Databases than it is to an application or web server.

Some enterprises use a central backup system to host and manage all backups. In that case, the responsibility for database recovery falls to that team and not to the Database Administrator. While that works for on-premises SQL systems and some Azure systems, Azure PaaS services manage backups internally and do not expose the workings to outside systems. This means you cannot enroll Azure SQL PaaS services in enterprise backup solutions and you will once again be responsible for database recovery. On a positive note, since the backups are now part of the service and behind a different control plane, they are immune from encryption or corruption schemes should your systems be compromised by ransomware.

SQL Backup and Restore Internals

This section is primarily for those who are not familiar with how SQL Server implements a transactionally consistent backup and restore process that allows for recovery to a specific point in time. This is not intended to be an exact technical description, merely a medium-level dive into the mechanics of SQL Server backup and restore so you can understand the process in the context of a transaction-processing engine and a data set. I am also not going to go into the exact syntax of each command. Microsoft has written multiple documentation pages on the RESTORE command that cover the technical details. Go use them.

Full Backups

SQL Server creates self-contained and self-describing backup files using a process described as a "fuzzy backup." The backup is transactionally consistent but not at a chosen point in time. Consistency occurs at the time the backup is complete or afterward.

By default, SQL Server will create a single backup file but can split the backup stream into multiple files for scalability. The process is identical to the single file method with the exception of the multiple file settings, so we will discuss the simpler process. When a BACKUP DATABASE command is executed, SQL Server begins the process of creating a SQL Server backup file. This file has a default extension of .bak.

Note   This section will not discuss the advanced topic of backing up and restoring filegroups in Azure. Azure SQL Services do not support backing up or restoring individual filegroups.

SQL Server starts by executing a checkpoint to ensure that all committed transactions are written not only to the transaction log, but any changed (*dirty*) pages are written to the data file(s). Then SQL marks the beginning of the backup in the transaction log. SQL then snapshots several data elements. It copies the Global Allocation Map (GAM), which marks the *Extents* (internal data file allocation units) and the database file definitions for all database files. It writes the file definitions along with some database metadata to the backup file. SQL then reads every allocated extent into memory and writes them out to the backup file. SQL is still processing transactions, and with the exception of a brief *latch* while the GAM is copied, there is very little that gets blocked except for a few global database changes. Compression and Encryption are applied as the extents are written to disk if those options are specified. Encrypted databases always generate encrypted backups.

Since only allocated extents are written to the backup file, the size is proportional to the amount of data in the database, not how large the database files are provisioned. When all extents are written to the backup file, a second mark is put in the transaction log indicating the end of the backup. The entire section of the log between the begin and end markers is copied to the end of the backup file but is *not* marked for reuse. If the "WITH VERIFY" option is specified in the BACKUP DATABASE command, a checksum is run across the backup file. The contents are *not* compared to the original database. As such, I do not recommend using the "WITH VERIFY" option as it adds time but no value and can lead to a false sense of security. As I stated earlier, the only true test of a backup is to restore it. SQL Server also resets the internal Secondary Global Allocation Map (SGAM) unless the backup is designated as "copy-only." The SGAM is a bitmap of extents changed since the previous full backup.

Transaction Log Backups

Transaction log backups copy the active portion of the Transaction Log to an external file. Transaction Log backups also begin with a checkpoint and copy only the used portions of the log up to that checkpoint. Once a log is backed up, the Virtual Log Files (VLFs) are marked for reuse. You can think of the transaction log as a giant tape loop that gets erased and reused after it is backed up. The Transaction Log works the same way in the Simple or Full Recovery model; the only difference is that Virtual Log Files may be marked for reuse after all transactions in that VLFs have been completed and checkpointed. Backing up the Transaction Log is not possible in Simple recovery mode.

Differential Backups

A Differential Backup uses the Secondary Global Allocation Map (SGAM) to identify any extents that have changed since the last full backup. A Differential Backup is always based on the previous full backup and ignores any prior differential backups. A Differential Backup also includes the current active log segment so it can be made transactionally consistent as of the end of the backup. Like the Full Backup, the log segment is not marked for reuse after it is copied.

Restore Database

When SQL Server is tasked with a RESTORE DATABASE command, the SQL engine begins by creating the database files exactly as they were on the source server. Any backup progress reported by the "WITH STATS = *nn*" option does not begin until the file creation has completed. SQL Server allows the "WITH REPLACE" option to force overwrite existing databases and database files. Azure SQL PaaS services do not support overwriting an existing database during a restore. If you need to replace an existing database, you can restore to a different target database name and then rename both databases.

The server then reads the backup file and writes the extents to the data file(s). Since the extents were read from storage in sequential order, the writes are often highly sequential. After all the extents are complete, the server writes the transaction log segment recorded during the time the extents were copied to the backup file into the empty transaction log file. SQL Server then replays the log segment. When SQL Server reaches the end of the log segment, it has three options:

- Restore with Recovery

- Restore with NoRecovery

- Restore with Standby

The simplest case is when the RESTORE completes with a database recovery. Any incomplete transactions are rolled back. The database is made available for new connections. This branches the timeline of the original database into the new database. New transactions are no longer part of the original database. No additional transaction log backups can be applied from the original database.

Restore Log

Although less simple, the more common case is when a RESTORE DATABASE command is issued with NORECOVERY. This places the log in a suspended state. No users can connect to the database as it not quite in a consistent state. This mode is used to move a recovered database forward to a desired point in time. Additional transaction logs can be restored using the RESTORE LOG statement also with either of the three options: RECOVERY, NORECOVERY, or STANDBY.

The final option, STANDBY, exists when databases use Log Shipping to maintain a copy of the primary database for read-only purposes. The pending transactions are temporarily rolled back and placed in a standby file. The database is brought online in a read-only state. Further RESTORE LOG commands can be issued but require an exclusive database lock – no other users are allowed during the restore. This technique is often used to maintain a copy of an active transactional database at Close of Business for use in Data Warehouse ingestion. As with NORECOVERY, any further log restores can use the RECOVERY, NORECOVERY, or STANDBY option.

Restore Differential

A Differential Backup can be restored as part of a point-in-time database restore process but only under very specific conditions. Differential backups are a way to speed up a Point-in-Time Restore (PiTR) while making efficient use of backup storage space. A differential backup stores only the extents that have been changed since the last full backup using a bitmap called the Secondary Global Allocation Map. As noted earlier, this map gets reset to zero when a full backup completes. The effect of restoring a differential backup is the same as if you restored all the log backups using NORECOVERY since the prior full backup, starting with restoring the prior full backup, of course. This can save time if your backup strategy has frequent log backups and long intervals between full backups. Like the other restores, you can restore with RECOVERY, NORECOVERY, or STANDBY.

Recommend a Database Backup and Restore Strategy

The most important element of a backup and restore strategy is the Service-Level Agreement (SLA) section on database recovery. If you do not have a formal SLA with the greater organization, you should at least write up a document on your SQL Database recovery capabilities and share it with your immediate management chain. Setting and managing expectations regarding what you can restore, how long you can keep a restored "extra" copy live, how far back you can reach both point-in-time and LTR, and what is required to replace the existing live database with a previous copy should all be covered by the SLA. The time it takes to restore a backup will be critical information in determining what you can promise as an SLA.

What it should *not* contain is the technical implementation of how you achieve these goals. Stick to strictly non-technical terms regarding times and expectations. Be realistic. Test your restore processes so you know how long it takes to restore a single system, a set of servers, or everything. Restore is especially important if you do not have any "hot" off-site DR capabilities.

Your strategy document on how you achieve the stated goals is going to contain all the technical details omitted from the SLA, including backup methods, backup frequency, testing procedure, monitoring, and alerting.

Let's use the Microsoft default backup strategy for Azure SQL DB General Purpose tier as an example. The SLA specifies point-in-time recovery for a minimum of seven calendar days but can be configured for as many as 35 days. In addition, the user can choose whether a differential backup is performed every 12 hours or every 24 hours as seen in Figure 15-1.

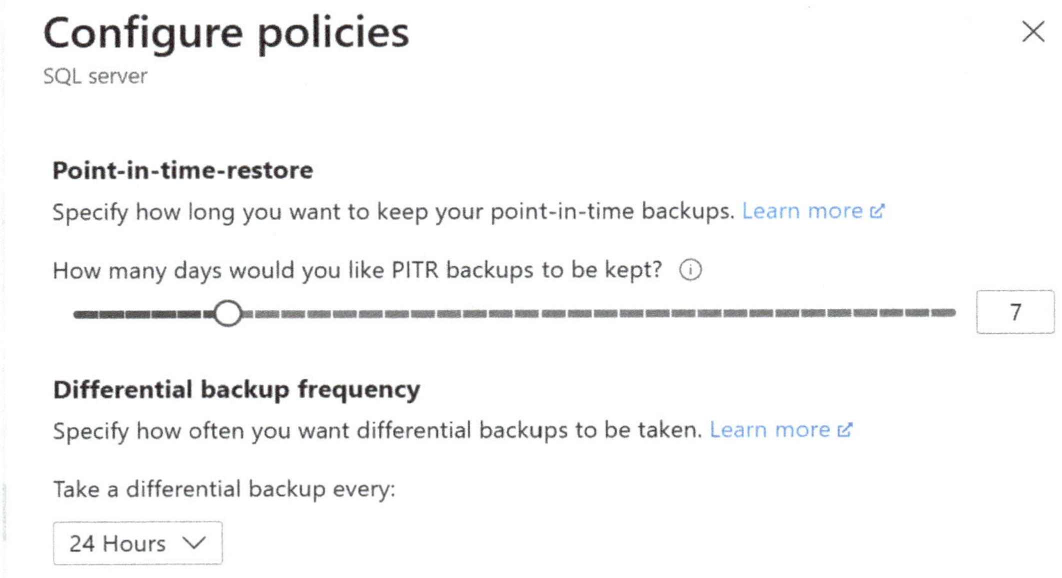

Configure policies

SQL server

Point-in-time-restore

Specify how long you want to keep your point-in-time backups. Learn more ☑

How many days would you like PITR backups to be kept? ⓘ

| | 7 |

Differential backup frequency

Specify how often you want differential backups to be taken. Learn more ☑

Take a differential backup every:

24 Hours ∨

Figure 15-1. *PITR Backup Policy Configuration*

This SLA conveys the desired outcome of the policy but shows very little as to how it is implemented. "Under the covers," Microsoft implements a Full, Differential, and Log backup scheme to meet this SLA. As you can guess, Full backups default to weekly *but* may be done more frequently if the Differential backup exceeds 30% of the size of the most recent full backup. At that point, there is little to no benefit from using a Differential backup. Log backups are every five minutes, but that time interval may be reduced depending on the amount of log volume generated. Given that there must be at least one full backup older than seven days to provide a baseline for PITR within the SLA window, the actual recoverability may exceed the SLA. This is acceptable and expected. The SLA is concerned only with the minimum you can deliver. You may need to exceed those targets some of the time in order to meet it at all times.

Perform a Database Backup by Using Database Tools

Creating a SQL Backup should be a familiar task for most of us. It is a fundamental DBA task. It is also one of the first tasks we automate. Almost all routine database backups should be automated. Manual backups should be for exceptions only. Microsoft even provides some basic automation tools "out of the box," and there are some very good automation scripts available in the Public Domain.

For those not familiar with SQL Server backups, some of the terminology may seem odd. SQL Server originated over 30 years ago and has inherited much from that time. "Devices" are where SQL backup files are placed. That includes tape drives, even though block storage has long rendered such storage technology obsolete. Removing or updating such nomenclature would make decades of scripts obsolete and break a lot of essential SQL functionality. It is better to just deal with some less-than-descriptive terminology.

Backing up a database from an Azure SQL Virtual Machine is not very much different from backing up a database on-premises. Backups to local storage are both simple and worthless. Unless you separate the backup from the original host instance, you have not really protected anything. On-premises, we accomplish that by backing up to a network share or having a central backup service "pick up" our local backup files and manage them centrally. Either way, we end up with protected files "off the box."

In Azure, we accomplish that by backing up to Azure Storage. You may want to refresh yourself on our discussion from Chapter 1 about the different types of Azure Storage. For SQL Backups, we typically back up to Azure Blob Storage. For all system backups, Microsoft recommends Geographically Redundant Storage (GRS). This makes a copy available in a different region – off-site backups are now just a matter of selecting the correct storage.

You can back up to URL from on-premises SQL, but it is a far better experience with everything in Azure. You no longer will need to explain why your SQL Server ate all the Internet bandwidth uploading a backup in the middle of the day.

In the following example, we will walk through creating a backup for a database hosted on an Azure SQL Server Virtual Machine. We will store those backups on Azure Storage (backup to URL). We will also create a full, differential, and log backup sequence that we will use to restore a database in the next sections. We will not go into provisioning or managing Azure Storage. We will discuss Azure Storage security, since it is the biggest change to the backup process from what you are familiar with.

Note   Beginning with SQL 2022, you can back up to an S3-type Storage. Connecting to S3 is not on the test as of publication, and therefore we will be exercising that capability at this time.

Backups to URL work almost exactly the same as local backups or backup to a network share with one major exception – security. With on-premises SQL the identity the SQL Service account used to connect to the NTFS or SMB resource. In Azure, we must use an Entra ID identity that the storage account can understand. Rather than hand out an Entra ID to each SQL Server wishing to save backups to a specific container, we create a Shared Access Signature (SAS) token. A SAS token combines identity with target name resolution and derives its authority from a specific Entra ID identity. Each token has a specific set of rights – you can issue read-only or write-only tokens – and a specific lifespan, days or hours if you choose. This token is stored as a Credential in SQL Server.

You can create a SAS token from the Azure portal, the Azure Storage Explorer tool, or – my personal recommendation – SQL Server Management Studio. SSMS does the "heavy lifting" of creating the token with appropriate permissions and storing it as a credential in SQL Server. The other methods require you to make the right choices and build a T-SQL command from the portal or tool output to save the credential.

Our example begins with our friendly database AdventureWorks2022. The database has already been backed up at least once to initialize the log sequence and placed in full recovery to emulate a production database. Figure 15-2 shows the default settings from selecting the SSMS Back Up Database Wizard by right-clicking the Adventureworks2022 Database name.

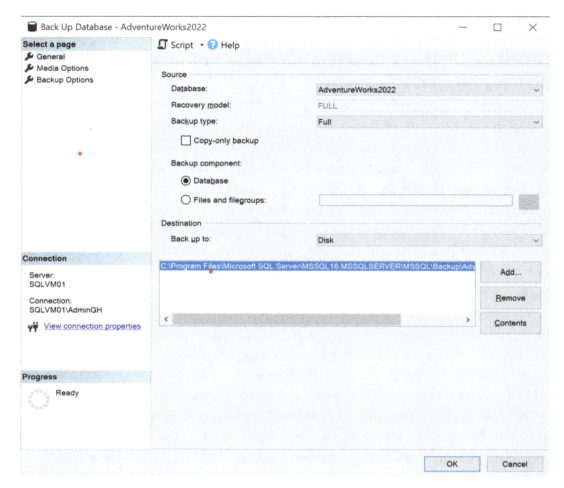

Figure 15-2. *SSMS Back Up Database Wizard Default Settings*

Notice the database is in FULL recovery mode so we can create Point-In-Time recovery backups.

Creating a Credential via SSMS

We will need to change the "Back up to:" option to URL and select "Add…" to open the URL Container dialog box. Changing the "Back up to:" target changes which dialog box the "Add…" button opens. The URL version of the "Select Backup Destination" dialog box is shown in Figure 15-3.

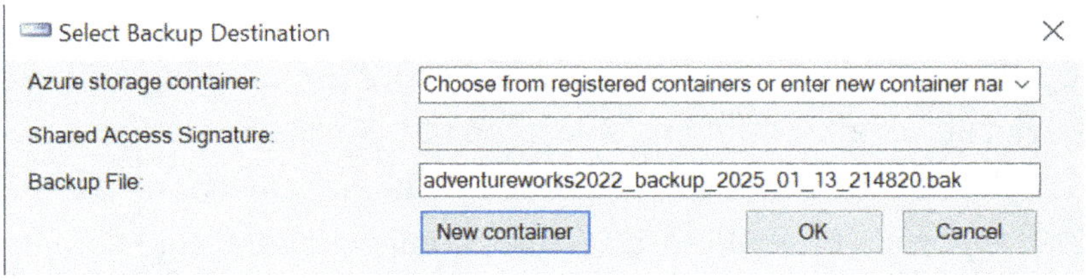

Figure 15-3. *Select Backup Destination – URL*

If you do not need SSMS to create credentials, you can enter everything here. If you are logged in to Azure, the Azure storage container drop-down is populated with containers you have access to. If you are not logged in to Azure or you need SSMS to create a credential for you, select "New Container." Despite the slightly confusing name, you will not be creating a new Azure Storage Container, you will be creating a new connection to an existing Azure Storage Container.

Figure 15-4 shows the also confusingly labeled "Connect to a Microsoft Subscription" dialog box.

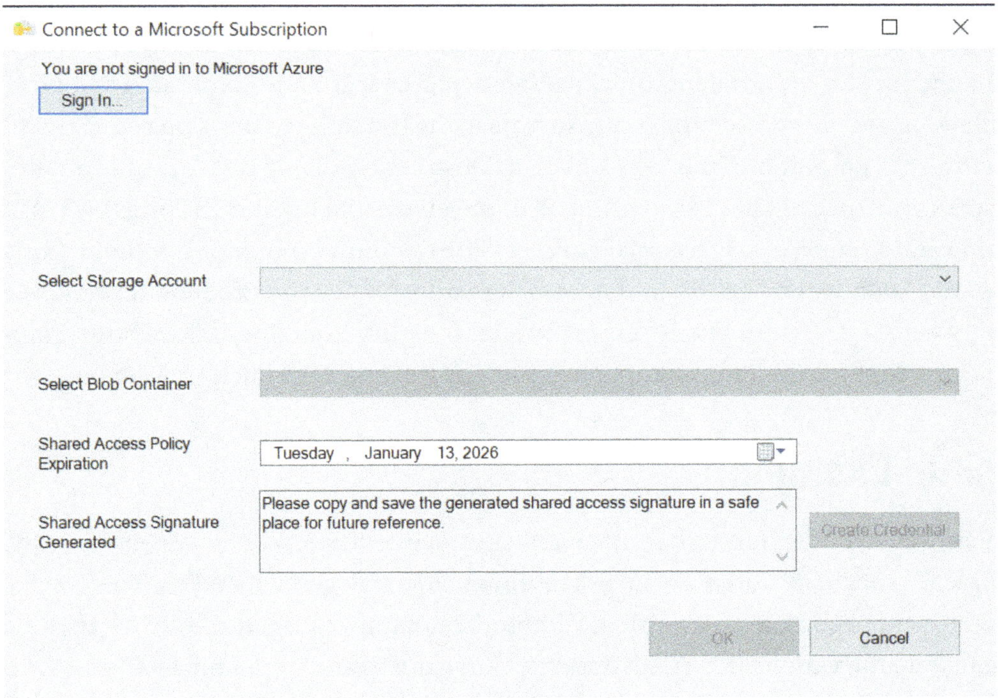

Figure 15-4. *Connect to a Microsoft Subscription*

Once you log in, you click the Select Storage Account drop-down, which will populate with a list of Azure Storage Accounts that your Entra ID account can access. Select the desired Storage Account and select the Blob Container below that. The Storage Account and Blob Container should be provisioned before you connect to Azure. You can use the Azure portal or the Microsoft Azure Storage Explorer tool to manage storage containers in Azure, including generating SAS tokens directly, but that process will not be detailed here. SSMS cannot provision Azure storage accounts or containers.

Note   The actual Storage Accounts used in this demo were deleted prior to publication. There is no need to try and access them.

SSMS does not consider Containers that do not allow SAS Token access as valid containers and will not list any such containers. Troubleshooting container access will likely be the most challenging aspect of executing a BACKUP TO or RESTORE FROM URL. Items to consider are network access, firewall rules, account permissions, and Storage Account configuration.

Once you log in and select an account and container, choose when the token should expire and hit "Create Credential." The Shared Access Signature Generated text box will populate. If you are connecting many servers using the same token, you can copy this signature and paste it into the Select Backup Destination dialog box for subsequent connections. You can check the existence of the credential in the SYS.CREDENTIALS system catalog view. The credential name will be the Blob Container Endpoint, and the credential_identity will be "Shared Access Signature." Since the Credential Name is a primary key, SQL supports only one credential per Blob Container. Close both dialog boxes to accept the default backup file name and return to the Back Up Database wizard.

Backup Example

The best way to understand a backup and restore sequence is to build and execute an example. We begin by outlining the exact sequence we are going to follow. This BACKUP example is more complex than strictly required, but I want to create a solid sequence to demonstrate the various RESTORE options. I am cloning and populating two tables in the database so we can easily see the progress through time as we execute the corresponding RESTORE process. The example begins with a database in FULL recovery mode with the transaction log initialized after a first full backup. The activity sequence is as follows:

1. FULL BACKUP

2. CREATE TABLE Person.Address2

3. TIME CHECK 1 (@TImeCheck1 = GetDate())

4. LOG BACKUP 1

5. POPULATE TABLE Person.Address2

6. TIME CHECK 2 (@TImeCheck1 = GetDate())

7. LOG BACKUP2

8. DIFFERENTIAL BACKUP 1

9. CREATE TABLE Production.Product2

10. TIME CHECK(@TImeCheck3 = GetDate())

11. LOG BACKUP 3

12. DIFFERENTIAL BACKUP 2

13. POPULATE TABLE Production.Product2

14. TIME CHECK (@TImeCheck4 = GetDate())

15. LOG BACKUP 4

With these backups and corresponding time captures, we can restore to any desired point in time and use differential backups to skip log restores. To avoid dating this book, I will have used DateTime variables to represent the different time captures. I am only including a single example of each type of backup. The only thing that changes between the first and subsequent log and differential backups is the target file name and the time the backup was taken. We will review the changes in the database during the RESTORE example.

Create Full Backup

The backup file path and name are chosen in the Select Backup Destination dialog box from when we created or selected the destination. Once you have created and stored a credential, the Azure Storage Container drop-down will populate with eligible containers. The default filename is a concatenation of the database name, backup type, and date and time. For this example we are removing the date and time portion of the filename.

Figure 15-5 shows the Media Options page of the Back Up Database wizard. Overwrite Media options are disabled since Azure Blob Storage does not support those file activities. Tape drive options are similarly disabled since Azure Blob Storage is not a tape drive, nor does it emulate one.

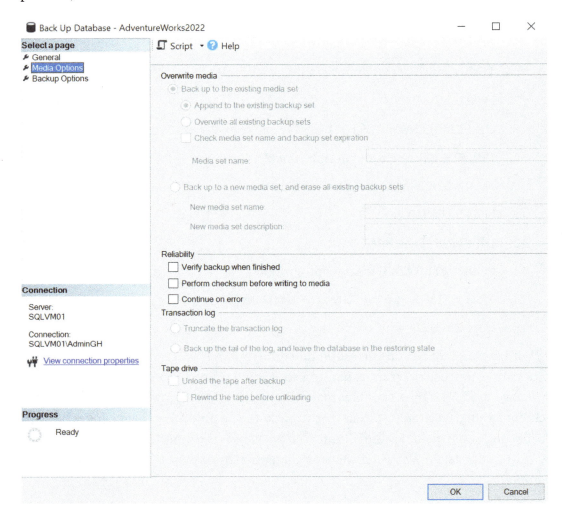

Figure 15-5. *Back Up Database Media Options*

The last page of the Back Up Database wizard is the Backup Options page. This allows us to add a description, set compression, and turn on encryption. Databases with Transparent Data Encryption enabled are encrypted automatically during all write operations, including backups. Figure 15-6 shows us an example configuration. Backup Expiration is disabled as Azure Blob Storage does not support the necessary file primitives.

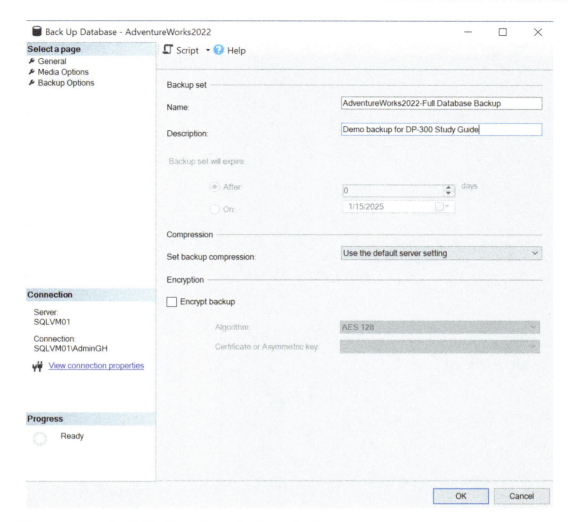

Figure 15-6. *Back Up Database Backup Options*

Selecting "OK" will begin the backup.

Create First Log Backup

When beginning the backup process, you will start with the BACKUP DATABASE option from SSMS, opening to the default "General" page shown in Figure 15-7. Note the "Full" backup selection. This is the first item we will change.

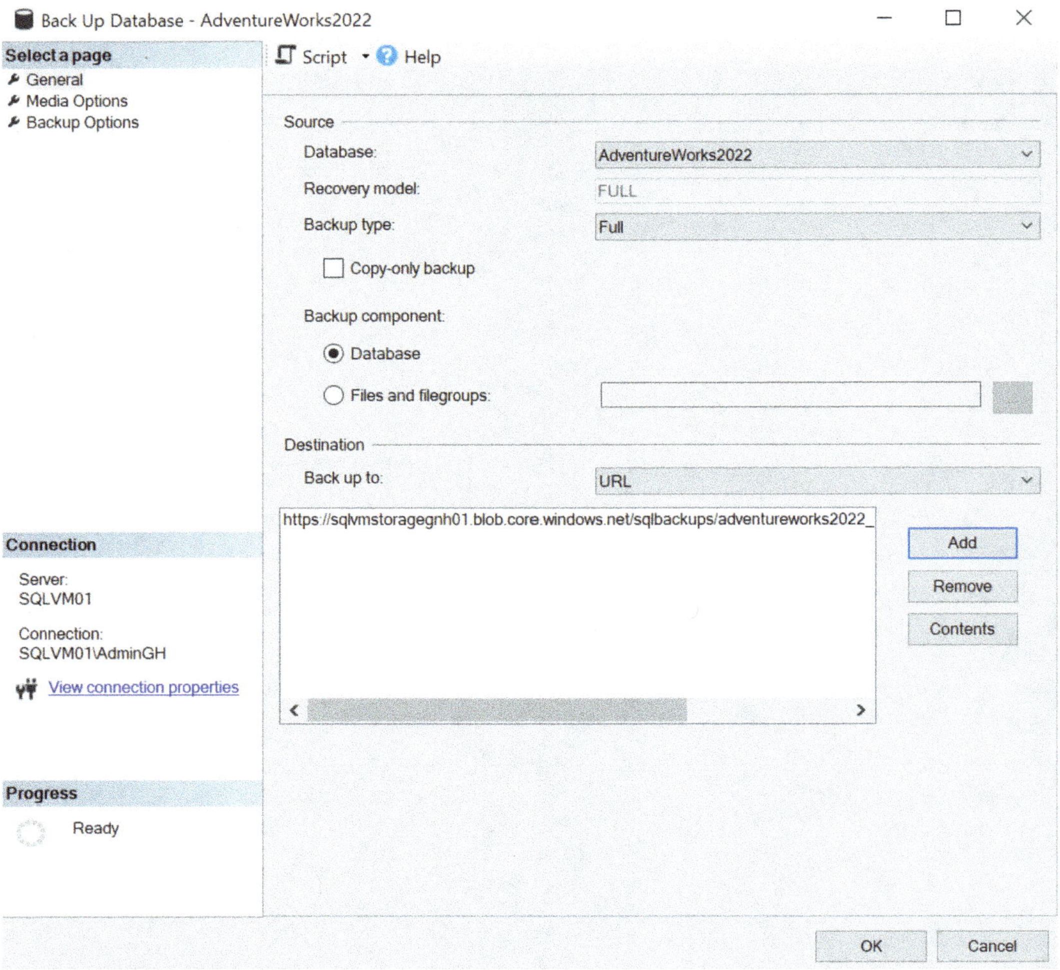

Figure 15-7. Backup Default Page (General Tab)

We will only review a single instance of the log backup process, even though we execute that process four times in this example, changing the target file name each time. Figure 15-8 shows the Back Up Database wizard set to *Transaction Log*.

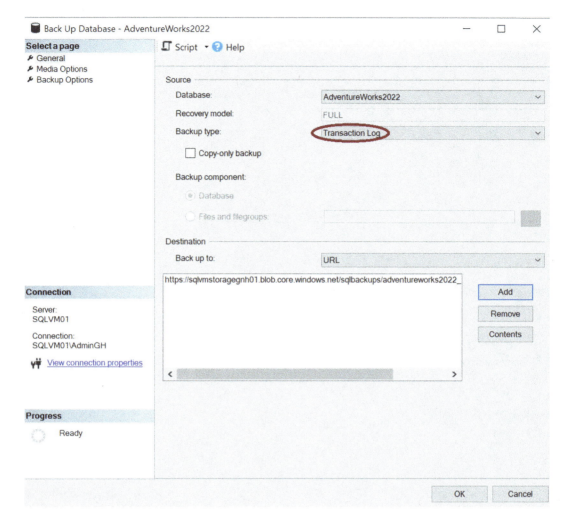

Figure 15-8. *Back Up Transaction Log*

Selecting OK will create a transaction log backup in the designated storage container. Selecting the "Copy-Only Backup" will *not* mark the transaction log for reuse and free up the backed-up Virtual Log Files.

Create Differential Backup

Again, we are only showing a single example of a Differential Backup. Figure 15-9 shows the Back Up Database wizard set to Differential.

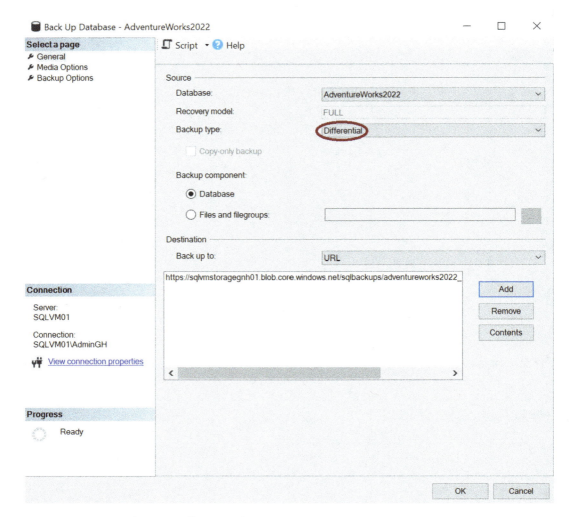

Figure 15-9. *Back Up Differential*

As with the backup Full and Transaction Log options, the rest of the wizard options are identical. The Copy-only backup option is disabled as a differential backup never resets any allocation maps nor marks log segments for reuse. A Copy-only option would have no effect.

Reviewing the Backups

After executing the complete sequence of table creation and population and the various BACKUP steps listed at the beginning of this exercise, we should have the files listed in Figure 15-10.

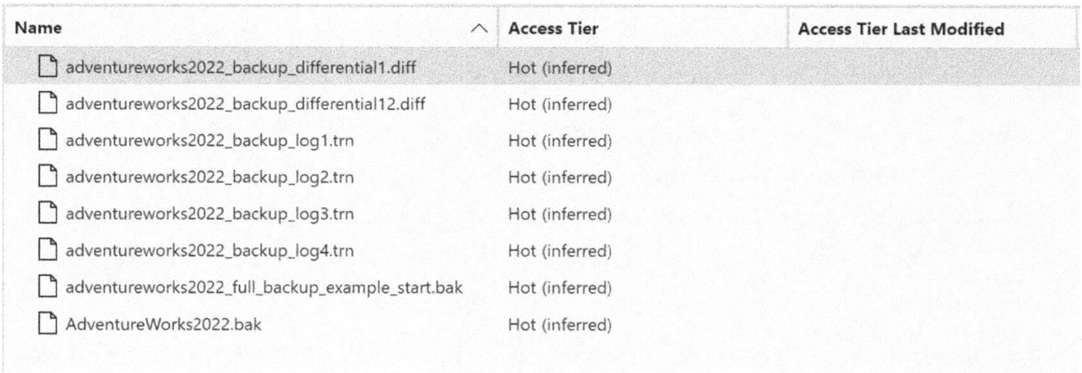

Name	∧	Access Tier	Access Tier Last Modified
📄 adventureworks2022_backup_differential1.diff		Hot (inferred)	
📄 adventureworks2022_backup_differential12.diff		Hot (inferred)	
📄 adventureworks2022_backup_log1.trn		Hot (inferred)	
📄 adventureworks2022_backup_log2.trn		Hot (inferred)	
📄 adventureworks2022_backup_log3.trn		Hot (inferred)	
📄 adventureworks2022_backup_log4.trn		Hot (inferred)	
📄 adventureworks2022_full_backup_example_start.bak		Hot (inferred)	
📄 AdventureWorks2022.bak		Hot (inferred)	

Figure 15-10. *Completed Backup Sequence Files*

Astute readers will notice two full backup files. "AdventureWorks2022.bak" is the original source database backup.

Note   As with all SQL Server backup files in Azure or on-premises, the file extension is purely cosmetic. SQL Server does not require nor restrict backup file type extensions. "BAK, "TRN," and "DIFF" are merely naming conventions.

Perform a Database Restore by Using Database Tools

In this section, we will perform a basic database restore, by walking through the SQL Server Management Studio backup and restore tool. The backup files are stored in Azure Storage, so we will be restoring from a URL. In this example, we will restore each of the database backups we created in the BACKUP database example immediately preceding this section.

When *restoring* any backup type, SQL offers these three recovery options:

- RECOVERY – Recover all committed transactions. Roll back incomplete transactions. The database is ready to receive new transactions via queries.

- NORECOVERY – Recover all committed transactions. Hold all incomplete transactions. The database is ready to apply additional Differential or Transaction Log backups.

- STANDBY – Recover all committed transactions. Roll back all uncommitted Transactions. Record all uncommitted transactions in an external file. Allow read-only queries to access a database. The Database is ready to apply additional Differential or Transaction Log backups.

We can choose multiple backup files in our Restore Database wizard. If we choose multiple files, the selected recovery model will only apply to the final file in the sequence. All previous files will be restored as NORECOVERY.

Example 1: Restore Full and Log to Standby

We begin a RESTORE the same way we began the backup. Right-click *databases* or an individual database and select Restore Database. This brings up the Restore Database dialog box show in Figure 15-11.

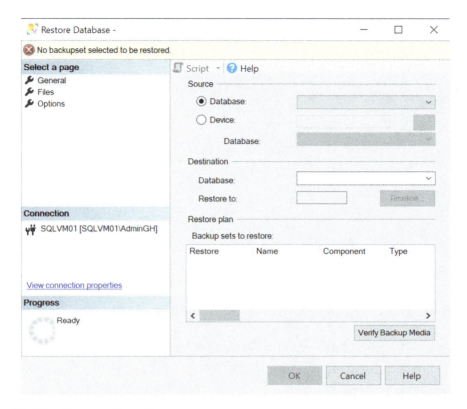

Figure 15-11. *Restore Database*

Here we have a few choices. If we want to RESTORE a database that was backed up from this server, we can leave the source as "Database." The Restore Database wizard will select entries from the internal MSDB database to locate files. If we are restoring from another server, we need to choose "Device." Since that is slightly more complex, that is the path this example will take.

Select "Device" and click the three dots to locate and select the files to RESTORE. This takes us to the "Select backup devices" dialog box we saw during the BACKUP example and shown in Figure 15-12.

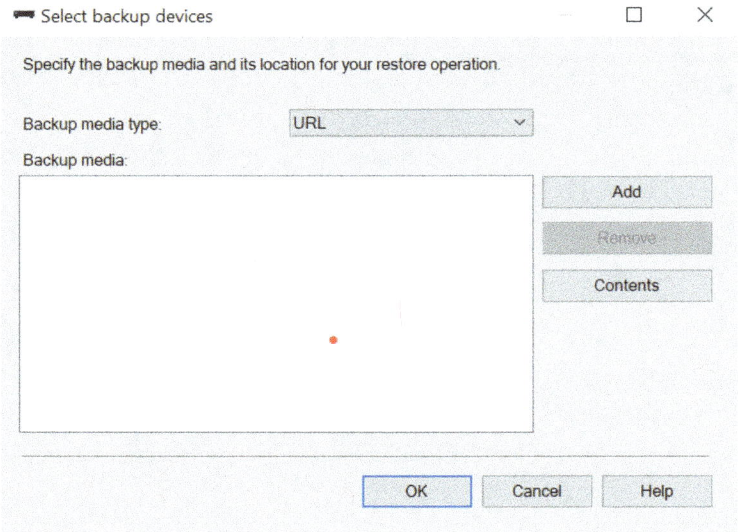

Figure 15-12. *Select Backup Devices for RESTORE*

Change the "Backup media type" to URL and select "Add" to open the "Select a Backup File Location" shown in Figure 15-13.

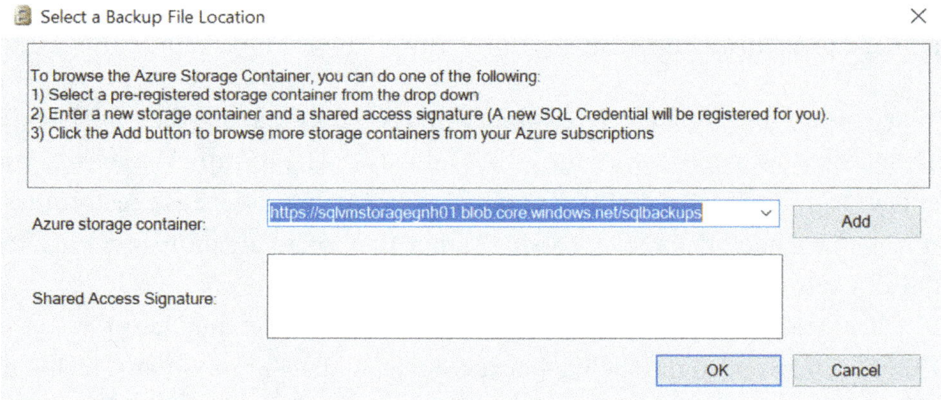

Figure 15-13. *Select a Backup File Location to RESTORE*

The "Azure storage container" list will include any Storage Containers that the SQL Server you are connected to can access. The SSMS dialog box cannot use the Credentials stored in SQL Server to access the contents. You will need to follow the steps outlined earlier in this chapter under the section "Creating a Credential via SSMS." You can also paste the Shared Access Signature if you saved it from that process earlier. Once you have a Shared Access Signature that SSMS can use and are connected to an Azure Storage Container, you will see a list of files in that container as shown in Figure 15-14.

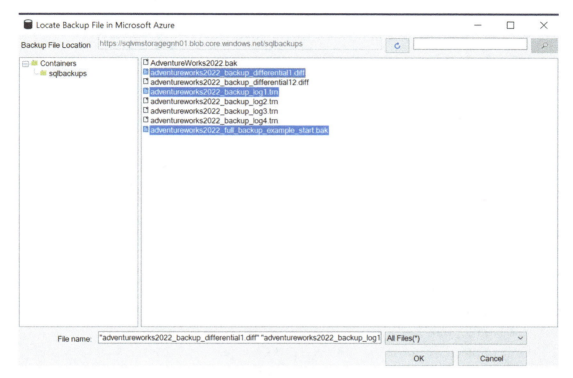

Figure 15-14. Locate Backup File in Microsoft Azure for RESTORE

For this example, we have selected three files, a full, a differential, and a log file. Clicking "OK" brings us back to the "Select backup devices" dialog with our selections as shown in Figure 15-15.

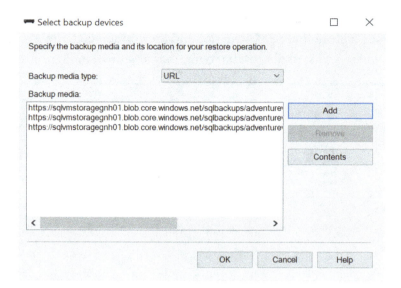

Figure 15-15. *Select backup devices for RESTORE – Populated*

Choosing "OK" executes a "RESTORE HEADERONLY" against each chosen file by the connected SQL Server. This data is sent back to SSMS to validate that your choices constitute a valid restore sequence. The restore sequence is also optimized and unnecessary files removed.

For example, if we chose to restore the FULL backup and LOG BACKUPS 1, 3, and 4, the system would only show the FULL and LOG 1 since LOG 2 is required to create a continuous log sequence.

In our example, LOG 1 is unnecessary since it exists completely between the initial FULL backup and DIFFERENTIAL BACKUP 1. Figure 15-16 shows the two files, FULL and DIFFERENTIAL, selected for RESTORE after SSMS optimized the RESTORE sequence.

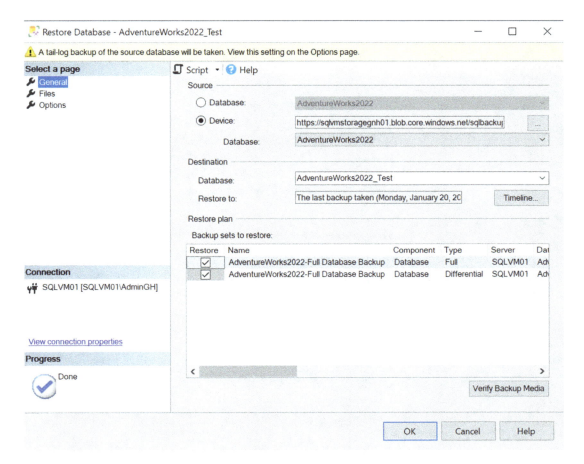

Figure 15-16. *Restore Database ➤ General ➤ Ready to Go*

Notice we are restoring to an alternate database name and not overwriting the existing database. Personally, I always restore to alternate names. It is much faster to rename databases than to "undelete" one. Azure PaaS enforces this behavior by not allowing RESTORE WITH REPLACE. Before we choose "OK" and restore the database, we should look at the Options page show in Figure 15-17. The default options may not be what we want or need.

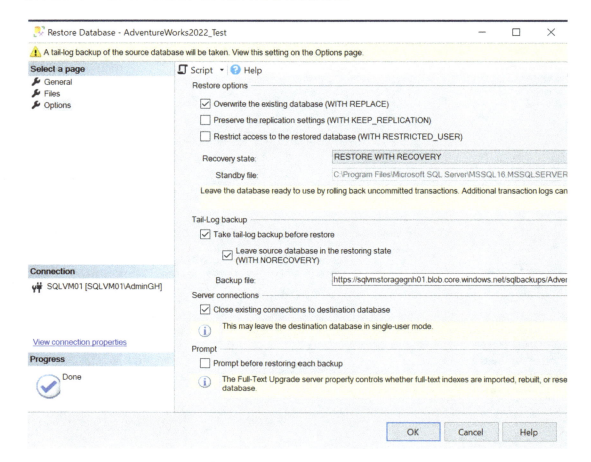

Figure 15-17. *Restore Database Options*

One of the first options we need to set or verify is "Overwrite the existing database (WITH REPLACE)." "WITH REPLACE" is part of the option name to connect the GUI tool to the underlying RESTORE command. We will explore that more in just a moment. If you are replacing an existing database, I strongly suggest always taking a Tail-log backup. This lets you "undo" any mistakes by having an up-to-the last second log backup. "Close existing connections to destination database" is also useful for overwriting an existing database. SQL cannot restore over an active database.

Choosing OK will create a new database and restore to where we chose. The RECOVERY option will be applied to the last file in the restore list.

Example 2: Restore Full, Diff, and Log

If we choose *all* the backup files in our container excepting the initial seed backup file, we get the results shown in Figure 15-18.

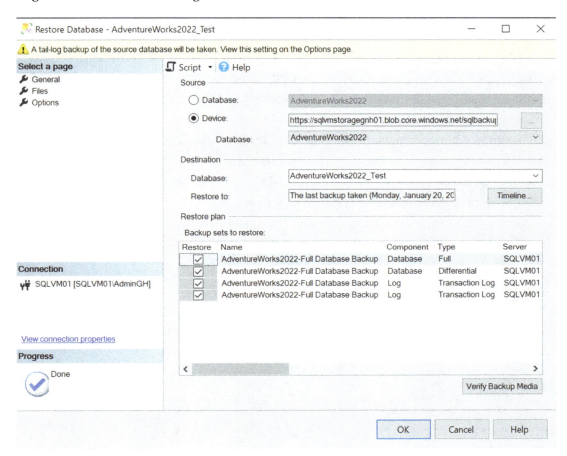

Figure 15-18. *Restore All Files – Optimized*

SSMS has optimized the restore process to restore a single FULL backup, a single DIFFERENTIAL backup, and the two log files that were created after the DIFFERENTIAL backup. This makes sorting through backup files much easier. Just let SQL Server and SSMS do all the work.

Perform a Database Restore to a Point in Time

One common RESTORE scenario requires restoring a database to a specific point in time. The desired time is typically immediately before a large intentional or unintentional data change. Either way, you need to restore a database to an exact spot to "undo" a data change. SQL Server allows you to select an exact point in time as part of the Restore Database wizard. This only applies when restoring one or more log files as part of a RESTORE sequence. If the designated restore point is within a selected log file, the restore is stopped at that point and the selected RECOVERY option is executed.

You access this capability by selecting the "Timeline" button on the "General" tab after picking the appropriate database backup files. Recall our discussion of file selection optimization from the previous example. Timeline will also apply optimization to the backup file selection process. Figure 15-19 shows a point in time selected that corresponds to @TimeCheck2 in our BACKUP example.

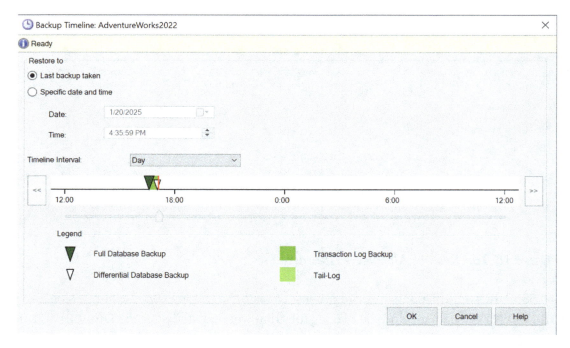

Figure 15-19. *Restore to a Point in Time*

Configure Long-Term Backup Retention

Long-term backup retention (LTR) is a feature of Azure SQL Database and Azure SQL Managed Instance. Long-term backup files are based on the default weekly full backup for all databases in the two PaaS SQL Services. You cannot pick the exact point in time you want the backup performed. Whenever the full backup completes is the only recovery point. This is generally acceptable since restoring a database backup from several weeks or months in the past seldom requires that restore to be from an exact point in time.

You access the control via the SQL Logical Server for Azure SQL Database or the Managed Instance Server blade for Azure SQL Managed Instance. Both are identical from that point, so we will only show the Azure SQL Database path. Go to "Data management" ➤ "Backups" as shown in Figure 15-20.

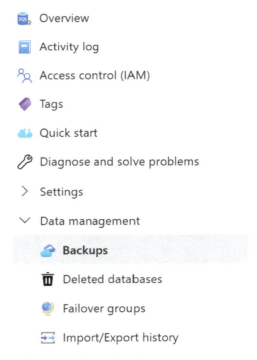

Figure 15-20. *SQL Database Backup Configuration*

Backup retention is considered a *Policy* by Azure. A Policy is simply a defined state that Azure enforces. You define the backup retention policy by selecting "Retention policies" as shown in Figure 15-21.

Refresh
Feedback
Configure policies
Remove LTR settings
Available backups
Retention policies
Configure and manage your automated backup retention policies below. Point-in-time restore (PITR) allows short-term backup retention of 1-35 days. Long-term retention policies enable you to keep full backups for up to 10 years. Learn more
Search for a database
Database
PITR
Diff. backup freq...
Weekly LTR
Monthly LTR
AdventureworksLT
7 Days
24 Hours
--
--

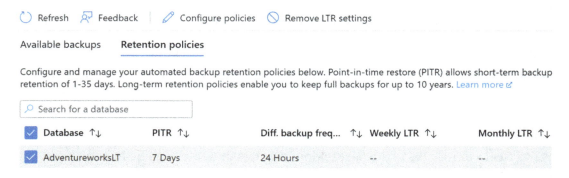

Figure 15-21. *Azure SQL Database Retention Policies*

This is the same blade where you select point-in-time recovery options. Those have been cut from the example for space and clarity. The options are self-explanatory as you can easily see in Figure 15-22.

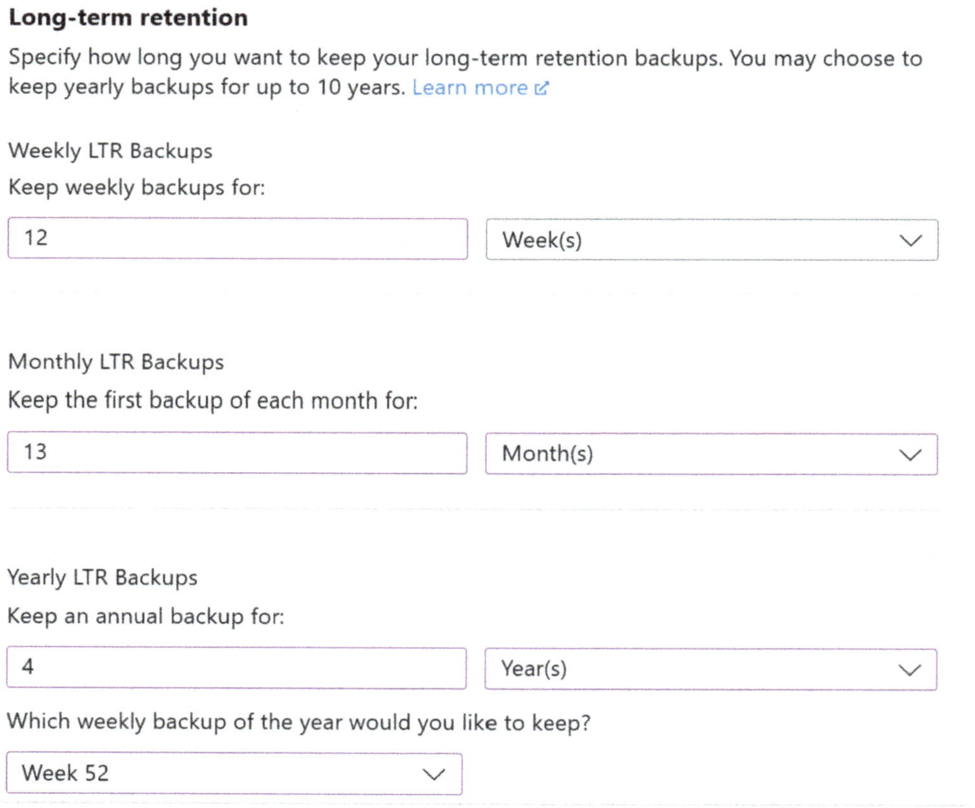

Long-term retention
Specify how long you want to keep your long-term retention backups. You may choose to keep yearly backups for up to 10 years. Learn more
Weekly LTR Backups
Keep weekly backups for:
12
Week(s)
Monthly LTR Backups
Keep the first backup of each month for:
13
Month(s)
Yearly LTR Backups
Keep an annual backup for:
4
Year(s)
Which weekly backup of the year would you like to keep?
Week 52

Figure 15-22. *Azure SQL Database Long-Term Retention*

Back Up and Restore a Database by Using T-SQL

The SQL Server Management Studio Back Up Database and Restore Database wizards are very powerful tools to help find and choose files to back up or restore. Like all GUI tools, they do not lend themselves to automation. Automation for SQL Server means T-SQL Scripts. Fortunately, the SSMS wizards also can help you with generating scripts. By comparing scripts to the Wizard selections, you can further your understanding of how BACKUP and RESTORE work in SQL Server. Figure 15-23 shows the Restore Database wizard from our earlier example with the Script button highlighted.

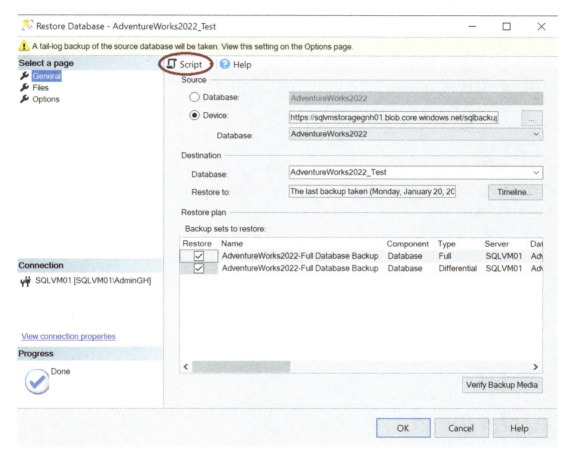

Figure 15-23. *Restore Database Script Option*

The resulting script with some reformatting for clarity is show in Example 15-1.

Example 15-1. Restore Database Example Script

```
USE [master]
BACKUP LOG [AdventureWorks2022] TO  URL = N'https://sqlvmstoragegnh01.
blob.core.windows.net/sqlbackups/AdventureWorks2022_
LogBackup_2025-02-01_13-24-47.bak'
    WITH NOFORMAT
    , NOINIT
    ,  NAME = N'AdventureWorks2022_LogBackup_2025-02-01_13-24-47'
    , NOSKIP, NOREWIND, NOUNLOAD,  NORECOVERY ,  STATS = 5
RESTORE DATABASE [AdventureWorks2022] FROM  URL = N'https://
sqlvmstoragegnh01.blob.core.windows.net/sqlbackups/adventureworks2022_full_
backup_example_start.bak'
    WITH  FILE = 1
    ,  NORECOVERY
    ,  NOUNLOAD
,   STATS = 5
RESTORE DATABASE [AdventureWorks2022] FROM  URL = N'https://
sqlvmstoragegnh01.blob.core.windows.net/sqlbackups/adventureworks2022_
backup_differential1.diff'
    WITH  FILE = 1
    ,  NOUNLOAD
    ,  STATS = 5
GO
```

The script begins with a BACKUP LOG statement since we chose to back up the tail of the log before replacing the existing database. I recommend reading the RESTORE documentation for a detailed explanation of each option.

Chapter Summary

SQL Server BACKUP and RESTORE is a core Azure SQL Database Administrator function, whether that is planning, executing, configuring, or verifying backups to meet recovery Service-Level Agreements. It may be the most important and visible function you ever perform for your employer, especially if you are a key part of a disaster recovery effort. While we all hope that such events do not occur "on our watch," we must diligently plan for the worst. Planning, preparation, practice, and testing are the keys to a successful database RESTORE, regardless of which SQL Service or platform you use.

CHAPTER 16

Configure HA/DR for Database Solutions

Back in Chapter 3 I remarked that the chapter and most of its subheadings, which are all based on the exam Learning Path topics, were all some form of "configure." We have the same situation here in this chapter. Back then it was about configuring Scalability and Performance. Here it is about configuring HA/DR solutions. This is where we get our hands dirty (figuratively) and start to implement the various Azure SQL HA/DR options. We have spent the last two chapters discussing the theory of HA/DR in general and as applied to Azure SQL along with some specific HA/DR solutions and how they compare with each other. Here we learn to configure and deploy those solutions.

One of the reasons I chose to join Microsoft was looking at how Azure implemented SQL HA/DR. Building an effective and stable multi-site cluster is one of the pinnacle skills of a DBA. I got paid reasonably well to do so by my clients. Looking at how much of the process is automated in Azure got me to reconsider the long-term value of that particular skill set. If you have built or even operated SQL Availability Groups (AGs) or Failover Cluster Instances on-premises, this chapter should smoothly extend that skill set. You should recognize concepts and map them to the technology you already know and understand as we proceed through the examples.

Configure Active Geo-replication

The word "Replication" is often overloaded in the SQL world, especially when talking with people outside of the SQL Database universe. Little "r" *replication* is a generic term for continuously synchronizing data sets such as databases or file systems. SQL often uses continuously streaming transaction logs to accomplish this goal. Big "R" *Transactional Replication* is a specific feature of SQL Server that synchronizes data via

© Geoff Hiten 2025
G. Hiten, *Administering Microsoft Azure SQL Solutions*, Certification Study Companion Series,
https://doi.org/10.1007/979-8-8688-1585-0_16

DML statements. In this discussion of Active Geo-Replication, we are using the little "r" definition. Active Geo-Replication does not have any relationship with big "R" Transactional Replication.

Active Geo-Replication can be used to create database replicas for both DR purposes and read scale-out. True DR replicas must be located in different regions than the primary, but there is no specific restriction on creating replicas in either a different region or the same region. Local regional replicas can be used for read-only scale-out. When determining a secondary server, you must avoid namespace contention. The secondary server cannot have a database with the same name as the primary database as database names must be unique on a server, even a logical SQL DB server.

Unlike some of our earlier walk-throughs in this book, for this example we will not be starting from "zero." We begin with two configured Azure SQL Database Servers. One of them will host our Primary replica, and one will be the target for our deployed secondary replica. For convenience, the example will use servers in the same region as the process for creating cross-region replicas is exactly the same.

We begin on the Data Management ➤ Replicas blade shown in Figure 16-1 accessed from the left tower menu.

Figure 16-1. *Azure SQL DB Replica Status*

Any existing replicas of this database are shown and managed here. Select "Create replica" at the top of the page. This will bring up a deployment blade since we are deploying a new database – the secondary replica. This blade has six sections labeled as follows:

1. Project details

2. Primary database details

3. Geo-secondary database details

4. Transparent data encryption key management

5. Backup storage redundancy

Project details display the subscription and resource group – this will be pre-populated with the source database subscription and resource group and cannot be changed. Primary Database Details display the primary database name and region. This will also be pre-populated and is unchangeable. Geo-secondary database details have the most complexity with three subsections. The Project details ask for the subscription and resource group of the replica database. Some organizations use different subscriptions and/or resource groups to manage DR resources. The choice is entirely up to you; both in-subscription and cross-subscription replicas are supported. Geo-secondary database details display the unchangeable replica database name and requires a selection for the replica server name. The replica target server name is the only item you must choose. Everything else can be inherited as a default. Geo-secondary database details also display the target region, inherited from the target logical server. Geo-secondary database details finally ask for elastic pool membership and/or target compute and storage provisioning. The default is to use the same provisioning level as the primary, but as a stand-alone database not an elastic pool member.

Transparent data encryption key management is only needed if you Bring Your Own Key (BYOK). Service-managed TDE is handled automatically. BYOK requires you to use the configuration blade to create or assign a user-defined managed identity and select the correct key. Recall from Chapter 6 that Azure Key Vault access is defined at the Logical Server level in Azure SQL Database. You must install or transfer BYOK keys outside of the replica configuration process prior to selecting a key and replicating the database. This is the same process as restoring a database with BYOK enabled to a different server.

The final section is backup storage redundancy. The selection defaults to the same level as the primary, but can be set to any level, regardless of the backup redundancy setting of the primary replica.

While this sounds complex and intimidating, the only entry that cannot be left as the default is the target database server name. Everything else can be left as the defaults, absent BYOK, as it is inherited from either the source database or the target server. As with all Azure SQL DB deployments, you will see a summary page with a monthly cost estimation as shown in Figure 16-2 before you finally deploy the resource.

Create SQL Database - Geo Replica   ⋯   ✕
Microsoft

Basics   **Review + create**

Product details

SQL database
by Microsoft
Terms of use | Privacy policy

Estimated cost per month
14.72 USD

Terms

By clicking "Create", I (a) agree to the legal terms and privacy statement(s) associated with the Marketplace
offering(s) listed above; (b) authorize Microsoft to bill my current payment method for the fees associated with
the offering(s), with the same billing frequency as my Azure subscription; and (c) agree that Microsoft may
share my contact, usage and transactional information with the provider(s) of the offering(s) for support,
billing and other transactional activities. Microsoft does not provide rights for third-party offerings. For
additional details see Azure Marketplace Terms. ☐

Basics

Subscription	
Resource group	SQLDB_RG_EASTUS2
Primary database	AdventureworksLT
Region	eastus2
Database name	AdventureworksLT
Server	sqldbsrver2
Compute + storage	Standard S0: 10 DTUs, 250 GB storage
Database level customer-managed key	Not configured
Database level user assigned managed identity	Not configured

Create   < Previous   Download a template for automation

Figure 16-2. *Azure SQL Database Replica Summary*

Once you deploy the replica, both the primary and the secondary replica will appear on the Data management ➤ Replicas blade as shown in Figure 16-3.

+ Create replica   ◯ Refresh   ◻ Feedback

Geo replicas for your database are listed below. Geo replicas reside on a different logical server from the primary and protect against regional failures or prolonged data center outage. Learn more ↗

Name ↑↓	Server ↑↓	Region ↑↓	Failover policy ↑↓	Pricing tier ↑↓	Replica state ↑↓	
⌄ Primary						
AdventureworksLT	sqldbsrver01	East US 2	None	Standard S0: 10 DTUs	Online	•••
⌄ Geo replicas						
AdventureworksLT	sqldbsrver2	East US 2		Standard S0: 10 DTUs	Readable	•••

Figure 16-3. *Azure SQL DB Replica Status with a Replica*

By selecting … at the left edge of the secondary database, you can choose from *Failover* or *Forced Failover*. Failover requires an active connection to the primary database so the transactions can be fully synchronized during the failover. Forced failover can result in lost transactions and should only be used during a true Disaster Recovery when access to the primary is lost. You can also stop data replication and leave the secondary as a stand-alone database on the secondary server from this menu.

You can deploy via T-SQL by using command ALTER DATABASE *<PrimaryDatabaseName>* ADD SECONDARY ON SERVER *<SecondaryReplicaServerName>* to create a secondary replica on a chosen server. This ties to the ability to inherit defaults for all fields except the secondary server name, again absent BYOK or having connected the secondary server to an appropriate Key Vault beforehand. All secondary replica settings will be set to the defaults inherited from the primary database. Changing those options is not supported via T-SQL during replica creation, but many can be changed later via portal or T-SQL.

Configure Auto-failover Groups

Auto-Failover Groups replace Active Geo-Replication with an enhanced service that includes group failover control and endpoint abstraction in addition to the fundamental capabilities of Active Geo-Replication technology. Instead of failing over as an individual group, databases fail over as sets. The scope of a failover group is one or more databases that are replicated between a single source server and a single target server. All databases in a failover group are failed together. Each failover group has a read-only and a read–write endpoint. This allows the databases to fail over without needing to update the application connection strings. Active geo-replication does not have this endpoint abstraction. For Azure SQL Managed Instance, all databases are enrolled in a single failover group.

People ask why both technologies exist when there is significant overlap between the two. The reason is time. Active Geo-Replication was deployed in Azure long before Failover Groups were created. Given the widespread use of Active Geo-Replication and a less than 100% feature overlap, Microsoft decided to keep both technologies Generally Available.

I often see confusion between local read-only replicas and global read-only replicas regarding how to access each. You can use the local read replica of the either the global read-only replica or the global read–write replica on SKUs (Hyperscale, Business Critical) that support local read-only replicas. Global is selected by choice of endpoint, while the Local selection is chosen via the ApplicationIntent=READONLY connection string option. You can also use the local Logical Server name (endpoint) for any replica with ApplicationIntent=READONLY to have local read-only access that does not fail over with the failover group.

Note   You do not have to configure Active Geo-Replication prior to configuring Failover Groups. Failover Group configuration will create the underlying replicas. The two technologies are completely separate and independent.

Active geo-replication begins at the *Database* level; we begin Failover Groups at the *Server* level. Like active geo-replication, we begin with the Data management entry and select Failover Groups.

Failover Policy

While Microsoft will allow you to defer the decision on when to fail over to them, Microsoft recommends not to do so. A Microsoft-initiated database failover will always depend on the underlying Region failure. As long as the region is functioning and the service has a recovery timeline, Microsoft will not initiate a service failover. Even if a failure is declared, there is a minimum of a one-hour "Grace Period" delay before forcing a service failover. You are far better off defining a failover policy that matches your specific availability requirements and needs; however, Microsoft considers their failure-initiated policy to be the only "automatic" failover option.

Configure an Always-On Availability Group

If you aren't already familiar with an Always-On Availability Group (AOAG) using on-premises SQL Servers, you may struggle with this section. I am assuming some foundational knowledge of the elements, components, and terminology around this technology. This section will focus on implementation details that are Azure specific and likely to show up on the exam.

Endpoint Redirection

An Always-On Availability Group abstracts the SQL endpoint connection via a *Listener*. The Listener is a Windows Server Failover Clustering (WSFC) Network Name object with one or more associated IP addresses. For on-premises SQL AOAGs in a simple two-node cluster configuration on a single subnet, each Network Name Object has a single IP address that "floats" between the two nodes, following the Primary Replica and acting as the SQL Connection Endpoint for external applications. On-premises, the network Address Resolution Protocol (ARP) advertises the binding of the two artifacts (IP and MAC address) so the other devices on the network can quickly update any changes. Unfortunately, Azure does not support "floating" IP addresses. There is no ARP. The Software-Defined Networking system in Azure ties the MAC (physical) address of a virtual NIC to a specific IP address. To remedy this, Azure uses a Basic Load balancer to host the "floating" IP address and redirects the connection to the correct underlying replica.

Alternatively, Azure supports the use of a Dynamic Network Name object (DNN) that is a different type of WSFC artifact to map a named endpoint to an IP address and port on a host server. DNNs can only be set up via PowerShell, cannot use port 1433, and do not support all SQL Server services.

Microsoft has designed a third cluster architecture that eliminates the need for a load balancer and has none of the shortcomings of Dynamic Network Names. Azure can now support multiple fixed IP addresses on the same virtual NIC. This allows us to place cluster nodes in different subnets, much like we would in a geographically distributed cluster, and assign a fixed set of IP addresses to each Cluster Network Name object with one address per subnet.

> **Note**   Given that Software-defined Azure networks are fully physically redundant, there is no need to create multiple networks in a cluster for heartbeat, backup, etc. One Azure Virtual NIC is sufficient and meets the WSFC redundancy recommendations.

Let's look at a couple of examples. First, we will examine a traditional/load balancer configuration using "floating" IP addresses, and then we will examine what that looks like using a multi-subnet design. Back in my consulting days I used Excel to track the design elements of WSFC clusters. I see no need to change that here. The following tables are simplified versions of the networking page of my tracking workbook.

Before we dig into the details, we should set the key parameters of these scenarios. This is good practice for the exam. Most of the questions set up scenarios of varying complexity and ask you one or more questions regarding the systems and their desired outcomes.

We have a two-node WSFC cluster with Default SQL Instances installed on each node. The Instances host a single AOAG with a Listener configured.

Table 16-1 shows the IP address assignments are for a single-subnet cluster. Clus01 and AOAG01 are both WSCF Network Name objects and can be assigned to either node. A load balancer hosts the actual IP address and redirects external connections to the correct host.

Table 16-1. *Single-Subnet Azure AOAG Cluster IP Addresses*

Name	Purpose	IP (10.90.10.0/24)
SQL01	SQL Host 1	10.90.10.10
SQL02	SQL Host 2	10.90.10.11
Clus01	WSCF Cluster Name	10.90.10.12
AOAG01	AOAG Listener Name	10.90.10.13

Table 16-2 shows the IP address configuration for a multi-subnet cluster with no load balancer required.

Table 16-2. *Multi-subnet Azure AOAG Cluster IP Addresses*

Name	Purpose	IP (10.90.10.0/24)	IP (10.90.20.0/24)
SQL01	SQL Host 1	10.90.10.10	NA
SQL02	SQL Host 2	NA	10.90.20.11
Clus01	WSCF Cluster Name	10.90.10.12	10.90.20.12
AOAG01	AOAG Listener Name	10.90.10.13	10.90.20.13

The Cluster Name Artifact in the Windows Server Failover Cluster Manager will show both IP addresses in an *OR* configuration, meaning that the Cluster will only allow one to be active at a time. SQL Server will only respond to that IP address if it hosts the cluster group containing the Network Name cluster entity. Your SQL client libraries need to be at least SQL 2012 or later compliant to properly connect to multi-subnet clusters.

Azure Template for SQL High Availability

Azure offers a Marketplace Template that uses the SQL IaaS extension we first discussed in Chapter 2 to create an Always-On Availability Group Host Cluster. All you need to supply are four prerequisites. These four prerequisites are as follows:

- Resource Group

- Virtual Network

- Domain Controller(s) in the same Virtual Network

- A Domain User with the following account Permissions/Items:

  - Create Computer Object

  - Domain Service Account for SQL Server

We begin by searching for *Marketplace* in the Azure Search bar at the top center of every portal page. We then enter the phrase *SQL Server with High Availability* in the Marketplace Search Bar. This brings up the selection shown in Figure 16-4.

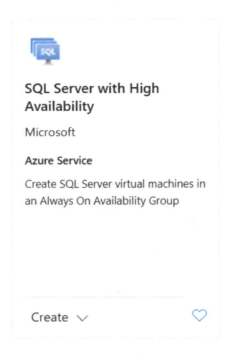

Figure 16-4. *SQL Server with High Availability*

Choosing this brings up a Template wizard that walks you through all the steps to create a working AOAG cluster. There is no additional charge for this template as this is all enabled by the SQL IaaS extension. You simply pay for the underlying SQL Virtual Machines. Choosing "Create" will bring you to a blade that looks much like the normal SQL IaaS deployment wizard but with some changes and an additional page as shown in Figure 16-5.

Create Always On availability group for SQL Server on Azure Virtual Machines
Microsoft

| Basics | Networking | WSFC and Credentials | Disks | SQL Server settings | Tags | Prerequisites validation | Review + create |

Figure 16-5. *Create Always On availability group for SQL Server on Azure Virtual Machines*

That is the additional page where you enter the cluster information. The first change you see is on the Overview page shown in Figure 16-6 regarding machine counts and names.

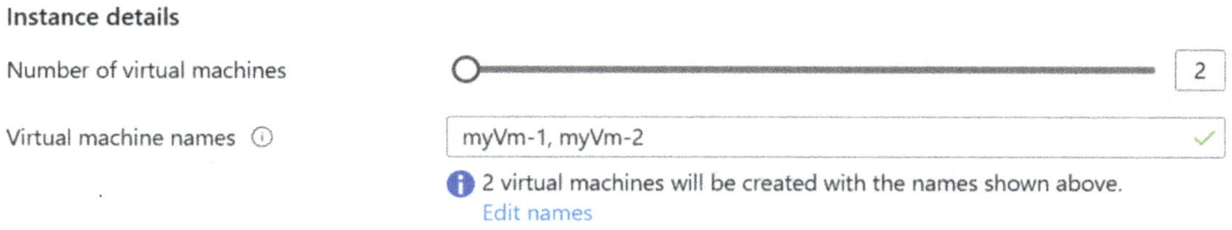

Instance details

Number of virtual machines

○━━━━━━━━━━━━━━━━━━━━━━━━━━━━━━ | 2 |

Virtual machine names ⓘ

| myVm-1, myVm-2   ✓ |

ⓘ 2 virtual machines will be created with the names shown above.
Edit names

Figure 16-6. *SQL AOAG Instance Details – Machine Names and Counts*

The wizard will build up to a nine-node cluster, and you can use the auto-generated names or edit them yourself. The other addition is the third page – WSFC and Credentials – shown in Figure 16-7.

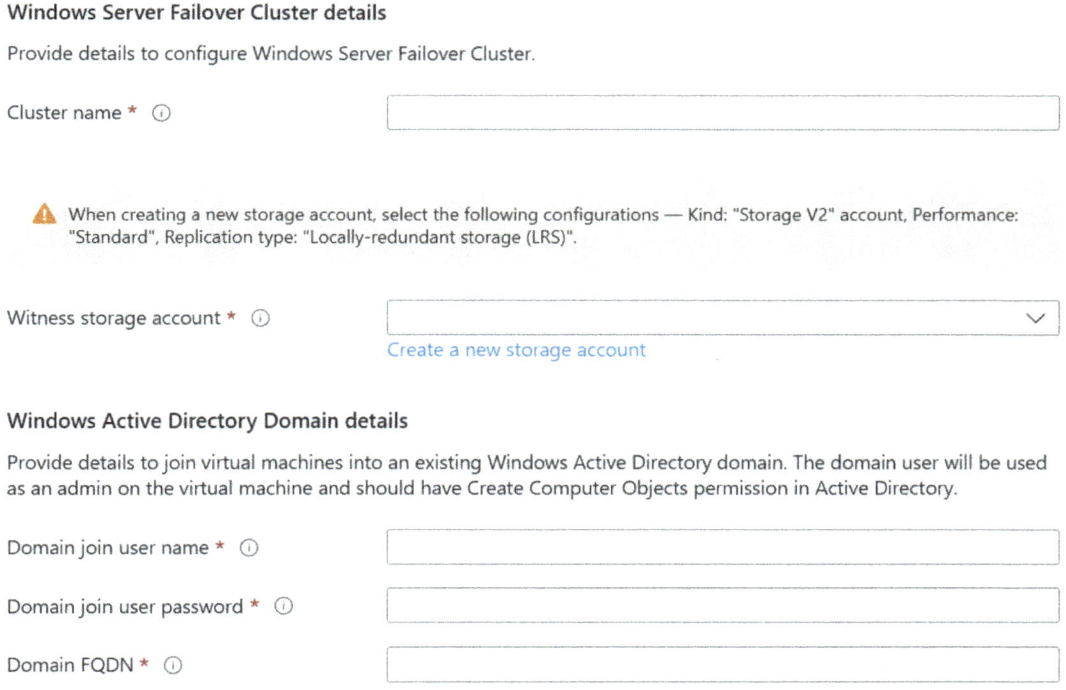

Windows Server Failover Cluster details

Provide details to configure Windows Server Failover Cluster.

Cluster name * ⓘ

| |

⚠ When creating a new storage account, select the following configurations — Kind: "Storage V2" account, Performance: "Standard", Replication type: "Locally-redundant storage (LRS)".

Witness storage account * ⓘ

| ⌄ |

Create a new storage account

Windows Active Directory Domain details

Provide details to join virtual machines into an existing Windows Active Directory domain. The domain user will be used as an admin on the virtual machine and should have Create Computer Objects permission in Active Directory.

Domain join user name * ⓘ

| |

Domain join user password * ⓘ

| |

Domain FQDN * ⓘ

| |

Figure 16-7. *WSFC and Credentials*

Once you have entered all the cluster-specific information as well as the standard Azure SQL VM information, the wizard will build you a WSFC cluster and create a new, empty Availability Group complete with a Listener. The AOAG options are added to the SQL Server settings page. Truly an Easy Mode to deploy an AOAG cluster.

Configure Quorum Options for a Windows Server Failover Cluster

WSFC Clusters use a voting system to determine what to do if the cluster detects a failure. It is a simple majority rules vote and happens in milliseconds if a failure is detected. The problem with a two-node cluster, or any cluster with an even number of nodes, is you can have a stalemate with each side getting 50%. This can lead to a "split-brain" situation where each part of the cluster can think it is in charge. We avoid that by having a third tie-breaker called a *"witness."* The witness allows for a single node to create a *quorum*, in this case a majority of votes, to react to a failure event.

Consider the following: A two-node SQL AOAG cluster loses communication between the nodes. Everything else continues to function normally. This cluster could be in Azure or on-premises; the situation and behavior are the same. Without a witness, the cluster cannot act. Each node believes it is a minority fragment and will cease operations, yielding to the supposed majority that "owns" the cluster decision-making process. With a witness still visible to both nodes, each node can request ownership, but only one will receive it. All Witness types can be *arbitrated*. They can be requested by multiple nodes, but only one will "own" the witness and add the witness' vote to the node vote. Both the winner and the losers "know" the outcome of the vote. Any node that cannot contact a witness automatically cannot count its vote. The default owner for a witness is the node currently hosting the Cluster Group.

Now that a subset of the failed cluster has a *Quorum*, the cluster can act. The majority node(s) can take over all resources, and the minority node(s) will yield. This may trigger a failover, depending on the settings of each Availability Group. Larger and more complex clusters have a specific logic chain to follow as various nodes go offline or come back online, but a majority vote with an optional witness is how it all works.

There are two Witness options for Azure SQL VMs:

- Disk Witness

- File Share Witness

A disk witness is typically used for Failover Clustered Instances where disk arbitration is already part of the configuration. AOAGs have no shared disks and almost always use a file share witness.

File Share witnesses can be stored on a variety of storage media, provided they support the necessary primitive commands for arbitration. One of the easiest ways to host a File Share witness in Azure is to use an Azure Blob Container. This is called a *Cloud Witness* and can be used for both Azure and on-premises SQL Virtual Machines. A Cloud Witness is especially useful for multi-site on-premises clusters as it gives a viewpoint from outside both hosting centers. If you look back at Figure 16-7, you will see the option to select or create a new storage account. WSFC will create a correctly configured storage container for Cloud Witness files. You can store multiple Cloud Witnesses for multiple clusters in the same Azure Storage container.

Configure Failover Clustered Instances on Azure Virtual Machines

Unfortunately, there is no Marketplace Template for Azure SQL Failover Clustered Instances. The IaaS extension does not fully support FCIs. This means that functionality like automatic backup, storage provisioning and management, and inventory is not available via the IaaS extension. You must deploy and install SQL "by hand."

I still suggest beginning with a SQL Marketplace image with a minimal configuration, even though you will have to reinstall SQL to create a Failover Clustered Instance. Begin by provisioning two machines (or however many you choose). You can even use the AOAG wizard to create machines and cluster them. Either way, you should delete any AOAG artifacts and uninstall all SQL instances. The reason to use a Marketplace SQL image is twofold. One, it pre-installs the IaaS extension. Even though the IaaS extension does not fully support SQL FCIs, some functions such as licensing are supported. Second, the SQL Install media is already copied to the *C:SQL ServerFull* folder on the VM boot disk, saving one of the most time-consuming steps in the deployment process, copying the SQL Server source media.

Once you have a cluster, the only Azure-specific step required is to provision shared disks. You can use Storage Spaces Direct to emulate a shared disk, or you can directly use shared Premium, Premium V2, or Ultra disks. Each choice has its own capabilities and limitations, but any of the three types can be shared. Microsoft will not ask this on the test, but there are also third-party storage options in Azure that support SQL Server Failover Cluster Instances.

Finally, install SQL from the local media and configure an FCI, much as you would on-premises. The load balancer vs. multi-subnet configuration choices we discussed earlier regarding AOAG clusters still apply here with multi-subnet being the recommended configuration for the same reasons as before.

Configure Log Shipping

Log Shipping is a fundamental HA/DR technology that relies on the fact that the transaction log represents a continuous timeline of transactions for a single database. Before we had *Log Streaming* to power AOAG data synchronization, we had Log Shipping. We can export via backup, copy the files, and restore the files to a different system anywhere in the world. Figure 16-8 shows the SSMS Log Shipping wizard found under Tasks by right-clicking the database name. This wizard is a very mature and comprehensive tool. It creates a series of SQL Agent Jobs that execute the complete log shipping scenario, including options to initialize the target database(s) via the wizard or manually.

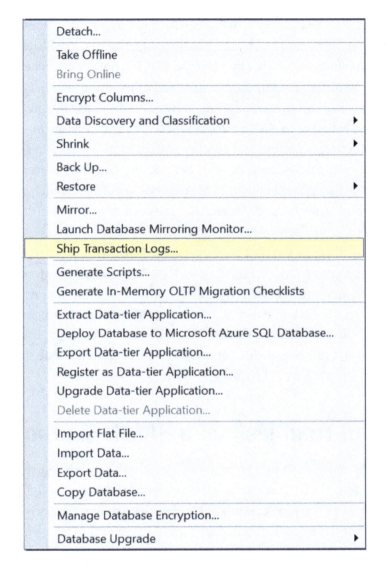

Figure 16-8. *SSMS Log Shipping*

Of course, you can always write your own scripts or adapt some you find online. Many people, including myself, have written custom log shipping scripts. My first attempt at writing log shipping scripts was back in the early 2000s because I needed to copy the backup files across the United States to a target data center. I was geographically protecting a set of SQL Servers based in Atlanta with a secondary data center in San Diego. This was where I researched the table set in the MSDB database that tracks all backups and how to properly query them. This led to my feature request to index those tables, which Microsoft added in SQL 2008.

The first thing the wizard does is arguably the most important. It configures log backups so they can be consumed by the log shipping process. It adds alerts to show if important elements fail. It does this by ensuring FULL recovery model and sets up log backups to a shared folder. Backups are configured as we discussed in Chapter 15.

The next step is to configure each target server and database one at a time. This includes creating a job to copy files from the initial folder where the databases land to a local folder for the target system. Azure storage may be used for either or both of the *primary backup landing folder* and the *copy to* folder for each target system. You can back up to a local file share and copy files to Azure Blob Storage or vice versa. You will need to properly configure security access to these container(s) as we discussed in Chapter 15.

Finally, the Log Shipping wizard configures RESTORE jobs on each target system, including whether to use NORECOVERY or STANDBY mode and optionally adding a delay between primary and secondary, capabilities that no other technology can offer. They certainly were not available in the built-in Log Shipping wizard back for SQL 2005. As with all wizards, the SQL Log Shipping wizard will create a script. This script will need to have portions run on specific servers (source, target) to create the correct jobs and alerts.

Monitor and Troubleshoot a HA/DR Solution

I wrote earlier that any system that you are not monitoring and measuring is out of control, by definition. HA/DR solutions are no exception. Regardless of the solution, you start by monitoring the baseline functionality of each participating server. In addition, you need to monitor the export, transfer, and application of the data synchronization. With log shipping, that is backup, copy, and restore. With Always-On Availability Groups, you monitor the transaction log forward and replay threads, using HA/DR DMVs to measure velocity and latency. It is a good idea to be familiar with the specific HA/DR DMVs available in all Azure SQL offerings.

Troubleshooting HA/DR is just as complex as creating a solution. Each element is critical to the overall functionality. We need these systems to be able to fail over successfully under the broadest possible circumstances within the SLAs we have promised our employers.

Do not get tunnel vision on troubleshooting SQL HA/DR issues. More often than not, the problems are due to network, storage, or permissions issues, not something within SQL Server. Keep an open mind (we call that a *Growth Mindset* at Microsoft) when approaching a troubleshooting session.

Chapter, Part, and Book Summary

With the completion of this chapter's "configure HA/DR technology" work, we have completed our exploration of Azure HA/DR capabilities as well as adding the terminology and vocabulary to build a complete mental model of how to think about SQL HA/DR both in Azure and on-premises. This completes our preparation for the DP-300 exam. I recommend re-reading Chapter 1's suggestions on test-taking, and *go schedule your exam*. Good luck.

Index

A

Active geo-replication, 349–353
Adaptive query processing, 243
Additive features, 60, 61
ADS, *see* Azure Data Studio (ADS)
AKV, *see* Azure Key Vault (AKV)
AKV access, 351
Always Encrypted, 144, 145
Always Encrypted with secure enclaves, 145, 146
Always-On Availability Group (AOAG), 29, 45, 84, 306, 311, 355–359
Anti-aliasing, 302
AOAG, *see* Always-On Availability Group (AOAG)
ARM, *see* Azure Resource Manager (ARM)
ASR, *see* Azure site recovery (ASR)
Asymmetrical keys, 126
Asynchronous communication, 309
Auditing
  Azure SQL DB, 158–160
  file management, 158
  managed instance, 160
Authentication
  data governance policies, 165
  entra ID, 108–110
  troubleshooting, 120, 121
  T-SQL, 122, 123
Authorization
  failures, 121
  troubleshooting, 120, 121
  T-SQL, 122, 123

Auto-failover groups, 353–355
Automated Azure deployment
  activity log, 274, 275
  ARM template, 269, 270
  Bicep, 271
  CLI, 272
  concept, 263
  monitor and troubleshoot, 273–275
  PowerShell, 272
  in progress, 273, 274
  Resource Manager, 263–265
  scaling up/down, 273
  tools, 265–269
Automatic query tuning, 232, 233
Automation scripts, 309
Automation technique, 77
Availability sets, 302
Availability zones, 303
AVM, *see* Azure Verified Modules (AVM)
Azure
  DBAs (*see* Azure database administration)
  implicit knowledge, 11
  networking, 14–17
  overview, 11
  storage, 12–14
Azure Active Directory, 108
Azure database administration
  roles, 22
  SQL offerings, 22–26
  virtual machines, 26–30

367

© Geoff Hiten 2025
G. Hiten, *Administering Microsoft Azure SQL Solutions*, Certification Study Companion Series,
https://doi.org/10.1007/979-8-8688-1585-0

Q